Tales of the New Babylon

Rupert Christiansen's previous books include *Prima Donna* (1984) and *Romantic Affinities* (1988) which won the Somerset Maugham Prize. He was educated at King's College, Cambridge, and after several years on the *Observer* is currently Associate Editor of *Harper & Queen* as well as opera critic for the *Spectator*.

RUPERT CHRISTIANSEN

Tales of the
NEW BABYLON

Paris 1869–1875

Minerva

For Caroline Dawnay

A Minerva Paperback
TALES OF THE NEW BABYLON

First published in Great Britain 1994
by Sinclair-Stevenson
This Minerva edition published 1995
by Mandarin Paperbacks
an imprint of Reed International Books Ltd
Michelin House, 81 Fulham Road, London SW3 6RB
and Auckland, Melbourne, Singapore and Toronto

Copyright © 1994 by Rupert Christiansen
The right of Rupert Christiansen to be identified as author
of this work has ben asserted by him in accordance
with the Copyright, Designs and Patents Act 1988

A CIP catalogue record for this title
is available from the British Library
ISBN 0 7493 1915 1

Printed and bound in Great Britain
by Cox & Wyman Ltd, Reading, Berkshire

Contents

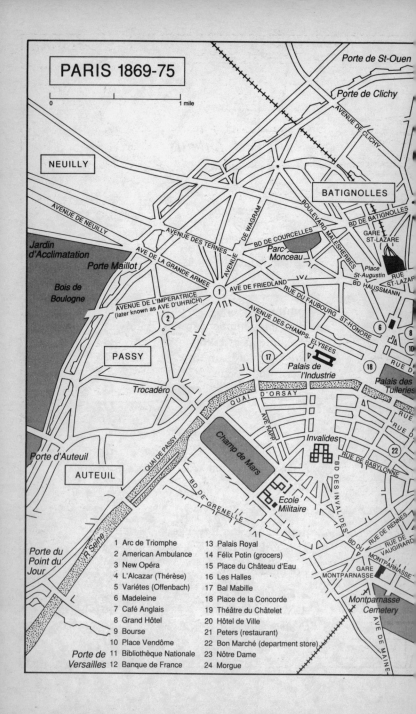

PARIS 1869-75

0 |———————————| 1 mile

Porte de St-Ouen
Porte de Clichy
AVENUE DE CLICHY

NEUILLY

BATIGNOLLES

AVENUE DE NEUILLY
BD DE BATIGNOLLES
GARE ST-LAZARE

AVENUE DES TERNES
AVENUE DE WAGRAM
BOULEVARD MALESHERBES
BD DE COURCELLES
Parc Monceau

Jardin d'Acclimatation
AVE DE LA GRANDE ARMÉE
AVENUE DE FRIEDLAND
Place St-Augustin
RUE ST-LAZARE
BD HAUSSMANN

Porte Maillot
Bois de Boulogne

AVENUE DE L'IMPERATRICE
(later known as AVE D'UHRICH)

RUE DU FAUBOURG ST-HONORE

①
②
⑥
⑧
⑩

AVENUE DES CHAMPS-ELYSEES

PASSY

Trocadéro
⑰
Palais de l'Industrie
⑱
RUE D
Palais des Tuileries

QUAI D'ORSAY
AVE RAPP

Porte d'Auteuil

AUTEUIL

Champ de Mars
Invalides
RUE DE BABYLONNE
②②
RUE D

QUAI DE PASSY

R. Seine
BD DE GRENELLE
Ecole Militaire
BD DES INVALIDES
BD D
RUE DE RENNES
RUE DE VAUGIRARD
GARE MONTPARNASSE
MONTPARNASSE

Porte du Point du Jour

Montparnasse Cemetery

Porte de Versailles

AVE DE MAINE

1 Arc de Triomphe
2 American Ambulance
3 New Opéra
4 L'Alcazar (Thérèse)
5 Variétes (Offenbach)
6 Madeleine
7 Café Anglais
8 Grand Hôtel
9 Bourse
10 Place Vendôme
11 Bibliothèque Nationale
12 Banque de France
13 Palais Royal
14 Félix Potin (grocers)
15 Place du Château d'Eau
16 Les Halles
17 Bal Mabille
18 Place de la Concorde
19 Théâtre du Châtelet
20 Hôtel de Ville
21 Peters (restaurant)
22 Bon Marché (department store)
23 Nôtre Dame
24 Morgue

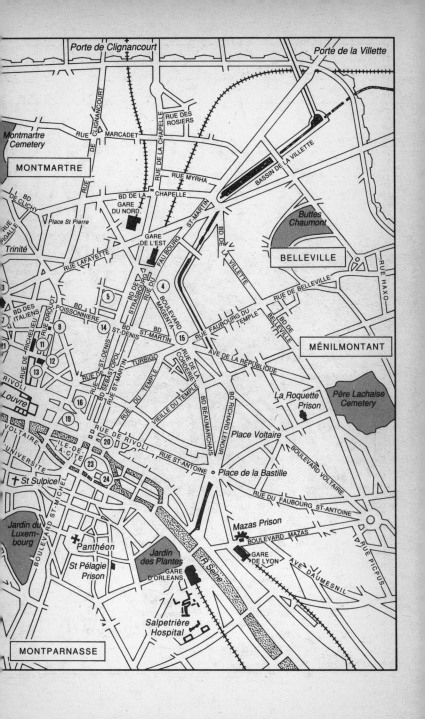

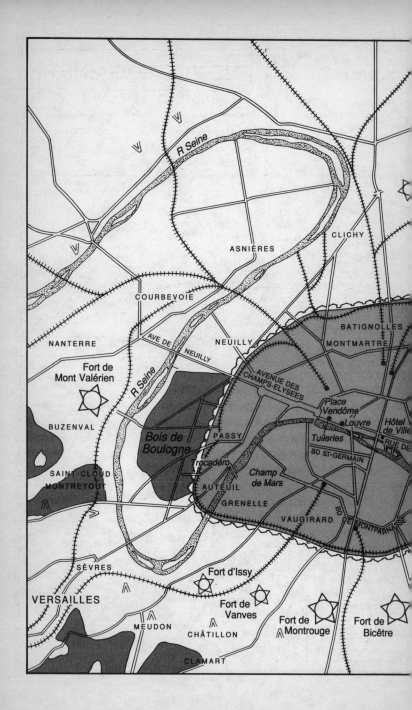

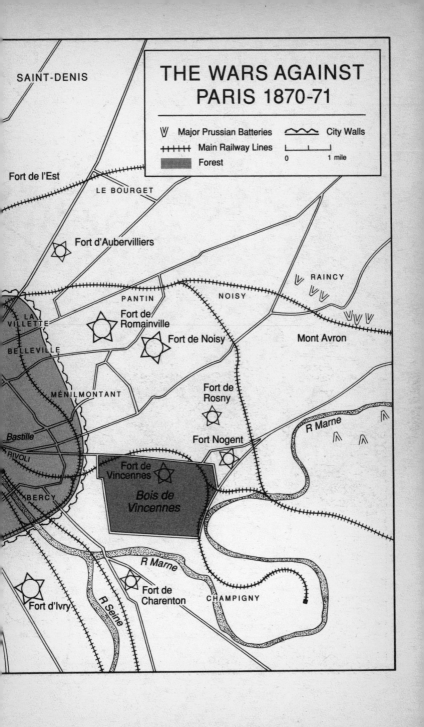

THE WARS AGAINST PARIS 1870-71

Major Prussian Batteries
Main Railway Lines
Forest
City Walls
0   1 mile

SAINT-DENIS

Fort de l'Est

LE BOURGET

Fort d'Aubervilliers

RAINCY

PANTIN

NOISY

LA VILLETTE

Fort de Romainville

BELLEVILLE

Fort de Noisy

Mont Avron

MÉNILMONTANT

Fort de Rosny

Bastille

RIVOLI

Fort Nogent

R Marne

Fort de Vincennes

BERCY

Bois de Vincennes

R Marne

Fort d'Ivry

R Seine

Fort de Charenton

CHAMPIGNY

List of Illustrations

Paris Partout!

A Guide for the English and American Traveller
in 1869;
or, How to see PARIS for 5 guineas

PARIS! – gay and beautiful Paris – rich in architectural treasures, teeming with historic associations of deepest interest – favoured in its genial climate – replete with endless novelty – the abode and dictator of European fashion – full of all that art and science can contribute to beguile the sense – its people renowned for their wit and daring – in fact, in sum, in total, THE PARADISE OF TOURISTS!

From London
Of the many different routes available, the speediest is that adopted by the South-Eastern Railway, whose accelerated special tidal trains leave regularly from Charing Cross, passing to Paris via Sevenoaks, Folkestone (indifferent refreshment room), and Boulogne. Weather permitting, the entire trip is of a duration of *c.* 10 hours. Return ticket, one month's validity, £3 10*s.*

Passports
Since a French regulation of 1860, English citizens are now exempt from the expense and annoyance of passports; but although by no means *absolutely necessary*, one of these documents, or a card of identity, is *most strongly recommended*.

Customs
Attention is generally paid only to cigars, on which a levy of 10 centimes per item is payable. Certain books and newspapers, of

an inflammatory or political tendency, can cause difficulties or embarrassment.

Money

25 Francs equal £1; 5 Francs equal $1.* The money of Switzerland, Belgium, Italy and Greece is the same as that of France.

Note It is customary in France, in walking or driving, to keep on the *right*-hand side, not on the left as in England.

Arrival in France

Outline of Recent History
1789 Capture of the Bastille
1792 Republic proclaimed
1793 Execution of Louis XVI
1804 Napoleon Bonaparte proclaimed Emperor.
   At the outbreak of the Revolution in 1789, one third of Paris had been occupied by ecclesiastical property. Since much of this was subsequently expropriated, and then sold to speculators or retained by the State, Napoleon availed himself of an opportunity to beautify the city, opening the rue de Rivoli, completing the Louvre Palace, and beginning the Arch of the Étoile.
1814 Abdication of the Emperor. Restoration of the Bourbon Louis XVIII
1824 Succession of Charles X
1830 Three-day revolution. Louis-Philippe, Duke of Orleans, proclaimed King. He completed the Arch of the Étoile, the Madeleine, enlarged the Hôtel de Ville, and repaired many neglected monuments, as well as widening principal thoroughfares. During this reign Paris was surrounded with the present fortified wall and ditch, and the detached forts erected.
1848 February Revolution. After two days' fighting, Louis-Philippe fled, and a republic was proclaimed. The words

* Any attempt to render these sums into modern equivalents is meaningless. See John Burnett, *A History of the Cost of Living* (Harmondsworth, 1969).

2

'*Liberté, Egalité, et Fraternité*' met the visitor's eye in every direction; they have now been erased. Louis Napoleon, son of Louis Bonaparte, King of Holland and nephew of the first Napoleon, elected by universal suffrage President of the French Republic.

1851 2 December. Discretion compels us to pass over the *coup d'état* which took place on this date. Suffice it to say that exactly a year later, Louis Napoleon was elected Emperor by universal suffrage, and the present regime, known as the *Second Empire* was established. In 1853 Louis Napoleon married the present Empress, Eugénie de Montijo. Since these events, works of public utility in Paris have proceeded at a pace quite stupendous, throwing into the shade everything previously achieved in any city in the world. Picturesque but insalubrious quarters of narrow and crooked streets have been cleared, the boulevards extended, railways constructed.

Today's visitor to Paris will find a population of between one and a half and two million. In 1860 the line of fortified wall which surrounds the city was made the municipal boundary: this wall is rather more than 22 miles in circuit, and has 66 entrances or gates.

The city is divided into 20 arrondissements, with their own administrations, over which are placed the Prefect of the Seine, Baron Georges Haussmann, and his municipal council. The modern fashionable quarter comprehends the bright and brilliant rue de Rivoli, Place Vendôme, Boulevard des Italiens and the Champs Elysées. The Palace of the Tuileries is the Paris residence of the Emperor and Empress; on the Ile de la Cité are the law courts, central police office, and the great hospital; there is nothing like 'the City' in London – the Bourse or Stock Exchange being close to the fashionable quarter. In the Faubourg Saint-Germain, on the left bank of the river Seine, stand the vast *hôtels* of the nobility, in which some of the traditions of old French society are maintained; in the adjoining Latin Quarter, many thousand students lead a life of riot and licence hardly to be understood by the foreigner. To the East, in the Faubourg S. Antoine, are numerous, manufactories and the

3

dwellings of those who work in them, formerly the hotbed of terror and insurrection. On the outskirts, as in the Faubourg S. Victor, Mouffetard, Belleville &c, are to be found the most wretched of the population; but Paris may at least be proud that it possesses fewer dens of misery, filth, and vice than the vicinity of Tottenham Court Road or Drury Lane can exhibit.

Hotels and Accommodation

Paris contains some 4,000 hotels and lodging houses, many of them bearing in their names evidence of the *entente cordiale* – hence the Hotels Chatham, Bristol, Windsor, Manchester, Brighton, Liverpool, Westminster, Dover, Bedford, Canterbury, Richmond, Lancaster, Clarendon, Nelson, Byron, Walter Scott, Prince Regent and several Albions, Londres, Victorias, Iles Britanniques, and Angleterres. Those on an expansive budget should note

Grand Hôtel, Boulevard des Capucines. A new hotel, financed by the Jewish bankers Pereire, of great show and size (not to be confused with its neighbouring rival, the Grand Hotel du Louvre against which it has been wrangling a costly and bitter legal suit). Seven hundred rooms, for which one can expect to pay 20 francs per diem. For all the splendou of its public quarters, designed by M. Charles Garnier, do not reckon on quiet, prompt attendance. There are few private w.c.s and many damp, dark corridors. More commodious to travelling agents for commercial houses than families seeking cheer and respectability. A lifting machine, operated by hydraulic press, raises clients to their floor, thus circumventing the fatigue of staircases. Electric bells operate throughout.

Hôtel Meurice, rue de Rivoli. Much patronized by visiting royalty and aristocracy. Our intelligence has it, however, that standards in this establishment have fallen since it passed out of private hands and into those of a joint stock enterprise, the Paris Hotel Company.

Hôtel de Calais, rue Neuve des Capucines. Frequented by the élite of American society. American breakfasts served (buckwheat cakes, fishballs &c.). Close to the American banking house.

4

Visitors intending to stay for longer periods should not hesitate to take a furnished apartment: a reliable agent can be found in *A. Webb*, 220 rue de Rivoli, tea dealer and wine and brandy merchant. Many English, American and Russians of more than moderate means prefer the leafy residential stretch of the Champs Elysées.

Restaurants and Cafés

Dinner is served between 4.30 and 8 p.m. Very large portions are the rule, and the visitor will find that one French appetite is sufficient for two Anglo-Saxon appetites.

The *carte*: nothing can be more bewildering to the stranger than to have this printed list, of some hundred dishes, placed in his hand, and he soon begins to feel uncomfortable at the contempt that his ignorance must inspire in the waiter. We therefore recommend – for reasons as much of economy as of personal dignity – that the visitor favours the fixed price menu of the day, available at all but the very smartest establishments.

For those who do not wish to risk the possibility of digestive contretemps, plain, wholesome English fare is offered by *Lucas*, in the rue de Madeleine (ham or roast beef, with boiled cabbage and mashed potatoes, 1 fr. 20c. English cheeses; half portions available); also by the well-established *Byron's Tavern*, rue Favart, *Taverne Britannique*, rue de Richelieu, and *His Lordship's Larder*, rue Royale. Beware signs in windows advertising 'Veritable Warranted Cheddar' or 'Stakes from London, Day and Night'.

The stranger should not as a rule venture below the third class, but he may safely patronize a new form of eating house, the *cremerie* or *bouillon*, in which simple dishes and collations are constantly ready for instant purchase and consumption. These places do not minister to the refinement or romance of dining out in Paris; no ceremony beyond eating and paying is attached to them; but they do have the advantage of the utmost *convenience*.

For those who wish to sample the full glory of Parisian cuisine, with expense no object, we would single out *Café*

Anglais, Boulevard des Italiens. Obtaining a table is not easy; there are times when those without *réclame* or a title seem to be tacitly excluded. The restaurant upstairs (in which smoking is not permitted) has long been the haunt of *la jeunesse aristocratique* – the Duc de Rivoli, Prince Paul Demidoff, the Marquis de Modena &c. A beefsteak costs 1 fr. 75c. The cellars, which contain over 200,000 bottles of wine, including some from the Château Lafitte vintage dating from the previous century, make a faery dining hall. The ground-floor café is but plain and *typique*, and open all night. Beware *cocottes*. *Véfour*, Galerie de Valois. Salmon mayonnaise (the receipt a closely guarded secret), 2 fr. 50c., highly recommended. The 36-page menu here lists twenty *hors d'oeuvres*, thirty-three soups, forty-six dishes of beef, thirty-four of game, as well as forty-seven of vegetables and seventy-one *fruits en compôte*. *Trois Frères Provençaux*, Galerie Beaujolais (not to be confused with its pallid imitator, the *Deux Frères Provençaux*, rue Dauphine), has four salons and eighteen private rooms; fine wines, cod with garlic a speciality.

Note Ordinary red table wine is usually drunk mixed with aerated water – this precaution is especially recommended in inferior restaurants.

Paris boasts at least twenty thousand cafés. The more salubrious of them present the visitor with a sprightly scene. Around are luxurious couches for your accommodation; mirrors, gilding, and tasteful adornments of decorative skill enrich the walls; whilst every art that can be used to attract and retain the visitor is brought into operation – the daily journals, draughts, chess, dominoes, cribbage and billiards. Excellent coffee, chocolate and liqueurs are supplied at reasonable prices. Ladies are at perfect liberty to frequent these saloons, and are numerously found there. The utmost decorum prevails, and the freedom and ease of conversation, carried on in a low tone, forms an additional attraction to these popular places of resort. Smoking is generally prohibited until the evening.

Coffee is served either as a *demi-tasse* (strong, black), or as *mazagran* (in a glass, with an accompanying carafe of water), or as *capucin*, with milk. Never tip, even for a single cup of coffee, less than 10c. Should you give less, you risk the embarrassment of an ironic shout of '*Un sou pour le garçon*!'

Tortoni, Boulevard des Italiens. Renowned for its ices and sorbets. *Café du Helder*, Boulevard des Italiens. Open after the theatre; food, at a price (half a chicken, 4 fr.!!) Well known for its *absinthe*, a spirituous liquor which, taken in any quantity, can be ruinous to both moral and physical well-being. *Café Leblond Favre*, Passage de l'Opéra. Stockjobbers from the Bourse breakfast here. Sherry cobbler, mint julep, American grog, and other Yankee potations purveyed. *Café de Suède*, Boulevard Montmartre. After-theatre suppers of goose *aux marrons*, sauerkraut and potato salad, served in private cubicles. Literary and journalistic clientele, of a radical political nature. A famous habitué is Le Guillois, the eccentric editor of the newspaper *Le Hanneton*. To publicise this he adopted the ludicrous habit of taking out a copy in public places, pretending to read it, and gasping loudly: 'This newspaper is remarkable! The critics are excellent, the drawings clever! And so much, for a ridiculously low price! Truly, this Le Guillois the editor is an astonishing man who deserves to succeed!'

Purchases

The visitor should note that Paris is the most expensive city in Europe. English sovereigns and half-sovereigns are generally accepted in lieu of native currency.

Much to be marvelled at are the *grands magasins* or *magasins de nouveautés*, huge emporia divided into several floors and departments. These stores offer a wide range of dry goods, drapery, haberdashery, clothing and furnishing. They are rigorously managed and quite respectable. Among smaller shops, American citizens may like to note the pharmacist *Swann*, rue Castiglione, by appointment to the American Embassy and the *American Cracker Manufactory*, Boulevard Malesherbes. Novel gifts for 'the folks back home' may be found at the establishment of *M. Paul Morin*, Boulevard Poissonière, whose jewellery is forged in that wonderful new metal, aluminium, which so impressed the Emperor at the recent International Exhibition that he commanded a dinner service made of the same. The

Maison Violet, newly opened on the rue Scribe, occupies a vast insular saloon, ornamented with frescoes and a superb chandelier of one hundred jets. The tone is essentially aristocratic. Inner boudoirs sell the paraphernalia of the *toilette*, notably the house's own exclusive 'Reine des Abeilles', or Queen Bee, cosmetic preparations, by appointment to the Empress.

Entertainments
Paris, the City of Light, is a veritable charivari of pleasures after nightfall; the visitor must only beware of not regretting the effects of a too-eager readiness to yield to the siren calls of its temptations and intoxications.

Theatres, lyric and legitimate
The Grand Opéra, rue Lepelletier. Properly, The French Opera, run up in a hurry in 1821 (to replace a building in the rue Richelieu, at the door of which the Duc de Berri was stabbed, and which was pulled down in consequence). In front of the portico three dastardly Italians tried to assassinate the Emperor and Empress in 1858, and now this building is being replaced too, by a splendid edifice designed by M. Garnier, due to open in 1871. The government provides 900,000 francs of annual subsidy. Performances on Monday, Wednesday, Friday, and often Sunday. The *Opéra Comique*, Place des Italiens. In this handsome hall are presented lighter works, by modern composers such as Auber, Halévy etc. The *Théâtre Italien*, Place Boieldieu. Here a select audience listens to Italian opera, in a season which lasts from November to April (after which the singers generally repair to London).

The *Théâtre Français*, rue Richelieu. The seat of the French regular drama – classic works and modern alike, with a government subsidy of 240,000 francs. Molière was once its manager; in latter years it has been the scene of the triumphs of Talma and Rachel. The manager is allowed to withdraw an actor from any other theatre to the Comédie-Française (as it is also known) on one year's notice. The *Odéon*, near the Luxembourg. A minor Théâtre Français, but not an inferior one. Here

Beaumarchais' play *Le Mariage de Figaro* was first produced in 1784; nine years later, the entire troop of actors was arrested by order of the Revolutionary tribunal. It has several times been burnt down. *Théâtre des Variétés*, Boulevard Montmartre. A neat and much frequented house, in which the amusing musical vaudevilles of M. Offenbach can be seen.

The infamous Boulevard du Temple, or 'Boulevard du Crime', on which the smaller theatres played the most lurid and distasteful melodrama, has now been destroyed to make way for the regime's march of progress. The *Théâtre Gymnase-Dramatique*, Boulevard Bonne Nouvelle, is respectable. The plays are moral and the performers all *married*.

Note Ladies do not patronise the pit, or parterre, of any theatre; gentlemen admitted here should in the interval ensure their places by tying a handkerchief around the banquette. Be also warned that at the Grand Opéra, the claque sit here. This disagreeable cohort, paid by the management in this and other theatres to respond favourably to the entertainment in question, should on no account be shushed or silenced in their mercenary activities. An attempt to abolish the claques in 1853 proved totally unsuccessful after a fortnight.

Tickets for all Parisian theatrical representations may be booked from a central office on the Boulevard des Italiens; avoid the profiteers who swarm outside the more popular theatres – their offers are always excessive in price, and frequently entirely bogus!

Cafés chantants. Spectators sit and listen to singing and music, sometimes of a coarse nature, executed by performers often outrageously overdressed. No charge is made for admission, but one will be expected to take refreshment, usually of an inferior quality. The company is not aristocratic, but the visitor need not fear annoyance or impropriety. The most celebrated of these institutions is *L'Alcazar*, rue du Faubourg Poissonnière. Here the fabulous Theresa, whose salary exceeds 20,000 fr. per annum, sings, twice a week in the winter season, ditties of a satirical and even saucy turn.

Bals publics. It is difficult to imagine scenes more curious or fantastic than those presented by these public dancing halls. At the most refined level, *bals masqués* are presented during the winter in the *salle* of the Grand Opéra – the pit being boarded over and joined to the stage. Gentlemen may be admitted (10 fr.) in plain evening clothes, but ladies should be masked or in costume. The gorgeous and glittering revelry of the polka, waltz, and mazurka reaches its climax at 1 a.m. Strict etiquette is by no means the predominating characteristic of the fair who resort to this pleasantest of pandemonia. It will be conceived that if a visitor should take the ladies of his family to witness this display, he must take them to a box as mere spectators, for to mingle with any of these too vivacious groups could be worse than indiscretion. Elsewhere public dancing halls abound. Some of the smaller establishments in the suburbs are little more than dens of all the vices: official efforts to curb their activities and proliferation have not been altogether effective.

In the centre of the city, more commodious establishments may be found, among them the *Salle Valentino*, rue S. Honoré. The architecture is a medley of the Moorish and Greek; the columns are gaily painted, and the recess is backed by mirrors which greatly enhances the brilliancy of the scene. There are a billiard table, a shooting gallery, a dynamometer for amateurs of muscular strength, and tables where trifles may be raffled for. The visitor may expect to see every variety of embrace, not excepting the ursine hug. Admission 2–3 fr. *Jardin Mabille*, Avenue Montaigne. A large circular space, with a pavilion for the orchestra in the centre, is reserved for the dancers, and lighted by a profusion of gas-lights suspended from artificial palm trees. A snug corner is laid out for refreshment; here the votary of Terpsichore may treat his partner to a refreshing lemonade. An immense covered saloon affords the visitor a secure asylum from bad weather. The company of this elegant garden generally comes under the description of 'the gayest of the gay', but licence is not carried beyond propriety. Admission, 2 fr. Would that the same could be said of the *Salon de Wauxhall*, rue de la Douane, which partakes of the character of the manufacturing arrondissements surrounding it, and is not much more respectably attended than the Holborn Casino! The police make forays on its bacchic excesses, and arrests are made.

A novel and hilarious diversion is provided by an American importation. In the *Roller Skating Club*, rue Jean Goujon, skating on shoes soled with rubberized wheels is demonstrated daily by 'Professor' Fuller, a master of the Art who claims to have been 'decorated by every Sovereign in the world with ice in his dominions'. The first such institution in Europe.

Sightseeing
Passing over the profusion of churches, monuments, galleries, and sights familiar to every tourist, we would draw the visitor's attention to the MARCH OF IMPROVEMENT evinced by this great city. In every quarter, at every level, Paris rises astonishingly anew. The sentimental antiquarian may mourn the loss of the old Paris and its romantic past; the strict moralist may deplore the glory accorded to Mammon throughout; but others must justly rejoice at the triumph of modern science and hygiene.

The wonders begin at the lowest level: Paris's new system of *sewers* consists of six main lines, fed by fifteen secondary lines, by means of which the city's whole storm drainage is conducted to a grand receptacle beneath the Place de la Concorde, whence it is discharged by a shaft – the most extraordinary of its kind – sixteen feet high, eighteen feet wide, and three miles in length. The sewers may be visited, via an opening in the Boulevard de Sébastopol.

The *foot pavement* may also be remarked upon. Twenty-five years ago, it was detestable, worse even than London's, and consisting in great part of large uneven stones, sloping from the houses down to the middle of the road, along which ran a copious and noxious gutter. The city is now widely blessed with smooth coatings of asphalt.

Les Halles. An immense establishment, adjoining the old Marché des Innocents, on which the market people had constructed a set of wretched huts that continued to form Paris's central market until very lately. In 1852 the present commodious and elegant Halles were begun from the architectural plans of M. Baltard, the result being eight large, lofty, and handsome *pavillons*, intersected by carriageways and joined by one immense roof of iron framing and glass covering. One *pavillon* serves as a fish-market, another poultry, another fruit and flowers, a fourth for butter, cheese, and eggs, two for butchers' meat &c. The vaults below, which may be visited, contain marble tanks and fountains for live fish, and underground tramways to the railway termini, by which produce is brought in from the country and rubbish removed without encumbering the streets. The whole site extends over five acres and has cost in excess of £1,500,000. Four million bricks in the vaulting alone, and five million kilogrammes of iron were used in the whole construction. There are eight electric clocks, public conveniences and extensive gas lighting.

Bois de Boulogne, four miles west of the Louvre. This favourite promenade was up to 1852 a regular forest, with walks and rides cut through. In 1852 the Emperor, determined to copy, or rather improve upon, the London parks, presented the Bois to the city of Paris, and, in concert with the Municipality, dug out the lakes and made the waterfalls, raised mounds, traced new roads, and converted the whole into the present and popular pleasant place of public resort.

At the north angle, near the Porte de Sablons, five acres have been given over to the *Jardin Zoologique d'Acclimatation*. Here are no wild beasts in the usual sense of the term, but only animals which may possibly be usefully acclimatized: yaks, tapirs, hemiones, viculas etc. Hitherto only the lama and the Tibetan ox have succeeded. There are pretty views from the crevices of artificial rockwork which has been reconstructed for wild goats and *mouflons*. Eggs, and cuttings and seedlings from the exotic flora with which the garden is planted, may be purchased.

La Morgue, Quai Napoléon. The lower orders in Paris are fond of theatrical horrors, but it is not easy to understand how so repulsive a phenomenon, rebuilt in 1864, can be tolerated in a civilized country. Entering this building, one sees a glazed partition behind which stand two rows of black marble tables, inclined towards the spectator and each cooled by a constant stream of water. On these tables are exposed the cadavers of those found dead or drowned, naked except for a strip of leather across their loins. Each corpse, often hideously bloated or disfigured, is thus left for three or four days, awaiting the identification of friends or family. Along the walls are hung the clothes and effects of the defunct. In 1866 the Morgue received a record 733 corpses – 486 men, 86 women, 161 infants. Of these 445 were identified: 285 had committed suicide by drowning, 19 were homicidal victims, 36 were hanged, 5 had shot themselves, 3 had been knifed, 6 charcoaled, 6 poisoned, 3 starved, and 82 had died suddenly on the street. Failed speculation on the Stock Exchange is said to be the greatest cause of suicide.

What, one must ask, is the use of such a monstrous proceeding? Few, surely, would recognize their oldest friend, naked, wet, and stretched out on a marble slab; and there are, in fact, numerous cases of persons not identifying their nearest relations, while others have wrongly laid claim to someone they knew not. A perpetual throng runs in and out of this loathsome exhibition, too many of them English and American tourists. There they stand, gazing at the hideous objects before them, sometimes with exclamations of horror, sometimes with utter vicious indifference. A poor madman, who fancies himself dead, comes every morning to see if he can recognize his own corpse, and is hardly to be driven away.

Transportation
There are thirty-one omnibus lines, which cover the city's main thoroughfares from 8 a.m. until midnight. Ladies may not ride on the upper level: fatal falls have been numerous as a result of tripping down the stairwell. Private cabs, hailed on the street and marked with red numbers, cost 2 fr. the hour. Small steamboats known as *mouches* (flies) or *hirondelles* (swallows) ply the Seine.

Post
Letters posted before the late-afternoon post-time are delivered in London the following morning.

Beware!

The flower girls at the *bals publics*, *cafés chantants*, and outside the theatres, as well as the wily advances of well-dressed and spoken women. The uncouth boldness of the street-walker will strike the visitor with immediate amazement and distaste: but how could one expect that under a lady-like appearance and language the Parisian gay woman hides the evil designs of a fallen angel, and laughs inwardly at the gullibility of her victims?

In markets, barter is the rule: let an inexperienced lady make her appearance, and she will at once be asked double the price that would be expected from an obviously sharp-witted French cook. There are no fishmongers in Paris: all fish are sold at market.

Jews selling lorgnettes, plated jewellery &c., who may also offer you licentious, forbidden literature and illustrations.

The concierge, or caretaker of apartment buildings. This person, if offended, has it in his or her power to give much annoyance, mislaying letters, misinforming callers, and speaking ill of you to tradespeople.

It is desirable to avoid the free discussion of politics. The police are ubiquitous and zealous, with wide powers of arrest and detention. The wiser course must certainly be to express yourself with great temperance in referring to the Emperor and government of France, and not to do or say anything that may serve to lessen the *entente cordiale* at present existing between our nations.

Part I

1 : *Autumn Pastoral*

The world knew Paris for its carnival flash, a crazy tinsel circus of all fleshly pleasures and all earthly magnificence. Moralists were chilled by the siren grin behind which rotted a greed and cynicism without parallel in nineteenth-century Europe. 'The religion of money is the only one today that has no unbelievers,' wrote Théophile Gautier. 'All very beautiful for the moment,' said another disenchanted romantic, Alfred de Musset, of a ball at the Tuileries palace, 'but I wouldn't give two *sous* to see the last act.' 'I think there never was a more corrupt, abominable city, nothing but a brothel and a gambling hall,' roared the splenetic Thomas Carlyle. He was not alone in his sentiments. By 1869 the knowledge that the curtain would soon fall on the extravagant spectacle the city had made of itself was coming uncomfortably closer. Government functioned without any clear chain of command or direction. Authority clouded, alliances shifted, certainties crumbled, as the French drummed their fingers and waited for the Second Empire to admit its own political bankruptcy and bring to an end – if not to a nemesis – an extraordinary episode in French history.

It had begun in the year after the revolution of 1848, when Louis Napoleon, nephew to Napoleon Bonaparte, was elected President of the Second Republic. In 1852, after a swift but bloodied *coup d'état*, he transformed a fragile democracy into an Empire over which his powers were more absolute than those of any other civilized monarch. Parliamentary assemblies, the legislature, the administration, the press, the armed forces were all made subject to one undivided power – the Emperor,

17

endorsed through an election that had a wide franchise but no real liberty behind it. Yet, after its first violent assault, Napoleon III's regime managed to sustain itself more by propaganda than by active repression. The Second Empire was a quiet tyranny – rarely beastly, often merciful, sometimes genuinely benevolent – which the prosperous and self-interested could easily ignore: there was such fun, such profit to be had from doing so. The police raids on socialists and republicans were quick midnight affairs followed by perfunctory punishments; censorship was a trifle comical; the pretence of justice acceptable to those wise enough not to enquire too closely. And it was in several respects a successful enterprise. Much of the Second Empire's social legislation was imaginative and generous. The centralization of bureaucracy led to an increase in efficiency. The liberalizing of trading controls stimulated growth and productivity. It was a society which gave opportunities and rewards, a society without the dreadful grey walls that surrounded the totalitarian tyrannies of our own century. The Second Empire may have been an autocracy, but it was not a prison.

Perhaps its most compelling strength was an apparently trivial one. It radiated glamour. It glittered and dazzled as it celebrated itself in a series of monuments and triumphs. The style was one of swaggering vulgarity, with plenty of gold trimmings, but it communicated an irresistible message. 'The Empire must be a succession of miracles,' one of Louis Napoleon's ministers advised him: the way to keep the loyalty of the French was to attract and distract their attention, be it in foreign wars, international exhibitions or massive public works – a constant bustle of advertised novelty and munificence. And nowhere was the Empire's capacity to present itself in alluring shop-window images more evident than at the château of Compiègne, to which the court customarily repaired for several weeks of the autumn, accompanied by a selection of guests carefully drawn from the ranks of the great and the good, favoured friends and valued allies. Pompous and absurd and mediocre as this November pastoral may sound to us today, for contemporaries the invitation represented a sort of divine call to a heavenly region in which all social aspirations would be consummated, all prayers answered. Some fundamental romance of the age was realized at Compiègne; and if Second Empire Paris had a dream in its soulless heart, it was there, some fifty miles from the city gates, that it was most tellingly displayed.

The Compiègne pageant began at the Gare du Nord, from which a specially chartered imperial train left at 2.33 p.m., the guests being summoned, at a month's notice, in three or four weekly batches of about a hundred – each known as a *série* – by the Lord Chamberlain. The expense incurred by an acceptance could be devastating: to make any sort of effect, a lady was expected to present herself in different costumes every day and evening, and gentlemen had to appear for dinner in court dress, of a fancy and unalterable kind. Somebody was once overheard at the Gare du Nord muttering that he had been obliged to sell his mill to pay for the visit; but as Felix Whitehurst, the worldly-wise correspondent of the *Daily Telegraph*, drily put it, 'those who are asked to Compiègne always go'.

And who were the favoured few boarding the 2.33 and steaming their way north-east into Picardy? The imperial family and its supporters among the Establishment, royal visitors (from Mad King Ludwig of Bavaria through Arab sheikhs to the Prince of Wales), card-carrying members of high society and dignitaries, of course; but what made the party interesting was the *arriviste* element, the people who had made it under the regime and whom the regime had the sense to recognize. They made Compiègne an intensely competitive place, as an anonymous English diplomat suggested:

. . . the most heterogeneous gathering of humanity it has ever been my lot to observe away from the gaming rooms at Baden-Baden, with which it has also one trait in common beside its outward elegance, namely, its absolute egotism, the unscrupulous hostility of each of its members towards his neighbour, like himself in pursuit of a favour, a possibly profitable transaction, or an intrigue.

A final layer of gilt was provided by a sprinkling of artists and intellectuals. Viollet-le-Duc, engaged with the restoration of the nearby château of Pierrefonds, and Prosper Mérimée, the author of *Carmen* and an old friend of the Empress's mother, came regularly: others privileged at least once included the painters Delacroix, Doré and Winterhalter, the sculptor Carpeaux, the architect Garnier, the composers Auber, Thomas, Gounod and Verdi, the writers Dumas *fils*, Flaubert, Gautier, Sainte-Beuve, Vigny, and the scientists Cuvier and Pasteur. They enjoyed it somewhat less than the others, but they were asked, and they went, they went.*

On arrival at the town of Compiègne an hour and a half later, the train disgorged, gawped at by townsfolk and tourists (whom hotels could charge as much as seventy francs a night for a room with a view). A magnificent crocodile of charabancs would briefly process to the fine eighteenth-century château and its hunting forest – a site associated with most of the rulers of France, from Charlemagne onwards, who had variously occupied, frequented or improved it: Napoleon Bonaparte and the Archduchess Marie Louise had celebrated their honeymoon there in 1810, for example. The château was thus a charged national symbol, which Louis Napoleon eagerly adopted, refurbishing it with a smoking room and pompous murals with titles such as 'Peace distributing Olive Branches to the Spirits of Agriculture and Industry'.

In its function as a grand hotel, Compiègne projected a fabulously luxurious front, the promises of which were not necessarily fulfilled behind. Guests were accommodated in suites which ranged from the five-star splendid to the one-star drab, and since a nervous sense of status was the glue for each *série*, their relative qualities provided a constant source of pique or crowing. Complaints to the Chamberlain – last year the *piano nobile* overlooking the park, this year a north-facing *grenier* – were numerous; and the painter Thomas Couture once ingenuously answered the Empress's polite enquiry as to his comfort with an assertion that his room reminded him charmingly of his first professional years struggling in a garret. But once your little white card had been assigned to its door,

---

* The first *série*, it was said, was for necessary people, the second for bores, the third for the fashionable set, the fourth for the intellectuals. But you never met anybody who was satisfied with the week to which he or she had been assigned.

there was little that could be done – the Compiègne operation was more meticulously planned than most French military campaigns, with a whole sub-world of servants (another embarrassingly expensive requirement for certain guests), luggage, supplies and transport to be considered.

It could also be unforgettably cold, despite some odd (and still extant) attempts at central heating. 'Siberia is two yards from my fireplace,' wrote the painter and author Eugène Fromentin. Others couldn't sleep for chattering teeth and icy extremities. Mérimée could hardly bear it: 'there are some corridors . . . which assure a jolly good cold to those who pass down them. I've no idea what happens to those who already have one. . . . You spend your time either freezing or roasting. We take walks from carriages in 7° below zero and then dance in a salon in which crocodiles would feel at home.'

But undoubtedly the most nagging worry for members of the Compiègne *séries* was the matter of etiquette. Court protocol during the Second Empire was an elaborate recreation of the rules and rituals that had prevailed in Napoleon Bonaparte's time. The regime may have established itself by violence and conspiracy, then confirmed its legitimacy on the basis of the results of a popular referendum, 'the will of the people', but it still needed to suggest, through its pomp and circumstance, a more transcendent dimension to its power. At Compiègne the most terrifying insistence of all was the imperial command to be at ease – for where then were the boundaries, what was the form? What would be taken as a joke, what would shock and offend? The dramatist Jules Sandeau rushed panic-stricken into Mérimée's room to beg him for the loan of a pair of ribbons which, he had discovered, were *de rigueur* for the top of gentlemen's white-silk evening stockings; Lillie Moulton, a pert young Daisy Miller figure married to an American banker, was 'never so mortified in all my life . . . speechless and confused' as when the unexpected receipt of a love poem from Gautier stunned her into being two minutes late for breakfast. 'Alas! it happened that just this morning the Emperor had desired me to sit next to him at the table, and the Marquis de Caux had been (and was still) waiting for me at the door to conduct me to my place on the sovereign's left hand . . . Prince Murat, who sat on the other side of me, kept saying "The Emperor is piping mad".'

In fact he wasn't, but such a dynamic of embarrassment – indicative of a much deeper social and political unrest – was as common at Compiègne as a cold.

The first evening was inevitably the worst: bags unpacked and a first toilet nervously made, guests made their way down to the Map Room at 7 p.m. The Emperor and Empress then received the new arrivals with 'words of compliment and welcome', which sometimes revealed a sinister depth of knowledge of an individual's life and situation. At 7.30 dinner was served, to the accompaniment of a military band, the tablecloth embroidered in the favoured Louis-Quinze style with silver-thread depictions of hunting scenes. A huge white marble statue of the first Napoleon Bonaparte, in imperial toga, dominated the *salle*.

They are a bottomlessly fascinating pair, this Louis Napoleon and Eugénie, upon whom posterity has found it impossible to agree. Born in 1808, Louis Napoleon was the son of Napoleon Bonaparte's brother Louis Bonaparte, the King of Holland,* and Hortense de Beauharnais, whose mother was Josephine, Napoleon Bonaparte's first wife. And nothing about him is more significant than his ancestry, for the simple reason that it gave him his unwavering sense of destiny: he lived with the one certainty that he had been born to renew the Napoleonic vision, to complete his uncle's unfinished business with France and the world. There was a gleam of the fanatic behind his drooping sensual eyelids – 'like a lizard which looks asleep, but isn't' as the Goncourts' journal has it – which compensated for so much else in his personality that was apparently diffident and deferential: as a child his grandmother Josephine had called him 'Oui-oui' because he was so relentlessly obliging, and throughout his life he maintained an equanimity of disposition that more impassioned temperaments found infuriating. His cousin Princess Mathilde, to whom he had briefly been engaged, once

---

* For the doubts concerning his paternity, see Jasper Ridley, *Napoleon and Eugénie* (London, 1979), pp. 14–15.

exclaimed: 'if I had married him, I should have broken his head open to see what was inside.'

After the death of Napoleon Bonaparte's son in 1832, he became the Bonapartist Pretender to the French throne, and twice unsuccessfully conspired – in 1836 and 1846 – against the Orléanist King Louis-Philippe. On his return to Paris at the outbreak of the 1848 revolution and his subsequent election as Prince-President of the Second Republic, he began a programme of reform much influenced by Saint-Simon's paternalistic version of socialism. Losing the support of the cantankerous and divided parliamentary assembly but confident in his personal popularity with the lower middle class, he decided to execute a *coup d'état*. On 2 December 1851 he proclaimed the dissolution of the governmental organs of the Second Republic. A plebiscite would be held, in which the nation was to be asked to endorse a new constitution which he, Louis Napoleon, would formulate. Paris initially reacted calmly enough to the news; but on 3 December barricades were raised and the more vociferous and hostile republican deputies arrested. On 4 December there was a catastrophic fracas when troops moving down the rue du Sentier were apparently fired on from a window: over a hundred men, women and children were slaughtered in the ensuing panic, the great majority of them law-abiding passers-by. Louis Napoleon was duly elected Emperor and the Second Empire was constituted, but Parisians never forgave him for this terrible episode, assuming it (unfairly) to have been a calculated gesture, intended to intimidate. Otherwise his assumption of a tyrant's prerogatives might have been more charitably regarded as necessary to 'national salvation' and history might remember him less ambivalently as a well-intentioned man who did much to improve the lot of the poor, encouraged industry and innovation, and rebuilt Paris according to the best modern principles.

But the subterfuge behind the coup and its innocent victims destroyed his moral credibility, allowing his enemies to interpret him as a monster of hypocrisy, whose many acts of kindness, lack of vindictiveness, personal charm and so forth were pure political cynicism. Perhaps they were: but Louis

Napoleon's great triumph as Emperor was to keep everybody guessing: he remained – and remains – an unknown quantity.

By the late 1860s something had gone out of him. Plainly tired and ill, he twiddled his thumbs obsessively, and ministers found him less and less able, or willing, to deliver the decisions expected of a tyrant. His habitual secretiveness – the mark of a practised conspirator – now seemed more like a desire to be left alone. There were times when his wife Eugénie, brisk and pragmatic, had no patience with him. Whether or not the *coup* continued silently to burden his conscience – 'you wear *le deux décembre* like the shirt of Nessus,' she had once snapped – he was worried about ensuring a Napoleonic future for France, freed of the chimera of republicanism. But as political opposition against him mounted inexorably, he realized that in order for the Empire to survive his death it would have to effect one final outstripping miracle – its own transformation into a democracy.

Eugénie would have preferred a firmer strategy. Intensely interested in politics, a Catholic reactionary, untainted by her husband's sentimental socialist streak, she was a woman of stern unimaginative principle never liked by the run of the French. She had been born, in 1826, to Spanish nobility (though her mother was half-Scottish) and her adopted country could not help but think of her in terms of another foreign queen, Marie-Antoinette – a bust of whom she did indeed keep in her bedroom. In her guttural Hispanic tones, she could be outrageously tactless and downright rude. As a girl her spunk had greatly impressed a notable friend of her mother's, Stendhal; later her aggression had been channelled (or so Paris rumoured it) into bullfights, which she would attend sporting scarlet boots, a dagger under her belt and a whip instead of a fan in her hand; as Empress, she continued in this role of gung-ho spectator, with occasional and dangerous bursts of direct participation. There was a sense of destiny in her too: 'I was born during an earthquake,' she once said. 'What would the ancients have thought of such an omen? Surely they would have said I was fated to convulse the world!' Many who knew her, and many who didn't, thought that she was just an adventuress with an eye to the main chance. Certainly as a dynastic alliance, marriage to Eugénie de Montijo contributed nothing to the Empire's consolidation. Rather the opposite: when the engagement was announced in 1852, the Stock Exchange plummeted; and for the next eighteen years, despite her energetic charities and scrupulous performing of her public duties, she remained a leaden political liability.

'Napoleon III made many mistakes,' wrote Maxime du Camp in his *Souvenirs*: 'the worst of which he can be blamed for . . . was that of marrying Eugénie de Montijo. . . . Around her hung an aura of cold cream and patchouli-oil. . . . Possessed of no passion except vanity, she dreamed of taking the leading role but was never more than a bit-player, dressed up in a splendour that she didn't know how to handle. . . .' Her better qualities – courage, loyalty, sincerity – were gritty ones which would make her impressive under the pressure of catastrophe; but her great redeeming virtue was her fabulous beauty, of the sort that changes minds and hearts. That moony and sallow expression, its doe eyes heavily accented with mascara, has dated badly – yet to her contemporaries she was the personification of loveliness, adorned with all the homage that the couture of the age could lavish upon it.

In private she was pious and practical in black, claiming to disdain the eclipsing opulence she radiated in public. 'My political dresses', she called her vast intricately brocaded crinolines: advertisements for the Lyons silk industry, necessities of her station, not to her sober taste at all. But whatever the costume, her self-presentation was as symbolically weighted as that of the Virgin Queen Elizabeth I of England, right down to the gold dust that she sprinkled over her luscious red hair.* Every passage of Eugénie's existence was deliberately and brilliantly staged. At Compiègne, for example, she was both sublime and relaxed, happily playing at being at play. The château had sentimental associations for her, since it was here that, following a first brief acquaintance in Paris in 1849, Louis Napoleon had begun his courtship in earnest. It was the

---

* Which had earned her the nickname of 'Carrots' during her unhappy stint at an English boarding school.

Christmas of 1852. The guests were amazed at how blatantly this obscure but exquisite young Spanish woman was being singled out. She hunted with spirit – Eugénie loved to be in at the kill – and tried her hand and eye with the Emperor's gun. On a walk in the gardens, she coyly marvelled at some dewdrops on a clover leaf; the next morning he presented her with an emerald brooch, sprinkled with diamonds, in its very shape. Five weeks later they were married in Notre-Dame.

Their life together was at one level not much of a success. Perhaps Eugénie truly loved only her sister Paca, Duchess of Alba; and she could certainly never forgive Louis Napoleon for concealing the news of Paca's death from her, while she was on a state visit to Algeria – an episode which culminated in some sort of nervous breakdown. Sexually, Eugénie had had one great thwarted teenage passion which resulted in a suicide attempt (poisoning herself with the phosphorus off some matches, dissolved in milk, so the story went); since that crisis, she had closed all access to her emotionally vulnerable quarters, returning the attentions of countless admirers with flirtation, satisfaction and indifference. It has been suggested that she was clinically frigid; it is certainly reasonable to assume that her love for Louis Napoleon was grounded in duty and ambition rather than passion, and that after she had provided him, in 1856, with the Prince Impérial, the male heir necessary to the perpetuation of the Napoleonic line, they ceased to have any erotic contact.

Unfortunately, Louis Napoleon, like so many men of his outwardly languid personality type, had an immense and somewhat ruthless sexual appetite. Although the tales of his debauchery subsequently became ludicrously garnished and exaggerated, it is clear that in the course of his marriage he went through several mistresses and many more casual liaisons, procured for him by his chamberlain, the Count Bacciochi. Sometimes the veils of discretion were none too thick, as on the occasion when the Princess Mathilde was sitting on the imperial train on the way to Compiègne, opposite Eugénie, the Foreign Minister Count Walewski, and other nobilities and dignitaries. The carriage was divided into two compartments, and when the train gave a sudden lurch the door between them slid open, revealing to Mathilde the sight of her 'très cher cousin' the Emperor, sitting astride the knees of Walewski's wife Marianne, 'kissing her on the mouth and thrusting his hand down her bosom'.

Eugénie was accustomed to bear her husband's infidelities with stoicism, and indeed had little alternative but to do so. What mattered was maintaining appearances: here Louis Napoleon was infinitely accommodating. He was someone who preferred a patina of politeness and deceit to open confrontation – a temperamental bias on which his entire strategy as ruler of France rested – and there are moments when one is tempted to sentimentalize him into a lonely and worried little man needing to be loved. Eugénie failed him in this respect, though, God knows, she did her duty; it was Louis, the Prince Impérial, on whom he lavished all his thwarted *tendresse*. He adored the boy, his 'petit Lulu', as he called him,* whose birth had moved him to declare an amnesty for those exiled or imprisoned after the 1851 *coup* and who was Compiègne's pampered mascot and favourite toy.

Apart from Eugénie, that is: at Compiègne she was most brilliantly herself – gracious, energetic, conventional, hopelessly banal in her quest for entertainment. The guest lists were of her devising, and the heavily gilded pastiche of *ancien régime* elegance in which the château was furnished reflected her taste. The *séries* were in sum her very own tiny triumph. Princess Pauline Metternich, wife of the Austrian Ambassador and herself a leader of fashion, believed that 'only a woman of the world turned Empress could have organized such gatherings. A princess by birth could never have managed it.' In other words, only a parvenu could have understood what other parvenus wanted – a touch of real class, with all modern conveniences and a chance to show off. This competitiveness became most evident in the matter of dress. Every day at Compiègne, the ladies changed their costume at least three times – moving from the soberly buttoned black silk of morning to the fantastic tulle and

* He once caught his son choking himself on a mandarin orange. Instead of snatching it away himself, he asked a courtier to do so. 'I could not do so. He would not love me if I did,' he explained sadly.

glitter of evening, with its revelations of *décolletage* and diamonds – and every time they looked each other coolly up and down. The most potent weapons in this subtle war of one-up-womanship were gowns designed by Frederick Worth, the English couturier resident in Paris. The son of a poor Lincolnshire solicitor, he had worked his way up through the drapery trade to become Paris's first notable male dressmaker. Not that he suffered people to call him that: in his Rembrandtesque-Wagnerian floppy velvet beret, he insisted that he was an artist in cloth, and to commission from him an original toilette – for the Compiègne *séries* of 1866, he was said to have made a thousand such – was not only to part with a great deal of money but to submit yourself humbly to his creative will. Building on a few basic models, he was certainly a superb craftsman and engineer, cleverly exploiting advances in textile production, but today his claims to genius look rather dubious. The ludicrous crinoline (which he finally abandoned in the late 1860s) was neither elegant nor practical, serving only to turn women's bodies into immobile vehicles for his heavy decorative fantasies and necessitating, for decency's sake, the wearing of long *pantalon* underwear; the colours he used after the introduction of aniline dyes in the 1850s – flame pink, magenta purple, bottle green, cruel violet, crashing yellow, Bismarck brown, jade and violet for widows – were violently garish; the trimmings and fringes which gave each gown its vital *haute couture* stamp of uniqueness ranged from the bizarre to the pointless.

But Worth's taste was perfectly attuned to an era of unbridled conspicuous consumption (his suburban villa was, according to one witness, 'a mass of gold, satin, plush, embroideries etc.; every chair was edged with gilt, and there were knick-knacks without end . . . [there was] an enormous silver bath in his dressing-room, while a fountain of eau de cologne played continuously in the adjoining room') and his clients, from Eugénie to the flamboyant American Mrs Potter Palmer and the *demi-mondaine* Cora Pearl, knew no headier joy than his fittings. 'Women dress for two reasons,' he cattily told an interviewer. 'For the pleasure of making themselves smart, and for the still greater joy of snuffing out the others.'

Aside from the daily parade of female sartorial splendour, the style of Compiègne did not altogether live up to its magical reputation. The Emperor did not care to linger at table, so dinner

Potage tortue clair
Crème de volaille
Brisotins de foie gras
Saumon Napolitain
Filet de Boeuf à la moderne
Suprême de perdreaux
Homards à la Parisienne
Gelinottes rôties
Salade
Petits pois
Ananas Montmorency
Glaces assorties
Café
Liqueurs

would be raced through in an hour, before the party repaired for conversation and dancing, both of a rather tame and stilted sort. An amazing fact, a novelty, an amusing anecdote was all that was required in the way of conversation. The Emperor set the tone. 'Did you know,' he asked Prince Richard Metternich, 'that it has been calculated that one *écu* lodged in the bank in the year AD 1 would by today have accumulated so much interest as to represent a sum larger than all the gold and silver on earth?' Polite or 'carpet' motions in the form of a genteel Sir Roger de Coverley or a quadrille would be accompanied by the operation of a mechanical piano. Sometimes the Emperor himself would obligingly turn the handle: he was totally unmusical, and executed the chore without the slightest regard for the rhythm or speed of the dance. Once the Duke of Atholl and some Scottish compatriots offered a display of Highland reels, their kilts and knees provoking a further quiver of embarrassment. Or there might be a little concertizing. His eyes rolling heavenwards, Gounod sang some of his own Spanish songs, which reduced the Empress, ever ready to dab her eyes with a handkerchief, to tears. Lillie Moulton was asked for some native

American *chansons*. ('Don't bother about singing anything serious, and certainly don't try anything classical,' Prince Richard Metternich advised her drily.) At the line 'O darkies, how my heart grows weary,' she saw that 'both their Majesties were deeply moved'; but having embarked on 'Nelly Bly', she found herself at a loss to remember the words. 'With shameless aplomb' she improvised:

> Nelly Bly wipes her eye
> On her little frock.
> Nelly Bly, Nelly Bly
> Dick a dick a dock.

Happily the Emperor did not notice anything wrong. 'What does "chickabiddy" mean?' was his only question. '*Ta chérie*,' she replied coyly, as he handed her a cup of tea.

The more sophisticated and cosmopolitan found these soirées deadly dull. One such, Pauline Metternich, was constantly trying to liven things up a little. This remarkable woman, who 'affected masculine manners', smoked cigars and arrived for her week's *série* with eighteen trunks and as many hatboxes, had, according to the Prince Impérial's English governess, Anna Bicknell, 'an extraordinary inclination for walking on the edges of moral quagmires, and peeping into them, with a profound conviction that her foot would never slip'. Amused by the unfounded rumours in the popular press about orgiastic goings-on at Compiègne, she remembered at the end of one peculiarly soporific session, the chamberlain turning the piano handle, two couples dancing, and others yawning on banquettes, how she and the Prince de Reuss had whispered to each other with melodramatic irony, 'Sodom and Gomorrah!'

But Compiègne was not innocent, even when its inhabitants were all yawning at 10.30 p.m. Despite the imperial command to be at ease, there were many ambitious people waiting, coiled, to make their various moves: in Zola's novel *Son Excellence Eugène Rougon*, the central character uses his invitation to a *série* expressly to lobby his cause with the Emperor, whom he finally corners during a game of quoits. (Unlike much of Zola's epic posthumous portrait of the Second Empire in the Rougon-Macquart cycle, this detail is credible.) Among all the trivialities, Louis Napoleon might suddenly let something diplomatically telling slip: 'I could not permit Prussia to make war on Switzerland,' he told the Austrian Count Hübner darkly. Nothing at Compiègne, however, can have been more pointed or charged than the notorious behaviour of Louis Napoleon's cantankerous cousin Prince Napoleon, known as Plon-Plon and as a snarling Republican sympathizer, on the occasion of Eugénie's birthday. At the end of dinner the Emperor had asked him to make a brief speech and to propose the Empress's health. Such was his hatred of her and what she represented that he refused. The chill that followed was recorded in a letter of Mérimée:

> 'You can dispense with the speech,' she said to him. 'Your speeches, which are always very eloquent, frighten me rather.' Grimace instead of a reply. A second call from the master of the house. His cousin said: 'I cannot speak in public.' Everyone was standing in silence. General discomfort. – 'Would you care to propose the Empress' health?' 'I would ask you to excuse me.' Everyone looked down at their plates, while Prince Joachim Murat proposed the toast, in a voice trembling with fury: we drained our glasses and made a dash for the salon.

In other accounts, it was noted that Eugénie gave Plon-Plon her arm as the imperial party grimly processed out of the dining-room – a gesture typical of her admirably steely nerve.

The programme of daytime entertainment at Compiègne was intensive. There might be outings – which precipitated more complaints about the cold – to Viollet-le-Duc's massive restoration of the medieval fortress of Pierrefonds, or to some standing stones beneath which tiny primitive skulls had been excavated: the Emperor was a dilettante archaeologist. One might simply wander round the estate and inspect the kennels, where Pauline Metternich's jape was to tease the fastidious Prince de la Moskowa by pretending to pick a flea off one of the hounds and stuffing it under his collar. There was a futile game of hide-and-seek, in the course of which a gentleman would lay a trail of paper which the ladies then followed. Archery was a sport which briefly commanded imperial attention, but Lillie Moulton had a hard time trying to introduce the Emperor and Empress to the vicious art of croquet:

> Both their majesties were highly interested; they examined everything with the greatest curiosity, unwrapped the balls themselves, and were quite anxious to begin . . . [But] Prince Metternich was so long and particular about telling the rules that he succeeded only in confusing all the beginners.
>
> The Empress was the first to play: her ball was placed so near the wicket that nothing short of genius could have prevented her from going through, which she did with great triumph; her next stroke went far beyond, and she worried it back by a succession of several pushing knocks into its position. No one made any remarks. Then the Emperor made a timid stroke, which gently turned the ball over. Prince Metternich remarked that he (the Emperor) should hit harder, at which his Majesty gave such a whack to his ball that it flew into the next county.

Eventually they gave up, 'bored to death'.

On wet days there were photograph albums, billiards, and a pinball machine. Forfeits, Consequences, spelling-bees, word games and quizzes were other common resorts. Lillie Moulton asked everybody to answer the same set of soul-probing questions about their personal tastes and beliefs. 'Do they invent intellectual pastimes in America?' asked the Empress catily. 'I thought they only invented money-making ones.' The Emperor took it all very seriously: to 'Which faults do you regard with most indulgence?' he replied 'Those which I can profit from', and he listed his favourite occupation as 'seeking answers to insoluble problems'. Someone else – often said to be Mérimée – set a celebrated nonsense dictation, which contained a large number of grammatical traps. The Empress made sixty-two mistakes, the Emperor and Pauline Metternich forty-two, Alexandre Dumas *fils* twenty-four, and the winner was an Austrian, Prince Richard Metternich, with only three. It was as near to strenuous mental exercise as Compiègne ever came.

At 5 p.m. the Empress received a select few in her Salon Chinois for tea. The invitation was much coveted, and often involved some little scientific demonstration designed to satisfy Eugénie's streak of naive, even gullible, curiosity about the world. Pasteur discoursed about the diseases infecting silk-worms and brought his microscope along. The Empress condescended to prick herself and provided a drop of blood for his slides: there was a polite rush to examine it, and more polite compliments. Some frogs used in the course of another experi-ment escaped from their box and hopped off down the nearest corridor to freedom, pursued by a posse of desperate footmen. 'Today it was a man who had invented a machine to count the pulse,' reported Lillie Moulton. 'He strapped a little band on your wrist and told you to concentrate your thought on one subject; then a little pencil attached to the leather handcuff began muffing up and down slowly or quickly as your pulse indicated. The Empress seemed much interested, and called those in the room whose pulse she wished to have tested. She said "Now let us have an American pulse." My pulse seemed to be very normal and the exhibitor did not make any comments, neither did anyone else.'

The more virile splendour of Compiègne was its hunting, conducted in fierce pagan glory once every *série*. The meet took place in the middle of the 36,000-acre forest, at a break known as the King's Well, off which led eight broad alleys. Those granted a set of silver coat buttons, emblazoned with stags' heads, were entitled to join the official cortège and to wear the full fancy eighteenth-century costume consisting of green velvet frock-coat trimmed in crimson with gold braid, white kid knicker-bockers, Hessian boots with heavy spurs, and a tricorne.* 'The French have not what seems our inheritance – the love of hunting *something*,' commented Felix Whitehurst, 'but they do love a spectacle' – and a spectacle this certainly was, punctuated by the baleful whooping of the horns. One observer, Madame Octave Feuillet, describes how 'hardly had the signal to start been given than the ground echoed dully as if an army of elephants was shaking it. Carriages, horses, and men charged into an infernal gallop across the forest. The speed of their pace

* Only Lord Palmerston spoiled the picture, when in his infuriating British way he stubbornly insisted on wearing his own bright red hunting cloak.

was such that the trees seemed swathed in a fairy mist. Through this same mist passed the huntsmen in their Louis XV outfit: one might have thought them ghosts of time past, summoned up for the occasion.'

None of this was just pretty picture-making. The Second Empire was always aware that it had to reinforce itself with imagery which suggested legitimacy and tradition as well as glamour and largesse, and all these procedures and uniforms, crowned by the magnificent ostrich feathers in the Emperor and Empress's headgear, were very deliberately drawn from models of royalist eras.

The evening after the hunt there ensued an even more fantastic ritual in the courtyard of the château. Thirty-two footmen in full livery stood in a broad circle holding flaming torches. A 'dog varlet' then appeared, bearing the head and antlers, skin and offal, of the stag which had died earlier in the day. With a flourish of trumpets, the imperial suite appeared on the central balcony. When the dog varlet dropped the carcass, the hounds – until then held at bay outside the circle and barking savagely – were released. But a crack of their Master's whip would check their advance, twice over, thus proving their impeccable discipline. At their third advance they were allowed to reach their reward, and 'then nothing could be heard except low growling and the cracking of bones between their powerful jaws'. Within ten minutes there was nothing left.

In comparison, the shooting constituted a standard sort of mass slaughter. On an average day, six goats, 338 hares, 1,311 rabbits, 306 pheasants and 27 partridges, subsequently distributed among the lower orders, were bagged. The Emperor scored 343 cadavers.

What to do after dinner remained the problem, and over the years of the *séries* increasing use was made of a small court theatre. Sometimes professional companies from Paris would arrive for the evening to give command performances of their latest boulevard success. Amiable farce rather than classical tragedy was the preferred genre: 'one passage in the first act threw the whole house, commencing with their Majesties, into the greatest hilarity,' reported *The Times* of a presentation of *The*

Chorus Girl's Husband. All this passed the time; but some guests needed more stimulation, and, especially with the advent of the fearless and fun-loving Metternich couple as a galvanizing influence, amateur dramatics were regarded as the most amusing means of avoiding post-prandial *longueurs*. *Tableaux vivants* were in vogue: Marianne de Walewska featured in *The Dream of Herculaneum*, Doré designed *Souls in Purgatory Being Led Forth by Hope*, the Marquise de Las Marismas dressed up as Ophelia, with Ambroise Thomas playing a medley from his new opera of *Hamlet* on the piano. *Sardanapalus on the Pyre with the Women of His Household* may have been more *risqué*.

Elaborate charades were the next fashion. *Anniversaire* (*Anne, hiver, serre*) for Eugénie's birthday, *Harmonie* (*armes, au nid*, in the latter of which the sight of the seven-year-old Prince Impérial as Cupid asleep in a bower aroused great enthusiasm), *Portrait* (in which the eight-year-old Prince Impérial forgot his lines), *Exposition*, *Pantalon*. Decorum was a delicate matter, and occasionally someone on stage would get overexcited and go too far: in 1866 the Goncourt brothers shook their heads wearily over the news that *Fourbu* (exhausted) had provoked Rouland, the former Minister of Justice, 'decked out in a wig and an idiotic costume, to play the clown with such fervour and a stream of low jokes that the Chamberlains had to stop him'. The divisions between good clean fun, not-in-front-of-the-ladies fun, and treasonable satire were all too easy to breach innocently.

From charades it was but a short step to more challenging projects. Octave Feuillet wrote a play in which the Empress herself, splendidly attired, took part – an experiment which, despite the ecstatic applause of the audience, she never repeated. In a week of terrible weather, an operetta was cooked up by the Marquis d'Aoust. 'The music of this is mediocre beyond words,' complained Lillie Moulton, who took a leading role. During the performance the *salle* was so hot that everyone's make-up ran and a fox-terrier belonging to one of the cast leapt up on stage to join its mistress. Most ambitious of all was a sort of masque entitled *Les Commentaires de César*, prepared in 1865 over four days of hectic rehearsal to celebrate the forthcoming publication of Louis Napoleon's pondered and ponderous biography of Julius Caesar. Prince Metternich played the piano, the Marquis de Caux appeared in drag as a *cocotte*, while the British consul Edward Blount impersonated the Marquis' sensational prima donna wife Adelina Patti, and Pauline impersonated the Spirit of Song (wearing a brilliant white petticoat embroidered with crotchets and quavers), an army canteen girl and a cab driver, as whom she sang a rollicking song about a recent cab strike that the Empress, acting as Regent in her husband's absence abroad, had crushed by putting in the imperial soldiery. The script was full of such contemporary references:

Madame de Pourtalès, as *La France*: Free exchange!
Madame de Galliffet, as *L'Angleterre*: No more passports! We will throw a bridge over the Channel!
La France: And extend the Boulevard Haussmann all the way to Piccadilly!

Leaving Compiègne could be a wrench: even the grouchy Flaubert admitted that he had been 'very much entertained', despite the hysterical request he dashed off from his room – number 85, second floor – to a friend in Paris, begging him to send up a box of 'ultra-chic camellias' for the Empress's birthday: 'don't forget, for Christ's sake'. Later he told Maxime du Camp that he wanted to import the experience into a novel about the Empire, 'with all the ambassadors, marshals and servants rattling their decorations as they bend to the ground to kiss the hand of the Prince Impérial'. He never did, more's the pity, but helped Zola with *Son Excellence Eugène Rougon* by mimicking the Emperor's voice and gait: Compiègne always provided good copy, good dinner-party conversation, and however grey the tedium or anxiety at the time, in memory it all invariably glowed rosily: for most guests the only question was whether one had made sufficient of an impression to earn an invitation for the next year.

One sour note: Lillie Moulton was furious on her last morning to be visited by the majordomo, firmly requesting a tip of 600 francs for the servants.

The last *série*, in 1869, was a bleak one. The Empress was in

Egypt, with a wardrobe of a hundred new Worth gowns, for the opening of the Suez Canal, and Princess Mathilde took her place as hostess. There were only forty guests, over one week, and the Emperor was preoccupied with politics, shuttling back and forth to Paris. In secret he received at Compiègne a brilliant deputy, Émile Ollivier, who might be trusted to steer a coalition government and keep the peace. Democracy, everyone knew, could not be far away now. One night the Emperor, whose problems included excruciating physical pain, managed to smile and dance the *carillon*, keeping some sort of party going until eleven o'clock. But when at the end of the evening he called for the refreshment of a late supper, the kitchen staff blushed and apologized – there were only two chickens and a ham in the larder, and no bread at all, except the hard, dry loaf, kept in the cellars for emergency army rations.

After the guests left, Louis Napoleon and his son spent five days at Compiègne on their own, returning to Paris on 21 November. Neither of them would ever see the château again.

2 : *The First Thunderclap*

The cab driver remembered how they had hired him late in the evening of Sunday 19 September 1869: a stocky young man, a respectable married lady, and her five small children, all neatly dressed in their best clothes. The young man had chattered tales of the amusements of Paris. At a crossroads in the scrawny and newly industrialized area of Pantin, neither urban nor rural, close to the north-east gates of the city, they stopped. The young man and the lady had climbed down, but two of the children began to whine on being told to stay behind, so they were taken along too, off across the Plaine des Vertus, past the silent factories, away from the rows of workers' cottages, towards some fields. 'What are you all doing here?' the cab driver casually asked the remaining children. 'We don't know,' one of them replied. 'We don't know.'

About twenty-five minutes later, the young man returned on his own, somewhat breathless. 'We've decided to stay here,' he said, hustling the children out. The cab trotted off and its driver thought no more about his passengers and their unknown midnight destination.

Early next morning, a peasant called Langlois was crossing the Pantin Fields, when he spotted a trail of blood, leading to a bloodstained handkerchief; close by was a freshly dug mound, about ten feet long and two feet wide. Kicking through the soil, he found a human hand, linked, as he then discovered, to a hideously mutilated body. Being a law-abiding, Empire-supporting sort of fellow, Langlois rushed off to summon the appropriate authorities. Within an hour a gawping huddle had gathered to watch him dig out the rest of the mound. What emerged was unspeakable and unprecedented: the mass grave of a mother and her five children, some of their corpses still warm and close to life. They had been axed, knifed, and strangled, literally torn to pieces: a total of a hundred or so wounds were later counted.

Carried through an already huge and ever-burgeoning crowd of hysterical jostlers, the bodies were transported to the morgue, examined, and photographed – the first time this medium had been used as an official adjunct to criminal proceedings. Later that day a bloodied kitchen knife was discovered in the field, but there was very little other evidence. The lady – for that was the social status she seemed to merit – wore a black silk dress and gold earrings. The autopsy revealed two further shocking facts: she was six months pregnant, and had been killed not by the knife or axe blows she had suffered, but by suffocation: the murderer, in other words, had buried her alive. Who the victims were was impossible to establish. Some of the children's clothes bore a tailor's label, Thomas of Roubaix, a large and busy manufacturing town near Lille, towards the Belgian border. It was not much of a lead.

The story exploded in the press, releasing a terrified excitement that would keep the Parisian imagination in a state of frenzy for months to come. The dead gaze of the unknown woman, stiff in the morgue surrounded by her slaughtered offspring, reminded the *Gazette des Tribunaux* of the statues of Niobe in the Uffizi; other newspapers speculated on the number of assailants involved – for surely one man, however monstrous, could not have perpetrated this deed alone? *The Times*'s correspondent grumbled about the police: 'the cocked-hatted rapier-bearing *sergents de ville* infest the boulevards and streets of Paris, but it seems that outside the fortifications people may be murdered by the half-dozen and buried at leisure'.

Then the first witness came forward. The proprietor of the Railway Hotel at Pantin remembered a young man who said he was a factory night worker had booked in a week earlier from Roubaix, scarcely occupying his room and interesting himself only in the mail that arrived for him. He had registered under the name of Jean Kinck. Late in the afternoon of 19 September an elegantly dressed lady had arrived with her children asking for this Jean Kinck. After establishing that he was out, she took two rooms, deposited some laundry and then left. The following morning Jean Kinck had returned, apparently with a companion, paid his bill and vanished. A search of his room revealed various blood-spattered objects and a letter which read: 'Wait. We aren't ready yet. Kinck.'

The hotel owner identified the corpses, and the police began to piece together their dossier. Jean Kinck was a self-made man, a model of Second Empire thrift and prosperity who had built himself a modest fortune of 100,000 francs and four domestic properties from the manufacture of industrial screws and brushes. Madame Hortense Kinck was an exemplary wife and mother, claimed her neighbours, a good and contented woman whose only known quarrel with her husband was his desire to return to his native Alsace. Madame Kinck preferred old friends and familiar circumstances, but Monsieur Kinck had insisted on going off with a young friend 'to view some property' near Guebwiller, with the plan of establishing a new factory in the area. Subsequently Madame Kinck became agitated: she had heard no news from her husband. As far as the neighbours could recall, she finally received a letter dictated by Jean – who had hurt his wrist and could not hold a pen – requiring their twenty-year-old son Gustave, a fine, strapping, even-tempered fellow, to join him with some money. Gustave had duly done so, and some days later Madame Kinck had mentioned a further note from her husband, asking her to come with the children to the Railway Hotel, 'where all would be explained'.

It was naturally assumed at this point that Gustave Kinck was the murderer, or at least that it was he who had been registered under his father's name at the Railway Hotel. The public began to clamour for an arrest. Everyone knew about Louis Napoleon's extensive secret service, the network of *écosseurs* or 'pea-shellers', the informers on whom the Empire relied for its security against subversives. Why was this great information machine now proving incapable of turning its cogs a little faster? To date all that officialdom could manage was a vain daily effort to erect fences round the Pantin Fields – barriers which would tumble within minutes, as the hordes of sensation-seekers pressed them down. Meanwhile the Emperor expressed his shock at an outrage against a family that represented all the bourgeois values his regime most passionately sponsored. Yet the murder also served the Empire well, providing Paris with an event, like the Great Universal Exhibition of 1867, which distracted the population's and the press's attention from the broader political crisis: the louring socialist and republican agitation, the drumming momentum of opposition massing against the imperial order, was temporarily quelled as the city held its breath, waiting on news of Jean and Gustave Kinck.

On 23 September there was a development. An *écosseur* who loitered in the low dives around the harbour at Le Havre informed the police that he had noticed a young man shopping around for false papers and a passage to America. A couple of days earlier he had booked himself and a companion into the Hôtel New York, signing the register as Herr Fisch, a German tailor who spoke no French. He was tracked down to a tavern on the front, where he was challenged with the question 'Is your real name Gustave Kinck?' He paled dramatically. Offering no resistance, he was arrested and marched along the harbour wall. Suddenly he broke away and leapt into the water with the clear intention of drowning himself. A stalwart caulker at work nearby dived in after him. After a furious struggle, the caulker managed to grab at the man's ankle and drag him ashore almost unconscious. He was then taken to a hospital. Hidden under his shirt, the police were excited to discover a large wallet containing Jean Kinck's papers – property deeds, receipts, identity cards – a gold watch and a silk handkerchief wrapped round 200 francs. They had their man.

But he was not Gustave Kinck. The next morning the celebrated detective Monsieur Claude, who had been put on the case, heard the feeble bedside confession of Jean-Baptiste Troppmann, a nineteen-year-old mechanic from Alsace. About a year earlier he had been sent to Roubaix by his father, another small manufacturer of industrial machinery, to install some equipment, and there he had made the acquaintance of Jean

Kinck and his family. Kinck and he had discussed money-making schemes, which he and Kinck had been pursuing together in Alsace. He had been an accomplice, but only an accomplice, to the murder of the family, holding the victims down while Jean and Gustave had slashed them into cadavers. Their motives were simple: Jean Kinck suspected his wife of adultery; Gustave had acted out of pure rapacity and spite. The three of them had then made for Le Havre in the hope of escaping France. He, Troppmann, was distraught with misery. He had wanted no part in it; he wanted only to die.

The story looked less than convincing, particularly in the light of a letter sent to a newspaper (from a source who obviously did not trust either the discretion or the efficiency of the Second Empire police) disclosing the fact that someone in Guebwiller had recently been suspected of impersonating Gustave Kinck in the course of attempting to cash a money order and collect a registered letter. Like a surgeon delicately probing a patient's innards, Monsieur Claude began the hunt for a deeper cancer of truth. He knew that he had only to wait for the nerves of a callow youth to give way under the pressure of captivity.

Yet Troppmann, although still physically weak, was not easily fazed. In impenetrable silence he endured the handcuffed train journey from Le Havre to Paris, passively allowing himself to be carried through the Gare Saint-Lazare to the shuttered police cab, apparently oblivious of the jeering crowds which would now dog his every public appearance. He was taken to the morgue, where he was asked if he recognized the corpses. Without removing his hat, without a quiver of emotion, he pointed in turn to Madame Kinck, to Emile, to Henri, Alfred, Achille and Marie. He then signed a statement, gently blowing the dust from the paper, testing the pen on his fingernail and replacing it firmly on the inkstand. It was a spine-chilling episode which convinced many of his guilt. Afterwards, he was locked in a cell of the Mazas prison, also occupied by two convict informers detailed to listen to his every word and watch his every move. The police's most pressing worry was that a second time he might succeed in killing himself.

The Pantin Fields now ranked as Paris's principal tourist

attraction – even the exiled Queen of Spain and her retinue had paid a visit. 'Booths and stalls have been erected,' reported *The Times*, 'and there is a great sale of wine and other drinks, of cakes, photographs of the place and of the victims, ginger-bread, fruit, newspapers, beer, red balloons and peacocks' feathers.' Street players re-enacted the crime; hucksters peddled fake relics of the Kinck family; broadsheets advertised scandalous revelations. An unlicensed hawker, arrested in the Boulevard Montmartre while flogging postcards of the Kincks, had screamed drunkenly, 'I am the Pantin murderer,' and caused a great commotion. The respectable weekly magazine *Charivari* complained that the whole affair was being trivialized by what we would now call 'the media circus', but itself showed no reluctance to detail the twists and turns of the tale. At Le Havre a banquet was organized to honour the plucky caulker who had saved Troppmann from drowning and delivered him back to justice. *Le Figaro* presented him with a gold watch; the poor man burst into tears when he was awarded a medal for gallant service to the Empire. There was an unseemly quarrel between various town halls over who was to host the Kincks' funeral: Madame Kinck's birthplace, Tourcoing, won the day, fifty thousand people lined the streets, the state paid the expenses, a subscription was opened for a grand stone memorial, and the Empress adopted as her godchild a niece of Jean Kinck's who shared her birthday. The Kincks were transformed into martyrs, symbols of the light of the Empire, and their funeral oration exhorted France to follow their shining example of family life.

Shortly afterwards, a butcher's boy was taking his dog for an early morning walk across the Pantin Fields. The dog stopped and began to scrabble at the ground with his paws. Further excavation revealed first a shovel and then – as everyone both hoped and feared – the rotting corpse of a young man, his hands tied behind his back, a kitchen knife implanted in his neck. Ladies fainted away at the appalling stink of decomposition, and the electrified onlookers let out a grim cheer when someone spotted the tell-tale label on the body's trousers: Thomas of Roubaix. This could be none other than the Kincks' eldest son, Gustave, buried (so the coroner would estimate) two or three days before his siblings.

Troppmann meanwhile was refusing food, and spent most of his waking hours leafing sullenly through back numbers of *Le Magasin Pittoresque*, an encyclopedia in weekly parts. His celebrity seemed not altogether to displease him, and he boasted that he could sell the right to photograph him for at least ten thousand francs. Taken back to the morgue to identify Gustave, he muttered 'Salaud!', 'Swine!', at the spectacle. 'What do you mean?' asked Monsieur Claude. 'Now Kinck has killed his eldest son,' Troppmann replied. 'I do not believe you,' said Monsieur Claude. Troppmann shrugged.

But the incident unleashed some daemon in Troppmann's soul. He soon began talking, at first slowly, then in a hysterical babble of anger and self-contradiction from which Monsieur Claude and his agents finally assembled a sort of personal history.

He had always been an outsider, this Alsatian boy, with no close friends that anyone had ever noticed, and a streak of solitary megalomaniac ambition. 'I shall do something that will astonish the universe,' a schoolfellow remembered him saying, and through his adolescence he became increasingly obsessed with the possibility of making a fortune. He read a lot – trashy adventure novels and scientific manuals; perhaps Jules Verne's fictions too – kept himself to himself, showed no interest in women, and had a violent temper. At home he filled his bedroom with crude chemical apparatus, on which he conducted complex experiments. He was bitter about the fate of his father, a clever and resourceful artisan who earlier in his life had been tricked by an unscrupulous partner and ended up bankrupt and alcoholic. His father's failure made his own motivation to succeed all the more intense: a feeling of being overlooked and hard done by soured Troppmann. In everything he went on to say about Jean Kinck, that note of bitterness sounded at a pitch of murderous envy.

They had met in a brasserie in Roubaix, and began to chat about Alsace and their shared interest in machinery and the money that could be made from it. Troppmann told Kinck about an invention he had been working on with his father – a revolutionary new type of papier-mâché filtering nozzle which he needed money to develop. Kinck was intrigued by this fervent young man, and invited him home to meet his wife Hortense, his son Gustave, already working in the family business, and the rest of his brood. In the following weeks Troppmann became a regular visitor and dinner guest *chez* Kinck, and when he moved to Paris to work on an installation in Pantin, he kept in touch with his successful older friend. He also hatched a plan to profit from his gullibility, his greed, his hypocrisy and conceit. For this much-respected and handsomely rewarded Jean Kinck was nothing better, Troppmann would claim, than a well-dressed middle-class crook who clearly wanted to steal his nozzle idea and manufacture the thing himself.

Troppmann played Kinck along, confiding that he had a lair in the cellars of an abandoned château in the middle of a forest in Alsace, where the prototypes for the nozzle were stored, and where he also had the means to counterfeit money in conditions of total secrecy. Kinck's appetite was whetted. 'I have found a room in which we can do everything we want,' Troppmann's letter read: come to Alsace, bring money, and I will show you. So Kinck went, and on the long walk through the forest towards this mysterious château, Troppmann slipped into his picnic wine flask a slug of prussic acid. 'Kinck lies dead and unburied in that forest; I will draw you a map so that you can find him. I killed Kinck *père* so as to gain possession of the money which he told me he had at his bank and which would be paid when he handed over the bond. I proposed to cash that bond by forging the writing and signature of Jean Kinck. Once I had killed him,' he continued blandly in his confession, 'it in some sense became a necessity for me to kill the members of his family, so that nobody would know that Jean Kinck had come to see me in my own part of the country.'

Troppmann stole Jean Kinck's wallet, but despite possession of all his identity papers, failed to cash the 5,500-franc bond, arousing suspicion in his bid to do so. He wrote to Madame Kinck 'on behalf of Jean Kinck', asking her to send cash by registered letter. This she did – but the Post Office refused to hand the letter over. He then wrote to Gustave Kinck, asking the boy to come to Alsace where he could claim the bond and take the cash to his father 'who has unexpectedly been obliged to return to Paris'. Like a lamb Gustave went, was also refused at the bank, and then accompanied Troppmann back to Paris, where he was murdered.

At the Railway Hotel Troppmann began to impersonate Jean Kinck. He wrote a series of letters to Madame Kinck, pretending to be acting as her husband's amanuensis, and sent telegrams, signed Gustave Kinck, proposing arrangements for her to bring more cash and the family to Pantin. In her anxiety, she caught an early train, arrived prematurely at the hotel, found nobody there, deposited her luggage, and returned to the station where Troppmann awaited her: a few hours previously he had bought a pickaxe and a shovel from a hardware store. He hired a cab, telling them that he would take them all to the house near the Pantin Fields where Jean was supposedly staying. And there he murdered them too.

Monsieur Claude was still not satisfied. How had Troppmann alone managed to dig a large pit in the time available to him between visiting the hardware store and arriving at the station? How had Troppmann managed to walk nearly a mile from the cab with a woman and two small straggling children, murder and bury them, and then return to the cab, all within what the driver reliably remembered as about twenty-five minutes? A polisher had come forward to witness that on that Sunday evening he had seen a woman with one child in her arms, another by her side, walking along the Pantin road, 'followed by three men, each holding a stout stick'. Troppmann's broken father had written his imprisoned son a letter asking him why he did not reveal his accomplices; other letters, all anonymous and quite possibly crackpot, threatened awful reprisals if he *did* implicate anyone else. The notion stuck: what was Troppmann holding back? Following his indications, the corpse of Jean Kinck had eventually been found. Squawking crows led the search party to his remains, propped against a tree, picked dry and hollow, only identifiable by the woollen stockings. But even then the dossier was not complete.

By the middle of October, Troppmann had come out of his stupor. His behaviour often showed a crazy sort of elation, as though nothing had happened at all, as though he had just been caught up in a misunderstanding. 'There were days when he laughed, joked and displayed his muscular force and skill, lifting heavy chairs between the thumb and forefinger of his left hand,' reported the *Gazette des Tribunaux*. 'He wrestled with a keeper. Last Sunday he danced.' Then he sent a letter to Monsieur Claude. He had more to tell, more to explain; previously he had lied, but now he would tell the truth. About two years ago, in his native town of Cernay, he had surprised three men in the act of burglary. One of them Troppmann recognized and subsequently blackmailed. Since that time he had been in some sort of league with these three criminals, and they had all been involved together in setting up the money-forging business in the ruined château. Troppmann's plan had been to rob Jean Kinck of the 5,500 francs and leave it at that. But one of his accomplices had insisted that he be murdered, and did so. The whole mess had followed that pattern: he, Troppmann, trying and failing, to restrain his accomplices from their bent for violence. Madame Kinck knew of her husband's schemes – they must murder her; Gustave likewise. Troppmann had not wanted to kill the children, but they had refused to stay in the cab, and the accomplices had argued that there must be no witnesses. There had been a struggle on the Pantin Fields, and the accomplices had come to blows with him: he had the scars and bruises to prove it. The next day they had fled to Le Havre, where he and one of the others had booked into the Hôtel New York.

He had not confessed all this before for one reason: he was not prepared to reveal identities. He explained: 'If I denounced one of them, the others would also be denounced, and a whole family would end up without bread. Therefore I will not denounce them. I shall face the consequences alone. There is enough unhappiness in my own family, without it spreading to other families, even though the leader of the gang deserves to be punished.'

You are not telling the truth, said Monsieur Claude. Was this not a delaying tactic, aimed at deferring the trial until 'the accomplices' had been traced? All Troppmann would add was that there was a wallet buried in the forest in Alsace which contained documents verifying his story. If the authorities would take him there, he could show them where it was; he even provided another map. The offer was ignored. I do not believe you, repeated Monsieur Claude. Did I not lead you to Jean Kinck? asked Troppmann. Why can you not believe me now?

The press showed no qualms about assuming guilt, and the public followed suit. Only a certain Dr Amédée Bertrand published a 'medical-legal' pamphlet, theorizing as to Troppmann's clinical condition. 'I detect a mental disorder,' he wrote. 'The structure and feeble irrigation of the criminal's brain provoked in him a cerebral compression which gave rise to an insane monomania. Troppmann hoped that his nozzle would become a national wonder and assure his family fortune. This *idée fixe* provoked congestion of the blood, increasing the size of his brain while diminishing its circulation.'

Bertrand's view was that this process had been reversed by the 'saline purge' suffered by Troppmann when he tried to drown himself in the harbour of Le Havre – a shock to the system which was gradually releasing the 'cerebral compression' and restoring his reason. Bertrand's neurology may sound somewhat naive, but it suggested a line of defence in the four-day trial, which opened after Christmas.

Six hundred citizens were daily admitted to the public gallery. The press box was packed with journalists from all over the Western world and a number of literary celebrities (such as Alexandre Dumas *fils*), waiting for their first long, hard look at this haunting and unfathomable creature. What they saw in the dock was a fresh and podgy-faced boy, dressed uncomfortably in his Sunday best suit. In prison, fear of another suicide attempt meant that he had not been allowed a razor, but his lawyer had insisted that a straggling black beard made an unfairly sinister impression, so he was put into a strait-jacket while a barber cut and trimmed him into a passably attractive chap, with a fine thick head of hair which he constantly smoothed and fingered. He seemed painfully daunted by the proceedings, replying to questions in low, provincial tones which at times could hardly be deciphered, at the levels of either volume or accent. But the most strange and hypnotizing aspect of Troppmann was his hugely splayed hands on which the thumbs were the same length as the index fingers – not worker's hands, but strangler's hands, freakish hands with the contours of evil to them: hands that somehow could have blindly slashed and wrenched to death a mother and her five children within the few allotted minutes.

The prosecution called over sixty witnesses and composed a compelling picture of the Kincks as a model of middle-class probity, industry and good-citizenship, betrayed by a treacherous proletarian whom they had befriended and trusted. Troppmann became not so much a murderer as a thunderclap of revolution, one of the wild animals ready to rampage over the sweet suburban pastures of the Empire as soon as the cage was unbarred.

The prosecution witnesses ranged from forensic experts who had analysed the blood on the clothing found in the Railway Hotel, to a man who had walked with Troppmann in the park of Saint-Cloud a week before the murders and listened to him boasting of how he could lay his hands on 25,000 francs and how he had once thrown a man into a river in the course of a scuffle. 'Did he stay in the water?' asked the judge. 'I don't know and I don't care,' replied Troppmann. A nightwatchman at one of the Pantin factories claimed to have heard various shouts, inter-spersed with cries of 'Maman! Maman!' on the night of the murders, but thought it was only some marital quarrel, which he decided to ignore. 'What you heard was me arguing with my accomplices,' was Troppmann's comment. 'I was begging them not to kill the children.'

His defence was conducted by Charles-Alexandre Lachaud, a celebrated lawyer with an appetite for taking on lost causes and a fair record of winning them back. Following Dr Bertrand's cue, Lachaud argued for a Troppmann driven insane by his desire to get rich, someone of intense seriousness whose only vice or even frivolity was the reading of twopenny fiction (such as Eugène Sue's blockbuster *The Wandering Jew*, which features a young man who so covets a rival's fortune that he kills a family of six to secure it). In a rhetorical effort to humanize the monster, he painted a touching picture of Troppmann's absolute devotion to his mother – at which point in the discourse the monster bowed his head and appeared to force back tears. It was the only vivid gesture of emotion he made during the trial, although there were many who interpreted it as a feint.

More crucially, he addressed the problem of the anonymous accomplices. Only one of the five defence witnesses could throw any light on the matter: unfortunately it was, quite literally, a grey and hazy light, cast by a fourteen-year-old apprentice wallpaperer whose record of veracity, according to his father's report to the police, was less than spotless. Nevertheless, his story had some circumstantial plausibility: walking across the Pantin Fields late one foggy evening in the company of a soldier, the boy had come across two men digging a pit, another man apparently curled up asleep beside them. They had exchanged a few perfunctory words, but because of the mists the boy and the soldier could not see precisely what was going on. The soldier could not be traced; the meteorological records suggested that the nights at the time had been clear. Similar sightings of Troppmann in the company of others were also inconclusive, so Lachaud concentrated on the buried wallet. Why had the police not traced it? Or had they traced it, and then suppressed its uncomfortable or embarrassing contents? Was Jean Kinck what he appeared to be? Were there larger dimensions to the activities in the forests of Alsace, so close to the German border? These questions were never satisfactorily answered.

Nor was the incomprehensible timetable of the murder of Madame Kinck and her children ever unravelled; nor the reason why Troppmann – in a position in which he had nothing to lose – refused to denounce his accomplices ever determined. 'You could say, if you like, that it is because of the daughter of the eldest of my accomplices that I don't want to reveal their names,' he told Lachaud once – but it was a straw of a pretext that he never clutched at again. Nothing could save Troppmann from a conviction on all counts and a death sentence: Lachaud had hoped to swing a verdict of insanity, but Troppmann's composed demeanour hardly encouraged it. 'He laughed! He laughed!' someone in the public gallery shouted, as he rose and turned to leave the court; but the reporter for *Le Moniteur* thought that it was only an involuntary facial twitch.

Back in his cell, he seemed indifferent. 'Oh, I quite expected it,' was his only comment on his fate. Earlier, letters he had smuggled to the prison pharmacist begging for poison had been intercepted; now they strait-jacketed him again, to await the result of the appeals. He ate and drank and read and slept and said very little. The public's fascination, over three months after the murders, was unabated. 'Everything has been said and it is perhaps too late to present my view of Jean-Baptiste Tropp-mann,' admitted the columnist of the satirical magazine *La Parodie*. But stories of monsters of this sort are like sweetmeats: people can't stay away from them, and keep on going back for more. 'On comes indigestion; and Paris will continue to have indigestion from the author of the massacre of Pantin until he has, well, umm, disappeared.' Everyone keeps debating the degree of his intelligence, the columnist continued. Is he so unusual? All workers in the heavily industrialized Alsatian region seem, like him, 'able and greedy'; but Troppmann has in many ways surely proved himself 'an atrocious imbecile':

He wanted a fortune, and to get it, what did he do? What spoils were his goal? He destroys an entire family not to grab at a lump of hard cash, but at cheques, deeds and titles difficult to exchange or realize, without thinking that the family might have legal heirs; imagining that, once the blow had been struck and the corpses were pushing up daisies, he had only to present himself somewhere or other in order to be handed the sum of the Kinck fortune and then to leave in peace of mind for America.

. . . He arrives at Le Havre completely unknown. He is on the point of embarking, when at the sight of the first gendarme idling along, he panics, and *piffff*, throws himself into the harbour. He is fished out and immediately confesses to the murder of Jean Kinck . . . He then has the good-heartedness to provide the most precise indications as to the whereabouts of a corpse which otherwise would never have been found, and whose discovery can only lead him to the scaffold. What incredible simple-mindedness! What sinister stupidity!

Even if this was indeed *une parodie* of the situation, there is no denying that Troppmann's conduct and motives were far from explicable or coherent, and in the days pending his appeal and Lachaud's plea to the Emperor for clemency, another piece of evidence emerged to confuse the matter further. A certain Madame Brett, who ran the Taverne de Londres in Pantin, had been called at the trial as a witness for the defence because she claimed to have seen Troppmann the morning after the murders, sitting in her establishment with three other men, all looking like provincials on an outing in their Sunday best. Troppmann, for some reason, furiously denied that he had ever been to this restaurant or so much as heard of the type of beer Madame Brett remembered serving them. She had now received a series of anonymous letters claiming that if she went to see Troppmann in prison, her resemblance to his mother would lead him to break down and reveal the identity of his accomplices. Madame Brett sent the letters on to the Empress, who in turn passed them to the Ministry of Justice, which asked her to present herself in Troppmann's cell and to see what happened. The result was disappointing – he announced that the letters were in the handwriting of one of his accomplices, but then fell into one of his impenetrable silences, his head turned to the wall. Why, everyone wondered, should anyone culpable have risked sending such letters in the first place?

The last doors were closing. On 13 January the appeal court rejected the request for a retrial and the Emperor refused clemency. On 16 January Troppmann was advised to take communion, and the prison chaplain heard his confession. He was as unmoved by the consolations of religion as he was by these signs of his inexorable end, asking only for the latest issue of *Le Magasin Pittoresque*, from which he had once learnt the recipe for the prussic acid that had killed Jean Kinck. His execution was set for dawn on 19 January, but the law forbade him to be forewarned.

It was an event made memorable by no less an observer than the Russian novelist Ivan Turgenev, then resident in Paris. He had been invited by Flaubert's *confrère* Maxime du Camp to join a small party of journalistic witnesses admitted to a privileged view of not only the guillotining itself – held in the courtyard of the prison of La Roquette, the gates of which would be thrown open at the last moment, allowing the public to take their salutary fill – but also the more intimately horrible spectacle of the ritual last half-hour passage from cell to scaffold.*

On his way to La Roquette at midnight on 18 January, Turgenev was struck by the explosive carnival atmosphere in the streets around the prison – the cafés and bars thronged with light and people, crowds already jostling for the best places, despite the bitter cold. Two cavalry detachments had been placed four deep at the gates, in case of riot. Received for the vigil by the governor in his apartment, Turgenev presented two bottles of Bordeaux, a ham and a box of cigars to add to the picnic spread of stuffed turkey, *pâté de foie gras*, sandwiches, punch and tea. He had no appetite for any of it. Troppmann, on the other hand, was reported to have eaten well and to be sleeping soundly. The party also included Monsieur Claude and his secretary, as well as other literary celebrities such as the playwright Victorien Sardou. The governor attempted to entertain his guests by laying out some of the letters that Troppmann had been sent, all of which he had refused to read. There was a twenty-page screed from a Methodist clergyman, analysing his guilt from a Protestant angle; there were pressed violets and marguerites from a sympathetic lady; and a wad of obviously lunatic scribblings from 'accomplices'. The conversation soon sank into a round of platitudes – about the trial, about capital punishment, about Troppmann's psychology and phrenology. Some little jokes fell sour and flat. There was a flurry of excitement when the executioner Heidenreich, alias 'Monsieur de Paris', arrived, accompanying the guillotine, which was trundled into the square on a cart, its pieces assembled by workmen who behaved 'as though they were constructing a

---

* Turgenev wrestled with his conscience before accepting du Camp's grisly invitation. The argument that the resulting essay would serve as a powerful polemic against capital punishment tipped the intellectual balance; while naked instinctual curiosity overcame any other qualms. An infuriated Dostoevsky (himself, of course, once condemned to death) raged against the whole exercise. 'It is the ostentatious delicacy that outraged me,' he wrote to his friend Strakhov. 'Why does he never cease to declare that he had no right to be present? His only *real* worry is the impression that his article will make.'

fairground booth'. The dummy drops of the blade provoked catcalls and applause. Heidenreich's air of patriarchal gravity, his elegant white hands, and his black coat, buttoned to the neck in military fashion, were remarked, but his presence made the atmosphere all the more intolerable. Variously the guests enquired after Troppmann, glanced at the clock, yawned, went downstairs into the yard to chat to the soldiers who had broken off for coffee, came back and sat down again. Eventually Turgenev dropped on to a sofa, wrapped his scarf round his ears to shut out the noise and tried to snatch some sleep.

Outside the horses whinnied as the crowd's murmur swelled 'in an unending Wagnerian crescendo, not rising continuously, but with long intervals between the ebb and flow . . . the rumble and roar of some elemental force'. The stink of alcohol was palpable, and the pothouses for a mile around glowed infernally in the darkness. A boy falling off a tree to his death caused hysterical laughter. Troppmann slept on.

At 6 a.m. breakfast and a priest arrived in the governor's room. Monsieur Claude clapped his hands for the party to compose themselves. 'Gentlemen, your hats and coats! It is time.' Through heavy doors, down long passages, and up dank staircases, they made their way down to Troppmann's cell, separated from the street and its tumults by three layers of wall. A black-haired, black-eyed boy with pink cheeks sat at the table. He received the deputation with barely a nod. Monsieur Claude removed his hat and – as Albert Wolff, another journalist present, records – announced to Troppmann that his pardon had been refused and that the moment of expiation had arrived.

'Do you want a glass of wine?' the prison warder asked the condemned man.

'No, I don't need anything at all,' replied the murderer of the Kinck family.

The warders removed his strait-jacket and gave him back the clothes he had worn at his trial. Troppmann dressed himself with the calm of a man about to go out for a walk, while Monsieur Claude asked him: 'Well, Troppmann, in your last hour, do you persist in your claims? Did you have accomplices?'

'Yes.'

'Do you wish to name them?'

'No.'

'And so, you continue to deny that you committed the murders in the Pantin Fields?'

'I struck nobody,' he replied in the utmost calm, as he pulled on his trousers.

'Troppmann, can I do you any last service?'

'Yes,' he replied.

'What is it?'

'In the drawer of this table is a letter for my mother.'

At this point Troppmann's tone faltered. Several of us turned away in tears; but to banish both his emotion and ours, the murderer continued: 'You will have to stamp it. I haven't got a *sou*.'

After he had kicked the heels of his boots against the floor to make sure his feet sat in them comfortably, the cell was cleared for a priest to give absolution. What sustained the boy, Turgenev wondered? 'Was it the fact that, though he was not showing off, he wanted to "cut a figure" before the spectators . . . Or was it innate fearlessness and vanity . . . the pride of the struggle that had to be kept up to the end – or something else, some still undivined feeling?'

Troppmann seemed to hurry of his own accord out of his cell, climbing two steps at a time towards the *salle de toilette*, the witnesses following him in an awkward crush, treading on each other's feet, knocking each other's shoulders. He sat unresistingly for the last shacklings and fastenings and obligingly bent his head forward for the last haircut. As a lock of thick brown hair fell on to his shoe, Turgenev was deeply struck by the whiteness and slimness of his boyish neck, laid bare for the blade. Once more Monsieur Claude asked him: 'Do you still insist that you had accomplices?' 'Yes, but I will not name them.' 'What is your last request?' 'Nothing.' 'Very well, let us go.'

The morning was damp and foggy, and nothing much could be seen; but when, moments before 7 a.m., the gates of La Roquette opened 'like the mouth of some enormous animal', the crowd's undulating crescendo exploded into a climactic thunderclap which hung heavy in the air. Out of a side door hurtled Troppmann, propelled by guards, his torso strapped and trussed. For one second he recoiled as though he had been punched in the stomach – Turgenev thought the boy was going to faint. Then he scrambled up the ten steps to the guillotine, and as he was pinioned flat screamed his last unyielding words: 'Dites à Monsieur Claude que je persiste!' 'Tell Monsieur Claude that I persist' – persist in claiming his accomplices, persist in holding his enigma. There was another long second's terrible and absolute silence, as though every sound had been rolled into a tight ball.

Turgenev turned away: a light knock, a swish, a thud, and Jean-Baptiste Troppmann was dead. In that final brief eternity, he had twisted his head convulsively in the wooden slot. One of the executioner's assistants pulled him by the hair back into place and Troppmann bit deep into his hand as the blade fell. In the ensuing dreadful release of tension, two men slipped through the barricade of soldiers and managed to soak their handkerchiefs in Troppmann's blood – a last souvenir of the Pantin massacre. Heidenreich quietly asked Albert Wolff for a cigar. Three doctors had bid for the honour of dissecting the body, but the state returned it to the family and anonymous burial.

Every murder holds a mirror to society's underbelly – its conscience, its values, its soul. Troppmann's story tells us about the way that the Second Empire's promotion of enterprise, commerce and profit as moral ideals could poison a fantasizing teenager; it tells us about the bourgeois' fear of the worker and the corruption of justice. None of these are unfamiliar phenomena; what makes the case more interesting is that it came at a point when the regime was painfully and silently beginning to realize that its time was up, and Troppmann served as a terrible portent of what might be to come next. The nation was obsessed with him: Flaubert published his great novel *L' Éducation Sentimentale* during the 'Troppmann months' and blamed its poor reception ('strangled at birth') on the fact that nobody could think seriously about anything else except the murder. 'The success of Troppmann,' as he put it to George Sand in 1871, was a diagnosis of 'the mental disorder of France'.

For some years, the case continued to be the focus of fantasy, speculation and paranoia. The Left pondered the possibility that Troppmann had been acting under instructions from Louis Napoleon's lackeys, and that the murder was a propaganda operation, designed to divert attention at a time of crisis; the Right liked to think that Troppmann was a Prussian agent – for Alsace was rumoured to be an area honeycombed with Prussian spies, and might not Jean Kinck have unwittingly stumbled on some secret industrial or espionage information?

There is no real evidence to substantiate either of these constructions, but Troppmann's trial did leave several questions naggingly unanswered. Was there a buried wallet, and why did the authorities show no interest in locating it? Or was it found, and were its contents considered too 'sensitive' to reveal? How could one man have single-handedly managed the massacre of the Pantin Fields? Who were Troppmann's companions in Paris and Le Havre? And what were his motives for persisting in his silence? Perhaps they were more personal than political. Some element of blackmail? Of revenge? Of homosexuality? Of a psychotic hatred of a smugly contented and prosperous nuclear family? We can only be sure that there was another dimension to Troppmann's story which nobody will ever know.

3 : *Monuments of Hypocrisy*

Some three weeks before the murder of Madame Kinck and her children, a different sort of crime had outraged Paris. On the night of 26–7 August 1869, some unknown person or persons had thrown the contents of a large bottle of black ink over a group of marble figures which decorated the façade of the opera house currently being constructed on a site north of the Tuileries Palace. The sculpture was entitled 'La Danse'; it had been unveiled to the public a month previously, the work of Jean-Baptiste Carpeaux, whose fleet and graceful style had won him several commissions from the imperial court and the special favour of the Empress.

The ink had sprayed over the flanks of two naked women, part of a ring dancing around the figure of an exultant Bacchus: the artist had chosen, in the words of the critic of *L'Univers*, to depict the revellers at the point at which 'exhausted, . . . they feel their legs weakening; giving way to the movement which impels them, they no longer have the strength either to continue or to stop'. Today, to the thousands who mill around the Place de l'Opéra, the spectacle this presents is about as erotically whiffy as the Statue of Liberty; but in 1869 it suggested something which took it far beyond the normal boundaries of academic sculpture and its respectable representations of nudity.

Carpeaux was summoned to inspect the vandalism and dashed off a furious telegram – 'Defiled by spite. General indignation. Letter follows. Carpeaux' – to the Opéra's architect, Charles Garnier, who was sunning himself in St Jean de Luz. In fact the indignation was by no means general. Carpeaux's supporters began a sort of vigil around the statue and placed a laurel wreath on its pedestal. Art students chanted anti-bourgeois slogans. But the press was divided, and in over two hundred articles various stands were taken on behalf of the Necessity of Public Decency, the Freedom of the Artist, the Vulgarity of Modern Art etc. The cartoonists had fun: 'Don't stare like that, it only encourages them,' snarls an old gent to his wife, mesmerized by the sculpture's goings-on; 'Are you mad, girl?' a mother asks her daughter. 'Going to the dance completely naked?' 'But, maman,' she replies, 'look at Carpeaux's group!' Then there were the jokes about all the sculptors in Paris throwing bottles of ink at their work, in an effort to win publicity.

As to the culprit, there were no clues. Could it have been another misprized sculptor? Or perhaps, in some Machiavellian attempt to rally sympathy, Carpeaux himself? 'It is impossible to say whether it was some fanatical upholder of the proprieties, or, more probably, some mischievous ruffian,' reflected *The Times*'s correspondent. On 30 August it was announced that another statue, of Acis and Galatea, in the Luxembourg Gardens, had been similarly attacked two weeks previously. The railway companies offered special day trips for those in the suburbs who might wish to view the evidence. The Théâtre Dejazet mounted a splendid *tableau vivant* of the spotted 'La Danse'.

Meanwhile, the Opéra's works management was receiving a flood of letters from chemists, stonemasons, dyers, decorators, stained-glass windowers, all proffering their recipes for removing the ink – no simple job, since the marble was highly porous and the offending substance had sunk deep. Following experiments with acids and jets of steam, whose failure greatly amused the crowds, 'a concentrated solution of alumine hyperchlorite, soda and lime, with hydrated alumine,' was applied twice in a thick paste and washed off with distilled water. It worked. 'And now,' mocked *The Times* on 3 September, 'people assemble to gaze at the place where the ink-stain was, and to wonder how very well it has been got out'.

The investigations of the police came to nothing.

Examination of the fragments of the guilty ink bottle, which had shattered against the marble, revealed that it had been – an ink bottle. On 8 September, however, came another turn of the screw, when a worker found a rolled-up sheet of paper at the foot of the statue, which some party had presumably thrown over the protective fencing. 'It is not the ink-stain which should be removed,' it read, 'but this statuary of revolting indecency. It must go, or else it will be smashed up.'

Over the coming months, the fate of 'La Danse' continued to be a minor political worry. There was some question of removing it to the relative privacy of a gymnasium or a dancehall. A collector offered to buy it off the state for 100,000 francs. Carpeaux, it was suggested, could be re-commissioned. The sculptor would have none of it. (He was enraged on another front too. The scandal had resulted in a flood of unlicensed postcards of the statue, which Carpeaux had impounded as an infringement of his copyright. A long and inconclusive wrangle followed, forming an interesting footnote to the problems thrown up by the new phenomenon of photographic reproduction.) He sent a framed and signed picture of 'La Danse' to the Emperor, and wrote to the thirteen-year-old Prince Impérial, whom he had recently sculpted, in the hope of soliciting his support. 'Between ourselves,' his tutor responded, 'I don't know whether the Prince, who has not yet seen your work, would be altogether competent to discuss or make any sort of judgement of its merits.' In the event, larger dramas conspired to make France forget 'La Danse', and by the time the Opéra Garnier opened in 1875, Carpeaux was dead, and his sculpture accepted. Ninety years later its weathered and decrepit state led to its removal: a reproduction now stands on the right-hand side of the building's façade, and the original is handsomely lodged in the Musée d'Orsay.

But why, precisely, had it given such offence? Perhaps because 'La Danse' communicated not the safely distanced and acceptable aura of classical mythology so much as the racket from the downtown taverns and halls of a city in which the manners associated with dancing had fallen quite out of hand. *The Times*'s correspondent missed the point when he described the sculpture as 'meretricious', if 'quite good enough for the tawdry edifice of which it forms one of the ornaments'. *Le Figaro* had a sharper idea of what Carpeaux was about. 'These are not the women of Phidias, of Cleomenes, of Praxiteles,' it surmised. 'No! these are women of the nineteenth century, women as we know them to be . . .' The critic of *Le Français* went further in accusing Carpeaux of merely sculpting some 'dancers of the Bal Mabille in their most daring postures'. Another cartoon: 'Where did you learn to dance like that?' shrieks a mother at her small daughter, who is violently thrusting her leg into the air. 'Why, from the statue in front of the Opéra,' she says.

That high-flying leg was the emblem of the cancan, which was not really a dance at all, more a frame of mind in which you danced. Some say that it came from Algeria, imported like absinthe by soldiers serving there; some that it was a variant of the polka, popular in the 1840s, and featuring a choreographed kick; but by the 1860s it had no rules at all, no fixed movements or rhythms, no beginning or end. 'Instead of moving in unison, with the maximum of elegance and grace possible, these dancers invent their own movements,' complained the *Revue et Gazette Musicale de Paris*. There were 'no agreed patterns, no routine, no uniformity: only a storm-charge . . . everybody following their own demon'.

The Larousse *Encyclopédie* of 1867 defined it as 'a very free dance, accompanied by indecent gestures and a swaying like the comportment of a duck . . . nothing more than a drunkard's lurching'. Forget the image of a saucy chorus line in white frillies: that is the *fin de siècle* gentrification for the tourists of what in the 1860s was a sexually predatory ritual, open to all comers, in which most women went knickerless, flashing glimpses of their genitals to the men, challenging them to thrust and enter, as the dance became hotter, faster, louder. To cancan was to jive, rave it up, freak out and go stir crazy, 'to dance as wildly as noisily, as furiously as you can' – thus Mark Twain in *The Innocents Abroad* – 'expose yourself as much as possible if you are a woman; and kick as high as you can no matter what sex you belong to'. In the frightened, fascinated eyes of the intellectuals, this was the working class showing its claws, signalling the aggression that it might one day let rip.

At Compiègne the guests may have been yawning their way through a Sir Roger de Coverley, the gentlemen chastely clasping their hands behind their backs, each turn scripted, each bow preordained; in the great court balls at the Tuileries Palace, the waltzes of Strauss or Waldteufel may have allowed a warmer lilt and some pleasant hint of physical proximity; but after midnight in the Salon de Wauxhall, in smoky dives such as the Assommoir du Temple – a billiard hall and doss-house in which, once a week, the straw was cleaned from the floor and a band shuffled in – in nameless taverns or *guingettes* under the city walls, anarchy was the only law. The police made their perfunctory raid, checking for public indecency and the presence of minors, then the whores crowded in, small boys stood on one another's shoulders to peep through the shutters, and merry hell exploded. 'When I dance I experience something akin to an attack of madness . . . The music enters and rises to my head like champagne. When the last bars ring out I am drunk. Then I have a fit of rage which cannot be compared to anything. My arms become weak, my legs as if adrift.'

So in her memoirs wrote the notorious Rigolboche, otherwise Marguerite the Huguenot, otherwise Marguerite Bedel from an industrial town in Lorraine, who looked, it was said, 'like a pig that has removed its spectacles', but who made her fortune by manoeuvring her legs through all angles, degrees, and contortions. The state of possession and exhaustion she describes is akin to the one suggested by the comportment of the female figures in Carpeaux's sculpture; the Bacchus in their midst could have been another star of the dance floor, Clodoche, otherwise Clodomir Ricart. He was a cabinet-maker, strictly an amateur who could be hired for the evening to liven up the proceedings. He came as the centre-piece of a team and concocted ever more bizarre routines, such as 'Les Pompiers de Nanterre' (*pompier* means 'fireman' and also 'cock-sucker'). His appearances were invariably sensational: one night, the Emperor, wrapped for anonymity in a domino, slipped in to watch him from a box at the Opéra ball. Later he summoned the phenomenon and acknowledged his genius with a gift of 400 francs.

'La Danse' also challenged a deep and confused hypocrisy.

The statue was intended to celebrate, or advertise, the activities of a theoretically respectable institution of national culture, heavily subsidized by the State and regularly patronized by the ruling classes. But Carpeaux had, in a sense, blown the cover. 'La Danse' showed the dance up for what it truly was: orgiastic, a stimulation and even a satisfaction of sexual appetite. Ballet was not the pretty, genteel entertainment, the innocent 'refuge of art and fantasy', the 'enchanted world' which the poet and aesthetician Théophile Gautier wittered on about. And perhaps Carpeaux's stone figures, insisted *L'Opinion Nationale*, were not half as obscene as the flesh-and-blood ballerinas inside an opera house, 'half-naked, gracefully raising one foot to the level of a shoulder while turning on the point of the other foot, leaning back in voluptuous and swooning positions and exhausting the art of revealing to the public things it has no business seeing'. Where lay the worse scandal? 'Is there not a huge contradiction between seeing a woman thrown out of a public dancehall for lifting her leg,' asks the Larousse *Encyclopédie*, 'while two hundred dancers, in short dresses, lift them even higher, to the universal applause of an audience in the opera house?' Behind the gauze and flummery, the opera house was peddling little more than naked sexual titillation.

'The man of fashion,' wrote Charles Yriarte in 1867:

has a horror . . . of anything artistic, which must be listened to, respected, or requires an effort to be understood . . . I wager that eight out of every ten subscribers prefer *Pierre de Médicis* to the fourth act of *Les Huguenots*, and *Néméa* to *Guillaume Tell*. And why? Simply because Louise Fiocre shows her limbs in *Pierre*, and her younger sister Eugénie shows much more than that in *Néméa*. And because, when you are a man of fashion with your box at the Opéra, and have listened to *Les Huguenots* and *Guillaume Tell* a hundred times, you would much rather visit it calmly and without going through violent musical emotions, recline in an excellent seat, equipped with excellent opera glasses, and indulge in the cult of the *plastique*. To the soothing strains of sweet and lively music your attention can wander from the calves of Mlle Brach or Mlle Carabin to the shoulders of Mme de N—, and during the interval, you can visit every box, or receive visitors in your own. That is the real Opéra.

There was an even more sordid reality behind such diatribes. The man of fashion did not stop at slavering through his opera glasses. He was more than a voyeur. The man of fashion surveyed the performers not as gas-lit fantasies, but as items on a menu which could be purchased at a price by certain privileged connoisseurs. The ballet was 'an exhibition of girls for sale', as Monsieur Graindorge, Hippolyte Taine's fictional commentator on Parisian life and times, insisted. 'From the stage to the auditorium, from the wings to the stage, and from one side of the auditorium to the other, invisible threads criss-cross between actresses' smiles, dancers' legs, and men's opera glasses, in a network of arousal and liaison,' agree the Goncourt brothers. 'One couldn't gather together in less space a greater number of sexual stimuli, of invitations to copulate. It's like the Stock Exchange.'

The Opéra, in sum, had the delicate whispered function of operating as the smartest brothel in Paris, one in which the Emperor kept his own *loge intime*, his private room. Its salon was the Foyer de la Danse, a dimly lit, mirrored and undecorated room in which the girls warmed up at the barre before a performance. Admission was obtained with difficulty, as demand greatly exceeded supply. Apart from the court and some very rich nobility, only members of the exclusive Jockey Club (properly, the Society for the Encouragement of the Improvement of Horse Breeding in France), who subscribed to eight boxes in the auditorium, could reasonably hope for access. And, once inside, there was another problem: the girls were 'managed' by their mothers, who gaggled at the stage door, ready to inspect, sift and barter with their daughters' suitors. 'Epic scenes took place there,' records de Maugny in his memoirs: 'I have seen maidens departing triumphantly on an admirer's arm after a good quarter of an hour's discussion with *maman*. I have seen some disappear secretly behind their duenna's back, leaving her prey to an epileptic seizure; and others carrying on brazenly beneath their very nose and receiving a volley of blows that would have terrified a street-porter.'

The stories are legion. When King Victor Emmanuel of

Piedmont visited Paris, he was said to have enquired whether it was true that French dancers did not wear knickers. 'If that is so,' he sighed wistfully, 'earthly paradise is in store for me.' The Emperor duly took him on a state visit to the Opéra, where, transported by the beauty of one of the *corps de ballet*, the King asked a flunkey what her price might be. Fifty gold louis, he was told. Victor Emmanuel was outraged at her exorbitance. 'Don't trouble yourself, *mon frère*,' interposed the Emperor, 'just charge it to my account.' There was Francine Cellier, kept by Baron Haussmann, who dressed her exactly like his daughter in order to avoid being spotted in public; Eline Volter, notorious for arriving late on stage, for reasons which would send the Jockey Club into fits of knowing winks and sniggers; Clara Pilvois, who was so ill-educated that she was said to have thought that the Edict of Nantes was a titled English lady and who took revenge on a cantankerous *maître de ballet* by launching into a gyrating cancan in the course of a performance in which she was meant to be impersonating a nun; and a Creole called Finette who became the mistress of the American painter Whistler, and once won 1,500 francs in a *bal public* by kicking a gentleman's hat off. Later in life she claimed to be the inventor of the feat of the *grand écart*, commonly known as the splits.

Tales of the liaisons between the men of fashion and the ballet girls became, not surprisingly, one of the great fictional and journalistic staples of the age. That the reality quite measured up to them one may doubt, although it is recorded that one Lolotte became the Comtesse d' Hérouville and Mlle Quinault-Dufresne married the duc de Nevers. There are certainly a number of countervailing anecdotes of the unassailable virtue of other *danseuses*: Zilia Michelet's book of religious reflections, penned in answer to attempts to convert her by the Abbé Théobald, is known to have 'excited the greatest interest', even though reviewers declared it to be 'quite incomprehensible'. Héloïse Lamy was 'seldom seen without a political journal', rushed home after a performance to write poetry, and subjected herself to a diet so rigorous that the joke went round that she never spat 'for fear of getting thirsty'.

According to the Goncourts' *Journal*, that most cold-eyed of documents, there were, in 1861, only about a dozen girls who had been properly 'set up' and only another dozen really delicious ones, with 'gorgeous faces, and perfect bodies'. For the rest, perhaps thirty wretched and vulnerable little creatures stood on offer, girls working desperately hard for a pittance of 600 francs a year, who, thought the Goncourts, 'made little impression without the gauze and their costumes. You had to be forewarned that they were pretty. They generally had only a footlights sort of beauty.'

It may not have been a very wicked business, but it was a sordid and indelible one, which 'La Danse' seemed shamelessly to flaunt. Carpeaux seemed to have forgotten that an opera house was a very serious matter. Financed by the public exchequer, significantly sited on an axis with the Tuileries Palace, the Louvre and the Comédie-Française, Garnier's vast new edifice, with its official title of the Académie Nationale de Musique, was designed to be a potent symbol of the order of the Second Empire (it was no accident that it had been outside the old opera house in rue Le Pelletier in 1858 that the Italian terrorist Orsini made his assassination attack on the Emperor and Empress) and the politics that lay behind its desire to endorse the dignity of French Art.

Not that the art on offer does the Second Empire much credit. The audience in the rue Le Pelletier wanted lavish entertainment with agreeable musical accompaniment, not challenge or originality. The genius of Hector Berlioz, for example, remained marginal: he died in 1869, having never heard his masterpiece *Les Troyens* performed in anything but a bungled and butchered fashion. Richard Wagner's *Tannhäuser* was virtually jeered from the stage in 1861, principally because the Jockey Club faction was enraged that the piece moved the ballet interlude from its traditional place in the second act to the first. The great ballet hit of the Empire was *Coppélia*, which transformed one of E. T. A. Hoffmann's most terrifying and ambiguous tales into a silly, harmless farce.

What mattered more than artistic content was the protocol of attendance; 'Grand opera' was the product best designed to accommodate the relevant demands. The formula for this genre (still-performed examples of which include *Guillaume Tell* by Rossini, *Les Huguenots* by Meyerbeer and *Don Carlos* by Verdi) went as follows: take some large historical theme, involving a political or religious clash and an amorous collision, but safely removed from any parallels which might call into question the Empire's credentials. Because nobody bothers to arrive for the first act and few remain in their seats for the fifth, make sure that you concentrate the highlights in the middle (an injunction which explains the relatively weak inspiration of the beginning and end of *Don Carlos*, commissioned by the Opéra, and first performed in 1867). Allow plenty of room for stopping and starting, cuts and additions – the management regarded composers' scores as little more than so many yards of fabric, waiting to be stitched and styled. Add a love duet; a song with a jolly tune; a dramatic oath-taking scene; some crash-bang-wallop climaxes, perhaps accompanied by flashing sword-play; a march and procession, featuring cheering crowds, flags, trumpets, and page-boys; and further opportunities for spectacular scenic tableaux (the collapse of palatial interiors and fairy grottoes, battlefields strewn with corpses, harbours complete with departing ships, mountain glens flooded by thunder and lightning). Most important was the provision of plenty of twinkling dance music for the interludes in which those delicious little girls could emerge to show their paces and their legs. Such episodes often had no dramatic relevance to the operas they interrupted: two hours into the 1869 revival of Meyerbeer's *Le Prophète*, for example, the gloomy tale of sixteenth-century Anabaptist martyrs suddenly picked up with a twenty-minute ballet set on a frozen pond and featuring dancers propelled by the latest craze – roller-skates.

In other words, a bit of this should be followed by a bit of that – and not too much of anything. It was a policy which brought the proceedings closer to the popular tourist vaudeville of 1869, *Paris-Revue*

Act One Gare Saint-Lazare, with a real train coming out of a tunnel
Act Two The Moon

Act Three The opening of the Suez Canal
Act Four An apotheosis of Paris, with Flower Maidens

than to the modern conception of an opera's dignity.

But the irony is that almost nothing in Second Empire Paris was more likely to reduce the audience to a state of catatonic boredom than an evening at the Opéra. Musically inept, lumberingly slow, ponderous with scene changes and intervals for applause and refreshment, all counterpointed by a succession of fashionable comings and goings and courtly bowings and scrapings, performances were stuffed with subsidy and kept alive out of a sense of duty rather than creativity, and ridiculed by anyone of taste or intelligence.

Fortunately, there was a constant carnival of alternatives: as Carpeaux's statue proclaimed, nobody could accuse Paris of not knowing how to enjoy itself. For the best Italian singers, there was the Théâtre Italien; for the more intimate and sentimental modern operas of Gounod and Bizet, designed for middle-class tastes, the Opéra Comique and Théâtre Lyrique. But the best musical fun of the decade had been had at the Théâtre des Variétés, home of Jacques Offenbach's sharp-witted operettas *La Belle Hélène*, *La Vie Parisienne*, *Barbe-bleue*, *La Périchole*, *Les Brigands* and countless one-act squibs, now largely forgotten. Their satire, concocted by Offenbach in collaboration with his regular librettists Henri Meilhac and Ludovic Halévy, deftly trod the line between providing amusement and causing offence, pricking the bubble of Second Empire pretensions to allow the necessary release of surplus hot air, without ever suggesting that there was much you could do about anything except laugh at it.

Offenbach was the Empire's licensed buffoon, its court jester, who knew the point at which to draw the line, if not to toe it. Under the suffocating plush and panoply, Verdi's *Don Carlos* was passing far more radical judgements on the evils of power and repression, but nobody had concentrated hard enough to notice. At the Variétés, however, keeping the audience's attention was scarcely a problem. If Meyerbeer was never-ending, Offenbach was over all too soon; if *L'Africaine* sank under the weight of high romance, then *Barbe-bleue* bubbled along on its bottom-pinching naughtiness. Offenbach's zest was irresistible. One of the investors in the Variétés was the senior minister, the duc de Morny – a figure who today would be described as 'fun-loving'. Alongside his more dubious speculative activities on the race course and in Mexico, he occasionally wrote the odd musical comedy libretto. Reports survive of civil servants twitching in a queue outside his office, while from behind his door came sounds of foot-tapping, hand-clapping *zimboom – zimbadaboom* as Offenbach gave a preview of his latest inspiration. Even the Emperor, normally noted for his lugubrious public demeanour, was seen to chuckle merrily at the fat old monarchs and lecherous Greek gods, invariably suffering from Wandering Hand Disease, stereotypes which in other circumstances he might have interpreted as dangerously insulting caricatures of himself.

Offenbach's greatest hour came with *La Grande Duchesse de Gérolstein*, premièred in the year of the Exhibition of 1867. It told the daft story of the ruler of a small tinpot German state so infatuated with a private in her army that she promotes him to Commander-in-Chief. The first night was a sensation, not only because of the operetta, but for the appearance of gentlemen sporting the new phenomenon of square monocles and Princess Pauline Metternich magnificently flaunting fashion in a gown of chocolate brown, without the customary crinoline. There was a last-minute backstage crisis too, when the Variétés' leading lady, the voluptuous Hortense Schneider, had a fit and slammed the door on being told that the Censor had forbidden her to wear military decorations on her costume. Outraged at this invasion of her artistic freedom, she refused to perform. The glamorous audience was becoming restive at the delay; the gallery began to heckle. Offenbach decided to take the ultimate risk, and struck up the Overture. It worked: Schneider, like the rest of Paris, surrendered to the demonic exhilaration of the music and came out of her dressing room. 'I felt like a circus horse hearing the tune to which he always trots round the ring,' she recalled in her memoirs.

Everyone adored it. The Emperor came alone, and then

brought Eugénie. The Kings of Bavaria, Portugal and Sweden came too, as did the Prince of Wales and the Sultan of Turkey, 'dressed like an English clergyman'. The Tsar wired from Cologne to order a box: having arrived in Paris, he went first to the Russian Orthodox church, then straight on to the theatre. The Pasha of Egypt was said to have gone forty times in six weeks. In a brilliant publicity stunt, Schneider (for many years the mistress of the duc de Gramont-Caderousse) drove her carriage to the gate of the Exhibition reserved for all these visiting royalties and heads of state. When challenged, she simply proclaimed, 'Je suis la Grande Duchesse de Gérolstein!' And of course the gate was flung open, and she passed through to wave at the crowds, considerably more of a celebrity than the King of Sweden.

But the most fascinated and amused member of the audience at the Variétés was the Chief Minister of Prussia, Otto von Bismarck. He was a man set on a mission to unite the real Gérolsteins, the muddle of small states, duchies and principalities which formed the patchwork of nineteenth-century Germany, into a single political and economic union. In 1866 he had won the Battle of Sadowa, effectively clearing southern Germany of the rival influence of the Austrian Empire and profoundly altering the balance of power in Europe. He was now an ace away from realizing his aims. How he and his Minister of War, the austere Helmuth von Moltke, laughed at the idiocy of the Grande Duchesse. 'C'est tout à fait ça!' he claimed. 'That's exactly how it is. We will get rid of the Gérolsteins.' Which he did; and, just for France, he had another, rather bigger, joke up his sleeve.

Truth to tell, after all this publicity and excitement, Offenbach's jokes began to wear somewhat thin. 'The public is tired of little tunes and so am I,' he said. From 1868 his shows mined a gentler, warmer vein. He stopped turning the pomp and prolixity of grand opera on its head and tried for an emotional note one tone deeper. The public, of course, lost interest, as the public always does.

Another great musical phenomenon of the 1860s was

simultaneously changing its identity. The *cafés-concerts* or *cafés-chantants* had developed into an institution unique to Paris. They presented their customers with what we would call a cabaret,* but one which was hedged around with various licensing restrictions. No charge could be made for admission, no scenery or dancing was permitted, no more than one performer could stand on the stage at a time, and all material performed had to be vetted by the censor. Within this tight framework, there flourished a rough and bawdy popular culture which educated opinion found ominous. As in the public dancehalls, as in Carpeaux's statue, the emotions it released seemed ready to spill over into rape and plunder and anarchy. A *café-chantant* was a place without respect or deference: it had no decency. In 1865 the Goncourt brothers visited the notorious Eldorado and watched with mounting distaste the antics of a comic in evening dress:

> He sang disconnected things, interspersed with chortling and farmyard noises, the sounds of animals on heat, epileptic gesticulations – a Saint Vitus' dance of idiocy. The audience went wild with enthusiasm . . . it seems to me we are heading for a revolution. There is a rottenness and stupidity in the public, a laughter so unwholesome that it will take another great upheaval, and the spilling of blood, to clear the air . . .

Other middle-class and intellectual observers found the atmosphere plain sordid. In 1867 the right-wing Catholic commentator Louis-François Veuillot went to the Alcazar and saw for the first time 'women in a café in which smoking was permitted'. And not just women, he added, 'but ladies'. To him it smelt of 'old pipes, gas leaks, fermenting liquor; and there is sadness at the bottom of it, that flat and eloquent sadness we call ennui. The physiognomy of the audience in general is a kind of troubled torpor.'

The main attraction of the Alcazar was Theresa, a former milliner's apprentice, sacked for singing on the job and distracting the other girls from their work, whose grainy and resonant

* Although the word *cabaret* in nineteenth-century French means only a low-grade drinking den or dive, with no implication of staged entertainment.

contralto makes her the forerunner of the great cabaret stars of the twenties and thirties. She was no beauty – 'she has, I believe, some hair; her mouth appears to stretch right round her head; she has great fat lips like a negro, and shark's teeth,' reports Veuillot – but her presence was unforgettable. 'She acts her song as much as she sings it. She acts with her eyes, her arms, her shoulders, her hips, shamelessly. There is nothing graceful about her; in fact she rather tries to shed feminine gracefulness.' Veuillot missed her deeper charm, the charm of an open, experienced sexuality, both sceptical and romantic, which could take all life's and love's knocks in its stride. Her songs looked like vacuous ditties on the printed page, and it was only when she opened that elastic mouth, shrugged those powerful shoulders, and swivelled those ample hips that they swelled with innuendo and burst into meaning. 'Rien n'est sacré pour un sapeur,' she winked, 'Nothing is Sacred to a Fireman'; or 'C'est dans le nez que ça me chatouille', 'It Tickles me up my Nose'.* From the top to the bottom of Paris, she was admired, quoted and imitated: the dauntless Pauline Metternich even took lessons from her, hoping to pick up some tips for her own comic musical turns.

But the authenticity of Theresa's talent couldn't long survive her success. She became a packaged, expensive, difficult star, too successful for her own good, and with the easing of censorship at the end of the decade, she lost her subversive edge and piquancy. The *cafés-chantants* began to clean up and become *cafés-spectacles*, presenting acts geared to the entertainment of tourists. Yet, in her heyday, it was Theresa who embodied the soul of the people of Paris – the Paris of the shop assistants and clerks and flower sellers and waiters – singing to them of their own lives and thoughts and jokes with a stylishness that transcended vulgarity.

In her streetwise scepticism, Theresa was typical of a culture

* Among other popular double-entendre titles were 'Com'on s'marie chez nous' (How to get Married down our way); 'Essayez-en' (Go on, have a Bash); 'Je garde ça pour mon mari' (I'm keeping that for my Husband); 'Je voudrais bien en tâter' (I'd love to get to grips with that); 'J'n' os'rai jamais dir' ça d'vant l'monde' (I'd never dare say that in public); and 'Comme elles sont toutes' (Così fan tutte).

which was not anxious to ask profound questions of itself or to light the scorching flame of moral idealism. What Paris craved was amusement: craved it obsessively, as though it might atrophy if it paused for reflection. 'Paris s'amuse,' wrote Pierre Véron, 'Paris amuses itself, on foot, on horseback, in a carriage. Paris amuses itself doing good, doing wrong; cheating and being cheated; laughing, weeping; hanging about, working hard; bankrupting, burning, killing itself.' The result was 'Chaos, chaos everywhere', as a columnist in *La Vie Parisienne* mourned in his review of the events of 1869. 'Rarely has a generation lived in all respects through so many changes of mind so quickly. Never has the object of today's admiration so often become tomorrow's laughing-stock.'

The reverse of this relentless superficiality was an officially sponsored public art full of grand opera and hot air, gilded pillars and polished mirrors. Napoleon III's regime faked itself, taking immense pains over the restoration of ancient monuments (as in Viollet-le-Duc's efforts to reconstruct the medieval castle at Pierrefonds); mastering the minor art of churning out reproduction eighteenth-century furniture, textiles and *objets d'art*; painting vast and meticulous panoramas of significant scenes from world history; promoting the brilliant decorative ingenuity of Garnier and Carpeaux. It amounted to a busy, sophisticated and expensive campaign to embody an imagery of imperial values – splendour, tradition, hierarchy – but its intentions and effects were hollow and heavy-handed. Second Empire art dated quickly and decisively. Far more fascinating is the work of a vanguard of artists and writers outside the Establishment, who developed a new realism with which to counter all this glittering unrealism.

Its most decisive weapon was the photograph, a medium that since its beginnings in the 1820s had developed technically and commercially with a rapidity which paralleled that of the railway: such, in fact, was its ubiquity, that Pierre Véron jokingly anticipated that by the year 2000 Paris would consist of seven million people of whom 3,975,000 would be photographers (and he was not far wrong). Already by 1869

73

some first primitive experiments with colour were being made, an increase in the speed of exposure had made snapshots possible, and the trade of miniaturist was as redundant as that of the ledger clerk is today. Big money could be made from portraiture. Through Disdéri's celebrated studio, for example, passed thousands of bourgeois and proletarian couples, posing hatchet-faced in their Sunday best, surrounded by some chosen trappings of their status. Forty-eight hours later they were delivered their prints, retouched as required, in the form of pocket-sized *cartes de visite*. Ordinary people could thus, for the first time in history, immortalize their appearances at the cost of two francs and a few minutes of their time: it was an extra-ordinary innovation.*

But was it art? The greatest poet and most original critic of the era, Charles Baudelaire (1821–67) was deeply exercised by photography's presumption, and insisted that it was not. It may serve 'travellers' albums, naturalists, astronomers, and anyone wanting precise archival records,' he wrote, but it could not lay claim to a deeper imaginative or spiritual reality, because art was not a matter of the exact reproduction of surfaces. The law thought otherwise. In 1862 it had decreed that photography should be covered by the same code of copyright as painting or sculpture, and the efforts of the Société Française de Photographie, a guild which had been holding pretentious exhibitions of framed work, nudes and genre scenes in imitation of the old masters, were vindicated. Beyond such empty aping, an

---

* A. B. North Peat intriguingly describes an early attempt to domesticate photography: 'Dubroni is the name of a young and most promising engineer, a pupil of the École Polytechnique. Laid up for several years with bad health, his mind remained as active as ever. Amidst the most intense bodily sufferings, he applied himself, night and day, to the study and perfection of photography, hoping to initiate the masses into its mysteries by simplifying the manipulations and turning photography into a drawing-room amusement within the reach of every purse. In this Dubroni appears to have been quite successful, inasmuch as his ingenious apparatus entirely does away with the necessity of an operating chamber. You have no longer to dread any stains or spots on your dress or hands, as the chemical operations are all accomplished with the *pipette*, a small instrument by means of which you can introduce into the camera obscura, through a little orifice, the different chemical baths which the plate must undergo previous to its bearing a picture.' Presumably the equipment simply didn't work very well: its popularity proved ephemeral.

experimenting photographer such as Nadar pointed the way forward to a more genuinely distinct aesthetic of the camera: his unretouched portraits of Second Empire celebrities and dignitaries still seem psychologically penetrating and communicate the familiar modern sense that the relationship between photographer and subject might be more than a matter of a straightforward business transaction. (He was also the first person to take exposures by electric light, and also pioneered aerial photography via his huge balloon, *Le Géant*, which carried a complete developing laboratory in its two-storey gondola.) The wider applications of photography to science, the law, medicine, anthropology and military reconnaissance came gradually. Like the microchip, the camera was an instrument so revolutionary to the way society communicates that its implications took a century to consolidate.

For painters it stimulated a new definition of the agenda. The photographer's ability to record physical appearances unselectively meant that the tradition of idealizing academic realism looked more futile than ever. What could a canvas convey that a photographic plate could not? Colour, the effects of light, movement, atmosphere, emotion? But the work of a Nadar showed how even these prerogatives might be threatened. So the competition worked both ways: if photographers aspired to be artists, artists had to be photographers too. Young lions of the modern school such as Edouard Manet (1832–83) and Edgar Degas (1834–1917) seem to have owned cameras, and many painters, the elderly Ingres among them, began to use photographic studies as a substitute for preliminary sketches. Manet built on photographs for the figures in his painting of an unphotographed event, the execution of the Emperor Maximilian. Corot's 'blurred' style was at least partially inspired by the 'coated-glass' photographic process. Capturing the open spontaneity and authenticity of a photograph, yet rendering it through the unique perspective of an artist's eye, in the medium of paint and brush: this crux was one of the seeds out of which the movement known as Impressionism came to parturition.

The catchphrase for the avant-garde in the 1860s was the title of a brief polemic that Baudelaire had tossed off in 1846: 'the heroism of modern life'. Stop painting ancient mythology and neoclassical perfection, was his injunction; seek out the epic beauty and drama of contemporary urban civilization, be it in the salons of fashion or the gutters of the underworld: follow the example of Balzac's novels. One young writer, Jules Vallès, coined the term *rualisme*, a punning variant on *réalisme*, to suggest the hard-edged streetwise focus that art and literature should now take. Baudelaire later befriended the young Manet, and although we do not know what they talked about, it is reasonable to assume that Manet heeded the great poet and allowed his cool, unprejudiced eye to cruise the boulevards and parks, as if flatly snapping them unawares. He liked to refer to himself in camera-like terms – 'I painted what I saw' was his shoulder-shrugging defence when criticized for distastefulness – but of course it wasn't as simple as that. In 1868 the Goncourts recorded meeting 'a strange, interesting and likeable boy' called Félicien Rops (whose wonderful ink drawing of the cancan is reproduced in this book). 'He spoke to us about the blindness of painters to what is in front of their eyes, seeing only the things they have been trained to see – like a contrast of colours, for instance – but nothing of the modern state of mind.' It was that 'modern state of mind' which Manet's camera was more profoundly registering: its sallow-faced inertia, the boredom and frustration beneath its scrabbling hunt for pleasure. There lay the reality.

In literature, there were parallel and sometimes intersecting trends. Repressed or at least inhibited by the Second Empire's censorship, French intellectuals withdrew from the grander Romantic arena and the vivid social and political conflicts depicted by Victor Hugo to focus instead on small and isolated patches of contemporary reality. One of Manet's early champions was an ambitious freelance journalist called Emile Zola (1840–1902), who wrote in 1867 of the way that the painter 'simply translates what he sees before him . . . He knows neither how to sing, nor to philosophize. He knows how to paint, that's all.' This is not astute or even remotely accurate, but it aligned writer and painter in the same Baudelairean camp, focused on the here and now of Paris, with a whiff of the unsavoury about their preoccupations. 'He sees women as Monsieur Manet paints them – sludge-coloured, with bright pink make-up' sneered one critic at Zola's second novel *Thérèse Raquin* in 1867. (He would have preferred the peach and rose complexions infallibly offered by the cheap romantic novels, formulaic and widely read, of the prolific comtesse Dash, whose ethics glowed with the same radiance as her heroines' cheeks.) The comparison should not be pushed too far, however. Zola preferred to think of his objectivity before his material as that of the biologist rather than the photographer, describing *Thérèse Raquin* as 'the study of temperamental disposition and the deep modifications of the organism under the pressure of environment and circumstance . . . I have simply exercised on two living bodies the analysis that surgeons make on cadavers.'

But Zola was no more doing this than Manet was painting 'simply what he saw'. He had indeed read bits and pieces of the latest Darwinian theorizing about heredity and its effect on behaviour; he had also read the introduction to Taine's *History of English Literature*, which infamously announced that 'virtue and vice are *products*, like sugar or sulphuric acid, complexes born out of the meeting of simple elements' – and rather pretentiously conflated it all into a literary manifesto. But the narrative voice in *Thérèse Raquin* often sounds like that of a first-year medical student writing an essay copied out of the best text-books (such-and-such, he will tell us, is 'a fact of psychology and physiology which often occurs in people who have suffered profound nervous shocks'); and the things that make the novel compulsively work, principally its tight, simple action and theme of crime, guilt and remorse, are as old as Shakespeare and Aeschylus. Later, Zola would develop a more sophisticated model, following the fortunes of two contrasting fictional families, the Rougons and the Macquarts, as they intermarry and interbreed their psychologies and physiologies against the panorama of the Second Empire – some die in alcoholic degradation, others rise to public prominence, their fates explicable in terms of what they have inherited from their parents. Yet even here it is the thrall of melodrama rather than the rigour of science that has kept readers turning the pages.

The idea of bringing photographic realism to fiction was carried to morbid lengths in the 1860s by the collaborative brothers Jules (1830–70) and Edmond (1822–96) de Goncourt. Baudelaire had written that art 'should plunge into the abyss to find something new'; in the preface to their depressing novel *Germinie Lacerteux*, published in 1864 and based on the secret miseries of their maid Rose, the Goncourts more fiercely decided that it 'must go down to the people, to the ugly and horrible'. In this activity they were not motivated by any Dickensian desire for social reform; they went there only because 'at the bottom of a civilization, the nature of things is retained'. Fiction for them grew not out of 'the imagination' but out of transplanted fact: 'the real novel is built on documentary evidence, or from nature,' they wrote in their *Journal*, 'just as History is built on written sources'.* Like Manet, they claimed only to write about what they saw, about what was there, with the single purpose of satisfying that criterion of art.

It was a desperate, hopeless and ultimately pathetic endeavour. Together they lived in hypersensitive seclusion on a modest private income, as infuriated by the sound of birdsong as they were by the vulgarity of the metropolis, despising virtually everybody around them with a venom more pathological than snobbish. They were reactionaries, élitists, aesthetes, dilettante historians and art critics who longed for recognition, but were possessed of nothing but contempt for the public and critics who could provide it. 'Three months almost without a visit or a letter, without even meeting an acquaintance on our eleven o'clock evening walks . . . half content not to be wounded by others and half sad to have only each other's company.' This, from 1867, is a rare confession of vulnerability. Much of the rest of the journal of the 1860s records with loathing the squalor of the poor ('its louse-infected pallets, its slang, its arrogance and meanness'), the triumph of suburban ordinariness, the spirit of commerce, the pretensions of the middle classes, the idiocy of

---

* It is interesting to speculate as to how such ideas would have been viewed by someone simultaneously peering through the opposite end of the literary telescope – Jules Verne (1828–1905), whose 'science fiction' adventure novels were very much based on fact.

the intellectuals, the mediocrity of the bohemians. They deplored the influence of the Jews. They banefully prophesied 'the Americanization of France'. Jules died in 1870, of syphilis: he had been nastily obsessed with sex. Edmond lived on in melancholy, loveless isolation, keeping up the journal he had begun with his brother, never mellowing, never gentle, but ever sharp-sensed and disenchanted. 'The Journal of MM. de Goncourt is mainly a record of resentment and suffering,' wrote Henry James in an essay on the occasion of its publication in 1888, '. . . copious as a memorandum of the artistic life', it is in 'abnormally small a degree a picture of enjoyment. . . . What they commemorate as workers is the simple break-down of joy. . . . *Nous avons l'agacement* ('we have the annoyance') might stand as the epigraph of the Journal at large, so exact a translation would [this] be of the emotion apparently most frequently with the authors.'

They stood on perhaps the furthest reach of one path of the avant-garde of their day, largely misunderstood, if not ignored, on their obscure eminence. The leading literary critic of the day, Charles Sainte-Beuve, in the last year of his life, 1869, read their strange novel of religious mania, *Madame Gervaisais*, with bafflement. 'It's not literature any more,' he told them. 'It's music, it's painting . . . it's something else you are after. As you say, it is movement in the colour of the soul of things. It is impossible.'

The Emperor could not understand – or approve – it either. 'It seems to me that literature exists in a milieu that lacks grandeur,' he confided to a member of the Académie Française. Nor for him Jules Vallès' *rualisme*. 'I would like to think that in my reign letters were flourishing in a high and elevated style – they should effect in the intellectual sphere what I have effected in the moral and political.' Literature, fortunately, defied him.

4 : *The Spermal Economy*

D r Tissot suggests a two-week curative regime for gentlemen suffering from impotence or, as he puts it, 'exhaustion resulting from too frequent voyages to Cytherea':

6 a.m. 6 oz. quinquina, 2 spoonsful Madeira
7 a.m. 2 oz. goat's milk, sugared orange water
12 a.m. roast chicken, a glass of Bourgogne and water –
followed by an hour's exercise
4 p.m. 6 oz. quinquina, 2 spoonsful Madeira
5 p.m. a ten-minute cold bath – followed by a nap and an hour's fresh air
7 p.m. a dinner of red meat, with red wine and water –
followed by more fresh air and exercise
9.30 p.m. Goat's milk, with vanilla essence

The restoration and cultivation of 'male vigour' was a medical imperative in Second Empire Paris, but not because of the city's constant stench of sexual possibility. The reason was more respectable. Uniquely in Europe, France suffered from a falling birth rate, and it troubled the government that a nation so economically thrusting and full of itself should be unable to expand its population. As explanation, it has been argued by demographic historians that French peasants practised primitive forms of contraception more widely than elsewhere, but this begs the question as to *why* they did so, quite apart from the inherent difficulty of substantiating the thesis (and in fact the number of offspring per marriage was consistently higher in the country than it was in the city, Paris rating only 2.65 against a national average of 3.1, according to a survey of 1865).

In any case, measures were taken, pamphlets issued, morals drawn. Had the situation resulted from an increase in mobility and restlessness, or of an easier availability of sex for money? A Dr Bergeret thundered that coitus interruptus or 'conjugal onanism' was infanticide, and the cause of uterine cancer and heart disease. A Dr Mayer agreed, and pointed to the distressingly late age at which the French averagely married – men 30–31; women 26–7 – as cause for concern. The Empire voted families tax relief and benefits. Eugénie handed out medals for exceptional dedication to motherhood; the prosecutions for abortion were severe. Divorce was impossible. The Société Saint François-Régis busily toured the poorer suburbs proselytizing the virtues of propagation. 'Be fruitful, conserve the individual, multiply, look to the future of the species,' counselled Dr Seraine in his manual *On the Health of Married People*.

France was consequently caught in a strange double bind. It wanted its citizens to have sex, but sex to order, and straitened by regulation. Sex, of course, refused to oblige, sex ran rampage – but the medical profession were at great pains to promote a moderate and healthy appetite. In *Hygiene and Physiology of Marriage*, one Dr Debay advocated that marital intimacy should only be undertaken in a mood of calm rationality, with the blood unheated, the stomach empty, the head unfuddled. The following frequency of copulation should be observed: between the ages of 20 and 30, two to four times a week, with a day off either side (the newly wed tendency to indulge 'five or six times a day' is deleterious, the doctor opines); between 30 and 40, twice a week; 40 and 50, once a week; 50 and 60, once a fortnight; older than that, forget it. To ensure strong and beautiful children – according to the popular pseudo-science of callipedia – wives should prepare for conception by eating red meat, walking briskly and sleeping as little as possible; husbands, on the other hand, should lie in hot baths, drink orangeade and content themselves with soup, salads and chicken. Throughout, a code of good manners should be maintained. Gentlemen should be alert to ladies' monthly indisposition, and ladies should be ready 'to simulate the spasm of delight: this innocent deception is justified inasmuch as it serves to attach a husband's affections'.* In his tract *Love*, Michelet recommends a husband to whisper a litany in his wife's ear: 'I am yours, I am you. I suffer for you. Take me as if you were my mother and my wet-nurse. Put your life in my hands. You are my wife and my child' – which may have been a trifle confusing.

It was widely thought that semen was a purified concentrate of blood, and that a man's stock of it was strictly limited; excessive emissions would drain one's life-force or 'spermal economy'. Masturbation was therefore not only a waste of a potential addition to the depleted French stock, but a sort of self-emasculation. The Larousse *Encyclopédie* of 1867 has much to say on the subject. A vice more prevalent in the South than the North, its early symptoms included a squeaky voice, fetid breath, bloodshot eyes and 'enlarged' sexual organs; eventually it caused digestive disorders, hallucinations, epilepsy and progressive enfeeblement. The case is recorded of an eighteen-year-old watchmaker who succumbed eight times per diem: eventually, he found himself the terrified victim of continual involuntary erections and orgasms which consumed him to the point of exhaustion, lunacy and death.

That was the grim spectre which haunted all sexual indulgence outside the tabulated pages of the doctors' manuals. Not enough of the right sort of sex, and France would die; too much, of the wrong sort (Dr Bergeret describes the oral variety as 'insanity of the genito-labial nerve'), and the individual would. But neither excess nor perversion caused as intense a horror as the idea of sexual infection – specifically, the syphilis which tainted the blood and carried itself inexorably from generation to generation, further debilitating French stock. In Paris alone there were thought to be about 50,000 cases of venereal disease,

---

* Female orgasm was a subject of great interest to men in this era. 'In thin women, it is evinced by a nervous spasm,' noted Edmond de Goncourt in his journal for 16 November 1870. 'In fat women, by a sort of convulsion. In the former, it is something more like a pulling out, a stretching. In the latter, a tightening, a contraction. Orgasm, *la petite mort*, gives the first an expression of ecstasy; the second, of apoploxy.' See Michael Mason, *The Making of Victorian Sexuality* (Oxford, 1994).

but nobody quite knew, not least because the standard treatment (mercury and potassium iodide) was of such variable efficacy. People would believe any number, any rumour. Mothers became terrified of entrusting their babies to wet-nurses in case their milk should be poisoned. Someone at the International Medical Congress of 1867 seriously proposed that all unmarried women in Paris not living with their parents should be compulsorily examined at regular intervals. The word *syphilomanie* was coined to describe the increasing number of doctors who detected symptoms of the disease in every boil, sore throat and rash.

The paranoia was screwed to a hysterical pitch by extraordinary changes in the pattern of prostitution, stimulated by Haussmann's eradication of the working-class areas of central Paris. In quarters such as the Île de la Cité and along what is now the rue de Rivoli had stood a good number of old-style, rough-but-ready brothels. When the Second Empire cleared the way for high-rent, high-profit blocks of apartments, offices and shops, the old-style, rough-but-ready occupants were evacuated. The streetwalking girls wandered away from their traditional purlieus in the Palais Royal up to the rich pickings of the glittering new Paris, cruising gullible tourists and fidgety gentlemen pretending to read their newspapers at pavement cafés.

In the constant bustle and throng it became impossible to distinguish between a lady respectably on her own and a girl for hire. 'One does not know nowadays if it's honest women who are dressed like whores or whores who are dressed like honest women,' complained Maxime du Camp; the Goncourts saw whores 'in the same toilet, the same costume' as the honest women, 'walking with children whom they resemble and seem to love'. A generation earlier, in the days of Balzac and Louis Philippe, the situation had been more clear-cut. There had been a few lovely courtesans, Marie Duplessis for example, sentimentalized into lavender romance by Dumas *fils* in *La Dame aux camélias*; there had been the good-time *grisettes*, pretty, hard-working proletarians, who wanted boyfriends and a good time, such as Mimi and Musette in Murger's *Scènes de la vie de Bohème*;

and there had been the dear old whores, who could be found in standard places and had for standard fees.

But in the Second Empire these distinctions had faded, as women increasingly took jobs which put them on ambiguous public display. Courtesans or kept women (another changing barrier) such as Blanche d'Antigny, Cora Pearl (whose real name was either Emma Crutch or Eliza Crouch) and Hortense Schneider became high-salaried musical-comedy starlets. The ballet girls at the Opéra were open to offers of protection. In the glamorous department stores it might be unclear whether the pert and smartly turned-out assistants were selling rolls of cloth or themselves. Florists, tobacconists, confectioners, souvenir shops were the merest front for their back-room activities. The mirrored restaurants on the boulevards were staffed by the unfamiliar phenomenon of female waitresses, 'picturesquely' attired – a brasserie on the rue Vaugirard even uniformed its staff in 'swimming costume' because 'the simplest clothes were the most beautiful'. Perhaps the ladies of the imperial court, parading their Worth gowns and perfectly pallid complexions in tableaux painted by Winterhalter, could be regarded as no more than the highest class of tart. It was a new version of the old game, marketed for a new sort of getting-and-spending society. Describing Paris as a city of 'universal prostitution' became a favourite cliché of the intelligentsia.

Great official effort was meanwhile being made to control and classify such activities. There wasn't much that could be done about those at the top of this slippery ladder – the courtesans, the kept women, the actresses, variously known as *femmes galantes*, *lionnes*, *grandes cocottes*, *grandes horizontales*, *filles de marbre*, or *amazones*. Colourful stories circulated about their sexual prowess, their wealth, their power, their calculated ruthlessness – and these became even more exaggerated in the years following the fall of the Empire, when a stream of salacious histories and memoirs were published with the ulterior purpose of emphasizing the decadence of the era to the morally born-again France. But the truth about them is actually rather drab.*

* A lot of the nonsense can be traced to the salacious Frédéric Loliée, whose *Les Femmes du Second Empire* (Paris, 1906) was widely read and translated.

There were very few of them – perhaps thirty in all Paris – and many of that number were simply women, unmarriageable because of their working-class origins, who had become rich men's mistresses. Some were connected with the theatre (and therefore assumed to be loose), some were free spirits who simply did not want to settle for the pieties of bourgeois life. Moralists and journalists were always keen to point an accusatory finger and apply the derogatory label, but only a mere handful of 'courtesans' were genuine prostitutes who had set themselves up on a pimp's credit and used their bodies as a means of paying off the interest, in the manner that the myth presents. Yet for posterity they made potent symbols of the rapacity and tawdriness that lay at the bottom of the values of Second Empire Paris: Zola's Nana, whose fortunes plummet as drastically as they rise; Manet's Olympia, her skin a cadaverous, diseased yellow, her hand slammed possessively over her most precious commodity, her stiffly defensive and empty glare, indifferent to the bouquet of flowers just left by one of her admirers – the whole painting a bitter parody of the warm allure of Titian's Venus of Urbino. This, Manet seems to tell us, is where sexual desire now festers.

But the real business began further down the social line. Prostitution in France was legally 'tolerated', on the grounds that, if enclosed and supervised, it provided a canal for baser instincts – rather like the hygienic institutions of sewer and public lavatory (the latter being another of the Second Empire's more earnest innovations). If the trade was registered with the police and followed a highly restrictive code of practice, which left it without any right to redress – a prostitute could not sue for non-payment, a brothel could not go bankrupt or take out a mortgage – then, it was believed, the spread of syphilis could be contained and certain pressures on the institution of marriage released. However great the naïvete in such a theory, it does seem that mid-nineteenth-century France suffered a much lower rate of syphilitic infection than contemporary England,* where there

* In 1867 a Dr Vintras published a brave pamphlet, 'On the Repressive Measures in Paris', estimating twice as much prostitution and venereal disease in London as in Paris, claiming that ten per cent of Londoners were infected and

was no comparable system of registration and surveillance. Yet Paris needed more sex than the system could accommodate. The abundance of money for leisure was also money which could buy you your desire – the Second Empire's deal was always that you could have what you could pay for, and it applied to women as much as to any other commodity. Under this dispensation, the old paternalistic controls broke down, throwing the market open to freelance operators. Demands became more sophisticated and the older whores bemoaned their clients' exigent tastes for oral sex and elaborately staged perversions. The decline in the number of registered brothels – from 217 in 1852 to 152 in 1870 – was evidence of an explosion, not a decline in prostitution. In 1870, about a 1,000 girls in Paris operated through these brothels, and about another 2,500 were registered as independent. But how many solicited outside the system, operating as part-time whores or casuals? Maxime du Camp guessed at over a 100,000 – a figure which implied statistically that any woman you saw walking on the streets was likely to be a streetwalker, that a *bonne bourgeoise*, veiled, hatted and gloved, carrying a bag of shopping or hailing a cab, might strip down to as ruthless a whore as the most brazen and bosomy of flower-girls. The reality of the figure was estimated by the police in 1869 as 30,000, and it may have been even lower, but the effect of the fantasy of the wider spread was to turn Paris into an erotic minefield. In any case, registering had few advantages. The independents carried identity cards, on which were marked both any convictions for infringements of the rules and the dates of an obligatory monthly medical inspection, initialled by the examining authority. The restrictions on where and how you could sell yourself were so tight that it was all too easy for the police to find a pretext to arrest you, charge you, dump you in a large communal cell under the supervision of a horrible old

that there were over 2,000 brothels. Such figures are unreliable, but not totally implausible. See Richard Davenport-Hines, *Sex, Death and Punishment* (London, 1990), ch. 5. In 1858, a Dr Diday had made the far-sighted suggestion that boxes of free prophylactics should be made a compulsory feature of every brothel bedside. See Alain Corbin, *Le Temps, Le Désir et l'Horreur* (Paris, 1991), pp. 117–41.

nun and in the gibbering and jabbering company of up to 200 of your colleagues, before sentencing you to a further week of imprisonment during which you sewed mailbags as another horrible old nun read you the joys of piety, chastity and remorse. Produce your card on demand. Wear a hat. Don't stand in front of an illuminated window. Don't touch anybody. Don't go anywhere near a park, a school, a church or a restaurant. Don't come out before 7 p.m. or stay out after 11 p.m.

They came from everywhere – one survey revealed eighteen Americans, twenty-eight English, fifty Italians, a Swede and six Poles – but would generally adopt one of a narrow range of professional pseudonyms, intended to convey something of their look, flavour, or age – never a Jeanne or a Marie, but many a Mignon, Carmen, Olga, Blondine, Brunettine, Ninette, Arlette. Three-quarters of them would change brothel at least once a year: life was certainly very dull when you weren't with a client: an eternal round of cards and lotto, *absinthe* and cigarettes, visits from the hairdresser, the same old jokes, more *absinthe* and cigarettes. A popular fantasy, doubtless with some foundation in reality, was the additional leisure pursuit of lesbianism, a practice resorted to rather as men turned to homosexuality in prisons.*

A lot depended on the fair dealing of the establishment's *maîtresse* – herself often at the mercy of the owner of the property. Each girl paid her a monthly sum for lodging, food and bills which could be as much as half her total earnings (average fees in an ordinary brothel would be in the region of 5–10 francs for an hour, or *la passe*, and 15–20 francs for a night, *le coucher*), but the exploitation often bordered on slavery, and in 1867 the desperate inmates of a brothel in Parthénay set fire to it in a bid to regain their liberty. Elsewhere there was a high and fast turnover, whether in the *maisons de luxe* in the Opéra district,

---

* When asked about her taste for lesbianism, Flaubert's splendidly uninhibited actress friend Suzanne Lagier ('the sort of woman who ought to be served up at a banquet' in the Goncourt brothers' view) explained it as a matter of being able to fart in front of other women without embarrassment 'which you just can't in front of men'. (*Journal*, 23 November 1862).

with their mythological murals, exotic perfumes and potted plants, or the rock-bottom *maisons d'abattage*, the knocking-shops around the city walls in which the clients would queue up the stairs for their fifty *sous*' worth. At the upper end of the market, money provided the excitement, the expense of the whore becoming intrinsic to her allure; at the lower end, only large quantities of alcohol made the proceedings bearable. It was the quiet and clean *maisons* with *touts conforts*, a discreet waiting room, frosted glass, tinkling bells, and trays of light refreshment (on which the *maîtresse* made her greatest profits) that were dying out in Paris★ as sex began to sell itself harder.

The registered independents lodged in *maisons de passe*, rooming-houses to which they could bring back their clients, procured by themselves or their pimps. Whatever trouble this arrangement caused, the girls at least remained identifiable – but it was not at all easy to see how or where the unregistered – the *insoumises* or *non-inscrites*, as they were known – played the game. The Prefect of Police, Charles Lecour, was tearing his hair out. 'They are everywhere,' he wrote in 1870, like rats or revolutionaries: 'in the brasseries, in the *cafés-concerts*, the theatres and the dancehalls. You encounter them in public establishments, railway stations, even railway carriages. There are some of them on all the promenades in front of most of the cafés, they circulate in great numbers on the most beautiful boulevards, to the great disgust of the public, which takes them for registered prostitutes violating the regulations and is hence astonished at the inaction of the police.'

But only if they were seen unmistakably soliciting could they be arrested, and all too often the evidence was ambiguous. It was the rarely foolish *insoumise* who betrayed herself by carrying the sort of hand-written phrase book, designed to help her chat to English and American visitors, that a girl in the Bal Mabille was observed employing:

Je vous aime   I like you
Que dites-vous?   What is that meant to mean?

★ Its continuing role in smaller communities is celebrated in Maupassant's irresistible story 'La Maison Tellier'.

Bonjour, monsieur   Hello there, mister
Où demeurez-vous?   Where do you live?
Que voulez-vous me donner?   What will you give me?
La nuit?   A whole night?
Une heure?   Just an hour?
Aujourd' hui   Now
Or   Cash
Beau   Nice
Mauvais   Not nice
Chaud   Cosy
Vingt francs   Twenty francs
Quarante francs   More than that
Voiture   Let's get a cab

There was a more suggestive *argot* of euphemism, recorded by Alfred Delvau in his *Dictionnaire Erotique*, which could be woven into conversation with the natives. *La danse* also meant love-making; *une cigarette*, a penis; *boire seul* (to drink alone), to masturbate; *aller se faire couper les cheveux* (to go and have your hair cut), to go to a brothel; *les Anglais ont débarqué* (the English have landed, a reference to the British army's blood-red uniform), to have one's period; *être de la Garde Nationale* (to belong to the National Guard), to be homosexual.

Even the more circumspect independent registered prostitutes could expect to be arrested two or three times a year, referring to their consequent terms of imprisonment as *une visite à la campagne*, a trip to the country. In his survey of Paris and its institutions, Maxime du Camp gives a vivid account of the arrival of a night's haul at the police station:

Their behaviour is very varied: some of them giggle; others seem half-asleep; the ones who have been beaten about try to look pitiful and weep; but the dominant emotion is indifference. They are numbed . . . staring wide-eyed into the fire as if they had never before seen burning coals. One of them – old, dried-up, lined – sits down on a stool, elbows on knees, chin on hands; her emaciated face, made even paler by her stringy black hair, reminds one of those bony statues that sculptors of the Middle Ages put in the portals of cathedrals: a fixed eye, a pinched mouth, a hard and reflective expression, she might represent the Threat of Beggary. In the lunatic asylums, in wards for the manic, you find similar figures.

Sometimes, stupefied with drink and soaked in alcohol, they let fly a flow of words which it seems will never stop. Implore, threaten, or scream at them to shut up, their slow, dragging voices continue to utter a stream of nonsense with the inexorable regularity of drops of water in a clepsydra. . . .

They are questioned: to hear them, you would think that the police are always mistaken, that they have a grudge, that they are being persecuted. If they are asked what the reason might be for this hatred, they don't know how to reply. All of them try to give a flattering account of themselves. 'I am not a wicked woman, like those others.' They have been arrested alongside ragmen and tramps – they reply: 'You know me and you know that I only like mixing with decent people.' The chief inspector writes down their replies in abbreviated form, and they all – despite the fact that few of them can read – follow the pen with their eyes, as if to guess the sense of the words they cannot decipher.

Their voices – hoarse from screaming, drunkenness and so on – sound dreadful; and their bodies all exude a strange smell quite unique to them . . . a mixture of filthy hair, old clothes and alcohol: it makes one's gorge rise. They plead for pardon, saying: 'It's at least six months since I was last arrested, doesn't that count for anything?' Sometimes they come up with remarks of almost sinister ingenuousness – one of them is accused of having been outside at midnight, an hour after the regulated period, and retorts: 'What do you expect, business is terrible!'

Often, when they realize that they are going to be sent to prison, they burst into tears and beg to be allowed to go home to feed their dog or their cat (they almost all have a passion for animals). The former practice of allowing them to take these creatures with them into the cells had to be stopped: the prison was turning into a menagerie. Or there's a child that they ask to be allowed to find, so that it can be entrusted to a neighbour for the duration of their imprisonment. As some poor woman speaks in a voice broken with sobs, the emotion spreads, and soon all the wretches are in floods of tears: for they cry, like they laugh, without really knowing why.

The prison of Saint-Lazare combined its function with that of a hospital for the venereally infected, where patients were forcibly confined until they were cured. It was dreaded for its harsh and humiliating regime and much criticized for its filth. Detection of the disease was rough, nasty and inaccurate. Every week the brothels were visited by one of the physicians attached to the vice squad; the registered independents were obliged to visit a dispensary at least once a month. As many as fifty girls an hour would be sat on the examination chair and submitted to the speculum: ingenious use of gold leaf and chocolate was made in hiding lesions, sores and other symptoms. The statistics show that the policy of registration was to some extent effective – in 1869, almost half of the 1,999 *insoumises* arrested needed treatment; but only one in every 116 of the registered.

Figures such as these increased the terror of infection, to the point at which Maxime du Camp could present the *insoumise* as both a symbol of the city's corruption and the direct agent of its approaching nemesis.

We are today faced with an Augean stable, into which people of all classes and conditions are hastening to pour their dung. Which Hercules will have the courage and strength to clean out the sewer? Never has the gangrene cut so deep. It has touched the quick, and will go on, if we are not careful, to break up the whole body. Where lies the remedy? In political reform, in social reform? I don't think so: we have always fallen victim to heated fever, when we have had recourse to that type of medication. No, the remedy is in moral reform: but who wants to listen, who doesn't smirk when that phrase is mentioned? . . .

Ask bosses why they seek women workers in vain, ask artists why it is so hard to find models: unregistered prostitution has seized them and will not let them go.

Everything seems to have conspired to produce this state of affairs, the results of which can be seen in the tables of marriages and births, which decline to an intolerable degree. Directly opposed causes lead to similar outcomes: poverty and riches pass the word to act in convoy: from industrial crises comes unemployment, emptying the factories and throwing on to the streets women who are pulled into debauchery to maintain a living that honest labour can no longer give them; the increase of public prosperity and individual fortunes naturally swells the desire for pleasure and an excess of vanity; money flows like water, and women have run out to grasp it and take their share.

Over women who were not prostitutes, this sort of thinking fell like a dead hand on their daily lives – they could neither work, nor socialize, say what they pleased, dress comfortably, nor enjoy themselves in public without being stigmatized or suspected of operating out of sordid motives. Few societies have so completely reduced women to sex objects as the Second Empire did – the age-old prejudice that prostitution was the sex's 'natural state' became a real and serious prejudice.

And there was a hypocrisy about it as well, which that great unmasker Gustave Flaubert refused to accept. The sight of a whore is profoundly thrilling to a man, he claimed, stirring 'so many elements – lust, frustration, the futility of human relationships, physical frenzy and the clink of gold – that a glance into its depths makes one dizzy. . . . During my first years in Paris, I would sit outside Tortoni's on hot summer evenings, admiring the sunset and watching the streetwalkers pass by. At times like that I used to bubble over with biblical poetry.'

As this may remind us, Paris's sexual preoccupation was part of its vitality as much as its decadence.

5 : *Social Engineering*

Sometimes, behind the ruthless triumphal clarity of Haussmann's new boulevards, you could glimpse something
of what people cloudily remembered as the charm of old
Paris – the 'dear, delightful, dark, dirty *rues*' as Felix Whitehurst
only half-ironically called the alleys of cholera and insurrection.
Close to the rue de Rivoli, for example, was the Carré Saint-
Martin, a small square to which gravitated the drunk and
destitute, sitting numbly on benches or sleeping under whatever
shelter they could find, kept alive by the few paltry coins they
occasionally earned from a session of machine-turning in one of
the ateliers nearby. The *écureuils*, they were called, 'the
squirrels', pathetically hoarding their empty bottles underneath
the trees, almost picturesque, almost harmless, until they found
their way on to the great shopping thoroughfares and slouched
against the walls, sullenly watchful, a revolutionary rabble
neutered and doped, but still slow-burning with untold resentment.

Elsewhere, the 'real' Paris, the Paris 'of romantic associations', the Paris that tourists had read about and *La Comédie
Humaine* had chronicled only thirty years previously, was being
systematically eradicated. Gone was the Liberty Tree in the
Luxembourg Gardens, last icon of 1789, torn down and replaced
with a statue by Carpeaux representing the four corners of the
earth and the glory of the Empire. Gone was the complex of
smells – sweet, savoury and foul – that had been as much part of
the city's landscape as its architecture. Gone were the thieves'
kitchens on the rue de Féves, torn down and replaced with the

grim stone of the Prefecture of Police. Gone the relics of a medieval street culture, with its chaos of pedlars shrieking licorice water, birdseed, shoelaces, umbrellas, potatoes by the bushel; its mountebanks, window-cleaners, plumbers, contortionists, jugglers, knife-grinders and charlatans. Gone was the intimate and relaxed elegance of the shady old boulevards, blasted into vast, noisy, demotic shopping parades, dominated by trade and traffic. Everything now was designed to conform to a logic of urban geometry: Edmond About's satirical character Colonel Fougas even ludicrously wondered whether the Seine might not be straightened out, because its curves were 'really rather shocking'. So rigid was Haussmann's planning that Victor Fournel fantasized about a city that by 1965 would consist of fifty boulevards each fifty metres wide, lined with indistinguishably standardized apartment blocks, focused on a huge central barracks linked electrically to a network of watchtowers. At regular intervals would stand some great monument, many of them moved brick by brick from their original inconvenient position so as to maintain the perfection of the symmetry. Every building would have its quota of oxygen fairly apportioned by an 'aerometer'.

Even now, continued Fournel, Paris had lost 'the variety, the surprise, the charm of discovery which made a walk in the old city a voyage of exploration across worlds ever new and unknown, a changing, living physiognomy which marked each quarter like a feature on a human face'. The charm of *flânerie*, one of Baudelaire's chief addictions – the art of 'hanging out' we would call it now – was lost in an environment dedicated to traffic, trade and cleanly lit asphalted highways. The Goncourts' distaste struck deeper. 'I am a stranger to what is coming, to what already exists,' their *Journal* recorded in 1860, 'as I am a stranger to these new unbending boulevards . . . no longer redolent of Balzac's world and conjuring up only some American Babylon of the future.' In all such complaints is something of our contemporary feelings about the imperative of conserving 'tradition' and 'community' against the depredations of a brutal, money-directed philistinism.

But more was at stake than intellectuals sentimentally

bemoaning their spiritual alienation. Tens of thousands of people were summarily removed from their homes and work-places to make way for the march – the spirit – of progress. 'Man in cocked hat calls and leaves paper (this is Monday),' explained Whitehurst. 'On Wednesday he returns with two other devils worse than himself, and not only gives you notice to quit, but fixes the day and the hour; and as the last box leaves the tenement one workman pulls down the door and the inspector makes a *bureau des démolitions* of the lodge from which your faithful concierge handed you – sometimes – your letters. You pass by on the Saturday, and all is a blank. Six grey Normandy horses, and four men much addicted to bad language, are laying the first stone of the rue Champignon, late rue de Chêne.'

Throughout the Second Empire Parisians lived as if over a continuous earthquake. Whitehurst scarcely exaggerated the speed of expropriation, and although the financial compensations might be generous, there was virtually no possibility of winning an appeal to stay where you were. Sometimes the point of the changes was hard to understand (Fournel was particularly amused by the faffing over the beautification of the inner courtyard of the Louvre: first they installed a fountain, then that became an equestrian statue, then a bank of grass and flowers, then another hole in the ground, then nothing at all), sometimes they seemed all too terrifyingly megalomaniac (one of Hauss-mann's last, thwarted but perfectly serious ideas was the emptying of all the city's cemeteries and the creation of a meticulously indexed necropolis thirteen miles out at Méry-sur-Oisc). Nothing and nobody escaped. Even seats in the theatres were now compulsorily numbered and ticketed. From the sewers to the chimney-pots, from the streetlights to the omnibus routes, everything was to turn as a cog in an unprecedented scheme of social engineering which the Parisians – whether they liked it or not – would drive into effect.

It couldn't work – inasmuch as human beings are generically resistant to schemes of social engineering – but it remains the nineteenth century's most radical experiment in shaping and governing urban society. Haussmann made real the idea of civic planning, not just in terms of specific architectural conceptions, but as an entire way of life, a system of interlocking elements which would both service and control its inhabitants. The influence of what was attempted and achieved in Paris between 1853 and 1870 is immeasurable: there is hardly a city in the western world today that does not evince its pioneering example, and even today an estimated sixty per cent of the city remains in some respect *Haussmannisé*.

Paris was not so much rebuilt as reconceived; and as with so much Second Empire policy, it is impossible to assess to what degree the motivation for this was political or altruistic, visionary or opportunistic, ideological or hygienic. From long before his first days at the Tuileries, Louis Napoleon feared the capital (as Hitler feared Berlin), and he knew that mastering it would be crucial to the Empire's existence. Paris in 1848 was volatile and anarchic, almost what sociologists today would call a 'virus city', expanding and responding with wanton unpredictability, beyond rational administration. Eight times within twenty years denizens of the working-class areas had thrown up barricades and shouted for revolution; epidemics of cholera had killed tens of thousands and the death rate was higher than that of London; crime spread in waves of comparably destructive effect; the traffic of carts and carriages was daily locked into a standstill along filthy, narrow streets.

Previous regimes had toyed with the edges of the problem. Commissions had inquired and proposed and tinkered. Minor improvements in highways and public health had had no major effect. What was needed was an authoritarian hammer blow; and one of Louis Napoleon's luckiest hours was finding someone prepared to wield it and bear the consequences.

Georges-Eugène Haussmann (1809–91) was a bear of a man, one of several civil servants interviewed for a job which required the unstoppable confidence of a steam-roller. A member of the appointments panel, Persigny, Minister for the Interior, later wrote that Haussmann 'showed off before me with a kind of brutal cynicism . . . full of audacity and cunning, capable of opposing expedients with expedients, snares with snares . . . I enjoyed the prospect of throwing this lion into the middle of the pack of foxes and wolves excited against all the generous plans of the Empire.' Persigny's expectations were fully met.

In 1853, Haussmann was inaugurated as Prefect of the Seine, and it could be said that for the next seventeen years he functioned as both Paris's mayor and its city council, wiping the floor with all other official municipal bodies. What Haussmann wanted, Haussmann could execute, without delay or impediment or red tape. A planning committee held only one meeting, after which he approached Louis Napoleon to suggest that things might move faster if its numbers were kept to a minimum. 'You mean,' the Emperor responded, 'that it would be best if there was nobody at all?' Haussmann nodded, and the committee was never heard of again.

The Emperor's involvement and interest, however, remained intense, and he was said to have conferred with Haussmann daily, directly after his immovable morning session with the Prefect of Police. Louis Napoleon was lucid as to his intentions. His eclectic reading during his years of imprisonment, his fond memories of the sweep and scope of Regent Street and the parks in London, his commitment to both Bonapartist absolutism and Saint-Simonian socialism combined to make him, in his peculiarly laconic fashion, a visionary – and Haussmann's brief was therefore not to play the creative artist, but to develop and realize ideas that the Emperor had already sketched out. Only in the underground matters of the water supply and drainage did Haussmann take a significant lead, proposing to his initially sceptical master an unparalleled extension to the existing system for which a century later the city would still be profoundly, if unwittingly, grateful.

But every measure taken was motivated by the same *realpolitik* and underpinned by the same logic. It reduces to this: push industry and the *sans-culottiste* tendency out of the centre of Paris, replacing its warren of dangerous slums with public monuments and commercial development attractive to a new class of clean-living, high-spending, Empire-supporting bourgeois. In other words, kill off a city built on the virus of poverty and give birth to a financially fecund city resting on clean foundations; bring Paris out of hiding and create public spaces open to surveillance;

keep the construction trade busy and happy, thus preventing a resurgence of the discontents which had led its workers to fan the revolutionary flames in 1848; and extend Paris's authority beyond its traditional boundaries so that the straggling jumble of suburban villages could be incorporated within the grand plan (this Haussmann achieved in 1860, doubling the extent of his territory with one stunning administrative stroke). Homogenize and segregate.

There were flaws in such thinking. Haussmann failed to provide sufficient public housing to accommodate either the exiled poor of the centre or the horde of immigrant workers which arrived to man the building sites. Nor did the planned mass social redistribution prove altogether feasible: short of forcible deportation, no way could be found of persuading all the inhabitants of long-settled communities to up sticks and move to areas they did not like or understand. When tenements were pulled down, their more cussed denizens would simply cram themselves into ever more crowded corners of the same neighbourhood, one jump ahead of the eviction orders.

An even more fundamental problem was money. Louis Napoleon upheld the Saint-Simonian principle that the more government invested in society, the more wealth and happiness would be generated. Whereas Paris had previously lived modestly off its income of taxes and levies, it now began borrowing against the collateral of that income and the prospect of an enriched city yielding yet more taxes and levies. For a time, this idea of running a 'productive deficit' seemed to work, and the fundamental economic thought behind the Second Empire (strong, stable government being attractive to investors, trade can be deregulated and credit extended, thus stimulating an atmosphere of confidence and enterprise, which produces full employment and creates a prosperity that in turn keeps the regime in power) gave the process the free financial rein it required. In 1858 Louis Napoleon helped it along further by authorizing the creation of an investment bank, the Caisse des Travaux de Paris, specifically to raise capital for construction. This institution allowed Haussmann to negotiate with private contractors and float a debt independent of the municipal accounts, a facility he used rather unscrupulously. In 1867 it emerged that he had secured loans for half a billion francs through deferred payment contracts and a complex system of discounting. The profits on these transactions went to the Bank Crédit Foncier – and the honest citizenry of Paris paid for them. The news that Haussmann planned another wave of expenditure in the suburbs further diminished his popularity, leaving people to wonder if they were in fact making the money they thought they were making.

Exposed by the brilliant investigative journalism of Jules Ferry's pamphlet *Les Comptes fantastiques d'Haussmann* ('The Fantasy Accounts of Haussmann', a title punning on the popular *contes*, or tales, of Hoffmann), the Prefect of the Seine could finally be nailed. In the more democratic atmosphere of 1869, he was obliged to submit his activities to the scrutiny of a public inquiry. The suspected irregularities were confirmed: over forty per cent of the municipal budget, they claimed, was being swallowed up in paying the interest on its debts. Despite the conversion of all the borrowing into one long-term loan, Haussmann's credibility was destroyed and early in 1870 Louis Napoleon recognized that he had no alternative but to dismiss his most faithful and effective servant. Haussmann refused to go quietly. 'A man like me,' he said, 'does not tender his resignation, any more than he hangs on to power. A man like me is either sacked or kept on. . . . I wish to take full responsibility for what I have done . . .' There followed a tremendous procession through the boulevards (for which he took 'full responsibility') culminating in the ceremonial surrender of his emblems of office. Haussmann left, as he put it, through the front door: to what extent he had personally benefited from his financial dealings – to what extent he was a crook – remains open to debate, but for the remainder of his long life he was a rich man, with a barony, directorships, a sumptuous villa in Nice and a handsome mansion in Longchamps to his name.

Some sharper-witted elements had long been taking a more subtle revenge on Haussmann's bullying. Everybody he expropriated was entitled to compensation, the level of which was settled by a public jury. To exploit the possibilities this presented there arose the intriguing new profession of indemnity broker-age. Practitioners would assist the passage of the evicted – for a fee of ten per cent of the jury's award. Versed in the art of hoodwinking or bribing the court's surveyors, they applied farcical ingenuity to the supplying of mean little backstreet premises with temporary splendours and forged account books that would raise the value of the property. It became quite a game. Victor Fournel cites the example of the owner of a little bar 'who by dint of crafty calculations, managed to have his premises demolished three times; and who, moving from one indemnity to another, ended up building a glossy marvel of a café – which he sincerely hopes to see demolished before he dies. He is about to retire and build himself a country house . . .' Given that as many as 800 properties were condemned every year, this ruse cost Paris millions. The cartoonists, led by Honoré Daumier, invented Monsieur Vautour, 'Mr Vulture', the archetypal Haussmann speculator, one step ahead and entirely ruthless.

But Haussmann understood with genius one profound neces-sity of the age: the modern city's dependence on its lines of communication, its capacity to move at speed. This applied to the sewers and water supply as much as to the roads and canals, as the statistics demonstrate (the length of the sewers quad-rupled, the piped water supply doubled, fifty-two miles of road added to the system, and the average width of a main street increased from twenty-five to between sixty-five and a hundred feet).

What enabled Haussmann more than any other phenomenon was the six-fold expansion of a railway network linking not only the entire country to Paris, but the entire continent as well. One can easily imagine the demand for steel and timber this boom stimulated, the rise in property values and, of course, the increase in individual mobility; but the effects also extended to the possibilities of transporting freight, post and food, even to the establishment of station bookstalls and the need for accurate timekeeping. Railways broke into the self-containment of small communities as they simultaneously opened up large ones. For Paris, encircled by a railway with spokes into the central termini, it meant both a vast international influx and an even faster, more localized daily influx of people either travelling across the city to work (previously almost impossible: you worked within walking distance of your home) or visiting shops and places of entertainment. Probably no city at any time has felt more immediately or dramatically the force of the cliché 'a change in the pace of life' than Second Empire Paris.

Another cliché is the notion that the chief reason for planning wide, straight boulevards was to allow for the strategic movement of troops in the event of rioting and to prevent the throwing up of barricades, but there is no evidence to suggest that this was anything more than a minor incidental consideration to either Haussmann or Louis Napoleon. Much more germane to their thinking was the imperative of expanding access to and from the railway termini, focus of the development of traffic, by striking single routes through from north to south (that is, from the Gare du Nord and Gare de l'Est, down the Boulevards de Strasbourg and Sébastopol, across the Seine at the Île de la Cité, and up the Boulevard Saint-Michel), and east to west (from the Gare de Lyon and Place de la Bastille down the rue de Rivoli, past the Louvre and the Tuileries to the Place de la Concorde). Haussmann's planning was not so much classical in inspiration as pragmatic. Its strength lay in its insensitivity to aesthetics, its readiness to flatten tradition and sentiment. The absolute priority was moving from A to B with the minimum amount of interference, in the minimum amount of time. Parisians may have sighed nostalgically for twists and turns, corners and dead ends, the ramshackle variety and spontaneity of centuries of organically accreted urban life, but Haussmann knew that their city needed air, light, space and mobility more than it needed romance.

The new Paris's greatest ally was a firm of maverick bankers, the Crédit Mobilier, led by the brothers Jacob and Isaac Pereire. More speculative and idealistic than their cautious Rothschild rivals, the Pereires took uninhibited advantage of the capitalistic liberty embodied in nineteenth-century Paris's infamous unofficial slogan 'Enrichissez-vous!' ('Get rich quick!'), investing brilliantly not only in railways (both domestic and foreign), but also in omnibus routes, cabs, water, street lighting, hotels, department stores and newspapers. They made their own fortunes and thousands of others by understanding what a railway civilization implied and what it would make people want and do beyond travelling by train (in his farce, *Les Chemins de Fer*, 'The Railways', Eugène Labiche has a provincial shareholder suggesting to the Board of Directors that dividends could be greatly increased by selling off the umbrellas that passengers left behind in the carriages: this is a joke the Pereires would have taken seriously).

The Crédit Mobilier was memorably described as 'the greatest gaming house in Europe'. The odds on raking it in were high: over its first full year of operation, 1852–3, the bank paid out a dividend of thirty per cent, and that figure was doubled, trebled, quadrupled. Chased by subsidiaries and imitators, Pereire money boomed, bred and sometimes burnt away. The heat rose dangerously in the late 1850s as the Gold Rush effect wore off; a Free Trade treaty with England in 1860 may have helped, but the American Civil War caused more difficulties. Having saturated Paris, the Pereires moved base to Marseilles in 1863 and decisively crashed in 1867. All the while, the amount of cash in general circulation was rocketing. Ordinary people accustomed themselves to bank accounts and small-scale savings; popular subscriptions for projects such as the Suez Canal (not a big success) thrilled waiters and shop assistants with the promise of fabulous ultimate returns.

So Haussmannization would have happened in some form without Haussmann: it was the spirit of the age that rebuilt Paris as much as the will of this one civil servant and his master, and it is important to remember that until his overspending came into question, Haussmann encountered very little opposition. Of course, it was not easy to oppose Louis Napoleon's regime, but even those dewy-eyed intellectuals appreciated that many of the changes were inevitable or beneficial, while the rest of society was kept happy by the consideration of the money that might be made from the upheaval.

Haussmannization became without doubt Paris's biggest industry, and even a summary list of what was constructed during its seventeen-year existence, through either public funds or private development, is staggering. The worst areas of inner-city decay were eliminated: the stifling and filthy shambles on the Île de la Cité became the monumental order of law courts, police headquarters, the extended Hôtel-Dieu hospital, and a flower market; a plan to join the Louvre to the Tuileries Palace, creating an imperial enclave on the scale of the Forbidden City in Peking, was never effected, but the flanking slums fell to the dazzlingly glamorous rue de Rivoli. More specific schemes included Baltard's elegant pavilions for Les Halles and five other covered markets, the reading room of the Bibliothèque Nationale, seventy schools, six town halls, six barracks, five new bridges and six extended ones, fifteen churches, four theatres, Garnier's Opéra, the storm drains (human excrement was still collected by night carts), the water pipes, parks for twenty-one residential squares, as well as the more grandly scaled Bois de Boulogne, Bois de Vincennes, Buttes-Chaumont, Parc Monceau and Parc Montsouris – all landscaped on the London model and fraternally open to all, with artificial lakes and grottoes, meandering paths and contrived panoramas, benches and refreshment rooms, the details of such amenities being a particular concern of the Emperor himself. Outside the city walls, Haussmann began developing a prototype of the modern industrial park, luring industrialists such as the steel magnate Cail to the Plaine Saint-Denis, where land was tax-free and the amenities dirt cheap.

Eighty-five miles of new roads were the arteries of this organism, mostly great tracks of wide boulevard or avenue, lined with evenly spaced rows of the same hardy little trees and dotted with standard items of street furniture,* leading to vast open crossroads (*places* or *carréfours*) signposted to one of the railway termini: the Gare Saint-Lazare (which by 1869, four years after its opening in 1865, was carrying thirteen million passengers annually, ten-and-a-half million of them surburban),

---

* Haussmann shared a common prejudice against electric light and refused to sanction its use for street lamps. Electricity was considered 'injurious to the eye . . . shedding a radiance which dazzles but does not illuminate'. See D. H. Pinkney, *Napoleon III and the Rebuilding of Paris* (Princeton, 1957).

the Gare de l'Est, the Gare Montparnasse (both opened in 1852), the Gare de Lyon, the Gare du Nord, and the Gare d'Austerlitz (reconstructed in, respectively, 1860, 1864 and 1869). These arteries throbbed: Parisian traffic doubled between 1853 and 1860 alone, announced the statisticians, and the 9,000 horses which daily steered the Boulèvard des Capucines in 1850 had become 23,000 by 1868.

The money was made out of the apartment blocks, those distinctive but unimpressive six-storey tapered edifices, which have remained the norm in stretches of central Paris until today. Architectural historians now lovingly catalogue the variations in detail that their iron- and stonework embrace, but the basic construction followed a strict code of regulation: specified height and depth, with an entrance wide enough for carriages and a courtyard for parking, ventilation and fire prevention. The old Parisian principle of separating the classes vertically – so that each block moved socially downwards as it moved geographically upwards, with the bourgeois on the first floor and the students and paupers crammed into the garrets – declined. The new blocks were more socially unified, and thinner walls and narrower public quarters and stairwells allowed developers to maximize rentable space. Life within could at times become painfully noisy and claustrophobic, according to Victor Fournel, 'combining extreme expense with extreme inconvenience':

Through the windows you receive the olfactory secrets of all the kitchens in the building; through the doors, the tramp of everybody using the staircase; through the fireplaces, the snatches of all the conversations and arguments. Below you, Madame suffers from migraine, forcing you, out of chivalry and compassion, to wear slippers and to walk round on tiptoe all week; opposite, Mademoiselle is taking piano lessons and has been practising for the last six months, from morning to evening, her book of exercises – a torture not to be described. Some children playing with a spinning-top in the apartment above is enough to render all work impossible. The squeaking of a chair or a cupboard door leaves you insomniac; a neighbour blowing his nose in the middle of the night wakes you with a start. You are hemmed in and hounded out by a swarm of noises which have to be endured to the bitter end. And as the last straw, should your concierge take a fancy to cabbage soup, then you too – either up the staircase or through the courtyard, or both at once – must swallow its every exhalation.

This domestic inferno he compares wistfully with '*le home anglais* . . . so peaceful and comfortable, its tranquil pleasures far removed from all exterior tumult' (the result, this view, of reading too much cosy Dickens, perhaps; although then, as now, it is true that a far higher percentage of modestly circumstanced Londoners lived in one-family houses than did Parisians.)

The great irony of Haussmannization is that it became a victim of its own success. Rents and prices rose to a point at which the city could no longer afford itself; and the covert design of remapping its demography (broadly speaking, through the attraction of the rich to the centre and the expulsion of the poor to the suburbs) was thrown into havoc by the necessity of importing migrant labour to man the building sites – the process of Haussmannization directly employed around twenty per cent of Paris's working population and the expenditure of 2½ billion francs. Over 50,000 provincials arrived in Paris annually through the later 1850s, and by 1866 it was estimated that only a third of the population was actually native to the city.* This worried the regime. Could this element prove to be the tinder for revolution? How were these men to be registered and monitored? Where were they to be housed? The notorious morgue, opened in 1864, in which all anonymous corpses were laid out naked for public identification, was the horribly necessary result of such a transience of population. Paris before Haussmann had been a city of tightly localized and immobile residence, every face and place ingrained in familiarity (only eleven per cent of businesses employed more than ten workers); but by 1869 it had become a city of masses, a kaleidoscope of the unrecognizable – a phenomenon as alarmingly novel to old Parisians as the related increase in the speed and volume of traffic. To be found like the Kinck family anonymously

---

* Between 1851 and 1870 it was estimated that the population of Paris increased overall from just over one million to 1,850,000 – of these something like one million were not Paris-born. Twelve per cent of the population was totally illiterate, sixteen per cent was employed in the building trade.

murdered on the scrubland of the suburbs far from home, railway visitors to the capital fallen victim to a boy of unknown associations who had booked into a hotel room, was like a nemesis on this modernity – a dreadful ironic apocalypse on a system which took unprecedented registering control over its subjects.

The Paris of tourists and consumerism was the other reality of Haussmannization. The city had become 'an object of luxury and curiosity more than of usefulness,' complained Fournel, 'a town of exhibition, placed under glass, hostelry to the world, the object of foreigners' admiration and envy, impractical for its inhabitants, but unique in the comforts and pleasures of all kinds it offers to the sons of Albion'.

The centre might well have seemed to resonate with the sound of English. Apart from the tourists, there were an estimated 9,000 British and 4,000 Americans resident in Paris, largely of the moneyed classes. The English set was led by the disgraceful Prince of Wales, who spent more time in Paris than he should have done, fraternizing with other British aristocrats voluntarily exiled in their search for venal pleasures less lavishly granted by London. Gaston Jollivet's souvenirs recall that young French blades of the time enjoyed posing as English nobs (sometimes to the extent of criminal impersonation); English breakfasts of tea, cutlets and oysters were standard fare on the boulevards between the hours of ten and midday; the fashion-able area around Parc Monceau was known as *le west end*; and in 1869 Felix Whitehurst noted the fashion for London tailoring ('Poole and Smallpage dress the Bois as they provide Piccadilly and clothe Hyde Park'). This English presence was a familiar irritant; but the nature of the American was a relative novelty to the general life of Paris, and one that was much discussed. Was this young democracy just absurdly vulgar and absurdly inno-cent? Or did its open spirit and energy mean that one day it might prove to be what the Huns and Goths had been to Ancient Rome? So the Goncourt brothers reflected on meeting 'a nice young American fellow', with 'a timid manner, a square head in which one senses prodigious nervous strength, the hardy, healthy, triumphant race to which he belongs. And we say to ourselves, "The world has been and is now governed by physical force; the nations which have exhausted their health are passing away." '

Ironically, the American community in Paris was dominated by effete Secessionist Southerners, drawn to the imperial pomp and rank denied them by hardy, healthy, triumphant democracy. The attraction was reciprocated by the Empress, whose maternal grandfather, Scottish by birth, had emigrated west (subsequently returning as the US Consul at Malaga), leaving her curious about, and sympathetic to, the New World. 'Paris is the heaven of Americans,' recalled the snobbish Dr Thomas Evans, Surgeon-Dentist to the Tuileries, writing in 1905. 'At no court in Europe were [they] more in evidence,' he gushed, bemoaning the latter-day invasion of the tourist classes, Daisy Millers and worse.

They were already there in the late 1860s: big spenders, or innocents abroad (like Mark Twain, attracted by the International Exhibition of 1867), splendidly catered for – if not at court then at a variety of institutions equally glittering, for which money rather than manners was the entrance requirement. The Grand Hôtel on the Boulevard des Capucines, for instance, a Pereire project opened by the Empress Eugénie in 1862 with the ingenuous remark, 'It's just like home' (or so it was reported), and boasting seven hundred rooms, as well as the innovations of electricity, elevators and ice-making machines. For restaurants, you were spoilt for choice, in a city which was already at a peak of its reputation for gastronomy. This was due less to the survival of immemorial traditions – for what people eat is as waywardly fashionable a business as what they wear – than to the development of a uniquely sophisticated food industry and the wealth of supplies accommodated in the new covered markets, with their cool underground storage chambers and effective administration. This facilitated both the processing of foodstuffs (margarine was invented in France in 1869) and their retailing (the still-extant grocery chain Félix Potin had a celebrated premises on the new Boulevard de Sébastopol which sold an astonishing variety of meats and pies, hygienically precooked and packed in a factory in La Villette).

Poorer neighbourhoods also relied on huge self-service restaurants, one step up from the charitable soup kitchen, such as the famous La Californie, which in its two daily five-hour sessions (7–12 a.m. and 4–9 p.m.) could accommodate 18,000 'workmen and ruined young men of various classes'. Its proprietor, one Monsieur Cadet, was originally a butcher, 'and usually reserved for the use of this restaurant 500 calves per month and 1,500 rabbits,' wrote A. B. North Peat, a young English diplomat, in wonder.

> Thirty butchers scarcely suffice to supply the amount of meat now required by 'La Californie' since he has put himself at the head of the concern. Precisely as the clock strikes seven M. Cadet, the said proprietor, presides over the distribution of soup and meat to the poor of the neighbourhood. Between half-past seven and eight the customers begin to arrive. Nothing can be more promiscuous than the crowd which frequents 'La Californie.' There may be seen the poor and industrious workman, who buys a piece of bread and a morsel of cheese, which he eats as he goes to his work; the *noceur* [reveller], who has spent his night in dissipation and comes in to drink a glass of wine and eat a crust; the tramp, who has slept in the open air, and the felon who adroitly contrives to evade even the Argus eyes of the waiters, and steals a plate of meat and a piece of bread deposited for an instant on a table, while its bearer answers a sudden call from an impatient customer. Every customer of 'La Californie' is expected to go in person to the kitchen and carry away to the eating-room the dish he prefers, for which he pays on the spot, being there supplied with a spoon and iron fork.

La Californie closed in 1868 on the death of Monsieur Cadet, but the notion of mass standardized catering, often involving elements of self-service, took wider hold further up the social scale. One particularly interesting phenomenon – the precursor of so much that we think of as American and mid-twentieth-century in origin – was the chain of cheap restaurants or *bouillons** owned by a Monsieur Duval, also originally a butcher. There were ten of these by 1868 in central Paris, 'extremely popular with all classes of society and may without hesitation be

---

* Which could unsatisfactorily be translated as 'snack-bar' but more literally as 'mouthful'.

visited by ladies', as Blanchard Jerrold's guidebook put it. They
were staffed by waiters and waitresses dressed primly in black
with white aprons, like the 'nippies' of Lyons teashops, the girls
with white, nurse-like caps too ('not unlike Sisters of Charity',
noted Baedeker). The furnishings and decoration were as uniform as the menu, offering simple dishes served at a speed, which
made them ideal for the office-worker's lunch break. Another
innovation, directed at tourists, was the fixed-price meal,
'comparatively recently come into vogue' according to
Blanchard Jerrold, for which one paid on entering the
restaurant.

Elsewhere, finding one's way around a menu could be
confusing. A sophisticated gourmet of sorts, Blanchard Jerrold
deplored the standard British unresponsiveness to the French
culinary genius:

> Madame Manchester pushed the Marennes oysters from her with
> disgust, vowed she could not sit in the same room with the melon;
> and finally, when a *foie gras aux truffes*, perfectly cooked, was put
> upon her plate, tasted, drew back from the table with an expression
> of unfathomable disgust, saying, 'Ugh! whatever is that? I never
> tasted anything nastier in my life!' This family has been a fortnight in
> Paris, and throughout had been dining off 'a good plain joint, sir' – I
> think at the Hotel Byron – all the time . . .

but was nevertheless forced to admit that 'counterfeit cookery is
a great trade in the French capital', and that the traditionally
grand restaurants could be forbidding to anyone nervous of
decoding the massive catalogues of dishes listed within their
velvet-bound *cartes*, let alone constructing a good dinner from
the infinite combinations they presented.

Such eating also demanded more time and attention than
suited the new pace of life: old-style devotees of *haute cuisine*
would order the day before and spend six or more hours
savouring the results, but now people wanted to get on to the
theatre or back to a railway station. Consequently several
famous establishments of the Palais-Royal area went into decline
(the Café de Paris, once frequented by Balzac, was forced to sell
up when its owner, Lady Yarmouth, who lived upstairs,

announced that she required silence from her tenants after she went to bed at 10 p.m., thus forestalling its valuable late-night supper clientele).

'Gastronomy has emigrated to England,' announced the Count d'Orsay, provoking great debate. It was certainly true that at the five-star level, other European capitals were learning to copy French models, but daily bourgeois cuisine remained much more interesting than it was in London or Vienna, and there were other innovations in public eating afoot. Geared to the tastes of the Sons of Albion and their followers were smart new establishments such as Hill's (York ham and pale ale, late-night theatregoers) and Peters (turtle soup, Welsh rarebit, Bourbon and literary celebrities). On Haussmann's expansive boulevards the relaxed sociability of café life flourished. The consumption of coffee increased phenomenally, thanks to the speed and efficiency of the newly invented hydrostatic percolator, which allowed each cup to be freshly brewed rather than stewed in a jug. Then there was *absinthe*, imported via the French troops stationed in Algeria: a seventy per cent proof concoction of crushed herbs diluted in sugar and water. The abuse of this *feu vert*, 'green fire', was so widespread that in 1865 there appeared for the first time in medical terminology the diagnosis of *alcoolisme*, alcoholism, a disease as dangerous to the health of France's stock as conjugal onanism, another dreadful sign of the degeneracy of the race.

Aside from those that offered floor shows or some musical entertainment (the Café des Aveugles, for instance, was noted for its entirely blind orchestra), there is a broad distinction to be made between the cafés such as Tortoni's, which concentrated on liquid refreshments (and perhaps a limited menu of ices and cakes, chicken and omelettes) with the diversion of board games, billiards and newspapers; and the cafés where this sort of service occupied only the street-front area of what was primarily a restaurant. Of this latter type, the most brilliant example was undoubtedly the Café Anglais on the Boulevard des Italiens. The clientele was both aristocratic and *louche*, the cooking original. Its chef, Dugléré, had been bought in, at a vast salary, from the sclerotic Trois Frères Provençaux and the simple elegance of his specialities – *boeuf flamande*, *pommes Anna*, crayfish bordelaise, larks with cherries, a sublime *mousse au chocolat* – invited the composer Rossini to dub him 'the Mozart of French cooking': not for Dugléré the dense baroque elaborations of the old school, with its inedible decorative flourishes.

Meals here were served *à la Russe* rather than *à la Française*: that is to say, courses appeared on the table in quick succession, turning the ritual into a sharply mapped journey through a series of contrasting tastes and textures, rather than the one vast spread, presented synchronically at the beginning of the meal, which the gourmet toyed with in a dilettante manner (much as we do now with oriental food). The introduction of gas stoves also made swift alterations in cooking pace easier to effect, allowing a chef an unprecedented degree of refinement and control over his creations. The trend, in other words, was towards food hotter, faster and more various.

The same could be said of everything else that Paris offered for sale, and nowhere did that fever pitch rise higher than in the new *grands magasins*, or department stores, which were revolutionizing both the practice and the psychology of selling. Here the purchase of a commodity became more than a commercial transaction based on fulfilling a customer's needs. Their remarkable success was based on the capacity to play on deeper and darker acquisitive appetites, stimulating desires as much as satisfying them, as potentially ruinous to women as the brothels were to men – or so thought the moralists. Zola's novel about one such Second Empire store, *Au Bonheur des Dames* ('Ladies' Pleasure', published in 1883) claims that it had become the focus of 'a new religion: churches, little by little deserted by those of wavering faith, were being replaced by [this] bazaar', filled by one sex alone: 'it was Woman they caught in the eternal snare of their bargains, after they had stunned her with their displays. They had awoken new desires in her weak flesh, they were an immense temptation to which she inevitably yielded, succumbing in the first place to purchases for the house, then won over by coquetry, finally completely enslaved.'

Zola's rhetoric may be overheated, but it is certainly true that the buying power of middle-class women was the market that the department stores primarily exploited, the focus of a strategy of retailing that remains basically unchanged almost a century-and-a-half later.

Essentially the *grands magasins* were draper's shops, where the customer bought rolls of cloth to make up into garments or furnishing. The more successful of these, fed by the mechanized output of factories in Alsace and Lorraine, slowly expanded to sell all manner of related goods – from umbrellas and carpets to scissors and brushes and leather and paper – which had previously been sold by tiny specialist concerns, staffed by one family and running on the basis of a low turnover and a high profit margin, with prices that were bartered. In an age of railways and boulevards, when large quantities of stock could be produced and transported at speed, such a policy became redundant. Thousands of little shops were starved to extinction by a few voracious big ones; high turnover, low profit margins, and fixed prices were the key weapons in the battle for survival.

The most influential of the *grands magasins* was Au Bon Marché, near Saint-Germain-des-Prés. In September 1869 its owner, Aristide Boucicaut, laid the foundation stone of what was planned to be the world's first-ever purpose-designed department store. One of the architects was the young Gustave Eiffel, who proposed an iron-framed interior consisting of several floors of galleries supported on columns, surrounding a magnificent central space rising to a glass roof: a still familiar model.* For various reasons this new Au Bon Marché would take nearly twenty years to complete, but its inception was a climax in Boucicaut's exemplary career. He had come up from nothing – from worse than nothing, some said. Diligence and sobriety had paved his way forward from his beginnings as an itinerant tinker, until in 1852, in his early forties, he had risen from a station as the least of the draper's lackeys to be *chef de comptoir aux châles* – chief salesman on the shawl counter. But he had a seemly ambition to improve himself further, and the Second Empire was happy to encourage it.

So Boucicaut and his wife – a former laundress of stern virtue

---

* The present Au Bon Marché remains on the original site, but is a twentieth-century reconstruction of Eiffel's building.

and impressive embonpoint – invested their thrifty savings in a partnership on a draper's shop in the rue du Bac, with a turnover of less than half a million francs a year. After a decade, that figure had rocketed to seven million, and with the bank's eager help, Boucicaut was able to buy out his partner for fifteen million and become sole master of Au Bon Marché. By 1869 the store had expanded organically along the street, consuming the premises of neighbouring businesses bankrupted by its own practices, a healthy blossom of Haussmann's ruthless urban ecology. With annual sales now totalling over twenty million francs, Boucicaut was ready to build a palace for his empire.

He had not been the first shopkeeper to pile high and sell cheap, nor the first to diversify; but he was the first to appreciate that a lady sought more from shopping than low prices. Au Bon Marché had those in plenty – as well as bargain-basement offers and seasonal reductions – but it also radiated an aura of devotion to Truth and Beauty that transcended the realms of Mammon. The principle of *serving* the customer was paramount. Goods could be delivered or ordered by mail; the staff were trained to follow your every caprice with abject deference (on pain of instant dismissal should any detail of a rigid code of professional conduct be ignored: Boucicaut was a 'philanthropic' – which is to say, profoundly authoritarian – employer, treating his minions like an enlightened slave-master and managing the store through a Byzantine hierarchy of seniorities). You could trust Au Bon Marché – there was no risk, there was every guarantee. All goods, *madame*, are labelled with their prices, and you are welcome to exchange or return them if they are unsatisfactory. Meanwhile, more insidious pressures to buy were being subtly applied. Au Bon Marché seems to have been the first shop to understand the attractive power of a window display; the first to plan its layout so that a customer would be lured inexorably from one purchase to another; the first to place a full-page advertisement in a newspaper. As Au Bon Marché served, so it also seduced.

In such an ambience, shopping became not so much a search for daily necessities as an intoxicating pastime, another of the diversions that gave Paris its getting-and-spending energy, its infinite ability to be distracted by the next novelty, be it decals, transparent parasols or the cricket club in the Bois de Boulogne.★ This buzzing nervosity had its positive effects. Neither Haussmann's Paris, nor Louis Napoleon's France, was the sort of tyranny that crushes the spirit of enterprise out of its subjects, and the Second Empire witnessed (and encouraged) advances in the science of everything from aluminium to margarine, the dry-cell battery to the compressed-air drill, Pasteurization to electroplating, and prototypes of the colour photograph, the gas engine and refrigerator, as well as the more ephemeral inventions of fashion. The spectacle of enormous material changes, achieved at unprecedented speed with money exploding over all quarters, combined with the knowledge that the pace of it all could only increase, bred an excitement that was often exhilarating. But it also drove the city's top note to the pitch of hysteria – a sound of emptiness, insecurity, anxiety, symptomatic of lives without purpose or direction, poisoned by the virus of boredom. 'The inhabitants of Paris are bored as nobody on earth has ever been bored before,' wrote Louis Veuillot in 1867. 'There is nothing to fear from a people that is bored, and nothing that one can do for them.' And what has caused this disease? The destruction of roots, tradition, community, he thinks: 'This new Paris will never have a past, and it will lose the past of the old Paris – all trace of it has already vanished for a man of thirty. Even the old buildings which remain standing no longer communicate anything, because everything around them has changed . . . Each house is now only a room in an enormous inn

---

★ In 1869 perhaps the greatest of such excitements was the *vélocipede*, an early form of bicycle. A prototype pedalled model had been developed earlier in the decade, but the substitution of solid rubber for iron on the wheels had made them smoother, faster and more physically tolerable. A road race along the eighty-odd miles from Paris to Rouen was won in 10 hours 40 minutes; a journal devoted to the subject was inaugurated; at L'Hippodrome, a successful vaudeville show entitled *Les Véloce-women* played to packed houses; and the newspapers noted that the Emperor's son, the Prince Impérial, had become a keen practitioner since his aunt Princess Mathilde had given him one of the machines for his thirteenth birthday. Of more lasting significance was the occasional sight of some brave eccentric riding from home to work on his *vélo* – a pioneer of the time when the bicycle would become an ordinary mode of transport rather than a weekend plaything. See John Woodforde, *The History of the Bicycle* (London, 1969).

through which everyone has at some time passed, but where nobody retains the memory of ever having seen anyone else.'

Haussmann's Paris lacked concentration and dignity. Its values were shallow, its soul bargained away to vulgarity. The Goncourt brothers, ever fastidious in their disgust, gloated over its decadence: dinner with the courtesan la Païva epitomized their fascinated repulsion. Originally a Polish Jewess, she lived in a mansion on the Champs Élysées (now the Travellers Club), completed in 1866 on funds mostly provided by her lover, a Prussian count with mines in Silesia. It was encrusted with the precious and splendid at every level – a bath and lavatory lined with silvered bronze, a staircase made from onyx, a salon extravagantly lined with the thickest crimson damask, ceilings crassly painted with mythological scenes of an erotic nature. Quite what it all cost, or how much of it was paid for, became a favourite matter of gossip. At la Païva's table – she was 'sotte, mais pas bête', 'stupid, but nobody's fool', and liked the company of better minds than hers – 'there was never any mention of the price of anything; one would only say that at such-and-such an establishment it cost 80,000 francs'. Her display of wealth was grotesque.

> Nobody who comes here realizes that this is the most uncomfortable house in Paris. It is impossible at table to drink a glass of wine and water because the mistress has had the fancy of using as bottles and carafes cathedrals of crystal, which you need a water-carrier to lift. In the conservatory, where one smokes after dinner, one is half-frozen by the draughts from above, half-stifled by the gusts of heat from the vents. Everything is more or less like that. A splendid tea is served; but ask for a glass of water . . . and it causes as great a commotion as it would in the humblest home.

Yet la Païva was a riveting phenomenon. 'All my wishes have come to heel, like tame dogs,' the Goncourts once heard her declare: 'she told the story of a woman who, in order to achieve a certain secret purpose, shut herself away from the world for three years, hardly eating the food she was oblivious of, absorbed in herself and in everything related to her plan. "And that woman was myself . . . and I achieved it." ' Such pointless greed and wilfulness made her a monstrous archetype of the age, as much a product of Haussmann's Paris and its possibilities as the 'stock-exchange speculator or photographer' who ate at Peters, replacing 'the artist, senior civil servant, officer, bourgeois, or sporting gentleman' who twenty years previously had eaten at Lucas's and set the city's social tone at a more sympathetic level.

In his satirical work *The Life and Opinions of Monsieur F.-T. Graindorge*, Hippolyte Taine made a closer study of the new Parisians. For Taine, the Haussmann generation – its prosperous middle class, at least – existed in a mental and emotional vacuum. Once the modern young man had thought about 'his toilet, his furnishings, his little image of himself, he had come to the end of his ideas . . . He has no violent passions, not even hotheadedness; almost all today's youth is like this, even in its foolishness. Excess scares them all, they channel their vices. They are by nature bourgeois – avoiding boredom, but also avoiding any sort of risk.'

No politics, no ambition, no passion; too much culture, too much refinement, too much physical comfort – Parisians remind Taine's Monsieur Graindorge of the busts of fourth-century Romans with their distant gaze and air of passive melancholy. The Paris which had once possessed Baudelaire as a maze of nightmarish incoherence had been unravelled, tidied and lit up. 'There are fences round land which was once wild . . . and crowds have filled the enclosure.' There was nowhere new for thrusting talent or imagination to colonize or dream, only a processing of life, 'like a wad of raw cotton, thrown into a machine at the doors of a great factory, which is turned uniformly and infallibly round wheels and spindles to become thread, cloth, fabric, a napkin or handkerchief to wipe a table or a nose'. In February 1869 the Goncourts wrote in their *Journal*:

> I read that now all the trees in Paris are starting to die. There has been enough mildew over the past few years. Ancient Nature is disappearing. She leaves a land poisoned by civilization; and the time is perhaps approaching when a natural landscape will have to be industrially manufactured, a time when modern capitals, hideous conglomerations of humanity, will have for shade and greenery only the cut-out and painted tin palm trees of a Turkish bath.

The New Babylon.

6 : *Too Much, Too Soon*

For seventeen years of the Second Empire, singing the *Marseillaise* was forbidden in France. To replace its barricade-trampling exhortations, a more plaintive and peaceable National Anthem was substituted – 'Partant pour la Syrie', an anodyne Crusader ballad in the style of Sir Walter Scott, purportedly composed by Louis Napoleon's mother, Queen Hortense:

> Partant pour la Syrie
> Le jeune et beau Dunois
> Alla prier Marie
> De bénir ses exploits.
> Faites, reine immortelle,
> Lui dit-il, en partant,
> Que j'aime la plus belle
> Et sois le plus vaillant

(As he left for Syria, the young and handsome Dunois prayed to the Virgin Mary to bless his exploits. 'O immortal Queen,' he asked her, 'as I set forth, grant that I shall love the fairest and prove the most valiant')

The melody was a drearily sentimental affair, which not even the most ardent of imperialists found inspiring, and there was universal relief, on musical grounds alone, when the legality of the *Marseillaise* was restored in 1870.

The rest of the Second Empire's old tunes had already spun out of fashion, as the wheels of Louis Napoleon's long-promised, long-delayed programme of liberalization began to turn faster. An authoritarian regime would metamorphose into a democratic one, with free elections, a free press and judiciary, and freedom to associate and dissent: ever since the Empire's inauguration there had been noncommittal mutterings about the desirability of such measures. 'To those who might regret that larger concessions have not been made to liberty,' Louis Napoleon said, 'I would answer: liberty has never helped to found a lasting political edifice, it can only crown that edifice when time has consolidated it.'

By 1869 he could no longer claim the excuse. Time had certainly consolidated something, and ten years of minor concessions had only left the majority of Paris's citizenry angrier, noisier and greedier for more. In the 1863 election the Empire had polled 5,308,000 votes to the opposition's 1,954,000; in 1869, the gap had closed to 4,438,000 to 3,355,000, with the Republicans dominating in the capital and almost all of the larger urban areas. Part of the Empire's problem was the failure of the old controls it had quietly exerted over the electoral system. France had a much wider suffrage than any other country in Europe, and voting was not marked by intimidation or false counting. Instead the corruption was more light-handed: the Empire was expert at baffling the semi-literate and illiterate with fusses over cards and registers, all of which made it much simpler to vote for the 'official candidate' than for anyone else. Around the ballot halls were displayed busts of the Emperor and banners proclaiming encouraging imperial slogans. Only the 'official candidate' commanded the help of ten civil servants, only the 'official candidate' could use white paper for his electioneering bills.

The success of this strategy, however, largely depended on ensuring the co-operation of a loyal network in each con-stituency – and this the Empire increasingly failed to do. Cynicism set in. Like its leader, the regime was ailing and ageing, unattractive to young blood. Opposition and republican parties became more adept at turning this electoral system to their advantage – corruption, after all, is not politically partisan – and people grew less afraid to speak their minds.

Louis Napoleon, meanwhile, was debilitated. He was a man peculiarly sensitive to physical pain – the condition known

clinically as 'hyperaesthesia' – which he endured uncom-
plainingly. Waves of gout, arthritis, haemorrhoids, neuralgia
and the stone washed over him. From the mid 1860s onwards,
he was a sick man. Yet in some ways he may have felt that his
pallid and enfeebled appearance worked to his advantage,
deceiving his opponents into underestimating his canniness. He
read the situation deeply; he preferred conspiratorial stealth to
frontal attack; and he had one great motivating wish – that his
beloved son Louis, the Prince Impérial, should succeed him on
his eighteenth birthday in 1874, at which time he and Eugénie
had secretly agreed to abdicate.

Meanwhile, he wrote in 1867:

> I must do something resolute and Liberal. I hesitate only as to
> timeliness. If I did something now, wouldn't it look as though I was
> trying to mitigate my failures in Mexico [i.e. the ill-fated attempt to
> sponsor the establishment of an imperial government under
> Maximilian] and in Germany [i.e. the failure to exact territorial
> compensations from Prussia after its victory over Austria in
> 1866]. . . ? In this position, would concessions not enfeeble me? I
> only want good. If I did not believe myself useful to this country, I
> would leave it without hesitation . . . what holds me back is neither
> uncertainty nor an empty infatuation with my prerogatives, but the
> fear of removing the means of re-establishing, in a country troubled
> by many diverse passions, that essential base of liberty – moral order
> . . . That has always been the problem. None the less, to convince
> people by decisive action, I would like to establish at a stroke what
> has been called the crowning of the edifice: and I want to do this for
> once and for all, since it matters to me and above all to the country
> that things are definitively fixed . . .

This is typical of Louis Napoleon. Weaving bluff and flannel,
procrastination and self-protection, into his good sense and
clear-sightedness, he commits himself to nothing. There is a
thread of humility and sincerity, but also the gush of hot air.

The tone was one that Eugénie deplored. Nothing about her
husband annoyed her more than his limp and wet grasp on his
authority. 'Don't you think he's going downhill?' she asked the
British minister Lord Clarendon after an interview with the
Emperor. 'Physically, perhaps, but mentally – no!' Clarendon
replied. 'Moi, je le trouve imbécile,' Eugénie sneered. 'I think

he's an imbecile.' She fancied taking up the reins herself: as Regent, so she thought, she could restrain the runaway horse with a tight backlash. The Second Empire should be baring its teeth and rattling its sabres, not faking a wan conciliatory smile. The road to liberalism was the road to republicanism, and could lead only to anarchy. 'Consistency is strength,' was her watchword. Now was the time to intensify the degree of control, not slacken it.

Eugénie had always been unpopular, an imported foreign princess who overspent and overdressed, perceived as the dubious offspring of an unsuitable marriage between a flamboyant Spanish count and a Scots girl whose father had been a wine merchant in Malaga. France saw no further than the fact that she was not French; and there is no doubt that Eugénie was a woman insensitive to French susceptibilities, with dubious alien loyalties. Nothing could restrain her tactlessness: at one level, she dressed the Prince Impérial in tartan and engaged an English governess for his education; at another, she publicly scorned ministerial decisions – 'on one occasion,' records the diarist Viel-Castel, 'she spoke with so much bitterness and hostility against French policy that the Emperor at last could contain himself no longer. "Really, Eugénie, you seem to forget two things – first, that you are French; and second, that you are married to a Bonaparte." '

Incapable of masking or moderating her feelings, Eugénie craved a sphere of action and influence. During the first years of her marriage, she threw herself into a vigorous programme of charitable visiting to which her briskly black-and-white temperament was entirely unsuited. Her habit of listening intently to everyone's complaints, granting injudicious favours and demanding instant reforms left the exasperated professionals (according to the Prince Impérial's governess, Anna Bicknell) 'strongly inclined to apply the homely phrase of "minding one's own business".'

But with her husband's apparent decline in health and motivation, Eugénie saw wider political horizons opening up to her. She plotted the idea of an alliance with conservative, Catholic Austria against the aggressive, upstart Lutheran cheek of Prussia, and strongly supported France's corrupt meddling in Mexico. The Italian nationalists and freedom fighters enraged her, as this encounter in 1862, witnessed and written up by the Austrian Ambassador Prince Richard Metternich, comically reveals. The Piedmontese *chargé d'affaires* at the imperial court, Count Nigra, has asked to present a petition.

Her Majesty: The moment is badly chosen, but speak.
Nigra: I would wish Your Majesty to desist a little from her hostility to us, and that she would use her influence to decide the emperor to retire his troops from Rome [where they protected the Pope from Garibaldi].
Her Majesty: I would drown myself sooner than lend a hand to your highway robberies. Oh! You want us to give in always and everywhere; you are insatiable; you call the subjects who have remained faithful to the King of Naples thieves; but what do you call yourselves?
Nigra stammered.
Her Majesty: You are the ones who pillage, you who rob others and who want to make us your accomplices. But just wait; the day of vengeance will come, you will see your Mazzinis and Garibaldis grow up under you, and, the day when you are hanged, I declare to you, it will not be I who will come to your rescue.
Nigra: Your Majesty is really too unfair, and to defend myself I will ask her if the King of Italy today is not doing at Naples what the emperor did in France yesterday.
Her Majesty (furious): Oh, don't say that to me, don't compare the emperor with your highway robber. The emperor did not take anything away from anybody; he found France abandoned, the throne empty, and he saved France by *crushing people of your kind*.
Nigra picks up his hat, leaps to his feet and leaves.

Nigra and the Empress weathered the storms to become oddly devoted, but others withered at the force of her blasts, and even Louis Napoleon would be observed surrendering abjectly rather than enduring such a tirade. It was no joke: the question of how to limit the damage she could wreak was a delicate political matter, and one important reason for maintaining press censorship was that wherever it was eased, a flood of tabloid-style libels against the Empress had gushed forth.

With a wife like Eugénie, the Emperor hardly needed enemies, yet she represented only one aspect of the opposition to his plans for an extension of democratic rights and institutions. From a left-wing direction came the resentment of republicans, socialists, and an urban working class whose favour the Empire had crucially failed to win. The problem had long exercised Louis Napoleon: in 1844 he had published a pamphlet entitled 'The Extinction of Pauperism', a Caesarist-Bonapartist-Peronist-Gaullist-populist proposal for a toughly paternalistic system of discipline and reward. When he came to power, noises were made about improving the lot of the poor, but little was actually done about it. The Second Empire preferred to let capitalism take its course, and economic historians cannot perceive any clear indication that the regime brought a real rise in average earnings, despite various improvements in the overall standard of public services and living conditions. Industrialization is always a mixed blessing to the worker, and the growth of jobs in the building and food trades must be balanced against the decline of traditional small-scale weaving and other artisanal crafts.

Louis Napoleon praised the honest worker and made constant propaganda of his claim to be his friend, although it was friendship at a cool distance that he had in mind – few sons of toil ever socialized in the Tuileries and the Emperor spent little time in the factories or on the farms. At arm's length, however, he encouraged their aspirations, and in 1862 the Empire paid for a delegation of 200 workers to visit the Great Exhibition in London, inviting them to return with *cahiers de doléance* – lists of complaints and ideas gleaned from the experience. The most enlightened aspect of his attitude to this section of society was his policy on education, developed through the later 1860s by the minister Victor Duruy. Apart from instituting free and universal primary education, Duruy also made important moves towards the extension of vocational training and the equal schooling of women.

This was an enormously expensive but sound investment. Cheaper but riskier was the decision, early in the programme of reform, to liberalize the law relating to labour. Combinations were authorized in 1864, co-operatives actively encouraged from 1867. Strikers – on whose behalf Louis Napoleon often interceded – were given more room for manoeuvre. This opening of the doors did not have the invigorating impact that the Empire hoped: the working class was not so easily bought, least of all when the rise in prices so far exceeded that in wages. It was misguidedly believed that permitting the negotiation of terms and conditions of employment was not the same as permitting the negotiation of broader political matters, but of course it was virtually impossible to enforce the distinction. Meetings called legally to discuss pay rises inevitably turned into anti-imperial rallies. Innocuous-sounding lectures with titles such as 'The Art of Raising Rabbits and Increasing your Income by 300 francs' or 'The Rise and Fall of the Crinoline' were fronts for much more serious debates. The strikes became increasingly menacing. In 1869, miners, weavers, and carpenters came out, as did whole towns such as La Villette and Le Creusot in what bordered on insurrection. At Aubin, soldiers killed fourteen striking miners in the course of a savage riot. The general view was that secret conspiratorial cells of a now radical movement known as the 'Internationale' – of which more later – were infiltrating and inciting peaceable workers' unions and combinations. One convicted member, a metal worker named Chalain, arrested and tried in 1870, spoke to his accusers in a virulent new language of class warfare. 'When you see a fabulous fortune, you say "national prosperity". We say "waste of capital, robbery and the humiliation of the working class". The one goes with the other.'

Even more dangerous to public order – because it appealed to the educated middle classes and to everyone's sense of humour – was a weekly pocket-sized satirical magazine called *La Lanterne*, which began publication in May 1868 following a partial relaxation of censorship. It was entirely written by Henri Rochefort, a deceptively Chaplinesque figure and one-time minor civil servant in Haussmann's office, who mounted a bitingly witty one-man journalistic show. 'He is the most popular man in Paris,' reported *The Times*'s correspondent, and with *La Lanterne*'s circulation at over 120,000 copies, this was no exaggeration.

What made Rochefort so irresistible was a brazenly subversive impudence the like of which Paris had not experienced since Louis Napoleon came to power in 1851. 'They have found a polite way of referring to despotism: they call it "personal government". Thanks to this euphemism, Nero, Caracalla, Commodus and Domitian are neither tyrants, nor vampires, nor cannibals. They are emperors who "govern personally".' That light, dry sneer reduced imperial pretensions much more effectively than head-long rhetorical bluster and left the government flabbergasted. After the eleventh issue, legal action was gingerly taken to suppress *La Lanterne*. Rochefort fled to Brussels and launched his venom-filled squibs from a safer distance. In Paris the air was thick with them, as battalions of imitative satirical magazines hit the streets and criticism of the imperial regime became ever more boldly hostile.

Louis Napoleon faced the stark alternative which confronts all unconvincing authoritarian regimes: to preserve his power, he could either do too much too soon or too little too late. But he had to do something. To date, all his liberalizing reforms had had an overall negative effect – antagonizing the hard-line imperial loyalists without winning the support of even the moderate republicans. The elections of May 1869 seemed to sound a death-rattle, not only because the Empire's vote slid so dramatically in the wake of its failures in Mexico and Italy, but also because of the ominously uncontrollable outbreaks of rioting which followed them nationwide. Felix Whitehurst gives an interestingly detailed account in his *Daily Telegraph* column of one such chain of events in the working-class area of Montmartre on the evening of 10 June – a point at which proceedings had been initiated against *Le Rappel*, a new and popular republican newspaper strongly linked to another exile from the Empire, Victor Hugo.

> By nine o'clock there was a mass of people, and at half-past a sea of heads was ebbing and flowing as far as the eye could reach. . . . Suddenly the demons of discord appeared on the scene in the shape of a dozen men, said to be 'students,' each armed with a long stick, on the end of which was a lantern; and then the riot broke out. Different parties formed up; some went to shout before the 'Rappel,' some to cry 'A bas l'Empire'.in the Rue Drouot, while a detachment

was told off to sing the *Marseillaise*, . . . there was also a little dance. But now let us look at the crowd. I should say there were 20,000 persons within rifle shot, packed as closely as sardines. What do they look like? Workmen! Oh! no; we are not in that quarter – the blouses, also supposed at the same moment to be dancing the same devil's dance, only in a worse way, are all by St Antoine. This Faubourg was described to me last night as a 'most respectable quarter.'

Out of this gathering of 20,000 persons, I should say there were 200 who wished for a real riot, 200 more who love to make a noise; and that the rest, composed of women and children as well as men, were mere lookers-on. Riot, mischief, and curiosity were thus repesented, and the crowd were all at the height of their enjoyment, the party of action just proposing to pull down something – the Empire, or at least a kiosk – when a change came over the spirit of their dream. Up the Faubourg Montmartre moves a body of darkly-dressed men, marching four deep, and halting at the Boulevard. A drummer advances, and then comes a gentleman in plain evening clothes, only wearing a scarf. He holds up his hand to the young drummer, who is about as high as change for a napoleon, and immediately a tattoo is heard. At that sound it is no exaggeration to say that every revolutionist fled like one man – no, like one old, nervous woman.

A lull followed. The Garde Nationale and police withdrew, the crowd dispersed and normal traffic resumed. But within an hour

the Guard and all the police left the spot; circulation of carriages even was not stopped – a fact which subsequently placed several cabmen in very false positions. At first quietly, but then noisily, the mob returned, and in five minutes it was evident to every one who had seen a street fight before that mischief was meant. There was a pause, almost a dead silence – a consultation of leaders, and a resolution to act. Then began one of the most ruffianly and disgusting scenes of wanton destruction which can be conceived. M. Rochefort's lantern-bearers opened the ball by smashing the lamps and turning off the gas; all available windows were then broken. 'The kiosks! the kiosks!' 'Vive *La Lanterne*, et à bas les kiosks!' and at it they went. In five minutes five kiosks and other buildings had fallen. I saw one cook – there were dozens of cooks and *garçons* in the mob – go in by himself with a large kitchen poker, and utterly destroy a kiosk in five minutes. 'Vive *La Lanterne*!' 'Let us have a barricade!' At it they went again. 'Vive *Le Rappel*!' 'Let us seize that omnibus!' but they could not stop it. 'That cab!' but the driver turned and fled quicker than cab has been driven within the memory of Frenchman. A house under repair was ransacked, and then the first barricade erected in Paris for years sprang up as if by magic in the Boulevard, just in a line with the Variétés. It was the very first one I had ever seen, and I confess that it did not strike me as a serious obstacle – any ordinary trooper would have taken it in his stride; but it was the beginning of an end which never can be allowed here. The destruction of poor people's property – of lamps belonging to the parish – of the living of that class which these destructives say they are benefiting, the kiosks, the fall of each of which ruined some poor old woman or crippled man – all, of course, for Liberty – then went on with a vicious rapidity which would disgrace the worst class of society in the worst city of Europe.

The authorities reappeared – behaving rationally, in White-hurst's view:

. . . it would be impossible for any troops or any police to have acted more firmly, more mildly, or with better temper. Again the scene changes, and the performance would be almost laughable if it were not so grave for many. The Guard and the police had closed every street leading out of the disturbed district, and shut up the whole of the rioters in the space between the Café Riche and the Restaurant Vachette. They were caught as fast as a polecat in a trap. Then came a simple manoeuvre. The police advanced up every street, driving the people before them, and at the end of the street there was a semicircle of police surrounded by an outer cordon of troops. Literally, they took them all. Once I thought there would have been a struggle opposite the office of the 'Rappel,' but the clatter of a few cavalry put an end even to that; and then it was all take and no give. For more than two hours the police continued to make captures. The soldiers held the position, and a body of police was sent out as skirmishers; and I really do not believe that they missed a man, except my iconoclastic cook – who, perhaps having other fish to fry, got off at the first beat of drum. I estimate the prisoners at from two to three thousand, and I certainly do not exaggerate. The order was, 'Arrest all!' and the order was fulfilled. When all the prisoners were taken away we were allowed to depart. The Boulevard was indeed a strange sight; besides ourselves there was not a soul to be seen, save one poor waiter from a *café*, who was immediately arrested by an outlying policeman. But in the Boulevard which we had deemed some ten hours before so calm and tranquil, we walked through a mass of domestic ruin.

Despite Whitehurst's dim view of the crowd's honour, this sort of behaviour could not be regarded as mere vandalism. It was undoubtedly a phenomenon of real political significance, perhaps even the harbinger of revolution: that night in Montmartre the retaliatory response was neither brutal nor craven, but it only staunched the wound.

In search of a longer-term solution Louis Napoleon turned to a politician who stands as one of the great might-have-beens of French history. Born in 1825, Émile Ollivier was a man of fervent moral and sentimental ideals, coloured by a sub-Wagnerian mysticism which babbled about the fusion of all classes, the regeneration of mankind and a universal brotherhood.* He began in politics as a Republican *Préfet* in Marseilles, but after the failure of the 1848 revolution (in which his father was imprisoned by Louis Napoleon), he withdrew to reassess his position, making his living as a barrister. Abandoning the red-hotness of his youth in breast-beating fashion, he arrived at the view that France had suffered from the influence of extremists and dogmatists and that something based on the English system of checks and balances of power was the remedy. His old friends on the left were antagonized therefore when he returned to politics and began, from the Republican bench, to parley with the more liberal elements of the Emperor's party. He had decided to trust Louis Napoleon's professions and to see where they could be taken. 'I do not confine myself to criticizing what we still lack,' he said, 'I give thanks for what is given to us.'

This tone of voice – variously described as snooty, schoolmasterly, smug, pi, and arrogant – was characteristic of Ollivier, a brilliantly fluent public speaker. It also irritated those who might have been his allies in the cause of moderation into

---

* In 1857 he married Blandine, the illegitimate daughter of Liszt and Madame d'Agoult, after knowing her only weeks. The wedding took place at midnight in the Duomo in Florence. 'I am marrying her not because her father is a solicitor, nor because her mother has influence with such and such a judge, nor because this or that social consideration urges,' he wrote, 'but uniquely for this mad reason that after having spent twelve days with her I saw that I loved her, that after having spent thirty with her I was convinced I adored her, and that after a month and a half I know that I can no longer live without her.' Blandine was indeed a great charmer: her salon included Berlioz, Wagner and many other avant-garde artists. She died in childbirth, in 1862.

thinking him a conceited opportunist, hiding personal ambition behind a cloak of unbesmirched virtue. But however insufferable he may have been, Ollivier was sincere.

In 1865 he received his first summons to an audience at the Tuileries. The Empress, in her odd, unpredictable way, decided that she liked him, and having blasted his ear with her views on the necessity for censorship, asked him to join a committee she led which was examining the treatment of juvenile delinquents. Ollivier was flattered by the attentions of royalty, and went on to deliver Louis Napoleon one of his perorations. 'Your government is strong enough to dare a great deal,' it concluded. The Emperor nodded impenetrably.

'He appears to be cold,' Ollivier wrote in his diary,

> but I think from timidity rather than from stiffness. One feels that he has a delicate, sensitive, feminine nature. I do not think he can be carried by assault; he must be acted on by slow and patient insinuation . . . He appeared to be weary intellectually: one feels that one would bore him quickly; at any rate the blasé can be seen under his pleasant manner . . . I do not know about what it was that he said: it is necessary to advance little by little. These words seem to me to sum up his true state of mind.

Ollivier was repeatedly called back to the Tuileries. The Empress became impatient with his talk of equality and fraternity, but the Emperor was impressed, and within a year or so Ollivier had become in effect his personal consultant on the question of liberal reform. From the Left, the accusations of double-dealing, shilly-shallying and downright treacherous collaboration multiplied. Ollivier lay low, biding his time and reading the stoical meditations of Marcus Aurelius. In the Corps Législatif, the middle ground was still thinly populated: it had to be colonized and developed.

But after the May elections had ignited an explosive summer of rioting, strikes and the Troppmann murders, even the procrastinating Louis Napoleon could delay no longer. Between the twenty-five pure Republican and the eighty diehard Bonapartist representatives in the new Corps Législatif were 187 moderate on at least some issues. It made a base on which

Ollivier believed he could realistically build. So, having sent Eugénie out of harm's way to preside over the opening of the Suez Canal, the Emperor asked him to lead a new government under a new constitutional arrangement to be known as the 'Liberal Empire'. The offer was accepted on 2 January 1870, but there were strings attached.

Ollivier would not be called Prime Minister, but Minister of Justice – because, the Emperor explained, the appointment of a Prime Minister would imply that the Corps Législatif had full power over the choice of ministers. This could not be countenanced: under the Liberal Empire, the Emperor could still appoint or dismiss ministers, call a plebiscite, and remained at least nominally the head of executive government, with various ultimate prerogatives. Window-dressing, sneered the sceptics – when would France be granted her liberty? But others were optimistic, and in London a *Punch* cartoon depicted the Emperor as Bad King John, forced at last to sign Magna Carta and acknowledge a limit to his tyranny.

Ollivier won some points too, notably the exclusion of Eugénie from all ministerial and council meetings, and his cabinet certainly represented a broader spectrum of opinion than anything that had preceded it. Through the early months of 1870 a vigorous programme of reforms was inaugurated hopefully. Powers of arrest and detention were reduced; stamp duty on newspapers was repealed and censorship of their contents eased; more initiatives were allowed to local government. Ironically, given the haste of the whole operation, this proved a case of too much too soon: the legislation was rushed through, badly drafted. Patched up, it came unstuck in the courts and much of it never became law. The new order's smile may have been warm, but it remained ineffectual.

Nor was the opposition assuaged. Only days after the Liberal Empire had thrown open its doors, a scandal threatened to shatter the fragile peace in Paris. A maverick cousin of Louis Napoleon's, Prince Pierre Bonaparte, notorious for his violent disposition and long unwelcome at court, published an article defaming a republican journalist. Via two colleagues acting as his seconds, the latter sent Prince Pierre a challenge to a duel.

Prince Pierre responded belligerently, hurling further crazy abuse of Henri Rochefort and his lackeys. In the ensuing scuffle, he shot dead one of the seconds, a man named Victor Noir.

This nonentity instantly became a popular hero and a martyr, his murder the symbol of the evil wreaked by Bonapartism. Twenty thousand people climbed five floors to pay their last respects to his body, and along the path taken by his funeral cortège, an estimated 100,000 lined the streets, ready perhaps for a call to revenge. Miraculously, it did not sound. As in the Montmartre riots, the timely appearance of a regiment of cavalry saved the day, allowing Victor Noir to be buried without bloodshed. The police made some arrests, but the subsequent trial was considered a farce that proved only how little the new regime was to be trusted. Having claimed that he acted in self-defence, Prince Pierre was acquitted of murder, ordered to pay compensation, and quietly hustled away to Belgium. Rochefort thundered: 'We weep for our dear friend Victor Noir, murdered by the bandit Pierre Napoleon Bonaparte. For eighteen years France has been in the bloody hands of these cutthroats, who, not content with shooting down Republicans in the streets, lay traps for them and murder them indoors. People of France! Have you not had enough?'

By the spring of 1870, the Liberal Empire was badly in need of a fillip. Louis Napoleon must have taken a deep breath before ordering a plebiscite, but he carefully phrased the proposition – that the people 'should approve the liberal reforms introduced into the constitution since 1869 by the Emperor with the agreement of the state institutions, and that they ratify the decree of the senate [relating to the new structure of government] of 20 April 1870'.

It was difficult for republicans and socialists honestly to vote against this, since the present was so indisputably an improvement on the past. None the less, Louis Napoleon took no chances, and special measures were enforced to minimize any antagonism. When, for example, it was officially announced that a plot to assassinate the Emperor had been intercepted, a newspaper which cynically suggested that this 'plot' looked very much like a fabrication of the police, designed to whip up support for the government, was swiftly prosecuted and silenced. Someone else was locked up for calling Ollivier 'a weathercock, Judas, apostate, turncoat' and another catcaller suffered likewise for writing that the Emperor was 'a rotting old man, worn out by debauchery, ruled by a Spanish wife and led by a Republican deserter'.

In the event, the results proved highly satisfactory to the Empire. Over seven million voted approval; only a million and a half demurred. The figures were celebrated in a brilliant ball at the Tuileries. In London Karl Marx guessed that Louis Napoleon would take such an endorsement as a sign that it was safe to stage another *coup d'état* and restore the original level of authoritarian control. But as so often happens in history, something else was creeping unnoticed up a side passage.

The rest of Europe regarded the France of the Second Empire with scepticism. In diplomatic terms, she was without doubt the least loved of nations, although her power and wealth meant that she did not lack flatterers and fair-weather friends. But Louis Napoleon was never able to cement any enduring alliances. Nobody trusted him – partly because of the duplicity behind his seizure of imperial powers in 1851, and partly because the French were regarded as territorially aggressive (particularly in relation to Italy). 'France must needs disturb every quarter of the globe and try to make mischief and set everyone by the ears,' wrote a vexed Queen Victoria in her diary. It was a common view, and a not unjustifiable one.

In the constant seesawing of the balance of power, which was meant to keep Europe at peace with itself, France's weight proved unsettling. The Russians deplored her support of the Polish revolt against their rule. Victor Emmanuel could not tolerate her troops protecting Rome and the Papacy from incorporation into the new Italy. The British balked when she bought a railway in an area of their special concern, Belgium. As a longer-term visionary strategy, Louis Napoleon was known to nurse vague schemes to lead a redrawing of the map of Europe – banishing the Russians from Poland and the Austrians from northern Italy, partitioning Turkey and establishing a buffer state on the left bank of the Rhine – but it was not clear how far he would go to achieve those ends.

More alarmingly real and immediate were the implications of Prussia's decisive victory over Austria in a brief war in 1866, fought over Prussia's occupation of the northern duchy of Holstein (a much-disputed region administered by the Austrians) and culminating in the Battle of Sadowa. France was caught short, outplayed in unscrupulousness. In the expectation of some sort of share of the territorial pickings, Louis Napoleon had indicated to the Prussian Chancellor Bismarck that he would remain neutral in any such conflict. But after Sadowa, Bismarck did not need to court anyone's favour. Prussia now dominated Austria and consolidated a formidably overweening power bloc across the centre of Europe. France's suggestion that Luxembourg might be ceded as a way of re-balancing the seesaw was rejected out of hand: it had got away with its interfering presumption long enough and it was time for others to take the advantage.

There was little Louis Napoleon could do about this, except to turn his diplomatic charms on to enfeebled Austria – which, being Catholic and conservative in its regime, was much favoured by Eugénie. He also attempted to institute a thorough reform of France's army: new armaments, new strategies, new soldiers were all required if France was to feel confidently defended against the clockwork efficiency of the Prussian military machine. This would have been an expensive and unpopular operation, opposed by various powerful sectors of government and public opinion which the Empire could not afford to alienate, and Louis Napoleon no longer commanded the political clout or energy to enforce his proposals. In retrospect, however, his assessment of France's military potential *vis-à-vis* Prussia's would look acute.

The French army was poorly trained, administered and supplied. Over the previous thirty years, it had spent most of its fighting time in North Africa, engaged in swaggering skirmishes with the Algerians, and it had virtually no experience of large-scale formal battle on European terrain. Nor was it big enough – only 300,000 against Prussia's million. Louis

Napoleon wanted to stiffen the farcically slack system of conscription and introduce large increases in the forces of part-time reservists, but the Corps Législatif smelt the whiff of militarism and voted through only a third of the necessary budget – not enough to make a substantial difference. 'Do you want to turn France into a barracks?' the Republican deputy Jules Favre asked the Minister of War, Marshal Niel. 'Beware that you don't turn it into a cemetery,' Niel replied.

In terms of the arms race, the French had the edge in one respect. Prussian superiority at Sadowa was marked by its use of the needle-gun, a novel breech-loading rifle accurate over a range of about six hundred yards, but the French version of the same model, the *chassepot*, was even more effective, with a longer range and a sword-bayonet attachment. Another potent weapon, the *mitrailleuse*, was being developed in secret, person-ally financed by Louis Napoleon. It was a prototype of the machine-gun, a bundle of twenty-five barrels, turned by a handle, with a range of two thousand yards and the capacity to fire a hundred and fifty rounds a minute. Had the troops been properly instructed in methods of using it, this could have proved a war-winning weapon. The Prussians invested more in heavy artillery: their steel breech-loading cannon (manufactured by the Krupp family) was a far speedier affair than the French bronze muzzle-loading equivalent.

What mattered far more, however, was Prussian morale. Under Field Marshal von Moltke, the army was rigorously disciplined and organized; forward planning, for all contin-gencies, was meticulous; there were lists and maps, there were bullets, belts, buttons and bandages. The French, on the other hand, ran their army on a combination of smug indolence and gung-ho improvisation. Despite its brilliant parade and reputa-tion for derring-do, people liked to say that its fundamental attitude was summed up in the shrugging phrase 'on se débrouillera toujours', 'we'll always sort it out somehow'.

Among the middle classes and in the press, there was a half-awareness of the situation, running dinner-table chatter about France's sinking prowess, chaos in the army, a lack of leadership and Prussia's burgeoning ambitions. In 1867, one General

Trochu published an angry but reasoned polemic, *L'Armée Française*, which contained frankly critical analysis of the force's shortcomings and what might be done to remedy them. The pamphlet was widely read – over three weeks it went into sixteen editions – hotly debated and then forgotten. Those such as the distinguished political columnist Lucien Prévost-Paradol, author of an influential book called *La France Nouvelle* (and later ambassador to the USA), who firmly and consistently believed that France and Prussia were 'like two trains hurtling towards each other down the same track', seemed fanatics, overrating the crisis. *On se débrouillera toujours*.

The government's private fears were focused on the likelihood of Prussia expanding its power southwards towards Austria and creating a German Empire, but in the event the flashpoint was struck over a completely separate issue – the throne of Spain. Although it had been vacant since a minor revolution in 1868 had led to the banishing of the Bourbon Queen Isabel, the country's Prime Minister, Juan Prim, remained determined that Spain should have a constitutionally appointed monarch. Throughout 1869 he had been approaching members of Europe's most important Catholic dynasties without success: no more interested than anyone else in a seat which promised little pleasure or profit was Prince Leopold of Hohenzollern, a scion of the Catholic branch of the Prussian royal family. On the diplomatic circuit, it was made clear that in any case France would have found his appointment unacceptable, inasmuch as it would have empowered Prussia at her most important southern border. No, no, said Bismarck, of course – out of the question.

There it stood, until a desperate Prim made a second secret approach early in 1870, this time via King Wilhelm of Prussia, head of the Hohenzollern family. Bismarck now began to machinate. His desire to unite all the German states under one flag might well be thwarted if Prim went on to offer the throne to a southern German Catholic prince with loyalties to other Catholic states which might band together to form a new bloc of alliances. If, on the other hand, Leopold did accept the throne, Prussia's honour and prestige would be publicly vindicated at

France's expense. How would she react to the snub and consequent humiliation? In the interests of his master-plan, Bismarck was ready to test the waters – and, if the temperature seemed right, to stir them up. Or, as he more grandiosely expressed it: 'A statesman must wait to listen until he hears the steps of God sounding through events.'

He pressed King Wilhelm and other Hohenzollerns to appeal to Leopold's sense of patriotism and played on the suscepti- bilities of his wife, a Portuguese infanta with ambitions. He also doled out bribes to crucial members of the Spanish parliament, obliged to put any candidacy to the vote. Leopold's resistance was finally worn down and in June 1870 Bismarck telegraphed Prim in Madrid to the effect that Leopold's name could be put forward. From that moment, having lit the blue touch-paper, he stood back and waited to see what sort of explosion would occur, claiming all the while that he had had absolutely nothing to do with it.

The French ambassador was informed on 3 July, and the news caused Paris a thrill of consternation – ironically only four days after Émile Ollivier had blithely announced that 'at no period has the maintenance of peace seemed better assured'. As Bismarck must have anticipated, a crazy chauvinistic fury at Prussia's brazen cheek swept the capital. Newspaper leader columns reminded France of what it had endured when the Habsburgs had similarly held the pincers over France in the sixteenth century. Eugénie, Prince Richard Metternich remarked drily in a letter, looked 'ten years younger' at the excitement, the fact that it was her native land at stake fanning her passions still further. 'She talked about Prussia the whole time,' reported Prévost-Paradol after an audience he had been granted a few weeks previously. 'Very worried about its progress, seeing only a huge disaster at the end of it etc. Very impassioned, obviously wanting war, talking about Prussian insolence and declaring: "It must cease . . . France's rank in the world is endangered. She must defend it or perish." ' In the Corps Législatif, Émile Ollivier knew that he had to be seen to be taking a strong line. His personal instincts may have been pacific, but the cause of war was already alarmingly popular, and at this stage of the game he wanted to make the Liberal Empire look resolute rather than lily-livered.

What Louis Napoleon was thinking remains unfathomable. Perhaps he believed that he could use the incident as a pretext for calling Bismarck's bluff and unmasking him as a shameless schemer and rule-breaker, an aggressive menace to the balance of power. Perhaps he believed that he could enlist Austria's support (and at least the neutrality of Britain and Russia) and fight and win a war which would have driven the Prussians out of southern Germany and away from the left bank of the Rhine. Perhaps he believed that a successful war would consolidate the new political order of the Liberal Empire and add some much-needed lustre to his own tarnished image. If any of this was so, he miscalculated badly. For he himself was too weary and decrepit to lead a war, and the French army was too bleary and decrepit to win one.

Then Prince Leopold suddenly withdrew his candidacy. Pressures from other parties – the Rothschilds, Queen Victoria and Gladstone, King Leopold of the Belgians – had been brought to bear, and the Hohenzollerns were scared off. Throughout Europe there was widespread relief: 'matters, if not yet absolutely settled, are now in the way of a satisfactory arrangement,' announced *The Times* of 14 July, and it looked as if the skirmishing of the affair would remain confined to the notional realms of diplomacy – a nasty business but not a fatal one.

But France required an outcome more positively gratifying to her *amour propre*. Her Minister for Foreign Affairs, the Duc de Gramont, was the toughest man in the cabinet – Bismarck also called him 'the stupidest man in Europe' – and he insisted that the firmest possible line should be taken. Prussia had tried to trump France; therefore France would positively trounce Prussia. The French ambassador, Count Benedetti, was instructed to ask for an audience with King Wilhelm, who was taking the waters at the spa of Ems. Benedetti had already been told to exact a countermanding of Prince Leopold's candidacy from the King; now he had to confront King Wilhelm and insist he issue a statement guaranteeing that the candidacy would never be renewed again. On 13 July, before the agreed time of audience, Benedetti accosted King Wilhelm on his morning perambulation. The King politely mentioned his satisfaction at Leopold's withdrawal but refused to consider issuing such a statement. Benedetti was later informed that the King had nothing further to say to him, and had therefore cancelled the audience. Later that day a telegram was sent to Berlin, relating the morning's events.

Reading it, Bismarck saw his chance to flourish what he called 'the red rag to the Gallic bull'. Editing the telegram so as to make its account of the Ems encounter sound like a dramatic ultimatum in which King Wilhelm had curtly snubbed Benedetti, he released the text to the press and the world. He was still playing brinkmanship, even though the stakes were now soaring beyond the rules of the diplomatic game.

France read 'the Ems telegram' on Bastille Day, and its impact was decisive. 'You see before you a man whose face has been slapped,' shouted Gramont. There was now no restraining the bellicose faction led by him and Eugénie, and if the political credibility of the Liberal Empire was to be maintained in the face of an electorate which bayingly concurred, there could be no shirking the challenge. In the Corps Législatif, only an elder statesman, Adolphe Thiers, hollered his opposition to the prospect of shedding torrents of blood over a question as academic as the Hohenzollern Candidature. But the war and the money to pay for it were easily voted through, the army was said to be champing at the bit ('if the war should last a year,' said Field Marshal Leboeuf rashly, 'we would not have to buy in so much as a gaiter-button'), Gramont lyingly hinted that support from Austria would be forthcoming and Émile Ollivier announced to the Corps Législatif that he would take responsibility for war 'with a light heart' – a phrase which would soon be his ruin. At the Opéra, the celebrated prima donna Marie Sass, brandishing the *tricolore*, sang the *Marseillaise*, and an audience led from her box by the duchesse de Mouchy rose to join in the chorus. It all looked stagily unreal. 'One felt oneself a supernumerary hired to fill the scene,' recalled Henry Adams in his memoir *The Education of Henry Adams*. 'Patriotism seemed to have been brought out of the government's stores, and distributed by grammes *per capita*.' On the streets, the mood was that of a chortling gung-ho bravado. Friends made only half-joking arrangements 'to meet in Berlin next month, for our victory parade'. 'Don't believe that people here regret this deplorable conflict,' wrote Gautier to the ballerina Carlotta Grisi. 'On the contrary, they are enchanted and I have never seen such a bubbling-over of happiness; all the medical students are enlisting as male nurses, and soon there will be no one at home but the sick and lame, and even they insist at the boards of appeal that they are fit to campaign. If anyone spoke in favour of peace he would be killed on the spot.'

'At last we are going to know the delights of massacre,' wrote a respectable columnist in *Paris Journal*, a respectable newspaper. 'Let the blood of the Prussians flow in torrents, in waterfalls, with the divine fury of the flood! Let the wretch who merely dares to utter the word "peace" be immediately shot like a dog and flung into the sewer!'

On 17 July the fashionable American couple Charles and Lillie Moulton arrived at the palace of Saint-Cloud, the Emperor's residence just outside Paris, to fulfil a long-standing dinner invitation. They had been on holiday at their country retreat and had not heard the news or received the note of cancellation. A horrified chamberlain received them at the door, but before the explanations and excuses were over, the Empress sent a note to say that having come so far, the Moultons had better stay. Protocol did not permit them to decline, and they were forced to endure an evening of silent social hell.

> You may imagine that I wished myself a hundred miles away. The Emperor never uttered a word; the Empress sat with her eyes fixed on the Emperor, and did not speak to a single person. No one spoke. The Emperor would receive telegram upon telegram; the gentleman sitting next to him opened the telegrams and put them before his Majesty. Every now and again the Emperor would look across the table to the Empress with such a distressed look it made me think that something terrible was happening, which was true . . . I was glad when the signal for leaving the table was given and we re-entered the drawing-room.

The Emperor was immediately surrounded by his gentlemen. The Empress moved a little way off, but without taking her eyes from her husband. The Prince Imperial stood by his father, watching him. Then the Empress advanced toward his Majesty and took his arm to leave the room. Just as she neared the door she looked at me, turned back, and coming up to where I was standing held out her hand and said, 'Bonsoir.' The Emperor stood a moment irresolutely, then, bowing his head, left the room with the Empress on his arm, the Prince following. . . .

I never in my life felt what it was to be *de trop* . . .

Next morning France made a formal declaration of war. The astonishing news was that Louis Napoleon would personally take supreme command of the campaign. It was not only the dismal state of the Emperor's health and morale that made this such an inexplicable decision; even more of a liability was his total military ineptitude – incapable of so much as reading a map, let alone plotting a strategy, he was also intensely squeamish and thin-skinned. It was a task for which he must have known he was hopelessly ill-suited, and once again, one can only wonder what his motivation for undertaking it might have been. Did he feel that he had to fulfil some expansionist Napoleonic destiny? Or was he driven by a depressive's suicidal fatalism?

To the rest of the world, it was certainly a war which looked appallingly unnecessary. France had provoked it, out of sheer pique, sheer preening vanity, and earnest, chorale-chanting Prussia would probably end up the pitiable victim – so went the general view. 'The greatest national crime that we have had the pain of recording in these columns since the days of the First French Empire has been consummated,' thundered *The Times*. 'It is still difficult to conceive what infatuation can have committed the Emperor Napoleon to a course which is as impolitic as it is criminal.' 'The Liberal Empire goes to war on a mere point of etiquette' was the view of the *Illustrated London News*, although the *Punch* cartoon preferred to depict it as a matter of 'six of one and half a dozen of the other'.

From Berlin, Queen Victoria's beloved daughter Vicky, married to Crown Prince Frederick of Prussia, wrote anxiously to her mother: 'The odds are fearfully against us in the awful struggle which is about to commence . . . our feelings are best expressed in Lord Nelson's words, saying *Germany* (instead of England) expects every man to do his duty.' Other Germans felt a similar rush of pious morality. Richard Wagner's future wife Cosima recorded in her diary how she told 'R. that the war is Beethoven's jubilee, the declaration of war was made on July 17, 1870, on December 17, 1770, B. was born. I only hope to God that there is a lucky seven in all this! R. says he is beginning to feel hopeful: war is something noble, it shows the unimportance of the individual . . .'

But in Paris, there was no such reflectiveness, as the pitch of giddy, partying excitement intensified. 'The war may be said to be popular,' reported the correspondent of the *Illustrated London News*.

The Senate went on Sunday to Saint Cloud to offer its congratulations to the Emperor at the decision that had been arrived at, and to express its devotion to his person and dynasty. Every evening the circulation of carriages is impeded by a procession of vehicles decorated with coloured Chinese lanterns, and conveying men bearing flags and sounding those immense *cors de chasse* [hunting horns] with which French sportsmen are in the habit of intwining their bodies, after the fashion of the serpent that clasps the Laocoon. Walking at the sides and following in the rear are crowds of men in blouses singing 'The Marseillaise,' or the equally popular 'Mourir pour la Patrie,' while the stream of loungers on the foot pavement of the Boulevards are every now and then swept aside by parties of young men with arms linked together or waving their sticks over their heads and shouting 'Marchons! Marchons!' at the top of their voices. The Parisians are, however, already tired of these senseless manifestations, and have come to regard them with complete indifference. It is not so with respect to the passage of the military through the streets en-route to the Strasbourg Railway station. They are invariably saluted with cheers, to which they respond with cries of 'Vive la France!' and 'à Berlin!' The cafés swarm with officers, many of whom will crush their carefully brushed black hats with their hands and still wear them to show that their occasion for them will not be for long. A morning or two since a large party of sailors leaving the Ministry of Marine promenaded the Rue St Honoré, preceeded by a flag and carrying brooms in their hands, singing to the tune 'Des Lampions,' 'Des balais pour Bismarck!' ['make a clean sweep of Bismarck']. It is in this frivolous spirit that the nation which pretends to consider itself the most civilised in the world enters upon a war the terrible issue of which few dare trust themselves to contemplate.

7 : *Too Little, Too Late*

The Empress bade her husband farewell on 28 July when he quietly boarded a train for the front at a branch-line station near the palace of Saint-Cloud. There was no grand parade before his departure: pallid, hunched, dropsically swollen and agonized by his kidney stones, Louis Napoleon was too enfeebled to make a swaggering public appearance, and the only visibly moved member of the party was the Prince Impérial, electrified at the prospect of accompanying his father to the war, and uniformed as a second lieutenant. Never bookish, this unreflective fifteen-year-old was embarking on his great adventure wide-eyed. The Empress made the sign of the cross on his forehead and told him to do his duty.

For the duration of the Emperor's absence, she had been appointed Regent. Ollivier and his cabinet were determined that her influence should be strictly curtailed and regarded the title as bearing no significance beyond that of constitutional necessity: ministerial decisions were taken without consulting her and she was kept barely informed of developments. Yet she was not a woman to be content at such a crucial juncture to function as a mere figurehead, and she therefore turned – fruitlessly – to the negotiation of foreign alliances. From Russia, nothing could be hoped; Britain was too concerned over the buffer state of Belgium to take anything but a neutral stance; the United States was still smarting from French interference with Mexico; while the new Italy would not co-operate while French troops continued to occupy Rome and 'protect' the Pope's independence. So Eugénie concentrated her efforts on the Danes (who could invade from the north, retaking Holstein) and the Austrians (from the south). Both would have had much to gain from a Prussian defeat, but neither would commit themselves until they saw irrefutable evidence that the French were well on the way to the overwhelming victory they so breezily anticipated: Eugénie's frank confession of her deepest worries to her friend the Austrian ambassador Prince Richard Metternich was a disastrous moment of weakness – to her face, he sympathized; to Vienna, he must have reported, at least implicitly, a gloomy prognosis.

For missives from the front were making it increasingly clear that French military prowess was not what it had been cracked up to be. As the Prussians mobilized according to a campaign plan formulated in 1869, moving half a million well-fed and ordered troops towards French Lorraine, their enemy literally did not know whether they were coming or going. Reservists were kicking their heels and reeling drunk in empty depots, awaiting basic equipment and instructions: in Douai, a third of a fine store of horse collars proved too narrow for any animal's neck; in Châlons, there was only one veterinary surgeon per twenty cavalry batteries. Railway lines were blocked by supply trucks unable to reach their destination, leaving whole regiments stranded and hungry: at Metz, France's chief war depot, there was neither sugar, salt, coffee nor rice. There were shortages of tents, cooking utensils, and maps of the frontier regions (later requisitioned from local schools); lack of food, or of cash to pay for it, led to pillage and sickness. Perhaps the worst of this vast management problem was the indiscipline and insubordination which crept virus-like through both seasoned and novice soldiers, unchecked by firm leadership.

The French notion – it could hardly be called a strategy – was to launch an offensive from Metz through the lower regions of Prussia, cutting it off from the southern German states, which were obliged by treaty to come to its aid. In a great empty show of resolution and aggression, the French risked a foray into Prussian territory and made a grab at the border town of Saarbrücken. It was a pointless gesture which led to a footling victory, but it had enormous value in terms of public relations.

Paris duly went wild with excitement when the news came through, and much was made of the story of how the Emperor and the Prince Impérial had taken part in the engagement, with the Prince pocketing as a souvenir one of the bullets which had landed close to his feet. The dispatch reported that 'he was no more moved' by the incident 'than he would be on a walk in the Bois de Boulogne' – a sang-froid which soon had the more sceptical Parisians snorting incredulously (a song went round: 'Et le petit prince ramassait les balles,/Qu'on avait mis là tout exprès', 'So the little prince picked up the bullets/Which someone had carefully laid down in front of him').

But everyone wanted to hear the good news: henceforth it would be in short supply. What followed Saarbrücken was a series of defeats – at Wissembourg, at Spicheren, and crucially at Fröschwiller, where a skirmish spiralled into a full-scale battle in which the French lost 11,000 men and laid Alsace open to the Prussian advance. France was blundering its chances away, and losing its confidence in the process.

Paris could not be fooled much longer. The public continued to whip itself into frenzies of patriotic fervour, fuelled by inexhaustible rounds of the National Anthem,* but there came a

* Two of the more histrionic renditions were amusingly reported to the readers of *Fraser's Magazine* in London: 'At the Gaieté the curtain rose upon a motley crowd of people, all dressed in the street costumes of '92. There were bourgeoisie, peasants, market-women, washerwomen with sleeves rolled up, men in bits of faded uniform brandishing ancient swords, the dresses exhibiting a preponderance of the red colour. In the centre of the stage stood the noted ballad-singer Theresa. She seemed to me to be the beau idéal of a street heroine of the revolutionary epoch. She was costumed in red skirt, with blue body, and white sash; her sleeves were rolled up, as if she had just come from the washtub; her dress was open with most artful negligence; and thus she sang the *Marseillaise*. Her powers of facial action are singular – her dark eye nearly closes, then expands with a spark; her strongly marked mouth crumples up, so to say, with scorn, her large frame trembles with fury, and her untrained voice seemed to break and falter from real emotion as she apostrophised Liberty . . .

At the Grand Opéra the *Muette de Portici* [by Auber] had attracted a large audience . . . Four acts of the opera only were given. More than the time that would have been occupied by the fifth was taken up with the patriotic singing of Madame Sass and M. Faure. Madame S. came out costumed as the Goddess of Liberty, and sang with a vehemence which culminated in hoarseness. It seemed to me ineffective as compared with that of Theresa, though the latter has no artistic culture whatever. Nevertheless, Madame Sass's *Marseillaise* was warmly encored, and after it Faure sang Musset's "Rhin allemand." This

point when the bad news had to be confronted. Ludovic
Halévy's diary records:

Saturday 6 August . . . at one o'clock Meilhac [his colleague] arrives –
drunk with excitement. 'A great victory,' he says, 'General
MacMahon has shattered the Prussians and taken twenty-five
thousand prisoners, among them the Crown Prince: it's Jena all over
again. Paris is ablaze . . . Come and see for yourself: it's amazing.'
He drags me out. The streets are full, their faces beaming.
Everywhere people are running around shouting: 'Thirty, forty,
sixty thousand prisoners' – the numbers rose in waves. We reach the
boulevard. Windows are bedecked, a huge crowd. . . . We enter the
Librairie Nouvelle [a bookshop]. A gentleman within says: 'I don't
know where this news is coming from. It's not pinned to the official
board outside the Stock Exchange. Nobody seems to know who
actually read it or where it came from.' I say at once: 'It's all a lie,
some Stock Exchange rumour'. 'Oh come on,' says Meilhac, 'that's
impossible. Let's go to the Stock Exchange.' We walk down the
boulevard. In the rue Vivienne, ten thousand people jam-packed:
Madame Sass [the prima donna], standing up in an open carriage

piece was hawked about the theatre beforehand. On it is a design of the German
Rhine, as an aged, long-bearded, gigantic figure, chained to a rock amid
rushing water.

After Faure had sung the piece of Musset, the crowd demanded that the
hymn of Rouget de l'Isle should follow. But the singer came out, bowed, and
returned without singing it. The audience thereon becomes furious, insane, and
clamours wildly for the *Marseillaise*. It could not comprehend this hesitation,
and some asked if Faure was a German; but it was speedily cleared up. A
regiment of the National Guard had halted for a little not far from the Opera
House. The cunning manager had slipped out and obtained the consent of the
commanding officer that some hundreds of the regiment, with their weapons,
should appear on the stage as part of the chorus while the *Marseillaise* was
sung. When the reluctant curtain at last did rise, and disclosed M. Faure with
the tricolour in his hand, surrounded by an enormous chorus, including
genuine soldiers on their way to the field of battle, with chassepôts and sabres,
the excitement of the audience was indescribable. They were as people who had
taken laughing gas; they shouted and cheered, they stamped, they beat the
backs of the seats with their hats; finally the audience lost its voice, its yells sank
to ineffectual screeches, and M. Faure took advantage of the moment to begin
the song. The artist made a good-looking soldier in the uniform of the Garde
Mobile, and his singing of the *Marseillaise* was extremely fine. He threw his
whole resource of dramatic power, of grandeur and pathos into it. When he
knelt at the words—

> Grand Dieu! par des mains enchaînées
> Nos fronts sous le joug se ploieraient!

and the vast chorus knelt with him, his voice was deep, fervent, thrilling.'

singing the *Marseillaise*. In another open carriage Madame Gueymard [another prima donna] also singing the *Marseillaise*. The chorus is taken up by all ten thousand voices. Flags wave. Absolute pandemonium. We meet Perrin. He says: 'It's not true.' It's hard to imagine a more unpleasant feeling. So much joy in them, so much grief in us . . . The rumour spread that the news was false. 'Impossible,' cried a large gentleman in front of us. (There is comedy everywhere and in everything.) 'Why impossible?' 'Look at Madame Sass, look at Madame Gueymard, singers at the Opéra. They must be well informed, they are virtually civil servants' [*sic*]. We made our way out of the crowd in despair.

The next morning Edmond de Goncourt surveyed a very different scene. 'A terrifying silence. On the boulevard, not a vehicle . . . not even the shouts of children at play . . . a Paris in which all sound seemed extinct.' The truth was out. 'Without a miracle, we are lost,' wrote Halévy. 'This is the end of the Empire. One may not mind much about that, but supposing this also means the end of France?'

Ollivier's government could certainly not last much longer. Despite the imposition of martial law on 7 August, it failed to hold its slim majority. A new ministry of diehard imperialists was formed by Eugénie on 9 August, and Ollivier slunk off to Italy, where he vainly tried to rally support for the French cause (much of the rest of his long life – he survived until 1913 – was spent licking his wounds and publishing tome upon tome of self-justification). The keynote was now one of decisive defensive action. An obscure general unable to raise his voice because of a bullet lodged in his throat was summoned to lead the new cabinet. But the Comte de Palikao (ennobled after campaigns in China) was a hard, cold-eyed character – 'the man who alone would be equal to the task of suppressing any serious disturbance in Paris', as the correspondent of the *Illustrated London News* chillingly put it.

This was now a vital consideration. It was not so much France as Louis Napoleon's Second Empire which faced defeat against the Prussians, and the war seemed to be developing a second front, with the possibility of a revolution becoming daily more imminent in a city which six weeks earlier had been unbuttoning itself for a pleasantly Liberal summer. The focus of the danger was the Garde Nationale, a civil militia called up in times of crisis since 1789: in Paris, its more specific responsibility was that of defending the capital's fortifications. The government could hardly ensure that it was only registered bourgeois, loyal to the Empire, who were entrusted with arms; yet equally it could not afford to provide the working class with the means to turn nasty on its masters. It was a tricky balance and, if it was not maintained, Paris might need to be defended from its defenders as much as from Prussian regiments.

The city rumbled with unfamiliar desperate energies. Precious works of art were boxed up and sent to distant cellars; Garnier's still-incomplete Opéra became a military store. Mass graves were dug in Montmartre. Trees in the parks were cut down, and the Bois de Boulogne became a massive grazing area for 150,000 sheep and 24,600 oxen, turning the elegant arti-ficiality of its *Haussmannisé* landscape into what Ernest Vizetelly described as 'hillocks of wool terminating in horizons of horn'. Efforts were made to dam the Seine and fill the ten-foot-wide moat which surrounded the city. Bridges were destroyed, tunnels blocked. On a broader national scale, a second centre of government was established in the western city of Tours, and all able-bodied unmarried males between the ages of eighteen and twenty-four were drafted into the reservist Garde Mobile.

'What's going on?' a little chorus girl from the Variétés asked Halévy's colleague Meilhac. 'Why does everyone seem to be moving house?'

'It's not a bad idea,' he replied, 'with all this awful news.'

'What? What news?'

'Well, that the Prussians have entered Alsace and Lorraine . . .'

'And that's bad is it?'

'I don't know whether it's bad, but it's certainly an invasion.'

'Oh, the *invasion* – oh yes, somebody was rattling on about that last night after dinner at the Café Anglais. Please could you explain to me a little of what's happening? I really ought to keep up with things, I don't want to look like an idiot.'

As such mam'zelles unravelled their blissful ignorance, the taut fabric of civil order was ominously beginning to tear. On 14

August, for example, there was a riot in the proletarian suburb of La Villette, when a band of a hundred armed men attacked a fire station. Their motives were dubious, but two combatants and one innocent were killed with several more badly wounded, the police made forty-two arrests and four death sentences were eventually passed on the agitators, suspected of belonging to the insurrectionary sect led by Auguste Blanqui. Nor was the tension confined to Paris: on 16 August, in a bizarrely dreadful outburst, a young nobleman-farmer living in Hautefaye, a remote village in the Dordogne, was mistaken for a secret republican and Prussian spy. He was brutally lynched by a mob of otherwise law-abiding villagers who finally tore his body to pieces and set fire to it.

The Emperor, still in dreadful pain whenever he moved, had by now yielded supreme command of the armed forces to Marshal Bazaine. The Empress had forbidden him to return to Paris for fear that his presence would incite further hostility, and in military terms he was now little more than an encumbrance and an embarrassment. 'Risk nothing by too precipitate action, and above all avoid any further reverses,' was his downbeat advice as he and his party retreated from the base at Metz to army headquarters at Châlons. Bazaine – a mediocrity – was only too inclined to obey such an injunction, and his caution meant that the Prussians were given time to sever his lines of advance and retreat. By 19 August, after several thwarted efforts to follow in the imperial party's path, his army was effectively besieged in Metz.

Louis Napoleon trudged a slow, anguished trail to Châlons, comforted only by the presence of his baffled yet still hopeful son. The journey was a humiliating one: at Verdun, they left the road for the railway, but it took eleven hours to assemble so much as a locomotive, a third-class carriage and a couple of cattle-trucks for the luggage. The townsfolk looked on without sympathy, their co-operation perfunctory. At Châlons they found the remains of MacMahon's army, defeated at Fröschwiller and now drowning its sorrows in drink. Alongside were eighteen battalions of the Garde Mobile reserves, mostly recruited from Paris and boorishly reluctant to discipline themselves in support of what was already believed to be a lost cause. Green and terrified country-lad recruits could not so much as aim a rifle, let alone fire a *mitrailleuse*. This, a month after its vainglorious dash to war, was now France's front-line army.

At Châlons an emergency conference took place, led by Plon-Plon, Napoleon's cantankerous cousin Prince Jérôme. It was decided to send the useless and dangerous Garde Mobile back to Paris immediately, with the Emperor following shortly after, nominally leading the army. To soothe insurrectionary sores in the capital, the tough and popular General Trochu was appointed Governor of Paris. Trochu was a Breton, of independent mind and views – so independent, in fact, that some said he was positively treacherous. His pamphlet *L'Armée Française* had leaked classified information, and his political sympathies were known to stand with the Orléanist faction rather than the Bonapartist. But Trochu was also a great maker of fine speeches, a master of the florid gesture and the hand-on-heart avowal. 'A grave injustice has been done to me by throwing doubt on my loyalty,' he scraped before the Emperor. 'I deserve the trust which Your Majesty is putting in me, and I promise Your Majesty that as Governor of Paris, I will furnish convincing proofs of my devotion to the cause.' Louis Napoleon was too weak and numbed by painkillers to argue otherwise, although he protested feebly that Eugénie should have been consulted before the post was confirmed.

Nor was the Regent at all pleased by Trochu's arrival, claiming powers over which she had no control. Her rapport with Palikao and the new hard-line, right-wing cabinet had been functioning smoothly and effectively, and she had risen magnificently to the role of disinterested patriot, tireless and steadfast. All her efforts were for France, not her own skin and jewels. 'I am not defending the throne, but honour,' she would say, austerely clad in a beige woollen dress and a black shawl. Nevertheless, she was not suicidal. The survival of the dynasty would be for the good of France, and it was not for her to abdicate. She therefore countermanded the Emperor's return to Paris, on the justifiable grounds that his washed-up presence would be politically inflammatory, tantamount to an admission of defeat and impotence. 'Just leave him alone to kill himself,' she is said to have hissed contemptuously at one point.

Back in Châlons, confusion over Bazaine's position changed MacMahon's plans daily. Then, on 22 August, after a break in the lines of communication was restored, a telegram was received from Bazaine announcing that he was about to break out of Metz and head north. Nobody realized that this message had been sent three days previously and that Bazaine was now besieged, so MacMahon's army set out from Châlons hoping to meet him *en route* and join forces.

Abroad, there was now very little hope for France. A head-shaking feeling that the country had brought misery on itself and deserved its drubbing was common throughout the neutral powers. France was a bad nation, Prussia was a good one: there was a certain divine rightness in the way things were going. 'I am very sorry for the sufferings of the French nation, but I think these sufferings are better for the moral welfare of the people than victory would have been,' wrote George Eliot to her friend Barbara Bodichon on 25 August. 'The war has been drawn down on them by an iniquitous Government, but in a great proportion of the French people there has been nourished a wicked glorification of selfish pride, which like all other conceit is a sort of stupidity, excluding any true conception of what lies outside their own vain wishes. The Germans, it seems, were expected to stand like toy-soldiers, for the French to knock them down.'

Not surprisingly, the note of crowing piety was even stronger among Germans. Cosima Wagner's diary of the period jumps up and down with bristling indignation:

R. says he hopes Paris ('this kept woman of the world') will be burned down . . . the burning of Paris would be a symbol of the world's liberation at last from the presence of all that is bad . . . R. would like to write to Bismarck, requesting him to shoot all of Paris down . . . It is curious how what is happening in Paris, which previously interested everybody, has now become a matter of such complete indifference . . . May the grace of God now descend on our magnificent German steadfastness, that the prize may be worthy of these dreadful and splendid struggles.

From Paris, the British ambassador reported to London that the Empress had 'much pluck, but little hope'.

In the Corps Législatif, Palikao did his best to keep up morale with a mixture of evasions and downright lies: 'I have good news,' he would say, 'but I cannot make it known.' In the small hours, trickles of soldiers wounded in the war's first engagements were disgorged covertly from the eastern railway termini.

On the front, the bungling confusions of the campaign multiplied. The Prussians had no idea that MacMahon was marching his army towards Metz. Having discovered from their scouts that Châlons had been evacuated, they assumed that he had fallen back on Paris – which would have been a strategically logical move – and prepared to follow him. But on 25 August, von Moltke conveniently came by a copy of the Parisian newspaper *Le Temps*, which conveniently informed him that MacMahon was now north-east of Reims, *en route* to find Bazaine, who was still assumed to be moving away from Metz. So now the Prussians swung round in an arc towards MacMahon, cutting him off from the possibility of a westward retreat.

MacMahon's troops plodded on through pelting summer rains, mud-spattered, hungry and exhausted. Tempers frayed: one battalion commander broke down and shouted at his officers: 'We are going to the devil with people who have no notion of what large-scale war is, and who are afraid, because they do not feel up to fighting the Prussians, and they know very well that they will all be beaten one after the other, because they are all ignorant and frightened.' The Emperor and his staff were still an encumbrance on their resources and a source of resentment: but on 27 August, Louis Napoleon made a great personal sacrifice and sent his son away to the safety of Belgium. Not a day too soon: for MacMahon now realized that the Prussians were about to corner him and that Bazaine was even more trapped than he was. A surprise engagement near the village of Beaumont turned into a screaming rout and resulted in the loss of seven thousand French, many of them drowned in the River Meuse. In the wake of this shocking fiasco, MacMahon fell back on the small citadel town of Sedan. He was now up against the frontier with Belgium, and had no other options. As one of the commanders, General Ducrot, so concisely put it: 'Nous sommes dans un pot de chambre et nous y serons emmerdés' – 'We're stuck in a chamber pot, and we're bloody well done for.'

In Paris the same sense of inevitability thickened like a pall. 'Last effect of war! The Grand Hotel is "concentrating" its visitors, and reducing the staff. The "lift" ceased to lift last night, and the legs of the four remaining Americans are crying aloud in consequence – that is, if legs can cry. Saw a fat lady in a fix': thus Whitehurst on 31 August. The same day Eugénie wrote to her mother:

> One can't vanish during times of danger and only reappear when things are looking brighter. Our destinies are in the hand of God, we do *what we must*, and each one of us has to prepare accordingly. Believe me, it is not the throne that I defend, but *honour* – and if, after the war, when there will no longer be a single Prussian on French soil, the nation no longer wants us, then believe me, I shall be glad of it, and far from the bustle of the world, I shall perhaps be able to forget how much I have suffered . . . Don't think that I have lost heart. I live in hope.

Yet, sustained by only the see-sawing stimulus of coffee and the sedation of chloral, there were periods when she seemed almost crazy – announcing one minute that she wanted to volunteer as a nurse, another that she would ride bareback through the streets like a latter-day Joan of Arc. Politically, she was caught with Palikao in a harshly entrenched battle of wills against Trochu, who wanted what was available of the army to marshal outside Paris and protect the city from its now virtually imminent and inevitable siege; Palikao and the Empress were adamant that to have so many malcontent soldiers twiddling their thumbs near the capital's radical and anti-imperial elements was tantamount to an invitation to revolution. They remained obsessively convinced that what mattered was MacMahon advancing to lift the siege of Metz and then joining forces with Bazaine. Despite this fundamental disagreement, Trochu extravagantly protested his loyalty to the Regent and the

Empire. When first presented to Eugénie, he had fallen to his knees and kissed her hand fervently. 'Madame, I am a Breton, a Catholic and a soldier. I will serve you to the death,' he gushed. What would you do if the Regent was attacked? someone asked him publicly. 'I should lay down my life on the steps of the throne,' he replied. Eugénie was not such a fool as to be anything but highly suspicious of such sentiments.

By the afternoon of 31 August the Prussians had begun to encircle Sedan. Battle began before dawn on 1 September, as the Prussians moved up through the outlying villages. Louis Napoleon – his cheeks rouged and moustache waxed – mounted a horse in his agony and rode prominently through the action, like some weird effigy of himself: as Eugénie knew, he was inviting an honorable death which would free him from the humiliation of his own downfall. But such mercy was not granted him: there was more to endure.

By 8 a.m., MacMahon had been wounded and the French were being pummelled by Prussian artillery. MacMahon's deputy Ducrot immediately ordered a general retreat from the town via the last remaining passage: already there seemed no possibility of anything except the avoidance of outright defeat. Then galloped in one General de Wimpffen, bearing letters from Palikao empowering him to take command in the event of MacMahon's incapacity – a decision taken in Paris the day previously. In Sedan, he was unexpected, and the confusion redoubled when he countermanded the retreat and proceeded to arrange for a dashing charge into the face of the relentlessly advancing enemy. The result was predictably disastrous, but Wimpffen maintained an absurd insistence, 'We must have a victory!' 'You will be very lucky if this evening you have so much as a retreat,' replied Ducrot with bitterness.

It was a brilliantly cloudless summer's day. From some hills three miles above Sedan, Bismarck, von Moltke, the King of Prussia and a host of German nobility joined with *The Times*'s correspondent and distinguished representatives of the major powers to observe the progress of an engagement that would reshape Europe. So clear was the light that through binoculars they could pick out the red trousers of the French soldiers and the escalating chaos within the city walls as Wimpffen desperately tried to marshal sufficient troops to launch one last break-out. Louis Napoleon refused to co-operate. As the Prussians tightened the noose around Sedan, the French troops outside the town were forced into a panic-stricken rout, jumping into the moat and clambering monkey-like over the walls: any more delay and a catastrophic massacre, if not a mutiny, would ensue. While Wimpffen was engaged in yet another crazy scheme to break out, the Emperor gave an order for the white flag to be hoisted. As he had resigned from any official military position, it was not strictly within his powers to do this, but he was prepared to take a peculiarly personal responsibility for surrender. 'Monsieur mon frère,' he wrote to the King of Prussia, 'Having failed to meet death in the midst of my troops, nothing more remains for me but to yield up my sword into Your Majesty's hands.' His hope was that by so self-abasingly delivering himself up as a prisoner of war he might persuade the Prussians to let his troops go free, on condition that they laid down their arms for the duration of the war.

But the Prussians saw no reason for clemency. In the warmth and eerie stillness of the evening, their army could be heard from Sedan singing the Lutheran chorale *Nun danket alle Gott*: righteousness had triumphed and justice must prevail. In parley with the truculent Wimpffen, von Moltke and Bismarck would not bargain or argue: the only question was whether the imperial regime or the nation of France had been defeated. To resolve this matter Louis Napoleon drove out of Sedan at 5 a.m. on 2 September to meet with the King of Prussia in the neighbouring village of Donchery. He was intercepted by Bismarck, who insisted that they sit in a tiny roadside cottage and discuss the political dimensions of the situation. Louis Napoleon's view was that peace terms had to be discussed with the Regent and the government in Paris; Bismarck knew full well that the Second Empire was unlikely to survive the news of Sedan. He left Louis Napoleon to pace ponderously up and down a path which ran alongside the cottage's potato patch. There was nothing more to say. When von Moltke arrived, it became clear that the Emperor was now in effect a prisoner of war. He was told that he could only meet with the King after Wimpffen had put his name to a total unconditional surrender.

(Madame Fournaise, the weaver who owned the cottage, did well out of the incident. Louis Napoleon thanked her courteously for her hospitality and gave her four gold pieces. Three of them, it is said, she kept to pay for her funeral and a fourth went with her to the grave. She further profited from the sale of the table and chairs used by the two leaders during their conversation; then she had copies made of the chairs which she sold to tourists, who still visit the cottage today.)

At Bellevue, Wimpffen signed at 11 a.m., and the Emperor met the King on the château's glazed veranda. One report of the encounter noted 'the contrast between the two sovereigns . . . the German tall, upright, square-shouldered, with the flash of success from the keen blue eyes from under the helmet, and the glow of triumph on the fresh cheek; the Frenchman, with weary stoop of the shoulders, his eyes drooping, his lips quivering, bare-headed and dishevelled'. They spoke stiffly, enquiring after the well-being of each other's families and praising the skill and valour of each other's armies. Louis Napoleon learnt that he would be detained at the castle of Wilhelmshöhe, near Kassel, held as a sort of hostage against whoever or whatever should succeed him as ruler of France. He asked only one favour: that he should not have to pass through the ranks of his defeated army. This being granted, he seems to have resumed his habitual diffidence. Retiring to bed early at Bellevue, he read a few pages of Bulwer Lytton's romance of the Wars of the Roses, *The Last of the Barons*. The remainder of his army and its generals spent the night in an improvised prisoner-of-war compound. There was nothing now between the Prussians and Paris except a hundred miles of open and undefended countryside.

Eugénie was given news of the defeat in the late afternoon of 3 September. She was not among the first in the capital to know: reports had been seeping through all day in the constant fug of rumour and counter-rumour, each new whisper contagiously believed. The telegram was solemnly handed to her by the Minister of the Interior. She stared at it mutely, then 'like some great tragedienne playing to an empty house', as Theo Aronson memorably put it, exploded into a scorching paroxysm of fury. 'She was pale and terrible,' remembered one witness. 'Her eyes were hard and brilliant with anger, her face distorted by emotion.' Out burst a tirade of incoherent, savage contempt directed against her husband's bungling, compromising cowardice and indecision. The attack was intensely personal and obscenely hateful. It welled up from years of pent-up resentment at his sexual infidelities and other marital incompatibilities, as well as rage at a war and a throne so clumsily lost, let alone nervous exhaustion and helpless fear. It was, however, the necessary acknowledgement of the terrible truth of her situation.

That night, in a late sitting of the Corps Législatif, Palikao confirmed the defeat and the Emperor's surrender. There were calls for abdication and threats of deposition, but they were superfluous – it was as if the Empire was simply crumbling away, the victim of its own hollowness. Trochu stood back and bided his time, ignoring summonses from Palikao and the Empress, but ready for any other call on his loyalties. He did not have long to wait. On the morning of 4 September a deputation from the Corps Législatif visited Eugénie at the Tuileries and begged her to abdicate. Futile but magnificent, she held firm, talking of her duty, her honour, her principles, her word. 'One can only give up that which is one's own, but never that which has been received in trust,' she said. 'The sovereignty is not mine to give. I shall never abdicate.' During this hopeless interview, several messages arrived from the Prefecture of Police. All over Paris they were smashing imperial emblems. In Lyons and other provincial cities, the republic had already been declared and it could only be a matter of hours, minutes even, before the imperial government lost its majority in the Corps Législatif. 'A bas l'Empire, vive la République,' they could be heard shouting outside, in emphatic counterpoint. As yet, there was no violence and Eugénie refused to give the order to shoot.

At midday a crowd largely composed of at least partially armed Garde Nationale, both bourgeois and artisan in character, invaded the chamber of the Corps Législatif, virtually unopposed by the police or the regular army. In the ensuing chaos, the radical deputies managed to command some sort of unity of assent to the idea that the death of the Empire and the birth of the Republic should be formally proclaimed from the balcony of the Hôtel de Ville, the town hall, where the revolutionary governments of 1789 and 1848 had also been inaugurated. A carnival excitement fired the ever-burgeoning horde of Parisians who now swarmed there, and Trochu, watching from his office in the Louvre, sensed that the hour had come. He rode out flamboyantly to follow the parade and, sure enough, was dubbed President of the new republic. Candidates for all posts and ministries were similarly selected with reference to the most basic political rule of thumb – the cheering or booing that calling out their names provoked in the crowd. The fun on the balcony of the Hôtel de Ville was led by a popular young radical deputy and fervent orator, Léon Gambetta, who was rewarded with the Ministry of the Interior; Jules Favre became Vice-President and Minister of Foreign Affairs; Ernest Picard was put in charge of Finance; and Henri de Rochefort, author and publisher of Paris's favourite satirical magazine *La Lanterne*, was hurrahed into a nice little sinecure. It was pure bloodless revolution. Political prisoners were released. Women stuck flowers down the muzzles of guardsmen's rifles and young men climbed lampposts to toss their hats higher into the air. The sun shone, within and without. 'We shook off the Empire as if it had been a nightmare,' wrote Juliette Adam. 'Light had drawn away the clouds, and although the sun's rays began to set . . . it seemed to us as though a day so luminous could banish shadows and darkness for ever.' 'Hail to thee, Republic! Thou art in worthy hands,' cooed the sixty-six-year-old radically chic George Sand. The defeat of Sedan and its implications were temporarily obliterated from Paris's consciousness: the Third Republic would see to the Prussians, the Third Republic would blow the war away.

So the Second Empire withered and perished. Trochu went to break the news to Palikao, who had just received news of his beloved son's death at Sedan and was too grief-stricken to care: he subsequently escaped to Brussels. But the Empress shook with fury when she heard of Trochu's turncoatery and remembered his empty protestations and florid bowing and scraping. Only her closest friends and servants remained in the Tuileries that afternoon, as the railings round the palace were wrenched apart and the gilded eagles on the imperial gateposts were smashed to pieces. She would be true to the last, she said, she would not flinch; she feared nothing except 'falling into the hands of viragos, who would defile my last hours with something shameful or grotesque. I imagined them lifting my skirts, I heard ferocious laughter . . .' It was an overheated scenario, born of her obsession with Marie-Antoinette; in fact, Paris that day showed surprisingly little interest in wreaking revenge on the Empress – had the mob wanted to drink her blood, it could easily have done so. But her presence in Paris could have become the focus for civil war, and her wisest counsellors, the Italian and Austrian ambassadors Nigra and Metternich, urged her to leave the country, taking – if it made her feel any better – the flame of the Empire and her Regency with her.

Finally, she agreed. In 1848, Louis-Philippe and his wife had fled from the Tuileries and revolution, leaving their dinner unfinished and with only fifteen francs between them. Eugénie's departure was scarcely more dignified or considered. Having packed one small handbag, she flung a heavy travelling cloak over a black cashmere dress that she had not removed for over a week and donned a veil. She had no money, nothing: her jewels had been entrusted to the safe-keeping of Pauline Metternich and from now she would be precariously dependent on kindness and luck alone. Her one companion was a lady-in-waiting, Madame LeBreton, who boasted a hundred-franc note and some change. Some of their routes of escape from the Tuileries were already blocked by the roistering mob, so, accompanied by three loyal courtiers and Nigra and Metternich, they made for the doors that connected the palace to the Louvre. But they were locked, and furious knocking had no effect, because by now all the museum staff had vanished. Valuable minutes were wasted while someone was sent to hunt out a master key, and the party then ran through the galleries, eerily emptied of all their paintings and treasures. Only Géricault's vast immovable canvas *The Raft of the Medusa* had not been packed up and sent to the naval arsenal in Brest for safe storage: the Empress is said to have paused thunderstruck in front of its depiction of ship-wrecked despair.

Eventually the little party emerged out of a side door and on to the Place Saint-Germain l'Auxerrois. A passing lad recognized the Empress, thrust his fist into her face, and shouted out his discovery. Nigra tried to silence him, as Metternich bundled the two ladies into a cab without a moment's formality or farewell. It was difficult to know where to go: most of imperial high society had decamped from the city and all the more obvious havens would be watched, if not overrun, by the new republicans. Madame LeBreton gave the driver – who remained miraculously oblivious of the identity of his veiled passengers – the address of a trusted friend of hers in the Boulevard Malesherbes. The cab passed slowly through the anarchic excitement in the rue de Rivoli, half of it charging towards the Hôtel de Ville, half towards the invasion of the Tuileries: to the latter, the imperial guard offered no resistance, and by 4 p.m. the palace was liberated. 'Property of the People,' was chalked on the walls, and every imperial 'N' desecrated. The Avenue de l'Empereur was renamed Avenue Victor Noir. 'They wrote up "Death to thieves" on all sides,' recorded the forlorn Monsieur Maillard, one of the last remaining domestic servants, in charge of the Emperor's china and glass. 'I have been unable to put things away in their proper places; they have not allowed me time to do so.'

Madame LeBreton's friend was not at home: the two ladies sat disconsolately on the stairs for a quarter of an hour, then wandered aimlessly on to the street, looking for another cab. Much the same thing happened when they tried another of Madame LeBreton's friends in the Avenue de Wagram: 'the servant in charge could only answer questions from the other side of the door, as by some misadventure he had been locked in.'

They were running out of ideas. The Empress then thought of applying to the American Legation, but neither lady had any idea of its address. Just as they were beginning quietly to panic, the brainwave came – if not the American Legation, then the American dentist. Dr Evans, who had so loyally attended to the teeth of the imperial household, was a charming and wealthy man, with excellent connections (indeed, he had been used as an informal gatherer of secret intelligence during the Civil War and had proved himself on several occasions highly sympathetic to the aims and activities of the Second Empire). His home was in the Avenue de l'Impératrice, and here the door was opened and the veiled ladies ushered into the study. But Dr Evans was out too, working on the kitting-up of an American-financed ambulance, or mobile hospital, which was to be sent out to succour the wounded at the front. His return had been delayed by the crowds celebrating the new republic in the rue de Rivoli; as he entered his study to greet his mysterious anonymous visitors, he saw only Madame LeBreton. The Empress was seated with her back to the door, 'lest the unexpected sight of her might elicit some exclamation from the doctor, and thus betray her identity to the servants'.

When the door was closed and the position assimilated, Dr Evans jumped to. They would make for Deauville, where his wife was taking the sea air, and thence to England: the Prince Impérial was now lodged in Hastings and the Empress could join him there to await further developments in the situation. The route to Deauville, via towns such as Mantes and Lisieux, was open and not treacherous: they would leave, along with Evans's English friend, Dr C—, early the next morning, on passports thoughtfully provided by Metternich and carried in the Empress's small handbag.

They left at 5 a.m. and managed to escape the capital unchallenged and undetected: at the gates of the city, Eugénie impersonating a deranged woman being taken from a lunatic asylum to relatives in the country. According to Evans: 'the Empress did not at this time fully apprehend the political consequences of the Revolution . . . she knew that the Empire, the French army and France had met with a series of terrible disasters, and believed that the war with Germany had practically come to an end at Sedan; but she did not seem to think that the Republic proclaimed in Paris was a necessary, or even a probable, final consequence of these events.'

What did obsess her was Trochu's treachery – and throughout the gruellingly claustrophobic thirty-six-hour carriage journey to the coast, she ranted and snarled and wept at the thought of it. Being the woman she was, such emotion must have sustained her.

They arrived at Deauville and the Empress and Madame LeBreton refreshed themselves in Mrs Evans's hotel. Dr Evans went down to the quay and picked out a sixty-foot yacht called the *Gazelle*. It was owned by an English baronet, Sir John Burgoyne. 'I drew him aside and told him I had a confidential communication to make,' Evans records in his memoirs, 'saying that I believed him to be a man in whose honour I could trust, and on whose silence I could rely should he be unable to give me the special assistance I was seeking. Sir John, in answer to my statement, opened his card–case, and giving me a card, remarked "I am an English gentleman, and have been in Her Majesty's service and in the army for some years." These words quite assured me, and I then told him frankly and without reserve how I happened to be in Deauville.' After a certain amount of humming and hawing, Burgoyne agreed to take the Empress and Madame LeBreton over to the Isle of Wight as soon as possible, despite the squally conditions in the Channel. Intriguingly, Burgoyne's account of the incident (in a letter written ten days later) mentions that shortly before the agreed hour of departure, 'I had the honour of a visit from a young Russian gentleman to whom I had only been introduced casually, who brought "a friend of his from Paris, who was anxious to see a yacht". I had the pleasure of showing them all over the vessel . . . and have little doubt that he was a spy, who suspected something.' Had the Empress been quietly followed from the Tuileries and had Trochu decided that it was better to let her slip away from the country rather than imprison her in Paris, where she would have remained a constant threat to the calm of the new republic? The story of her escape certainly remains almost absurdly incredible, and the gutter press coloured it further by suggesting a romantic involvement of the Empress and her handsome American dentist.

Sir John Burgoyne received his passengers on board.

The Empress was very much agitated and sobbed bitterly, and on my saying to her, going over the side, 'N'ayez pas peur, Madame,' she replied in English, 'I am safe with an English gentleman.' I then introduced her to my wife, who told her the last three days' news, and read the papers to her. At seven o'clock we left the harbour and had some very heavy weather with a nasty sea running, but the *Gazelle* is a very fine sea boat and behaved splendidly; but I fear the Empress must have suffered frightful discomfort, although we did all in our power to make her comfortable. I landed with the Empress at Ryde a little before seven on the 8th; and she left at midday via Portsmouth to join her son.

According to the memoirs of the comte d'Hérisson, 'the Empress did not take the trouble to thank Sir John Burgoyne, and Lady Burgoyne had a year afterwards to give personal expression to her astonishment at the omission before it was rectified'.

Meanwhile the world contemplated the defeat at Sedan and the fall of the Second Empire. 'May we all learn what frivolity, conceit and immorality lead to!' wrote Crown Princess Vicky of Prussia on 6 September to her mother, Queen Victoria.

The French people have trusted in their own excellence, have completely deceived themselves: where is their army, where are their statesmen? . . . Gay and charming Paris! What mischief that very court, that still more attractive Paris, has done to English society, to the stage and to literature! . . . It would be well if they would pause and think that immoderate frivolity and luxury depraves and ruins and ultimately leads to a national misfortune. Our poverty, our dull towns, our plodding, hardworking *serious* life has made us strong and determined; is wholesome for us. I should grieve were we to imitate Paris and be so taken up with pleasure that no time was left for self-examination and serious thought.

On the same day, a poster was pasted around 'that still more attractive' city:

THE ENEMY IS ADVANCING TOWARDS PARIS, IN THREE ARMED FORCES

French Republic, Ministry of the Interior

The enemy is on the move towards Paris. The defence of the capital is assured.

Every citizen will be inspired by the great duties which his country demands of him.

The Government of National Defence counts on the courage and patriotism of one and all.

6 September 1870.

The President of the Government of National Defence

Governor of Paris,
General TROCHU

Part II

8 : *The Siege*

5 September 1870

After nineteen years in political exile from the Second Empire, the great poet and novelist Victor Hugo returned to his homeland, now once more a republic. He was sixty-eight, grey-haired, eagle-eyed and possessed of overpowering confidence in his own genius. Arriving from Brussels at the Gare du Nord, he was received by a hysterically enthusiastic crowd, which burst into spontaneous mass recitations of his poetry and pelted him with flowers. 'I shook more than ten thousand hands,' his diary records, with a characteristic note of self-congratulation.

Over the ensuing months, Hugo would continue to bask in all such tributes to his own importance, envisaging himself as the symbolic embodiment of the true spirit of France. If they had offered him the presidency, he would have accepted it; meanwhile his bottomless windbag exhaled massive belches of oracular patriotism addressed to the Parisians, the Prussians, all humanity, anyone who could be bothered to listen.

> Paris has an anchor, a civilization fermenting within her, that the Red French of the Republic placed in her crater . . . The city was full of all the explosions of the human soul. Tranquil and troubled, Paris awaited the invasion. The volcano needed no assistance . . . Cast Paris to the four winds, you will only conduce to make from every grain of its ashes the seed of the future. This sepulchre will cry out 'Liberty, Equality, Fraternity!' Paris is a city, but Paris is also a soul.

And so on and on.

6 September
Edmond de Goncourt, after attending a dinner at which the more sceptical views of other members of the intelligentsia were voiced:

> We talked of the great defeat, of the impossibility of defending the city, of the ineptness of the eleven members of the Government of National Defence, of their distressing lack of influence over the diplomatic corps and neutral governments . . .
>
> Someone throws into the conversation the idea that 'precision armaments don't suit the French temperament. Shooting fast, charging with a bayonet is more our soldiers' style. If they can't do that, they're paralysed. The *mechanization* of the individual isn't our thing. And therein lies the superiority of the Prussians today.'
>
> Renan [theologian and historian] raised his head. 'In everything I have studied I have always been struck by the superiority of German intelligence and the German capacity for hard work. It's hardly surprising that in the art of war – which is, after all, an art, inferior but complex – they should have attained this superiority . . . Yes, my friends, the Germans are a superior race!'
>
> 'Oh indeed no,' the others choroused.
>
> 'But yes, I insist – highly superior to us,' Renan continued heatedly. 'Catholicism is a *cretinization* of the individual: all education provided by Jesuits or monks arrests and suppresses the highest virtues, while Protestantism develops them.'*
>
> The sweet and sickly voice of Berthelot [scientist] recalled our thoughts from these high-faluting sophistries to more menacing realities: 'My friends, perhaps you didn't know that we are surrounded by enormous quantities of petrol, left at the gates of Paris and never brought inside the walls because of import duties. If the Prussians take possession and throw it into the Seine, they will make a stream of flames which will burn up both river banks. That is how the Greeks destroyed the Arab fleet.'

8 September
Tales like these multiplied, criss-crossing the boulevards and newspapers, colliding with and confusing each other. Everybody had a prognosis of the enemy's advance on the capital, or a

---

* When this section of Goncourt's *Journal* was finally published in 1890, Renan vigorously denied ever having entertained such views. But see p. 386.

privileged gloss on the truth behind the latest official report – and their tenor was often weirdly optimistic. The Prussians went to war with the Second Empire, ran the argument, and they had decimated it: but they had no quarrel with the glittering benevolent phoenix of Republican France. And in any case, how *could* Paris be besieged? Even the Prussians would not show such cheek. The operation was unthinkable, impractical, insane. 'In the cafés, on trains, in drawing-rooms, hordes of honest folk who knew nothing whatever about it, claimed that it was as clear as day that investment of the city was mathematically impossible. *Mathematically*,' wrote Edouard Cadol. 'You can imagine how that adverb became fashionable, and one would appear presumptuous, even potentially treacherous, if one cast doubt on the validity of that "mathematically".'

It was reported that Jules Favre, the Vice President, had returned from negotiations with Bismarck empty-handed. In a communiqué sent to the embassies he declared France unbowed, if severely bloodied: 'We will not cede so much as either an inch of our territory or a stone of our fortresses.' This gung-ho assertion came to have a bitterly hollow ring. The worst news was that despite another round of diplomatic negotiations, Britain, Austria, and Russia all refused to intervene on France's behalf. The conflict could not be allowed to mushroom, and France would have to pay the price for her initial aggression alone.

9 September
Felix Whitehurst reported in his *Daily Telegraph* column the official orders 'for all strangers who wish to leave Paris to go at once'. A favourite hangout of the expatriate community, Thorpe's, closed its doors, 'but a cunning American has opened another "bar" ' to serve those who remained. A decree also closed all the theatres and places of entertainment – a measure which badly affected morale. The city was now thoroughly militarized. Camps were set up in denuded parks and squares. Line upon line of soldiers marched down the boulevards or paraded in the Champs Élysées. The regular clatter of drilling and musketry, the ugliness of barricades and placards, filled

streets which weeks earlier had been quietly residential or bustling and commercial.

12 September

Juliette Adam, married to the politician Edmond Adam, took a more sternly cheerful line. In her diary she is every inch the Roman matron, tireless and tearless. Like all housewives, she was becoming preoccupied with the problem of filling her larder for the grimmer contingencies.

> I'm trotting about all over the place getting in my provisions, I need so many things! I'm showing all my domestic genius in my research. I dream of nothing but Australian mutton, Liebig ham, Chollet vegetables, groceries and victuals. My pockets and gown and arms and hands are always chock-full when I come home. If I find a new jam, I imagine the surprise it's going to give in three months' time to the friends I invite to eat it. If I see heroes spring up around me, I shan't weave wreaths for them, or deck their houses with garlands, I shall offer them a jar of the new preserved carrots.

Paris, it must be remembered, was in the habit of shopping daily for fresh supplies. Hoarding and storing food was not a normal domestic practice, and canned and preserved foods, like Juliette Adam's carrots, were still a novelty. One of the contemporary pioneers in this field was the grocer Félix Potin, whose name is still familiar on French tins and bottles.

13 September

Queen Victoria, writing from Balmoral to her daughter Crown Princess Vicky of Prussia: 'In England I can assure you the feeling is far more German than French, and far the greater part of the press is in your favour. All reflecting people are. The Pall Mall has excellent articles. You should take it in.' (The 'Pall Mall' was the *Pall Mall Gazette*: its articles on the Franco–Prussian situation were written by none other than the Marxist Friedrich Engels.)

An inventory taken of the furs left in the Tuileries Palace by the Empress:

> One Swansdown cloak, lined with Silver Fox.
> One black velvet mantle, trimmed with Marten Sable.

One black velvet circular cloak, lined and trimmed with Chinchilla.
One velvet pelise, lined with Weasel, with Sable collar.
One Otter skin cloak.
One blue Cashmere opera cloak, lined with Swansdown.
One black Cashmere opera cloak, lined with Swansdown.
One hunting waistcoat, lined with Chinchilla.
One black silk boddice, lined with Chinchilla.
One grey silk boddice, lined with Chinchilla.
One Marabout muff.
One Sable muff.
One Silver Fox muff.
One Ermine muff.
One Chinchilla muff.
One Otter muff.
One Otter's head muff.
One Marten Sable boa.
One collar of Sable tails.
One collar of Marten Sable heads.
One pair of Chinchilla cuffs.
One pair of Silver Fox cuffs.
One green velvet wrap, lined with Canadian fur.
One carpet of Thibet Goat skin.
One white Sheepskin carpet.
One set of Otter trimming.
Two caracos of Spanish Lamb skin.
8¾ yards of Chinchilla trimming.
27 yards of Sable tail trimming.
One front and a piece of Black Fox.
Four strips, a wrist band, two pockets, two sleeves and one
    trimming of Black Fox.
Two Swansdown skins, in pieces.
Fourteen Silver Fox skins.
Six half skins of Silver Fox.
Twenty Silver Fox tails.
One Otter collar.
Three tails of Canadian fur.
Two Marabout collars.
Some odd pieces of Chinchilla.
Four large carpets of black Bear skin.
Two small carpets of black Bear skin.
One brown Bear, with head.
One stuffed Bear.
One white Fox rug.
One caraco, one petticoat, and one waistcoat of chestnut coloured
    plush, trimmed with Otter.

19¾ yards of Otter trimming.
Two Pheasants' skins
Three white Sheepskin stools.
One Sable dress trimming.
Three Sable skins.
Two squares of Chinchilla.
One Weasel tippet and two cuffs to match.
Two pieces Swansdown.
Two Pheasants' wings.
One stuffed Fox.
One pair of Otter gloves.
3½ yards of Skunk trimming.
Two court mantles bordered with Ermine.

14 September

A proclamation issued by General Trochu, Governor of Paris and President of the Republic of France, addressed to the Garde Mobile and Garde Nationale:

> With our formidable fighting force, the daily guard in Paris will never be less than 70,000 men. If the enemy pierced the fortifications by storm, or by surprise, or by an open breach, he would meet the barricades which are now being built, and the leaders of the enemy columns would then be defeated by the attack of ten echelons of reserves.
>
> Have complete faith, then, and know that the fortifications of Paris, defended by the persevering effort of public spirit and by three hundred thousand rifles, is unapproachable . . . I thank you for your patriotic concern for the cherished interests which are entrusted to you.
>
> And now, to work, in the nine sections of the defences! Let there everywhere be order, serenity, devotion! And remember, as I have already told you, that you remain in charge of the policing of Paris in these days of crisis.

Since nearly a quarter of a million regular soldiers were either imprisoned or besieged throughout the war zone, the loyalty and efficacy of the Garde Mobile and the Garde Nationale was indeed crucial to the capital's defence. To what degree could they be relied on? The Garde Mobile consisted of around 100,000 conscripted reservists, and although they may have been distinctly amateurish (twenty-eight battalions were made up of Bretons, many of them never off the family farm before and unable to speak more than a few words of standard French), they were relatively disciplined and untainted by political partisanship. The Garde Nationale was much more wayward. Created in 1789 as a civilian militia, it had always been regarded with suspicion by governments, and Louis Napoleon was not the first to restrict its size and powers because of his fear of the likely results of arming potentially revolutionary sections of the population of Paris.

Now, however, it had to be taken seriously, and by the end of September it numbered two hundred and fifty battalions, containing over three hundred thousand Parisians of all classes, ages and walks of life. Units were recruited and administered by each of the city's twenty arrondissements and the rank and file were permitted to elect their own officers. This meant that the most Red, poverty-stricken and disaffected areas of Paris, such as Belleville, were in effect being allowed to regulate their own armies. Moreover, the organization was *ad hoc*, the drilling, uniform and training disorderly: the only constant factor was the pay: one franc fifty per diem, with an allowance of seventy-five centimes for wives at home.

Service was part-time, and nothing very rigorous was demanded in the line of military endeavour. The basic function of the Garde Nationale was to watch over the immense perimeter of the city's ramparts. These had largely been built in 1840 and provided Paris with an impressively tight belt of security. The whole city was surrounded by a thick, thirty-foot-high wall, with a deep ditch in front of it and ninety-four bastions dotting its course. Beyond this wall were sixteen detached forts, forming a thirty-two-mile cordon; behind it was a circular military road and railway, as well as a network of telegraph wires and intersecting boulevards. The Garde Nationale manned the wall in round-the-clock shifts: Francisque Sarcey describes a typical day in the life of his unit, foregathering in its arondissement before marching out to patrol.

The zealous and the novices arrive at 7 a.m. precisely – the military hour! – because that's what a real soldier would do. The more cunning ones begin to emerge only between 7.30 and 8 a.m. from the surrounding streets. They are full of the scalding-hot soup or coffee recommended by the Consultant Committee on Health and Hygiene as a protection against the effects of the disturbing morning fog. By 8 a.m. everyone has piled up. We have to get moving. Officers run about shouting; we all pull in our stomachs or fiddle with our shirt-fronts. A head count is taken. At this point, even to the least perceptive eyes, it becomes clear what has long been the problem with the Garde Nationale.

Next to an old man with a white beard stands a baby-faced young one . . . the honest faces of peaceable bourgeois jostle with the martial figures of old campaigners; numerous pairs of spectacles bear witness to a regrettable level of myopia and red noses to the services of the wine merchant. It is, in sum, the strangest jumble of physiognomies imaginable. . . .

We arrive at the bastion at about 11 a.m. Lunchtime. Some of us dig into the depths of a rucksack for something that's been packed back home; others make for the outdoor stalls; others disperse into the local taverns. At this point it is difficult not to think of a day's Garde Nationale duty as an excuse for a pleasant out-of-bounds promenade. Bottle after bottle is emptied, round succeeds round, and even the officer's braid is no guarantee of immunity from the lamentable consequences of visits to the wine merchants.

There would have been only one way of stopping men from falling prey to this vice: to oblige them, by means of physical force if necessary, to undertake some exhausting labour: building shelters, pitching tents, driving carts – all of which needed doing. Instead, from the start to the close of day, we walked up and down the tents in which we would rest in the evening. Some of us played at *bouchon*, others at whist or piquet. A lot of people just hung around, or read the paper, or slept in the sun.

This kind of behaviour was not particularly subversive, perhaps, and the government must have believed that it was better to tolerate a certain slackness than to enforce a harder line which might provoke a backlash. The Garde Nationale provided employment for those with no other means of honest subsistence, at a time when the siege had effectively paralysed the Parisian economy, and kept some sort of leash on the feckless. Yet there were units with a sharper edge than Sarcey's, filled with men not content with getting drunk and bored, men who might turn violently against the government at any moment, on any pretext. So Trochu and his cabinet could only ever keep one eye on the Prussians: there was also an enemy within. 'Virtually the whole defence revolved around a single factor,' wrote General Ducrot in his history of the siege, '*Fear of insurrection*. . . . One was constantly obliged to face two enemies: one which, night and day, tightened his ring of fire and steel; the other which at every instant was awaiting the moment to hurl itself upon the Hôtel de Ville.'

15 September

A new body, describing itself as the Central Committee of the Twenty Arrondissements, published an alarming manifesto. Behind it, so they said, were crazy Reds from the Internationale, but it commanded wide support in the working-class districts of the city. Among its demands were expropriation of all private food supplies and the institution of a system of total rationing, alongside the accusation that the Government of National Defence was cravenly prepared to negotiate or even surrender on any terms. This was not altogether untrue: secretly, Trochu and other conservatives were sceptical of Paris's ability to withstand the siege and, even more secretly, afraid that victory for the republic would give the radicals and Reds in Paris their head – something which the army command, with its monarchist sympathies, could not have tolerated.

Mathematically or not, Prussian forces had by now begun to encircle Paris. Railways, roads and bridges had been blown up, villages occupied and requisitioned. Still a crazy optimism prevailed. If there was going to be a siege, it could only be short – a week, a month before the armies that remained in the provinces marshalled themselves to bring relief. Paris was impregnable, divinely sanctioned. There was no cause for alarm. In fact, there was a certain thrill of anticipation at the adventure in it all. As Henry Markheim, a young Oxford graduate teaching English in the city, put it: 'Paris is in the feverish state of a man about to fight a duel: we puff at our cigar, flourish riding-whips, look at ourselves in the glass, and ask our seconds "if they ever saw us so cool".' Many of those who could have afforded to leave preferred to remain – some because they considered it scarcely worth the bother of decamping; some, simply because they did not want to miss out.

Strangely, the migrant traffic was busier into the city than out of it. Fleeing the onslaught of the Prussians, desperately in search of the capital's charity, trundled trails of dispossessed peasants, pushing loaded wagons or carrying pathetic bundles, their children and animals alongside. Native metropolitans turned up their noses and told patronizing stories about their country cousins' lack of sophistication. Sarcey recounts the one about the landlord who gave over the first floor of one of his apartment blocks to a family of such refugees. One day the concierge informed him that some very unpleasant smells were permeating the stairwell and the neighbours were complaining. The landlord went to investigate. In the yard, a cock and chickens were strutting about; the hallway was covered with straw and feathers and muck, dead rabbits, strings of garlic and onion; in the bedroom, ducks sat happily in the washbasin. The farmer followed him from room to room, proudly explaining to this flabbergasted city gent how he had ingeniously adapted to these new conditions.

'And what about the drawing room?' the landlord asked in dread.

'Monsieur is in there,' replied the farmer with a burst of pride.

He opened the door. In a corner, grunting on a filthy litter, reposed a huge, sweating pig.

'Good lord,' exclaimed the landlord. 'Why on earth is he here, when there's a perfectly good courtyard outside you could put him in, along with the chickens?'

'I can't put him down there,' sighed the farmer, 'because harvest is coming up, and there's nowhere else to store the barley.'

16 September

The government received hundreds of letters from all over France, offering advice and information. Many of them proposed plans to assassinate the Prussian leaders. Here is the self-sacrifice of a would-be Charlotte Corday.

To M. Le Président

Forgive the liberty that I take in writing to you, but, seeing my fatherland in danger, I cannot, despite my sixteen years and my sex, withhold from offering to save it or at least to do all that I can . . . I ask to be put in the most dangerous position: with the grace of God and my own courage, I am almost certain of attaining my goal.

Alas! for a long time now I have been tormented with this idea, but I did not want to push myself forward, fearing that I believed myself to be stronger than I was, and above all because I was not free to act as I wish, being under the tutelage of my parents whom I love very much and fear to anger. But now I think that nothing can hold me back and neither M. de Bismarck nor His Majesty King William frightens me – any more than their seven armies do. Please, monsieur, reply to me at once, so that I may know what I should do. As I cannot sign this letter or give my address, since I must not worry my family, please sir, reply to me in the columns of the newspapers and believe in the sincerity of my words – for a girl of sixteen would not propose herself for something which she did not feel she had the strength and courage to do . . .

A reply, as soon as possible, for time is pressing: they are advancing upon us!

I greet you, your servant devoted to *France*, mother of all

X

18 September

A national holiday, celebrated as normal in blazing late summer sunshine. As his contribution to the general jauntiness, Felix Whitehurst relayed to his readers a pedantic Prussian pun ('when a Scotchman or a Prussian makes a joke, it is the duty of all to laugh – it is so rare an event') reported in the *Gazette de la Croix*.

THE FALL OF THE EMPIRE

L'Empire respire (breathes) – May 8 [following the referendum]
L'Empire aspire (aspires) – July 14 [Bastille Day]
L'Empire tire (fires) – 2 August [first shots in the war]
L'Empire retire (retires) – 6 August [following first defeats]
L'Empire empire (worsens) – 14–31 August
L'Empire expire (expires) – 2 September

The *Morning Post*'s correspondent, Tommy Bowles, sounded a more anxious note: 'The postal service has been as regular as in the most ordinary times up to this morning, but the mail which left London yesterday morning appears to be the last that has been able to come right through. The letters, due this morning at 10 o'clock, have not yet appeared, nor does anybody know when they will appear.'

Victor Hugo addressed the nation again: 'Rouen, draw thy sword! Lille, take up thy musket! Bordeaux, take up thy gun! Marseilles, sing thy song and be terrible!'

19 September

Paris did not yet altogether know it, but the capital was by now totally invested by the Prussians, and all its normal lines of communication were severed.

An attempt by the foolhardy General Ducrot to defend the strategically significant plateau of Châtillon to the south of the city failed. Frightened and inexperienced soldiers, poorly briefed, routed when the Prussian field gun battery started firing shells. In the mist and panic, Mobiles began firing on each other and a division of the North African zouaves finally ran screaming back into Paris. Many of them were later arrested in Montparnasse, rolling around drunk. Earlier in the day there had been rumours of victory, so the reality of the fiasco seemed all the more disgraceful. The cynical left-wing view was that the exercise had been less than a wholehearted military operation, more something designed to give the impression that the government was taking a strongly bellicose line.

20 September

Versailles surrendered to the Prussians without the firing of a single shot.

Following the arrests in the wake of the previous day's débâcle, General Trochu issued a proclamation:

> I am firmly resolved to put an end to such grave disorders. I command all defenders of Paris to seize these stray men, whether they were full soldiers or Gardes Mobiles, who entered the city in a state of inebriation, spreading scandalous rumours and dishonouring by their behaviour the uniforms they wear. *Articles 213, 218, 250, 253 are punishable by DEATH.*

Twenty-one of these deserters were later 'marched round the ramparts with their hands tied behind their backs, their coats turned inside out, and then led from the Porte de Maillot to be shot'. But people said that this was just a bit of dramatic staging, *pour encourager les autres*.

21 September

In secrecy, Jules Favre again attempted to negotiate with Bismarck, this time in the Rothschilds' château at Ferrières, some miles east of Paris. Bismarck, nonchalantly puffing at a cigar throughout the interview, refused any concessions, let alone an armistice. He demanded occupation of the fort of Mont-Valérien and the surrender of Strasbourg. 'You are trying to destroy France,' Favre moaned, before bursting into tears. But Bismarck was not the man to be impressed by such feeble histrionics. In a corner of the room Field Marshal von Moltke sat reading *Martin Chuzzlewit*.

When news of the negotiations was leaked to the press, the left was enraged that peace should even be contemplated. The government retorted that it was necessary to establish what the Prussians wanted from the war.

A left-wing newspaper, *Le Combat*, printed a letter reflecting one lesser but persistent problem of the siege:

> While the working people of Paris adopt an attitude befitting the citizenry of a revolutionary fatherland confronted by immense peril, a scandal, too little noted, insults our manliness. The gilded prostitute of the Boulevard des Italiens displays its shamelessness as if the Empire was still in its heyday. . . . These stone-hearted girls, who have done so much for Bonapartism by emasculating and depraving the young bourgeoisie, stand there, drinking beers, smoking cigarettes and making love in full view of the world.

What could be done? There were several calls for a mass expulsion: Paris's infamous *filles* could be let loose on the Prussians in a venereal version of germ warfare. But all that happened was a slackening of the surveillance and medical examinations of the registered prostitutes and a flood of the unregistered to the ramparts, where rich pickings were to be had during the Garde Nationale's lunch hour.

22 September

The substantial percentage of Paris's population which had voted for and actively supported the Second Empire had evanesced, fallen silent or swiftly changed its mind. Many of Louis Napoleon's closer confederates had of course left before the siege was invested, and it is to the Republic's credit that there was no witch-hunt among the lower social strata. But where did all those everyday imperialists go? What became of all the engraved portraits of Eugénie hung over the mantelpiece in suburban salons? How did all those who had accepted imperial patronage and basked in imperial favour reconcile themselves to their error of political judgement? Don't ask me, replied the man in the Auteuil omnibus, it's not my fault.

Paris was in the mood to pass the buck: and because he was absent, imprisoned, defeated and brought low, unable to pass it on to another culpable party, that buck stopped with Louis Napoleon. 'It is amusing to observe,' commented the *Daily News*'s Henry Labouchere, himself a republican sympathizer:

> how everyone has entered into the conspiracy to persuade the world that the French nation never desired war – to hear them, one would suppose that the Rhine had never been called the national frontier of France, and that the war had been entered into by Badinguet, as they style the late Emperor,* against the wishes of the army, the peasantry and the bourgeoisie. Poor old Badinguet has enough to answer for already, but even sensible Frenchmen have persuaded themselves that he, and he alone, is responsible for the war. He is absolutely loathed here. I sometimes suggest to some Gaul that he may possibly be back again some day; the Gaul immediately rolls his eyes, clenches his fists, and swears that if ever Badinguet returns to Paris, he (the Gaul) will himself shoot him.

23 September

A balloon called *Le Neptune* was successfully launched from the Place Saint Pierre, carrying 125 kilograms of mail and piloted by Jules Darouf. It remained airborne for over three hours and travelled over a hundred kilometres before landing near the

* In reference to the pseudonym he had used to escape from imprisonment in 1846.

The Bon Marché, most sophisticated of Paris's
grands magasins or department stores, mid 1860s.

A typical grand reception – possibly a wedding banquet
– in Second Empire Paris.

Louis Napoleon.

Louis Napoleon and
Eugénie, impersonating
bourgeois devotion,
photographed by
Disdéri in the mid 1860s.

Eugénie shows off the baby Prince Impérial at Compiègne.

An early photograph of the Prince Impérial,
with his anxious father standing at the right.

The murdered Kinck
family in the morgue.
Said to be the first
photograph ever taken
in connection with
police evidence.

The darker side of Haussmann's Paris: the rue Champlain, c. 1865.

◀ Carpeaux's *La Danse*:
the ink stain spattered
the hips and haunches
of the nudes on the
left of the picture.

Cancan by Félicien Rops.
The contrast with
Toulouse-Lautrec's later
images of the dance
is marked.

◀ Cora Pearl,
impersonating
respectability.

One of 'the dear, delightful, dark dirty *rues*' (Felix Whitehurst) decimated by Haussmann.

Louis Napoleon's birthday officially acclaimed by the residents of an 'asylum' in Vincennes. The Emperor's bust is displayed in the doorway.

Haussmann's improvements: in the distance can be seen the shell of Garnier's new opera house.

Baron Georges Eugène Haussmann.

Caricature by 'Zut' of Eugénie, 'the Spanish cow', whose fart alarms her useless little husband (right). On her back sits Emile Ollivier, with whom she was falsely rumoured to be conducting a torrid love affair; below, the Prince Impérial.

town of Évreux. Two days earlier an attempt to launch *L'Union* had failed when the fabric tore during inflation, but from now there would be few hitches in this miraculous traffic. Every two or three days another balloon would leave the city from one of several sites. Sometimes their baskets carried as much as 400 kilograms of mail and as many as five passengers. The longest flight – that of 24 November – lasted nearly fifteen hours and ended up in Norway; others reached Belgium and Bavaria. Out of a total of sixty-eight balloons, only two were lost (both at sea), not counting the small paper balloon carrying 4 kilograms of postcards which was shot down over enemy lines on 30 September.

These balloons became Paris's principal means of communication with the outside world, administered by the privately managed Compagnie Nationale Aérostatique. Only a very few foot couriers ever managed to pass through the Prussian lines, and even fewer managed to pass back in again (although one wonders what can have been behind the advertisement carried by *Le Figaro*: 'A great number of persons of my acquaintance are desolated at the absence of news of their families. I believe I have found a perfectly simple and practical means to achieve a happy resolution. I need an intelligent man, who can furnish good references, to come and find me at 8 rue Drouot, between 8 and 10 a.m. The successful candidate will earn 1,000 francs a week.'). Other attempts at establishing secret telegraph links were swiftly detected and destroyed by the enemy – a cable running under the Seine to Rouen, for instance, was severed on 27 September after barely twelve days of operation. The sky was thus the only real option; it was not an easy one.

Balloons had previously been used for military reconnaissance, but never significantly. They were impossible to steer, vulnerable to the slightest changes in the weather, and anything but a pleasurable or picturesque form of transport – they were, rather, a source of profound terror for a civilization which still conceived of human beings as by nature earthbound. One reason that there were not more balloon flights during the siege was the shortage of people willing to risk manning them. Nor was the manufacture straightforward or cheap. Each balloon, around fifty feet in diameter, took about twelve days to complete and required intensive labour. Huge strips of calico were minutely inspected for flaws or holes, then oiled and varnished, before a line of a hundred or more seamstresses manually sewed them together. Each basket, apart from personal supplies, was kitted out with:

> a barometer, a thermometer, a mariner's compass, a miner's lamp, several ropes, twenty strips of paper, each 65 ft. long, and destined to try the direction of the wind, an oriflamme bearing the balloon's name, a paper triangle like a kite, with which to make observations on the currents and the speed, a parachute, between 300 and 400 bags of ballast, each containing 33 lbs of fine sand, an iron grapnel, 4 ft. high and 2 ft. 7 in. broad, a guide rope 656 ft. long half in mat-weed, half in hemp, two grappling ropes &c.

The total weight, without passengers, was well over a ton.

Various efforts were made to simplify or improve this technology. How to navigate an aerial course was the scientists' preoccupation, and many earnest experiments were made with rudders, all of them flops. *Le Combat* described one of the most ambitious of these abortive dirigible models, as 'heavier than air, ovoid-shaped, driven by two propellers, one vertical the other horizontal, fired by a little steam engine of two horse-power, with two flat and inclined wings. This apparatus has been constructed at the expense of the Committee of Armaments for the *arrondissement* of Grenelle, and its inventor, M. Vert, has offered it to the Republic free of charge'.

The siege stimulated Parisians to some much odder propositions, and the Scientific Committee of the Defence of Paris monitored an amazing range of visionary ideas. These included glass bombs, paper bombs, and precursors to the horrors of chemical and germ warfare such as a scheme for 'decomposing the air above the Prussian encampments so as to asphyxiate them' and for catapulting shells with typhoid- and smallpox-infected matter on to the enemy lines. (Another use suggested for human remains was to convert them into gas: one Dr S. claimed to have found a formula for distilling cadavers and obtaining a substance which 'gave a very clear light, more powerful, softer, and infinitely more economical than oil gas'.) Mobile ramparts. Underwater boats. A hot-water gun. A musical *mitrailleuse* which would deafen all those within range through a barrage of cacophony. Most bizarre of all was the notion of a giant hammer, six kilometres in length and weighing ten million tons, which would be lifted by means of a number of balloons and then dropped on Versailles, crushing King William, Bismarck, von Moltke and the entire Prussian command in its stunning wake.

24 September
'The one irritating feature about being thus shut up,' complained Tommy Bowles, 'is that, so far, we have not had any excitement to justify it all. Not a bomb has fallen, not a horse has been eaten as yet, and one's dinner costs just the same money and consists of precisely the same elements that it always did.' With the commercial, industrial and intellectual inertia as well, ennui began to set rottingly in. For Jules Claretie, nowhere was more melancholy than a mainline train station. 'Cushions from the carriages are piled up in the waiting room. Useless trains, left in place in the station, are covered not with black coal, but the fine grey dust of inertia. These things radiate an air of boredom as if they were living and feeling beings.' A short dreary ride into the suburbs came to seem like a liberating adventure. 'To leave Paris! To leave it for an hour, for a day, to return again in the afternoon: to see trees, a patch of sky, tufts of grass – what bliss! *Saint Mande*! shouts the conductor, then *Vincennes*! At the stations, ironic posters seize your attention and pull at your heart: *Bal du Grand Casino de Vincennes*, *Voyage circulaire en Alsace et dans les Vosges*, *Train de plaisir pour Nancy*. Hoardings of last summer, pieces of ancient history!'

Such pervasive melancholy led on the one hand to a loss of libido – 'we felt *so* virtuous' recalled John O'Shea; 'There was little marrying or giving in marriage at the time: Paris was a model of continence. *Sine Baccho et Cerere*, the Cytherean goddess lacks worshippers. If we were frigid, we deserved no praise for it' – and on the other to what the American Ambassador Elihu Washburne called 'demoralization' – '[the]

city government practically fell with the Empire, and in the absence of governmental and political regulations, there was much disorder; the streets were filled with the most obscene and disgusting literature, and the vilest caricatures were cried on the streets by men and boys and sometimes even by young girls.' The *filles* on the Boulevard des Italiens, the piles of uncollected garbage, the lights turned out early: Haussmann's metropolis drooped, a limp and seedy shadow of itself.

'Poor Paris,' mourned Claretie, 'how sad it looked, and yet at certain times on certain days, how superb was its aspect!' It reminded him of a friend who suddenly falls sick and is threatened by death. 'The traits of the loved one suddenly assume a new beauty. You reproach yourself for not having appreciated somebody whom misfortune may now take from you. So it was with Paris. Assailed, it immediately appeared with an unexpected physiognomy, a proud one. The more she was buffeted the more one was seduced and overwhelmed by her. Paris *en fête* was something distressing. Paris in mourning was irresistible.'

25 September

A Sunday which glowed in glorious autumnal sunshine. 'They could stand it no longer; the afternoon was too fine,' wrote Labouchere.

> Stern patriotism unbent, and tragic severity of demeanour was forgotten. The Champs Elysées and the Avenue de la Grande Armée were full of people. Monsieur shone by his absence; he was at the ramparts, or was supposed to be there; but his wife, his children, his *bonne*, and his kitchen wench issued forth, oblivious alike of dull care and of bombarding Prussians, to enjoy themselves after their wont by gossiping and lolling in the sun . . . At the Arc de Triomphe was a crowd trying to discover what was going on upon the heights above Argenteuil. Some declared they saw Prussians, while others with opera glasses declared that the supposed Prussians were only trees. In the Avenue de l'Impératrice was a large crowd gazing upon the Fort of Mont Valérien. This fort, because I presume it is the strongest for defence, is the favourite of the Parisians. They love it as a sailor loves his ship. 'If I were near enough,' said a girl near me, 'I would kiss it.' 'Let me carry your kiss to it,' replied a Mobile, and the pair embraced, amid the cheers of the people round them.

Spies

An obsession, amounting to persecution mania, with the presence of spies in the city was another feature of the social psychology of this first phase of the siege. Almost any unknown quantity was vulnerable to suspicion – a foreigner, a strange dialect, a deformity, an inexplicable absence, a flickering candle shining from a window at night. 'The possibility of being taken for a spy makes you feel like one,' wrote Nathan Sheppard. 'You return furtive glances with glances as furtive. You colour in trying not to colour. You become ill-at-ease in the endeavour to seem unconscious. If you have a passport or a letter, with the signature of someone in power, that is exactly the document with which a spy would provide himself. Whatever you say seems to be exactly what a spy would say.' There were endless comic misidentifications – putative Madame de Bismarcks were arrested several times daily – as the more zealous members of the Garde Nationale enjoyed the opportunity to exercise a little authority and create a little stir. A sewer worker who poked his head out of a manhole at the wrong moment was shot dead. The duchesse Tascher de la Pagerie, 'a brilliant ornament of the imperial court', was confined and investigated. Even public figures such as the Maréchal Vaillant and the great caricaturist Cham were apprehended. Entire professions – lamplighters, blind beggars – were scrutinized, and no conspiratorial possibilities seemed too far-fetched. An occasional genuine discovery, such as the treachery of the male secretary to Étienne Arago, the Mayor of Paris, confirmed the insane logic and fanned the flames of paranoia.

Beneath it all was what Sheppard called 'the intolerable tension of expectation. . . . One really knows nothing of what is going on, and there is an all-pervading sense of something that is going to happen, and which may come at any moment. This gives a sense of unreality to one's whole life. . . . Something is coming – is on its road – is impending. We know not what it is, or what it may be; nor how it will come, nor when it will come. The solid earth seems turned to smoke.'

27 September
Edmond de Goncourt's *Journal*:

> Paris is worried about its daily sustenance. Women gather in fiercely gesticulating groups; and in the rue Saint-Honoré I come across a rowdy assembly, banging against a grocer's closed shutters. One of the women explains that the grocer has sold a smoked herring to a Garde Mobile for fifty centimes. He has stuck it on the end of his baton, with a placard reading: '*Sold for fifty centimes by an officer of the Garde Nationale to a poor Mobile*'. A few yards away, I hear two women behind me sighing that 'there is no longer anything to eat'. And yes, that's what the exiguous displays of charcuterie indicate – a few sausages wrapped in silver foil and some jars of preserved truffles. . . . The white marble tables of Maison Lambert, at this time of year normally laden with venison, pheasants, and game, are bare; bowls which should be full of fish are empty. Inside this little temple of culinary appetite a very thin man walks up and down in a melancholy fashion. Yet a few steps away, in the gaslight which shines on to a wall of tin boxes, a fat cheerful girl sells pots of Liebig's Meat Extract.

28 September
In a public meeting the painter Courbet advocated the destruction of the column in the Place Vendôme, claiming it to be a monument to imperialism, offensive to republican sensibilities. He further spoke in favour of removing every trace of Napoleonism from the city. At the same time, a commission was set up to supervise the publication of the Emperor's secret papers and private correspondence, discovered in the Tuileries. Goncourt met someone working on the project, and was sceptical. 'In nothing that he said, implied, or revealed, did I find anything truly curious or unexpected. Fat payoffs to men whom everyone had always suspected of having received them; embezzlements which were a secret to nobody . . . not a single intimate document, not a letter which can add anything to the history of the human soul.' There was, however, an album of photographs of the Empress in her masked-ball costumes. One of them depicted her dressed 'in the Greek style, clothed in almost less than nothing'. There was talk of having the photograph engraved, as a way of demonstrating the moral decadence of the imperial court. 'I could not prevent myself,'

Goncourt continued 'from indicating a little contempt for this means of revolutionizing the masses.'

But at a time when entertainment was in short supply, Paris relished any little tabloid-scandal novelty. So it tut-tutted cheerfully at the news that the Emperor's forty-two cousins had received pensions amounting to 1,310,975 francs per annum; that General de Failly had been granted 1,200 francs for sugar plums; that the Prince Impérial's baptism and its attendant hullabaloo had cost 898,000 francs; that Prince Achille Murat's debts had been paid off twelve times; that Badinguet's old girlfriends had not been financially forgotten.

All these details made excellent copy for the newspapers – forty-eight new ones were published between 4 September and the end of the year, embracing all manner of opinion and character. One of the titles, *Les Nouvelles*, appeared four times daily; another, *Le Moniteur des Citoyennes*, was specifically aimed at women; another, *Le Trac*, at the frankly terrified ('un journal des peureux'); another, *La Réprouve*, at those who felt that the whole business was the fault of miserable sinners.

29 September

Was President Trochu the right leader for such a dark hour? He was not, certainly, an inspiration. Biding his time, privately pessimistic and reluctant to risk lives on dubious military ventures, he had proved stubborn and somewhat unimaginative – Bretons, Sarcey reminds his readers, 'bang nails into walls by using their foreheads like a hammer.' What Paris wanted meanwhile was action: dramatic, immediate, triumphant action. 'If only Monsieur Trochu had guts!' boomed Juliette Adam. 'I don't know why I always picture him to myself with the sanguine expression of a gentleman. People who see and listen to him keep repeating, "He is a very distinguished man". I would prefer that he was an energetic corporal. Being so distinguished has no relevance to the brutal exigencies of an extraordinary situation.'

1 October

Queen Victoria writes from Balmoral to her Foreign Secretary:

The Queen is so glad to see how firmly and *resolutely* Lord Granville refused to be dragged *into* mediation and inference, though it must be very difficult to avoid it.

The Queen feels so very *strongly* the danger *to this country* of giving advice which will not help the *one* party, and may turn the very powerful other party, already much (and unjustly) irritated against us, into an inveterate enemy of England, which would be very dangerous and serious.

She also feels that, if we offer advice, we shall be asked to give promises for eventual action one way or another, which may be very serious for us and drag us into intervention; for we could not say, if we pressed our advice, that we would on no account act.

2 October
Another broadside fired from Victor Hugo's cannon.

Attack Paris, ye Prussians! Blockade it, surround it, bombard it.
Just try.
Meanwhile, winter will draw in.
And France.
Winter – that is to say: snow, frost, rime and ice. France –
that is to say: fire.
Rest assured, Paris will defend itself.
Paris will defend itself furiously.
To the firing line, o citizens!

'When we are starved at home, and chance being riddled by amateurs in arms if we go out to seek meat, when the enemy is not only at the gates but inside them, we really don't require poetry written prose-fashion, and printed in large type,' sighed Felix Whitehurst. 'Still Victor Hugo appeals to sentiment, humanity, and general fraternity! Bosh!'

3 October
The American General Burnside paid a secret (and fruitless) diplomatic visit, passing through the lines of investment. He spoke to Trochu: according to one witness, Wickham Hoffman of the American Legation, the President gave a histrionic performance.

He told us that France had been very wicked, that she had fallen away from the true Catholic faith; that infidelity and scepticism were rampant in the land; that the misfortunes which had come upon her were deserved; that they were visitations for the sins of the people; but that, when they had repented and humbled themselves, he had faith that the punishment would pass from them. He continued in this strain for a full twenty minutes, speaking very eloquently; then pulled out his handkerchief, and saying, 'Excuse my emotion', he wept.

The low thud and distant boom of war reached Paris every morning in counterpoint, its message ominous but meaningless. Reports of the fall of Strasbourg and Toul were officially confirmed, but according to Labouchere, 'many refused to credit the news'.

Some analysis of the military situation from the *Pall Mall Gazette*, as recommended by Queen Victoria:

It is a surprising fact, even after the inconceivable blunders which have led to the practical annihilation of the French armies, that France should be virtually at the mercy of a conqueror who holds possession of barely one-eighth of her territory. The country actually occupied by the Germans is bounded by a line drawn from Strasbourg to Versailles, and another from Versailles to Sedan. Within this narrow strip the French still hold the fortresses of Paris, Metz, Montmédy, Verdun, Thionville, Bitche, and Phalsbourg. The observation, blockade, or siege of these fortresses employ nearly all the forces that have so far been sent into France. There may be plenty of cavalry left to scour the country round Paris as far as Orléans, Rouen, and Amiens, and even further; but a serious occupation of any extensive district is not to be thought of at present. . . . [The German hold on French soil] remains limited to barely one-eighth of the whole extent of France; and yet France, though she will not own it, is virtually conquered. How is this possible?

The main cause is the excessive centralization of all administration in France, and especially of military administration. Up to a very recent time France was divided, for military purposes, into twenty-three districts, each containing, as much as possible, the garrisons composing one division of infantry, along with cavalry and artillery. Between the commanders of these divisions and the Ministry of War there was no intermediate link. These divisions, moreover, were merely administrative, not military organizations.

. . . They were organized for political, not for military ends.

They had no regular staff. They were the very reverse of the Prussian army corps, each of which is permanently organized for war, with its quota of infantry, cavalry, artillery, and engineers, with its military, medical, judicial, and administrative staff ready for a campaign. In France the administrative portion of the army (Intendance and so forth) received their orders, not from the marshal or general in command, but from Paris direct. If under these circumstances Paris becomes paralyzed, if communication with it be cut off, there is no nucleus of organization left in the provinces; they are equally paralyzed, and even more so, inasmuch as the time-honoured dependency of the provinces on Paris and its initiative has by long habit become part and parcel of the national creed, to rebel against which is not merely a crime but a sacrilege.

Next to this chief cause, however, there is another, a secondary one but scarcely less important in this case; which is that, in consequence of the internal historical development of France, her centre is placed in dangerous proximity to her north-eastern frontier.

4 October

The capital's mortality rate began to rise alarmingly. The mean figure of the previous five years for the first week of October had been 754; only days into the siege, it was 1,483. Paris was becoming filthy. Huge piles of ordure and garbage accumulated and festered in each arrondissement, the out-of-city dumps being inaccessible. There was also a decline in the quality of the water supply (following the severing of the aqueducts which brought in fresh flows from the hills, and some inefficient filtering of the Seine). Despite a compulsory vaccination programme, small-pox spread rapidly, chiefly among the refugee peasants. Then there was cholera, and with the cold and damp, fatal pneumonia and bronchitis. 'But those who had the direst sufferings to undergo were not the destitute, for charity took them under its wing,' wrote John O'Shea '. . . nor yet the artisans, for they had their thirty sous a day in the National Guard, when they had nothing else,' but the *petits employés*, those who had been thrown out of small jobs in factories and offices, 'whose fixed salaries had stopped, who were too proud to beg, and had no credit at the restaurant. They did suffer, and terribly, especially during the excessive cold; and they did not complain, but died.' Others lined the boulevards hawking pathetic siege souvenirs, or rucksacks, buttons, belts and scarves, mugs of coffee and evening newspapers to the Garde Nationale.

Ambulances

The charitable impulse amounted, in the view of Dr Nass, to a symptom of siege fever – especially among the middle- and upper-class women who needed some forum to compensate for the loss of peacetime arenas. Displaying an air of self-mortification, through a black woollen or bombazine dress and a chastely swept-back unbraided coiffure, became the most fashionable of poses. The wealthier among them turned their houses into *ambulances* – in effect, improvised temporary hospitals – and waited in keen anticipation to nurse the wounded.

At first, it was all a bit of a joke: there weren't enough victims of the Prussians to go round, and ladies were said to be at loggerheads in the fight to net the better-looking and more romantic ones. Pale and interesting cavalry officers being at a premium, most of them had to make do with drunk or syphilitic members of the Garde Mobile with sore feet and coarse tongues.

Society ambulances of this kind were run by – among many others – Madame la Baronne de Rothschild, in the rue Laffitte; the Duchesse de Galliéna, rue de Varennes; the Comtesse de Bauzuy, Boulevard Malesherbes; the Princesse Troubetskoi, rue Clausel; and the Baronne de Ladoucette, rue de Chaillot. At the Comédie-Française, where the foyers and green room were kitted out with beds, beautiful young actresses such as Madaleine Brohan moved seraphically from one fallen hero to another, wiping the sweat from fallen heroes' brows with cambric handkerchiefs and reciting the more ethereal passages of Byron. Not to be outdone, starlets and courtesans followed suit. Blanche d'Antigny took to a white apron in her splendiferous *hôtel particulier* in the Avenue de Friedland, and offered kisses at five *louis* each to raise funds for medical expenses; Cora Pearl tore up her fine linens to make shrouds.

There was, of course, also a remarkable amount of hard and dedicated work, done in dangerous conditions against a background of appalling suffering. Juliette Adam, for instance, spent many long and shattering days and nights in the vast Palais de l'Industrie, previously an exhibition hall, which combined an ambulance, an administrative centre (for the nascent Red Cross Society among others) and a store for dressings and medicaments. Crossing a room filled with the desperate screams of amputees – some sharp and searingly conscious of the pain, others moaningly delirious – she saw 'Madame X., a woman of the highest reputation at Eugénie's court. She had no make-up on, and was excessively badly dressed. I felt an unconquerable revulsion, and couldn't but ask myself whether certain women of the old official order, whether these rodents of France's honour, whether these lunatics had, as we have, the right to do good?' The answer, in Sarcey's view, was emphatically yes. The spirit of unselfish devotion and generosity rose up in Paris like some miraculously springing fountain. 'Who knows,' he wrote, 'perhaps from this siege will date an era of regeneration for us . . . this war has forced us to face up to many moral faults which we have insufficiently questioned; it is up to us to correct them, and to renew France. The war has also brought forth many fine qualities which we did not suspect in ourselves . . .' Such was the sustaining visionary hope of the intelligentsia during the siege: that from the ashes of the New Babylon would rise some higher moral order, chastened and purified of its materialism and venality.

Yet the legacy of the Second Empire still hung heavily over Paris. In military medicine not least: as the number of casualties expanded, the extent of medical disorganization and incompetence became alarmingly apparent. The contrast with the enemy was marked: the Prussians made wholehearted use of Lister's recent advances in antiseptics (virtually ignored in France, except by scientists such as Pasteur), had four times as many doctors as the French army and (owing to compulsory vaccination) a rate of smallpox infection four times lower. They used properly equipped, purpose-built medical wagons and trains to transport the wounded. They provided every soldier with a sterile first-aid kit and a medical card worn round the neck – both items which could save crucial minutes in an emergency.

French arrangements verged on the chaotic. There was no

centralized monitoring of vacant beds among the many ambulances in Paris or any arrangements for the separate housing of the contagious. The Garde Nationale was used as stretcher-bearers, and many of them behaved little better than marauding thieves. A hopeless variety of farm carts, omnibuses, hackney cabs and other rolling stock took the wounded from the front and frequently finished them off.

If you reached a bed alive, your chances of survival hardly improved. Most of the ambulances were hopelessly insanitary – one of the most notorious, for instance occupied two stories of the Grand Hôtel du Louvre, just below the floor still occupied by the foreign correspondents. The death rate there was something in the region of fifty per cent. Almost every amputation proved fatal as a result of the infections bred by what were known then as 'miasms' in the poorly ventilated atmosphere and heavy drapery and carpets. Walk in perfectly healthy except for a cut finger, they said, and you would be putrid with gangrene within hours.

Your best hope was to be taken to the American Ambulance, established on the Avenue d'Uhrich (formerly the Avenue de l'Impératrice). Drawing on experiments made and knowledge acquired during the Civil War, it represented the last word in medical modernity. Among its founders and planners was Thomas Evans, the imperial dentist who had enabled Eugénie's escape from Paris. Instead of being housed in an existing building, it consisted of a series of tents, interspersed with orange trees and pomegranate bushes: Sarcey compared it to a Swiss mountain village or a child's toytown. Largely staffed by Yankee volunteers, it became the fashionable hub of the American community and its charitably inclined ladies and gentlemen: special mention, please, of the extraordinary services rendered by Mr Joseph K. Riggs, Mr William R. Bowles, the admirable Mrs Conklin, the tireless Dr Swinburne, pioneer of a new method of reforming fractured bone.

Several factors contributed to the success of the American Ambulance – a simple but effective system of under-floor heating and ventilation; the oil-smeared impermeable canvas of which the tents were constructed; the use of antiseptic oakum dressings and warm-water compresses rather than lint; a pharmacy which eschewed lotions and potions in coloured jars with meaningless labels, relying instead on the salubriousness of fresh air and clean water, and the pain-killing effects of quinine and opium; mattresses and pillows filled with naturally antiseptic seaweed; innovatory lavatorial arrangements, including flushing cisterns and wooden seats (which flung the zouaves and peasant Gardes Mobiles into consternation: accustomed to more primitive arrangements, they almost superstitiously refused to use them, preferring the more spontaneous but less hygienic crouch).

Beyond such material improvements came the less tangible benefits of high morale. There were musical recitals and concerts, tourneys of chess and backgammon, an unhygienic tortoise-shell cat, and singing caged birds. The wonders of the American Ambulance's coffee-wagon, used at the Battle of Appomattox but resident in Paris since its appearance at the 1867 Exhibition, also brought joy to the field. This, according to the winged verbosity of Evans, was 'an ingenious arrangement' constructed by Messrs Dunton of Philadelphia on temperance principles. It contained

> enormous coffee-pots, and other reservoirs for tea and soup, with receptacles for sugar and for crockery, and three large boilers for heating water. The whole was set upon wheels and was drawn by two horses; it was provided with a seat for the driver and distributors, and with a fireplace so judiciously contrived beneath the boilers, that the fire, kept alight by the current of air created by the motion of the 'establishment', brought the water to the boiling point, by the time the vehicle reached its destination; when the coffee and tea being placed in their respective receptacles, the welcome brew was ready, in the course of a very few minutes, for distribution among the multitude of eager applicants that never failed to gather around it on its passage.

7 October

Son of an Italian grocer, the firebrand orator and Minister of the Interior Léon Gambetta nervously mounted a balloon, the *Armand-Barbès*, alongside a cargo of a hundred kilogrammes of mail and sixteen carrier pigeons. The plan was that he should make for the delegation of the government which had its headquarters in Tours, beyond the war zone, take over the Ministry of War and rally the provinces to the aid of the capital. He was also instructed by Trochu to discourage the holding of elections, the results of which might weaken the Republic's mandate.

As the balloon rose into the air, piloted by one Monsieur Trichet, Gambetta unfurled a *tricolore*. Four and a half hours later, having narrowly missed Prussian fire, a safe landing was made a hundred kilometres away in the Somme, and Gambetta made his terrestrial way to Tours.

The sixth instalment of the Tuileries papers was published. It showed the complicity of Louis Napoleon's secretary, the Count Bacciochi, in his extramarital affairs and also suggested that the Secret Service had been keeping the Emperor himself under surveillance, opening his private correspondence and documenting his most intimate movements. Some of the smarmy letters the Emperor had received on the publication of his biography of Julius Caesar caused widespread mirth.

A decree announced that slaughtered meat would be proportionally divided between each of the twenty arrondissements. Cards would be issued to all citizens, marking an individual ration of a hundred grams a day. A further order established the regulations for the hygienic slaughter of horses: veterinary inspection would take place Monday, Wednesday and Friday between 8 a.m. and 11 a.m., at the Horse Market.

8 October
From the heights of the Moulin de la Galette, in Montmartre, a revolving electric searchbeam began to cast a nightly watchful light over 3,300 metres of dubious territory.

Lest anyone become too sentimental about the reformed nature of the Parisians, *Le Gaulois* reported a sordid crime:

Since the beginning of the siege of Paris, the nuns of the Hôpital Cochin have distributed daily, to needy persons, milk for the sick and for children.

A woman, living in an adjacent street, presented herself late last Tuesday and demanded her usual ration. The nuns told her that very little milk remained, but that they would nevertheless give her what they could. Then one of them took the little iron canister that she held out with such ill-mannered peremptoriness, returning it to her three-quarters full. The woman started kicking up a row on the grounds that she was in the habit of appearing every day and did not understand why nobody had thought to keep aside her entire ration. She then left, muttering menaces . . .

The next day, on the morning before the crime, she arrived at the normal time, and her anger seemed to have increased . . . Finally, on Thursday, she found her way into a corridor which led to the nuns' office, grabbed a kitchen knife off a table and waited. When the nun had finished her milk distribution and was returning to the office, the woman fell upon her and stabbed her right side. The nun expired yesterday.

At midday, outside the Hôtel de Ville, about four thousand of the Garde Nationale assembled noisily to demand immediate municipal elections. Hostile to Trochu's government, they represented what middle-class Paris thought of, darkly and vaguely, as 'Belleville' – an area occupied by dangerous working-class Reds, one of several arrondissements which were virtually no-go areas to the police. 'Vive la commune!' they shouted, in reference to a form of government which they would conduct themselves. General Tamisier tried to address them, but was shouted down. 'Citizens, there is a voice more eloquent than mine,' he threatened. 'Cannon.' Then there was a counter-demonstration by loyalist battalions of the Garde Nationale, but Trochu remained adamant that force should not be used to disperse the crowd. By 6 p.m. calm was restored, but, as Whitehurst believed, 'it might have been most serious'.

10 October

Labouchere announced to his readers that he had given up believing anything he read in Parisian newspapers. Three times a week a Prussian Prince was killed and an army relieved Metz. A herd of 1,500 oxen, 'impelled by patriotism', had stormed the Prussian lines. A quarter of a million soldiers were marshalled in Rouen and would attack the enemy in Versailles at any moment. 'Is there a contest to test the limits of human credulity?' he asked. Still, it relieved the monotony, as did the flood of siege humour: jokes about cats, jokes about rats being rationed, jokes about deaf old ladies trying to buy train tickets to Nice, jokes about stingy shopkeepers, about Bismarck and Badinguet. The great enemy was boredom.

'Paris, once so gay,' Labouchere continued

> has become as dull as a small German capital. Its inhabitants are not in the depths of despair, but they are thoroughly bored. They are in the position of a company of actors shut up in a theatre night and day, and left to their own devices, without an audience to applaud or to hiss them. 'What do you think they are saying of us in England?' is a question which I am asked not less than a hundred times a day. My interrogator usually goes on to say that it is impossible that the heroism of the population has not elicited the admiration of the world. It seems to me that if Paris submits to a blockade for another month, she will have done her duty by France; but I cannot for the life of me see that as yet she has done anything to entitle her to boast of having set the world an example of valour.

The Women's Club

Although forbidden to purvey their customary programme, the theatres and dancehalls of Paris were not left empty during the siege. Their new tenants were *les clubs rouges*, the Red Clubs, talking-shops for working men which had sprung up ubiquitously since the Republic lifted the last restraints held by the Second Empire. The debates were sometimes anarchically hilarious, sometimes thunder-and-lightning serious, but almost invariably radical in tone. Journalists reported their proceedings in detail: they made irresistible copy.

One particularly interesting episode centres on the attempt of a 'democratic maniac' called Jules Allix, presiding over a *club rouge* at the Trait Gymnasium, to establish a Women's Club. Some of his ideas about social welfare and communal work-rooms were enlightened, but he never stopped talking, and the organizational role of the sex in question seemed confined to that of applauding him. More dubiously, he proposed forming a posse of women who would engage in espionage work armed with the 'Prussian finger': 'a little indiarubber thimble . . . at the end of it is a small sharp tube containing prussic acid. The Prussian approaches; you hold out your hand; you prick him; he falls dead. If several Prussians approach . . . she who has the

Prussic finger pricks them one by one, and remains tranquil and pure, having round her a circle of corpses.'

The meeting on October 9 at which this scene was proposed ended, not surprisingly, in hysteria, but it set people thinking. That day Paris was placarded with posters headed 'Amazons of the Seine' and signed Félix Bélly. He was a visionary character who had won himself notoriety a few years previously when he tried to raise money for a scheme to dig a canal through Panama, and he now announced the formation of this new legion, which would render 'all such domestic and fraternal services as are compatible with moral order and military discipline'. An enlistment bureau in the rue Turbigo was open from 9 a.m. to 5 p.m., and contributions of superfluous jewellery were invited. There was no lack of response. At the bureau, 'the staircase was completely thronged with applicants and their escorts, and one observed that by far the great majority of Amazons presenting themselves for enrolment, were women of a certain age, and evidently accustomed to hard work, often muscular, and not unfrequently over-stout,' wrote the sneering Ernest Vizetelly. 'They appeared principally to consist of *femmes du peuple*, cooks, washerwomen, and such like, with a fair sprinkling of shopwomen and seamstresses, the youngest among them being not less than five-and-twenty.'

Sadly, the police intervened. Such amateur vigilantism was forbidden, and the membership fees that Bélly had exacted from these would-be Amazons were confiscated. But women were not left silent. Most of the *clubs rouges* allowed women speakers and they were vociferous in street demonstrations, notably on the subject of food. The outstanding politicized figure of the era was the schoolteacher Louise Michel, strident and inexhaustible. She led the Women's Vigilance Committee in the working-class area of Montmartre and ensured that although its functions may have been charitable, its mood was belligerent. 'Here in Paris, we breathe an odour of death. Treason is rampant,' she proclaimed. 'We must not let the people sleep. Let us be on our guard.'

13 October

There was an ardour too, an intensity to the Siege. Lovers felt more in love, tears flowed faster. Geneviève Breton, a daughter of the intelligentsia, was passionately engaged to the brilliant young painter Henri Regnault, bravely serving as a sharpshooter. Her diary palpitates agonizingly with the drama of the situation:

> I was deep in meditation when he came in. I have for so long now been in the habit of self-restraint that instead of throwing myself into his arms with a cry of deliverance and joy, I remained sitting motionless and trembling at my little table. And here is another of my sufferings: to feel a beating heart, burnt up and consumed in a cold, awkward envelope which can show nothing of what impels it . . . a few muttered words, my cheeks covered with hot embarrassment . . . behind such wretched and unsatisfactory expressions, what can he perceive?
>
> He went down on his knees before me and gravely recounted his day. He had been to Noisy to find his sharpshooting kit and had not wanted to forewarn me, fearing my fear, wishing to avoid worrying me – my dear and best beloved.

Joans of Arc

Another sort of female fervour was evinced by a series of girls who believed themselves to be the second Joan of Arc. All over France seraphic voices were heard, visions – of the Virgin Mary, of the Maid of Orleans herself – seen. Lucien Nass described some of the victims of these delusions.

> Cathérine Panis, a twenty-year-old hysteric, was in service to a Madame de M. in the town of Saint-Laurent de l'Ain . . . She too had visions: the Virgin appeared to her, a chaplet in one hand, a sword in the other, and said: 'Go to Paris, and deliver France from her enemies.' Her mistress treated her as if she was a lunatic, but to what end? She made her way to Paris, where she arrived on 14 October: she left again having met up with the personages she had a mission to see (orators in the Clubs, doubtless). She crossed the Prussian and French lines, entered Orléans (the obsession with Joan of Arc again), stayed there for three days and ended up running aground at her mistress's with two sous to her name. The most extraordinary fact of this story, recounted by the curé of Saint-

Laurent-de-l'Ain, is that members of the government asked for Catherine's name and address in case they needed to get in touch with her!

Another incarnation of the girl from Lorraine came in the shape of Amélie Seulart, who signed her manifestos simply 'Joan of Arc II'. One of these placards, pasted to a wall in Paris, revealed to the members of the provisional government how France in particular and humanity in general could be saved by Woman:

The flag or banner of Womankind proposed to the French and to other races as a symbol of Universal Brotherhood. The flag of the veritable public and pacific law, one and indivisible, destined to unite all peoples and nations.

GLOBE

Creations of a source of life in the union of two elements one masculine the other feminine

The Future

Earth, paternal side, to man is earthly power — Air, Nature Mother creator of worlds uniting man and woman in the past, present and future in the name of the son the daughter mother of the eternal spirit — Water, maternal side, to woman is spiritual power

father
Equality through the creating mother
No more war

Yes, I am Joan of Arc, the rainbow, the dawn, the Maid come down from the sun of justice so that tyrants may tremble and those of good heart be reassured

—————————

Amélie Seulart, Joan of Arc II

15 October

From Goncourt's *Journal*: 'This evening, in the street, a man strolled in front of me, his hands in his pockets, whistling away almost gaily. Suddenly he stopped and blurted out as if he had just woken up: "My God, things are going badly." '

17 October

Reported by J. Arsac:

The mother of the Gracchi, Cornelia, is not dead! Read this true story.

As she was about to sit down to dine, a fine lady of the Faubourg

Saint-Germain learns of the death of her only son, a simple Mobile, killed by the enemy.

Grief overwhelms her and, her eyes glazing over blankly, she falls inertly into an armchair.

Her servants surround her and do everything they can to bring her round.

Nothing! It was as though she too were dead . . .

Seeing this, an elderly retainer, losing her head, cried out: 'Oh, if only the young sir hadn't been a brave young man who only wanted to fight, if only he'd been a coward, we could still be embracing him now!'

At these words, the mother suddenly recovered herself, her tears ceased to flow, and a noble smile lit up her face: 'Joseph,' she said to a servant. 'Put flowers on the table.'

From the diary of P. Schuler, a Swiss resident of Paris:

It is the anniversary today of the French entry into Berlin, following the Battle of Jena (1806). At this time the present King Wilhelm was aged about ten. Seeing with what tenacity he is now pursuing the destruction of France, one might almost say that the young prince had sworn – as Hannibal once did – everlasting hatred of the enemy.

18 October

The town of Châteaudun in the Eure-et-Loir fell after heroic resistance. Five thousand Prussian soldiers had attacked the peaceful little place at midday; by 9.30 p.m., eighteen hundred of them had been killed, but the town was a blazing ruin.

The town of Châteaudun had done its duty to France. We will remember.

20 October

First published in 1853 but banned under the Second Empire, Victor Hugo's *Les Châtiments* (Chastisements) now appeared in its first French edition. It caused nothing less than a sensation: six thousand lines of diatribe against Louis Napoleon and his regime, a collection of odes, ballads, elegies, satires and reflections, all dedicated to 'the Muse of Indignation', a virulent anti-tribute to the men who had destroyed the Second Republic, full of insult, mockery and rage. Such magnificent fury, such an inexhaustible tirade, was inspirational to Paris – a channel for its besieged emotions which the government's penny-plain exhortations could not provide.

23 October

A sad, damp day described by Jules Claretie:

> As much as it can, Paris grabs and holds on to the little successes which are announced in loud voices at the front door of the town halls: sorties, the more or less significant or useful operations. On Friday Ducrot tried to take Malmaison. He killed a large number of the enemy. That evening, the rumour spread round Paris that we had captured four Prussian cannon and that twelve thousand members of the *Landwehr* found themselves trapped in Gennevilliers. Today Ducrot's report brings us the truth: no defeat, a well-executed reconnaissance, but two lost cannon – and cannon at this point are rare, despite the civic subscriptions and the production lines.
>
> How depressing all this is, and how melancholy one feels at certain times! Yes, the mob is admirable, it is taken hold of by any glimmer of hope and shouts 'Vive la République!' It asks to march, to fight, to die – but when one comes up close to individuals and judges things more calmly: what sadness! And how mediocre all this seems beside the grandeur and horror of the situation!

Claretie then stumbled upon a patriotic march, made by four thousand children:

> . . . little ones, frail ones, fifteen-year-olds, four thousand Republican pupils in blue pantaloons, grey blouses and red belts, all wanting – they too – to march against the enemy. They are armed with the agility and intrepidness of adolescents. Burn hayricks, plunder funeral processions, dig up the dead, uproot potatoes and bring them in, feed those who remain, pick up those who fall . . . this is their role! . . .
>
> Others, the smallest, four, five or six years old, are being exercised in the Palais-Royal, blowing their little trumpets, banging their little drums and manoeuvring their harmless guns like grenadiers with their *chassepots*. Blond heads, pink lips, wearing policemen's helmets or shakos . . . Present arms! Fire! . . .
>
> They are the France of tomorrow, and these little heads will not forget these weighty matters. They will remember. They will do better than we have done.

We can perish. There are those behind those who fall at the hands of men, and they are these children!

24 October
An aurora borealis glowed in the sky, presage of triumph or disaster.

25 October
Between the city ramparts and the Prussian siege lines lay an unholy circle of territory, its diameter varying from one to four miles. A bombed-out, evacuated realm, patrolled by sharp-shooters and inhabited only by peasants who had stubbornly refused to budge. The braver of them foraged in the fields, risking Prussian bullets for the potential profit in a sack of potatoes or a barrow of turnips. Occasionally, Parisians would be allowed out here too, on the pretext of visiting a sick relative or inspecting some abandoned property. There must have been some black-market traffic, some collaborating here too: in *Lettres à un Absent* (Letters to an Absent Friend), Alphonse Daudet tells the sad little story (with more truth in it, doubtless, than most of the maniac spy reports in the newspapers) of a desperate *gamin* who smuggles some newspapers to the enemy in return for a little money. Overcome with remorse, he confesses what he has done. His father proudly takes the money back to the Prussians and is never seen again.

Tommy Bowles accompanied two potato-gathering ladies out to Rueil, 'a little town about as large as Richmond':

> We found in it probably as many as thirty inhabitants. I asked one of them – a poor old fellow, half blind – why he stayed when everybody else had left. 'Why should I go away?' he replied; 'I know the Prussians . . . I was a prisoner among them for six months under the first Napoleon; and then, what can they do to me? I have nothing to lose; I am old and worn out; seventy-nine I am; I cannot see. If I left my cabin I should die on the road, and I may as well be killed here.' Another inhabitant here came up. 'The Prussians,' said he, 'but they are charming, the Prussians – they let us gather our potatoes, and it is all we have to live upon in the winter. They come and walk about the town; two or three pass in this street every day, and then they return home – to La Malmaison. The other night they

came and slept in the barracks because it rained, and in the morning they went away quietly.' 'But why didn't you send and tell your own troops that they were here?' 'Oh, pour ça – ça ne nous regarde pas.' ['That's none of our business'] This is not an uncommon view of things in the surrounding villages. The peasant wants to live and so long as he is allowed to do that, he does not take the least interest in either of the armies that happen to be fighting over his home. . . . The object of our visit was a woman who was said to possess a little store of vegetables, and we stumbled up a ricketty staircase into her garret. She was just serving out to her children the morning soup – made of horse, as she confided to me – which smelt very savoury; but in a minute she produced from under a mattress a heap of potatoes, onions, and lettuces, and plunged into a desperate bargain with the two ladies, which ended in the acquisition of three big sacks of potatoes, wherewith the convoy successfully re-entered Paris.

27 October

Leaving Paris permanently was obviously a more difficult matter, and the only safe passage out of the city through the Prussian lines was that negotiated by the American Legation, which alone maintained diplomatic channels to Bismarck. This was the day which brought the last substantial exodus of the siege. Fifty vehicles containing Britons, Americans and Russians assembled at the Porte de Charenton. Barely forty-eight hours' notice of the *laissez-passer* had been given. At Créteil the cavalcade was met by a party of Prussian officers, punctilious and irreproachably polite, who minutely inspected every signature on every piece of paper. After much shaking of hands and clicking of heels, the carriages were escorted to Versailles and to unoccupied France, thence to Belgium, the northern ports and England.

30 October

'I wonder what has happened in Europe,' asked Felix Whitehurst. 'This makes forty-two days since I have seen an English letter or paper.' In fact, only one important international issue had emerged in the previous six weeks. In defiance of the treaty which had terminated the Crimean War in 1856, the Russians were refortifying the town of Sebastopol on the Black Sea, thus defiantly restating their threat to the independence of neighbouring Turkey.

In Paris, the futile recapture of the village of Le Bourget to the north-east of the city on 27 October – falsely greeted as a turning-point in France's fortunes – was now humiliatingly reversed, at the cost of twelve hundred French lives.

The good news was a relaxation of the regulations forbidding theatrical performance. 'In order not to shock public opinion,' wrote Labouchere drily, 'the programme of their entertainments is exceedingly dull. Thus the Comédie-Française bill of fare for yesterday was a speech, a play of Molière's without costumes, and an ode to liberty. Fancy, for an evening's entertainment, a speech from Mr Cole C.B.; the play of *Hamlet* played in the dresses of the present century; and an ode from Mr Tupper.'

31 October

An unnerving day dominated by what Whitehurst called 'a revolutionette'. It was provoked by a number of circumstances and events: the government's continuing refusal to allow any municipal elections (which would undoubtedly have brought more Reds and socialists to power, undermining the already fragile control of the city); the announcement that Thiers was proposing to negotiate from Tours an armistice on the basis of the cession of Alsace (news that pleased the Stock Exchange, but not Belleville); and the tragic slaughter of the recapture of Le Bourget, followed by confirmation of the rumours that Metz had fallen (Bazaine would later be court-martialled for his surrender, which was considered to border on treachery).

So the Reds exploded, and for twenty-four hours the chances of the government being elbowed out by a radical commune looked real. What happened, in brief, was this. The flamboyant and buccaneering Gustave Flourens – he had fought, Byron-like, against the Turks in Crete – led several of the Belleville battalions of the Garde Nationale to the Hôtel de Ville. He had long wanted, he said, to have 'a very serious talk with our friends in the Government of National Defence' and this was his way of doing so. A huge crowd, drawn from all classes and occupations, gathered round, chanting the run of anti-government slogans, and the loyalist battalions of the Garde Nationale either would not or could not dissipate the tensions. The correspondent of the *Illustrated London News* continued:

After vainly attempting to force the main entrance to the Hôtel de Ville, they at length managed to penetrate into the building by a side door which had been left unguarded. The mob soon thronged most of the apartments, and even invaded that in which the members of the Government were deliberating. Flourens, Félix Pyat, Blanqui, and others proceeded to form themselves into a Committee of Public Safety, naming M. Dorian as their president; and Flourens, mounting the table at which the Government of National Defence were sitting, intimated to them that they were under arrest. The new Committee, having secured the official note-paper, &c., next set to work to issue various decrees, to which, however, no attention at all appears to have been paid. About eight o'clock in the evening General Trochu and M. Jules Ferry were released by the 106th Battalion of National Guards, who broke into the apartment where they were confined; and some six hours later, while the Committee of Public Safety were deliberating as to their course of action, a couple of battalions of Breton Mobiles succeeded in entering the Hôtel de Ville by a subterranean passage from the adjacent barracks. These were soon followed by M. Jules Ferry, with a large number of National Guards, and the Commune party were forced to quit the building. During its occupation by the rioters the damage done to the Hôtel de Ville was enormous – furniture being destroyed, mirrors broken, and pictures injured. In addition to this many articles were stolen, and it is stated that no less than 3400 dinners were served, besides innumerable casks of wine broached.

'The whole affair seems to me to be inconceivably ridiculous,' wrote Tommy Bowles.

An accepted government with all the outward signs and appurtenances of authority is suddenly replaced at its own council-board by a few individuals without striking a blow in self-defence; then these same individuals are ousted in turn, also without striking a blow; and finally they embrace all round. Surely this passes the wildest bounds of burlesque. The day will have taught the Parisians one thing, that the dreaded *spectre rouge* is a very harmless turnip-headed ghost after all . . .

Ridiculous it may have been, but it had repercussions, the all-round embrace proved treacherous, and the *spectre rouge* was not harmless or turnip-headed after all. The crisis had been resolved not by force, but by persuasion, with the government promising immediate municipal elections (on 3 November) and an amnesty for all those participating in the invasion. Then, like the finale of one of Offenbach's operettas, the 3 a.m. exodus from the Hôtel de Ville brought the government leaders to the portals arm in arm with the communards. It was an empty gesture of amity: with a shocking bad faith which caused Juliette Adam's husband, the Prefect of Police, to resign, the government then reneged on its word and arrested twenty-two of the leaders of the fracas, as well as cashiering sixteen commanders of implicated battalions of the Garde Nationale. Such reprisals were at the very least clumsily handled and stupidly provocative.

1 November
From the diary of Raoul B., Garde Nationale:

> O poor and beloved France, today it would need a miracle to lift you from the abyss into which you have so permanently fallen. Today I hope for nothing more, I believe in nothing more on earth except God whose mercy is infinite. May he heed the fervent prayer of a believer that I addressed him in the night! To have suffered so great a fall in barely two months – to fall from such a height – all because of one man to whom our cowardice made us accomplices.

2 November
From the diary of Geneviève Breton:

> 'I hear that Metz is betrayed. Henri, sitting by the fire at Kate's, is doleful, silent, desolate; we feel that misfortune is upon us, that a terrible shame is crushing us. 'Where have you come from, Geneviève, at this hour?' he asked, touching my damp clothes.
> 'From church.'
> 'And you have prayed there: God no longer protects France; he has forgotten us.'
> 'No, it is we who have forgotten him. France wanted to do without God. She abandoned Him and now she cries out that the God she has abandoned, abandons her.'

3 November

The government could not risk holding full elections at such a delicate juncture, so as a sop to the braying of Belleville, it held a plebiscite instead. A vote of confidence was carried by 557,996 votes to 62,638 – a majority of nine to one. Less satisfactory, however, were the elections of arrondissement mayors. Several extremist Reds were returned to office, and they took revolutionary powers upon themselves – one district, for example, refused admission to the police; another instituted compulsory primary education. After the Draconian centralization of the Haussmann era, local town halls became places of real power and decision-making again.

6 November

The popular journalist and pundit Edmond About published a controversial column in *Le Soir*, as Thiers negotiated with Bismarck. We must negotiate, he said. 'We have lost the match. Let us play fair and pay up.'

In fact, Bismarck had refused to negotiate with Thiers, on the grounds that – given the events of 31 October – the government he represented had no real authority to speak for France.

7 November

Edmond de Goncourt in the salon of Victor Hugo:

> In the shadowy light cast on his antique furnishing, on an autumn day darkened by the mouldering colour of the walls stained with cigar smoke, in the midst of this old-world décor in which everything appeared vague and uncertain – things as much as people – Hugo's head stood in bold outline and made a grand impression. His hair is streaked with rebellious white locks, after the manner of the prophets of Michelangelo; on his face hovers a strange placidity, an expression which is almost ecstatic . . .
>
> When I asked him if he was able to find his way round Paris, he replied to me roughly thus: 'Yes, I like Paris as it is now. I would not have wished to see the Bois de Boulogne when it was full of smart carriages. I am pleased that it is now a hole in the ground, a ruin – it has nobility, it has grandeur! But you shouldn't think that I condemn everything that has been done in Paris: the restoration of Notre-Dame and the Sainte-Chapelle is very fine, there are doubtless some

beautiful houses.' When I say that the older inhabitants of the city feel displaced, that we feel Paris has been Americanized, he replied: 'Yes, it is true. Paris is Anglicized – but thank God it doesn't resemble it in two ways: the comparative mildness of our climate and the absence of coal. As for myself, my personal taste, I prefer the old streets . . .' When someone talks of the great arterial boulevards, he says: 'It's true, this government has done nothing to defend the city from outsiders: everything has been done to defend it from its own population.'

According to a subsequent informant of Goncourt, Hugo was at this time also actively appreciative of another long-standing aspect of Paris – its sexual life. Every evening throughout the siege he would make his way to Madame Meurice's respectable lodging-house, where a selection of women of all stations lined up outside his discreetly rented room, ready to be selected to feed his priapic appetite.

9 November

A balloon letter sent by a *bon bourgeois* professor of medicine, Frédéric Desplats, to his wife in Boulogne, soberly summed up the increasingly dismal situation in Paris:

> The weather is cold and damp and that makes us more sad and discouraged. To brighten up my solitude, I have made a fire, using the little wood and coke that I still have. No further developments in our position. A government decree has just mobilized a section of the Garde Nationale, bringing the strength of the fighting army up to 100,000. It embraces men of 25 to 35 either unmarried or widowered, without children; married men without children of 35 to 45, and married men with children of 35 to 48. These measures should have been taken two months ago. It's a little late now, it seems to me. In a few days, General Trochu will make various offensives; the Prussians aren't moving, they hem us in and their only goal is to take us by famine. It is cowardly, this way of fighting, and they have succeeded by sheer weight of numbers and long-term preparation. If the armies in the provinces don't intervene, it is certain that they will further succeed in forcing us to capitulate . . . They dare not or cannot bombard us. I wonder if they are also afraid of antagonizing the neutral powers? The fact is that those powers could have stopped this miserable war if they had wanted to. However, Prussia evidently can only make peace with an established government . . .

Since the Le Bourget business, there has been no fighting. While we wait for our fresh food supplies to run out, nothing is stranger than the aspect of the streets. Everywhere you see cabbages, salad, turnips, potatoes. A cabbage sells for a franc to one franc fifty, potatoes for six francs a bushel, a rabbit for fifteen francs, a chicken for ten francs, there's plenty of dripping – horse and donkey fat which costs two or three francs a pound, and is excellent. In the market, you see cats where you used to see rabbits and they're greatly in demand. A nice bit of donkey costs four francs a pound, butter thirty francs a pound. . . .

The emergence of horse, dog, cat and rat as part of the Parisian diet became a staple of conversation. Edmond Deschaumes, a teenage schoolboy, scribbled the latest excitement in his diary:

At evening class, Digard came back from lunch with one of his uncles at his office in the Hôtel de Ville and told us some amazing news. On the Square in front of the Hôtel de Ville is a rat market. Ordinary ones sell for thirty or forty centimes, fat and fleshy ones go for sixty. At the same time he told us about the lunch menu that his uncle had offered him. It was made up of minced saddle of cat, mayonnaise, and cutlets of dog with petits pois. Digard licked his lips greedily, looked important and declared in an unanswerable fashion: 'I had a slap-up meal of rat cooked in my uncle's restaurant.' He added that *salmi* of rat was also on the menu, and that for dessert he enjoyed a pudding of horse marrow.

This Lucullan cuisine did not, however, seem to agree with our excellent friend. We watched him suddenly turn green, as if his meal had sent him reeling. Little by little he resumed his natural colour and declaimed to us the poem by Théodore de Banville, *Ode to Rats*.

> In a remote corner of the park
> Rats, seated on their rear ends,
> Watch Monsieur de Bismarck
> Under the shade of the trees of Ferrières
>
> With their eyes inflamed with anger
> And their pink tongues hanging out,
> The little black, white and brown rats
> Recite to him in chorus the following:
>
> White cuirassier, what has led you
> To want this extraordinary war?
> Ah! Murderer of Kings –

It's because of you that they're eating us!

But you will pay for this crime:
And because it is you who is killing us,
We will make our way, us little rats,
To Prussia, where our pointed teeth

Will eat into the brick of your towers
And the gates of your fortresses,
More famished than the vultures
Whose wings will beat noisily in the air

Mercier, who is really good at reading out loud and who regularly gets the prize for history, told us that the rats who are saving Paris aren't the first patriotic rats and that the vast legion of Egyptian field mice caused the destruction of Sennacherib's army by gnawing through the straps of the shields and the strings of the bows of the Assyrian soldiers.

10 *November*

A report from Berlin, published in *The Times*:

'Deserters from Paris state that General Trochu is preparing a grand sortie, in order to restore his prestige with the populace. The Germans have constructed fresh batteries on the heights of Raincy, opposite Noisy; and on the heights of Montmagny, opposite St-Denis; and at Bezons, and at Courbevoie.'

And from Brussels:

'A despatch here from Berlin asserts that Paris will not be bombarded, Count Bismarck having acquired the conviction from what transpired during his negotiations with M. Thiers that the French capital has only sufficient provisions for one month, and that it will be certain to capitulate within a brief period.'

'The fact is that we are getting bored,' wrote Tommy Bowles. '*Anything* that lasts two months becomes a nuisance, I don't care what it is.'

11 *November*

A rant of a letter to *The Times* from England's greatest sage, Thomas Carlyle – notoriously Germanophile, Francophobe and slightly dotty and senile. Paris he had always loathed, and he could muster no sympathy for it even now. The siege was 'the hugest and most hideous farce-tragedy ever played under this sun', but it would do France 'a great deal of good . . . a terribly drastic dose of physick . . . and well will it be for her if she can learn her lesson honestly. If she cannot, she will get another, and ever another; learnt the lesson must be.'

He concluded: 'That noble, patient, deep, pious and solid Germany should be at length welded into a nation and become Queen of the Continent, instead of vapouring, vainglorious, gesticulating, quarrelsome, restless and oversensitive France, seems to me the hopefulest public fact that has occurred in my time.'

14 November

Wonderful news! In the evening, a poster hits the placards announcing 'with indescribable joy that a blood-spattered carrier pigeon has brought a report from Gambetta via Tours. 'The Army of the Loire has retaken Orléans after a two-day struggle. Most of the action was concentrated around Coulmiers, on 9 November.'

Strategically, however, this was problematic. Trochu had been planning a massive break-out in a north-west direction. He now had to consider the harder option of moving the operation south-east, in order to join up with the victorious Army of the Loire.

'I know this very odd character who can hardly be unique at the moment,' wrote Louis Moland in a balloon letter.

> He is the man of provisions. The personage of whom I speak has a household consisting of four other people: his wife, two children and a maid. I think that he has amassed enough supplies to feed them for a year. He hoards in every nook and cranny of his home boxes of sardines, boxes of dried meat, boxes of dried vegetables . . . He showed me his provision of sea-biscuits – enough for a voyage of exploration to the North Pole. 'I have fifty kilos of rice,' he told me. 'Fifty kilos!' I exclaimed. 'What do you want to do – exterminate your family?'
>
> 'If I have to, if circumstances become critical, I will be generous to my friends,' he winked. 'And then they won't make fun of me any more.'
>
> I will not mention the piles of chocolate bars, two or three sugar

loaves, the huge pots of Brittany butter, the cases of candles. He has forgotten nothing, he even has a store of bottles of mineral water lest it should become difficult to procure drinking water.

Some chickens get fatter, for, better or worse, in his kitchen. Hams which he doesn't dare touch lie covered in the pantry. Noah's ark can have been scarcely better supplied. I would like to visit his cellar: it must be a curious sight.

16 November

At the frontiers of the siege there was regular official parleying between the French and the Prussians. The Comte d'Hérisson described the way it functioned – with just a hint of complicity between the prisoners and their jailers.

At the end of the bridge of Sèvres which belonged to us, there was a little house half knocked to pieces by shells and riddled with bullets, which was called 'The House of the Flag of Truce'. At the end of the bridge there was a barricade composed of all kinds of things. Before getting over it, we put our horses under cover and the trumpet sounded the cease-fire.

As soon as the trumpeter of the post on the other bank had sounded the German call corresponding to ours, we escaladed the barricade and waved our white flag.

The two calls could be heard a very long way off, for in those regions there reigned in the intervals of firing an extraordinary, solemn, mournful, and almost supernatural silence – the silence of death, that which on earth preceded the appearance of living beings. You might have heard a gnat fly between the advanced sentries posted on both banks, and you might have said that even the Seine, gliding slowly along the desolate landscape, had stilled the murmuring of its waters.

The Prussian officer bearing the flag of truce then advanced along the bridge from his side, as I did at the same time from mine. The middle arch of the bridge no longer existed, it had been blown up by dynamite. We halted on our respective sides of the yawning gulf and entered into conversation. I am bound to confess that my interlocutors were almost always young officers of distinguished bearing, of whom there are so many in the German Army. There are many drawing-rooms where conversation is carried on with less gracefulness than we displayed. We put on new gloves figuratively and in reality to converse.

When everything went on thus it was perfect, and I bore with a good grace the genial *badinage* to which I was treated by a sort of adjutant who commanded the advanced post of Sèvres, and who, as soon as he saw me, sent a mounted orderly to apprise the Prussian officer told off for the duty of parleying, whose quarters were away from the banks of the river.

These jokes lacked variety, and in the end they were reduced to one, always the same.

The animal took a few paces along the bridge and called out in German.

'Good morning, captain. You are thinner than you were when I saw you last.'

As I did not see any use in altering my formula so long as he did not change his, I invariably replied,

'I am in training and on strict diet.'

The fair idiot would reply,

'You have nothing to eat when you are hungry.'

To which I always answered,

'If you want anything do not distress yourself about it. You know the proverb – "Where there is enough for—" '

19 November

A horrible massacre of innocents near the village of Bondy. About sixty impoverished men, women and children foraging for food were shot dead – some of them by French crossfire. The incident was kept as quiet as possible.

Pigeon Post
From the *Illustrated London News*:

Notice has been received at the English Post Office that a special despatch to Paris by means of carrier pigeons has been established at Tours, and that such despatch may be made use of for letters originating in the United Kingdom and forwarded by post to Tours. Every letter must be posted without any cover or envelope, and without any seal, and it must be registered. No letter must consist of more than twenty words, including the address and signature of the sender; but the name of the addressee, the place of his abode, and the name of the sender – although composed of more than one word – will each be counted as one word only. No figures must be used; the number of the house of the addressee must be given in words. Combined words joined together by hyphens or apostrophes will be counted according to the number of words making up the combined word. The letters must be written entirely in French, in clear, intelligible language. They must relate solely to private affairs, and no political allusion or reference to the war will be permitted. The charge for these letters will be 5d. for every word, and this charge must be prepaid, in addition to the postage of 6d. for a single registered letter addressed to France. It is notified that no guarantee can be given of safe delivery.

There is something deeply touching and even sublime about the role played by carrier pigeons during the siege – they are its unwitting heroes, honoured by a law protecting their entire kind from being shot for human consumption (a law impossible to enforce, but, it appears, widely upheld). They were of two categories: departure and arrival pigeons. The former, numbering 1,100, belonged to societies in the north-eastern industrial towns of Roubaix, Tourcoing and Laval. 'Confided by their owners to the Mayor of Paris shortly before the investment,' writes Ernest Vizetelly, 'they were lodged at the Jardin des Plantes

until required from time to time to carry out despatches to the north or west. Usually ten copies of each despatch were remitted to M. Casimir Derode, who had charge of the birds, and were fastened, under his superintendence, to one of the tail feathers of as many pigeons as there were messages to send out.

The arrival pigeons – those which were despatched with the balloons to bring back word of their safe descent, together with news from the provinces – were principally furnished by MM. Vanrosbeck and Deronard, of the Société de l'Espérance, and by MM. Cassier, Trichet, Noblécourt, Laurent, Goyet, and others. M. Cassier's dovecote, situated at Batignolles, in the centre of a somewhat carelessly ordered garden, was faced by a little pavilion, which the Post Office agent, charged to signalize the pigeons' return, used as his look-out station. On its arrival the pigeon entered its house by an opening in the roof, which, while allowing the bird to enter, did not permit its egress. A glance enabled the proprietor to detect the particular pigeon which had returned, as it was usually very fatigued, and would at once seek its habitual place in the dovecote it had quitted a few days previously. Not unfrequently the pigeon was found to have been wounded, either by some bird of prey or by shots from a German rifle. The season being, however, altogether unfavourable to these feathered travellers – as the autumnal mists obscured their sight, and the cold paralyzed their strength – far more lost their way on the road than fell victims to the enemy's projectiles.

La Presse's moving account of the arrival of a pigeon in the dovecote, empty-feathered and exhausted:

> Weak, emaciated, famished, it fell like a stone on to the shelf which surrounded the dovecote; . . . It arrived, like the runner from the Battle of Marathon, dying, losing blood and gathering in a supreme effort all of its energy and fidelity. Its master, who had been watching its hesitating flight through the sky for ten minutes, had recognized it: he reached out his arms and took it gently, poor exhausted bird, in his cupped hands, and kissed it as if it had been a sick child. . . . Did the pigeon understand this paternal caress? Did it even recognise its master? I do not know – but it turned its round head with a gentle, stroking motion; its mouth half-open, it lay in the man's hands as if fainting with lassitude and joy; it felt itself to be safe, and it rested trustingly in the cupped hands of he who had seen it born and grow.

The quills attached to the pigeon's feathers contained several thin sheets of collodion. Unrolled and magnified via a magic lantern projector, these contained as many as 100,000 words of official dispatches and private correspondence, reduced by a primitive form of microphotography pioneered for the Exhibition of 1867. The equipment and personnel necessary for the processing had been flown out of Paris by balloon on 12 November. Although a near-fatal accident involving some burst bags of ballast forced the crew to jettison some crucial items, the unit eventually reached Tours, where a centre of operations was established. Of all the technological advances employed in the Franco-Prussian war, this is perhaps the most remarkable.

20 November

One of the great popular heroes of the siege was Ignace Hoff, a Sergeant in the 107th Regiment. Compared to (and probably confused with) the trappers of Fenimore Cooper's novels – Hawkeye, Leatherstocking, the cunning of the Sioux and Mohican – he was said to have killed forty-nine Prussians, in an independent fashion. 'Hoff had been known to dig a hole silently during the darkness,' O'Shea writes, 'and ensconcing himself there like a fox in his covert, to wait the livelong day till he got an opportunity at nightfall to creep out stealthily behind a sentry, flash a knife into his ribs, and while a horrid gurgle in the throat proclaimed another dead man, get back on all-fours to his comrades, chuckling and elated. I only wonder he did not scalp those he killed.' His motivation, according to one journalist, was the death of his old father at the hands of a Prussian.

22 November

A young Englishman, Edwin Child, employed by a smart Parisian jeweller's but now keenly doing his bit in the Garde Nationale, wrote home:

> Dear Mother,
> Being a filthy wet day and my boots having fallen unfortunately the worse for wear, I thought it a splendid opportunity to let you know I am in the land of the living, althou' I look upon my trouble as almost wasted, the 3d. for the stamp included, as I more than doubt if these epistles ever reach you. This system of writing through the air may be very poetical but it is far from assuring. If by chance you receive this, send William or Alfred to see Gladstone and tell him if peace is not enforced before Xmas, I'll spoil his breadbasket to use a pugilistic expression. Fancy rats, wine and bread for a Christmas dinner. It's barbarous. Happily there is an enormous supply of tobacco so that there is little suffering as yet.

23 November

Nor was there ever any shortage of alcohol during the siege – in fact, it seemed as though some secret spring of the stuff had suddenly been tapped, so endemic did drunkenness become, especially among the murkier battalions of the Garde Nationale.

And when they weren't drunk, they were merely feckless. In his old age, the novelist Anatole France reminisced about his days in the ranks of one such outfit.

> The commander of our battalion was a fat local grocer. He commanded no authority, I have to say, because he sought to keep his customers happy.
>
> One day, we received the order to participate in a sortie. They sent us to the banks of the Marne. Our commander looked splendid in a brand-new uniform which didn't suit him. He mounted a charming little Arab horse which he'd procured from somewhere or other and of which he was very proud – a little white horse, adorably graceful

and frisky. Too frisky in fact – that was the ruin of the poor grocer. As he was prancing about with the creature, it reared up high, fell on its back and killed our commander, by crushing his kidneys.

We weren't terribly sorry about this. We took the opportunity to stop, break rank and stretch out on the grass. We remained lying there all morning, then all afternoon. In the distance, the artillery thundered . . .

Towards evening, on the road which overlooked the river bank, we saw some sailors running. Many of them were blackened with powder. The wounded wore bloody bandages. These fine fellows had fought hard, but they had yielded to ill-fortune.

What was our clever notion? We started shouting: 'Long live the navy!' This exclamation, which the sailors deemed ironic, had the effect of incensing them. Some of them rushed down at us, brandishing their bayonets. That looked dangerous. We hurried off the grassy slopes and made for the flat. As we had had a good rest and the pursuers were exhausted, we escaped without difficulty.

We arrived back in Paris. But our long period of idleness weighed down on us and we were extremely hungry. So we felt no scruples about pillaging a bakery which we encountered *en route*. Happily, the proprietors had time to slip away. And we weren't murderers.

That was the way we carried on. I'm not boasting about it, I really am not. But I like the truth . . .

24 November

The American Ambassador Elihu Washburne celebrated Thanksgiving:

Visions of beef-steak, broiled chickens, hot rolls and waffles for breakfast; roast beef rare, turkey and cranberry sauce, roast goose and apple sauce, plum pudding, mince pie, pumpkin pie and Livermore cheese for dinner; but not as bad perhaps as it might be; we make the best of the cruel situation. Our thoughts go out warmly to the great unbesieged world. A few gather at the Episcopal Church at eleven o'clock; . . . Dr. Johnston, Dr. Swinburne, Mr. Curtis, and also many ladies present. The Episcopal service is read and the pastor makes a little address. Returned to the legation at noon; always something to do, which is a blessing. The people here who have nothing to occupy themselves with are perfectly desperate. A Thanksgiving dinner at a restaurant on the Boulevard des Italiens given by two of our American gentlemen. Quite a little table full and all quite jolly; but the portion of turkey to each guest is painfully small. Toasts, little speeches, till half past ten, when the guests retired, most of them to go to a little Thanksgiving party given by one of our compatriots.

25 November

The mortality rate continued to rise alarmingly. Figures for the previous week show 2,064 deaths, as opposed to a mean five-year average of 780.

One sector of the population to be appallingly hit was the remaining German community in the city. Before the war, Germans had provided a plentiful source of cheap labour, especially in the catering trades. Most of them had returned to their homeland at the outbreak of hostilities, but those who stayed were not eligible for rations or benefits. They were left to the mercy of charity, which only the American Legation felt like providing. 'The poor Germans keep coming more and more, starved like woodchucks out of their holes,' Washburne wrote. 'A poor Prussian woman, Mrs Schultze, who gave birth to a child a week ago, died three days since, leaving six little children; but a good old Huguenot minister and his good old Huguenot wife, God bless them, have found them out and will have them cared for. The fifty-franc note I had sent the poor woman was found in a little box in a drawer after her death, where she had carefully laid it away.'

Poverty and disease were compounded by the breakdown of the city's sanitary arrangements. Ironically, the collection and disposal of sewage was another profession staffed by Germans, and in its absence Paris stank. Dumps of human and animal excrement lay ignored in the streets. The closing of public laundries and the shortage of soap increased the squalor. The decline in the quality and amount of filtered drinking water favoured the spread of cholera, while smallpox raged unabated through the helpless refugee peasantry, packed with no conception of urban hygiene or vaccination into garrets, hovels and alleyways.

26 November

A charity soirée in aid of the ambulances was held in the salon of that celebrated man-about-town, occasional essayist and theatrical jack-of-all-trades Arsène Houssaye. After an overture played by the small orchestra and the recitation of an ode to Charity, written by Monsieur Houssaye himself, there followed a long and varied programme of verse, drama, and music, including duets from *Rigoletto* and *Il Trovatore*. In the interval, refreshments were served, at a price. A cup of chocolate cost twenty-five francs; a glass of Château d'Yquem 1861, twenty francs; a little *foie gras* on a bread roll, five francs; tea, punch or *vin ordinaire* twenty-five centimes. A glittering audience of glamorous personages paid twenty francs each for admission. The conversation, reported *Le Gaulois*, was 'not exactly bois-terous', but everyone made an effort, with every handshake, every smile bespeaking one word 'Courage!'

It sounds a good deal jollier than the matinées at the Comédie-Française – reams of blank verse and extracts from the tragic drama for which 'the actresses wore morning dress, and the actors the tail-coat and white kid-gloves of society, the effect of which', complained Tommy Bowles, 'was extremely depressing.' *The Athenaeum*'s correspondent agreed – it was as though everything was deliberately made 'as severely disagree-able as possible – recitations were to be unaccompanied by scenery or orchestra, and were to be as dull as they could be made; add to this an icy-cold house . . . and no more light than was absolutely necessary' and you wonder why they bothered. 'But poor Paris hankered after a change of ideas, and longed to drown, if only for a moment, the memory of ever-present sorrow. The theatre once opened was besieged: pale rhapsodies of Corneille and Racine were applauded to the echo; the audience, usually so fastidious and intolerant of trifling defects, sat patiently through endless "stage-waits" . . . it hailed the bombastic emptiness of the *Cid* with acclamation, and laughed and wept by turns over the lugubrious strophes of the *Châtiments*.' (It was wryly noted that many of the actors and actresses who had been most obsequious before Louis Napoleon and Eugénie were now only too happy to declaim violently republican verse excoriating them.)

In his little book of observational essays Gautier described an auditorium in which the lamps burned at only a fraction of their normal power. This duskiness flattered the stage and the actors . . . the audience came to see, not to be seen. There were relatively few ladies and their austere outfits, in black or grey, had no need of glittering illumination. The men, for the most part, hadn't bothered to take off their National Guard uniform. Hats were few, kepis numerous. The auditorium, you might say, felt something like a military camp. On the apron stage, in what was once the Imperial Box, convalescent wounded from the ambulance [housed in the theatre foyer and Green Room] watched the play – and all eyes turned on them with tender interest. There were arms in slings, hands and heads wrapped in bandages; but what commanded most attention was a young fellow, his face covered by a large strip of cloth – he looked like one of the Tuareg in the Sahara, veiled up to their eyes . . . in one of his nostrils was a bullet which, so they said, could not be removed – it didn't stop him from being very attentive to the tears of Andromache and the passions of Hermione.

At the Opéra, the same atmosphere prevailed through morally uplifting concerts of serious music (much of it Germanic and Beethovenian). *The Athenaeum* records the 'graveyard chill' of the place: 'every instrument seemed to have a frozen echo, and a perfect cloud of steam issued from the mouths of the chorus as they rose and commenced to sing'.

Some of the most vivid performances in besieged Paris were to be found in the churches, where priests gave fund-raising sermons. 'I have never heard anything so brilliant in my life,' gasped Albert Vandam, at the Abbé Duquesnay's effort.

Not the slightest attempt at thrusting religion down one's throat. A good many quotations on the advantages of well-doing, notably that of Shakespeare, admirably translated, probably by the speaker himself. Then the following to wind up with: 'I do not know of a single curmudgeon who has ever been converted into what I should call "a genuine alms-giver", by myself, or by my fellow-priests. When he did give, he looked upon the gift as a loan to the Lord in virtue of that gospel precept which you all know. Now, my good friends, allow me to give you my view of that sentence: God is just, and no doubt He will repay the loan with interest, but after He has settled the account, He will indict the lender before the Highest tribunal for usury. Consequently, if you have an idea of placing your money in that way with God as a security, you had better keep it in your purses.'

All very well – but this, like every other public entertainment was stiflingly genteel and depressingly high-toned. For those with less exalted tastes, for those who just wanted some light relief, nothing was provided or even permitted. Without a circus, without dancing or popular tunes, it is hardly surprising that so much of the working class turned to drink for solace.

27 November

Gustave Flaubert, in Croisset, near Rouen, wrote to his dear old friend and ardent republican George Sand in Nohant:

> I am dying of shame. It's the truth. Consolation only irritates me. What really distresses me is 1, men's ferocity; and 2, my conviction that we are about to enter into an era of stupidity. It will be utilitarian, military, American and Catholic. Very much Catholic! Just you wait! The war with Prussia has completed the French Revolution, and destroyed it.
>
> But supposing we win, you retort! Such a hypothesis is contrary to all historical precedent. When has the South ever beaten down the North, or Catholics dominated Protestants? The Latin race is dying. France is about to follow Spain and Italy. And the rule of the boor begins!
>
> What a come-down! What a collapse! What misery! What abominations! Can one go on believing in progress and civilization, when all this is going on? What use is Science, since these people, full of scholars, commit abominations worthy of the Huns! And worse than theirs! For they are systematic, cold-blooded, and self-conscious, without the excuse of either passion or hunger. . . .
>
> There is no shortage of cliché: 'France will rise again! Never despair, it's a salutary punishment, we really were too immoral etc.' What everlasting nonsense. One does not recover from a blow such as this.

29 November

The beginning of the long-awaited *grande sortie* – Trochu's attempt to break out of the siege through the south-east of the city and thence to join up with Gambetta and the Army of the Loire. Despite the secrecy surrounding the operation, the tension inside Paris had mounted feverishly as vast numbers of soldiers were marshalled and egress from the city gates was forbidden to all civilians. 'Pale, we reach the sublime cliff-face,' wrote Victor Hugo, 'and kick the plank into the void.'

On the morning of 29 November, placards tersely proclaimed the beginning of a new initiative in the campaign. 'I shall only re-enter Paris dead or victorious,' they quoted General Ducrot, who was to throw pontoons over the Marne, establish bridge-heads and lead one hundred thousand soldiers across into enemy-controlled territory. Owing to rain-swollen tides and other miscalculations, this did not proceed according to plan. Many of those who made it over were pummelled by enemy fire and the casualties were appalling. The action would continue for several days, and Paris was issued with only the briefest of reports on its progress. As, for example, at 9 p.m. on that day: 'The object the Governor had in view has been attained.' In other words . . .

30 November

Eugénie had ended up with the Prince Impérial, leasing for a modest £300 per annum a house called Camden Place, in the Kent village of Chislehurst, about ten miles from central London, and by chance the former home of an early *amour* of Louis Napoleon. 'When I am free, I should like to . . . live with you and Louis in a little cottage with bow windows and creeper,' he wrote to his wife wistfully from house arrest in Wilhelmshöhe (Camden Place, today maintained as a golf clubhouse, is rather grander than that).

That morning, Queen Victoria visited Chislehurst. She did not much care for Eugénie, but the entry in her journal shows her prepared to be civilly sympathetic to her plight.

At the door stood the poor Empress, in black, the Prince Imperial, and, a little behind, the Ladies and Gentlemen. The Empress at once led me through a sort of corridor or vestibule and an ante-room into a drawing-room with a bow window. Everything was like a French house and many pretty things about. The Empress and Prince Imperial alone came in, and she asked me to sit down near her on the sofa. She looks very thin and pale, but still very handsome. There is an expression of deep sadness in her face, and she frequently had tears in her eyes. She was dressed in the plainest possible way, without any jewels or ornaments, and her hair simply done, in a net, at the back. She showed the greatest tact in avoiding everything which might be awkward, and enquired after Vicky and Alice, asked if I had had any news, saying, 'Oh! si seulement l'on pouvait avoir la paix.' ['If we could only have peace!'] Then she said how much had happened since we had met at Paris and that she could not forget the dreadful impressions of her departure from there. She had remained as long as she could, but once General Trochu had allowed the Chambers to be taken possession of by the populace, there was nothing to be done but to go away. The garden had been already full of people who were entering the Tuileries, and there had been no troops to resist them. The night before she had lain down fully dressed, on her bed. The crossing had been fearful. Afterwards she talked of other things. The Prince Imperial is a nice little boy, but rather short and stumpy. His eyes are rather like those of his mother, but otherwise I think him more like the Emperor.

Paris, 4 p.m.

The Governor of Paris has been at the head of his troops since the day before yesterday.

The army of General Ducrot been crossing the Marne since morning, using pontoons the fixing of which was delayed by a sudden and unforeseen swelling of the river.

The action continues over a huge perimeter . . .

This great operation, developing on a large scale, cannot without imperilling security at such a moment be further explained in detail.

Paris, 5 p.m.

There has been brisk action on several fronts.

The conduct of the troops has been admirable. They have reached their positions with tremendous energy.

All divisions of General Ducrot's army have crossed the Marne and have occupied the posts assigned to them.

The heart of the engagement is at Coeuilly and Villiers-sur-Marne. The battle continues.

'This evening,' wrote a palpitating Juliette Adam: 'we had another piece of excellent news. M. Albert Liouville told us that he had read in an English newspaper how our fleet, composed of several ships, of which the *Victorious* was one, has captured the entire Prussian fleet. Albert Liouville went to take the newspaper to M. Dompierre d'Hornoy, the minister, who was overcome with wild joy and cried out with an exaltation that still moves M.

Albert Liouville: "If this news is true, it is the greatest feat of battle this century." '

1 *December*

An important organ of radical thought in Britain, the *Fortnightly Review*, publishes a powerful essay symptomatic of a turn in informed public opinion about the war. Entitled 'Bismarckism', it was written by Frederic Harrison, the Positivist philosopher and liberal journalist, and it takes a prophetically long view of the situation free of preconceptions or sentimentality. He had no time for French puffed-upness – 'Frenchmen have given utterance to much unwarrantable language about the "sacredness of French soil", "Paris the city of the world"; the peculiar and special sanctity of a republic and the enormity of assaulting Paris. Count Bismarck never said a truer word than this, that the honour of France is of precisely the same quality as the honour of other nations . . . To bombard Paris is no greater outrage than it would be to bombard London' – but he had no time for the Carlylean picture of 'noble, patient, deep, pious and solid Germany' either. Sick of 'the schoolboy view of the war', he sought to take 'the political view . . . a question like this is not a law-suit, nor is it a personal quarrel. It concerns the future well-being of Europe.'

He went on to emphasize the uniquely militaristic nature of the Prussian monarchy, pointing out that its history, its traditions, its ideals are simply those of war . . . the whole state organization from top to bottom is military . . . the only European state organized on a military basis as completely as any State of antiquity.' In the last generation, he reminded his readers, Prussia had fought 'two wars of conquest against Denmark; a war of conquest against Southern Germany; bullying Switzerland; bullying Holland; oppression in Slesvik; oppression in Posen; oppression in Hanover, Saxony, Frankfurt, Hamburg'. We have heard plenty about French chauvinism, he adds, but 'we never hear of the chauvinism of Prussia'. The Germans, in his view, 'are now carrying on war with inhuman cruelty', while 'thanking God for his mercy by platoons'.

What has come over the English mind that it acquiesces so calmly in the sanguinary acts of this war? The Germans have not exactly pillaged. 'The wise "require" it call.' But they have stripped one-third of France utterly to the bone. The ransacking of the villager's home, seizing his cattle, and 'requiring' his daily bread and the seed of his land, may be strictly according to the rules of war; but it is still inhuman cruelty. It deliberately reduces him to starvation. The bombarding the civil portion of cities may be a right of war, but it is still inhuman cruelty. The burning of towns and villages wholesale – twenty we were glibly told of in one telegram from Berlin – may be a military necessity, but it is inhuman cruelty. Plundering citizens by threat of instant death, the placing them on the engines, the massacre in cold blood of irregular troops, and still more of villages suspected of aiding them, may be a mere measure of self-defence; but I call it inhuman cruelty. It is the murder of non-combatants or prisoners – and therefore terrorism.

What Harrison feared was 'the passing of the undisputed supremacy of force to such a power as Prussia . . . more unscrupulous and ambitious than Napoleonism itself'. This power, he believed, must be checked 'by diplomacy if possible; but by arms if necessary . . . in the highest interests of European peace and progress'.

He turns to France, and pays tribute: 'It is the fashion to sneer at her efforts, to deny her courage, and to undervalue her resources. For my part, in spite of wild speeches and divided counsels, I call the resolute front of her actual rulers heroic. . . . I call the willingness of Frenchmen to bear every extremity rather than a dishonourable peace heroic. And above all, I call the defence of Paris, the unity of its multiform population, and the resolve of its attitude heroic.'

He hopes, finally, as did so many moralists, that 'all that France loses in material ascendancy in Europe, she will gain in moral ascendancy'.

2 December

The fighting continued in and out of dense woodland, the French having achieved nothing of substance. The previous day a short truce had been agreed and the battlefields cleared of casualties. Following a vicious renewal of the attack this morning, the French were routed near the village of Champigny. Paris read only the good news – which between the lines was no such thing.

The painter Edouard Manet took part in the fighting today as a lieutenant in the Garde Nationale. 'What a racket!' he wrote to his wife Suzanne. 'However, it was all over very quickly. Shells passed over our heads from all sides. The result was satisfactory, according to this morning's proclamation made by Trochu.'

Anatole France had an even blander version of the day's events. He and his friend Fernand Calmettes, manning the Fort de la Faisanderie, read Virgil's pastoral *Eclogues*, to the counterpoint of shells and havoc. 'While on the horizon of the grey and devastated countryside Prussian batteries trailed white smoke over the hills, we two, sitting on the bank, a stack of guns beside us, our brows leant over a copy of Bliss's edition of Virgil (which I still own and cherish), exchanged views on the golden world which the poet's delicious imagination had created.'

3 December

At dawn, Ducrot ordered his army to cross back over the Marne. The church of the Trinité was overnight converted into an ambulance capable of receiving up to seven hundred wounded. A notable British resident of Paris, Richard Wallace, the natural son of the extremely rich and unpleasant Lord Hertford, had recently inherited from his father a fortune and a beautiful house, the Bagatelle, in the Bois de Boulogne. In one of many enormously generous gifts made to Paris during the siege, he donated 200,000 francs towards providing fuel for the poor. It was a timely gesture: the temperature was below zero and sinking.

4 December

MILITARY REPORT

Enemy losses have been so large during the glorious days of 29 and 30 November and 2 December that, for the first time since the beginning of the campaign, beaten down in its power and pride, it yielded a river – in its presence, in the clear light of day – to an army which the day before yesterday it had attacked with terrible violence.

This, it must be emphasized, is something unique in the war of 1870 – a blessing on the efforts of any army which did not exist two months ago. It can be explained by the patriotism of the elements which compose it and by the strength which the population of Paris has, through its support, inspired in all defenders of the capital.

The army, reunited at present out of the range of attack, draws fresh powers from a brief rest which it had the right to expect from its commanders after such exhausting combat. Some battalions will be replaced, and with the utmost energy we will proceed to restructure certain parts of our organization. The Governor of Paris, Trochu, remains at the head of his troops, ready to supply all requisite needs. General Ducrot addressed the troops of the Second Army thus:

Vincennes, 4 December 1870
Soldiers!
After two days of glorious combat, I have led you back over the Marne, because I was convinced that fresh efforts, in a direction in which the enemy will have had time to concentrate its forces and prepare its tactics would be futile.

Had I continued on that course, I would have sacrificed thousands of noble lives uselessly. Far from serving the cause of our deliverance, I would have compromised it severely, even to the point of leading you to irreparable disaster.

However, as you will understand, the struggle is only suspended for a moment; we shall resume it with resolution: so be prepared, restock your munitions and supplies with all haste – and above all lift up your hearts to the supreme sacrifice which the holy cause, for which we do not hesitate to give our lives, demands.

The General in command of the Second Army
A. DUCROT

Juliette Adam: 'Our troops have passed back over the Marne and are camping in the Bois de Vincennes. Why? They tell us that it's less cold in Vincennes than in Champigny. But have we stopped fighting? If so, are we going to allow the Prussians to recapture the little bits of territory that we recovered with such effort, at such a price, with so much blood spilled, so much sacrifice? I lack the courage to believe this.'

5 December
Mean temperature, for the second day running, of less than $-3°C$. Casualties flooded back into Paris from the front, filling

every available ambulance, and there was no further gloss that could be applied by the propagandists to their reports on an operation which had basically failed to break through the investment and cost 12,000 French lives. As if to rub salt into the wounds, Trochu received the following icily proper letter from Field Marshal von Moltke.

> Versailles, 5 December
> It may be useful to inform Your Excellency that the Army of the Loire was yesterday defeated near Orléans, and that this town was occupied by German troops. If however Your Excellency sees fit to convince himself of this fact through one of his own officers, I should be happy to furnish him with a safe conduct for his passage.
>   Accept, dear General, the expression of the high consideration with which I have the honour to be your humble and obedient servant,
> Chief of Staff, Count von Moltke.

Unlike the recent news of the capture of the Prussian fleet, this was all too horribly true. Gambetta had received news of the sortie too late to act upon it rationally (the balloon in which it was posted had drifted as far as Norway, in what was probably the longest-ever such manned flight) and had been confused by one of the dispatches' reference to the capture of Epinay. Believing this to be the town south of Orly, he assumed that the sortie had succeeded, and that Parisian troops had finally broken through the Prussian lines. The Army of the Loire rushed to join up with them. Unfortunately, the Epinay referred to was Epinay-sur-Seine, an insignificant village in the northern suburbs. An inexorable line of Prussians drove Gambetta back, forcing him to evacuate to Orléans and retreat to Bordeaux, which now replaced Tours as the centre of the Provisional Government.

6 December
Trochu replied to von Moltke thus:

> Your Excellency has seen fit to inform me that the Army of the Loire was defeated near Orléans, and that this town has been reoccupied by German troops. I have the honour to acknowledge receipt of this

communication, which I do not believe I can verify by the means suggested by Your Excellency.

Accept, etc.   The Governor of Paris, General Trochu

7 December

Thick snow. No pigeons homed for the last three days.

The Central Commission of Public Hygiene announced that the whiteness of bread is no sign of its excellence. In fact, much of the goodness is removed by the refining process, and the citizens of Paris should be assured that the rougher, browner bread is more nutritious than the gentler varieties. The more cynical newspaper columnists chuckle grimly at this fortuitously timed scientific discovery.

The question of food – of the extent to which Paris could be kept healthily victualled – was becoming ever more real and urgent. To date, the eating of rats and cats had been something of a joke, at least to the middle classes, and the consumption of the flesh of more exotic creatures a matter of bravado rather than necessity. Supplies could be supplemented by improvised market gardening (Albert Vandam's cunning Algerian man-servant also ran a nice line in breeding rabbits in a stable) and some form of fresh vegetable could always be obtained at a price. Everybody hoarded: Vandam noticed the way that at the slightest rumour of peace, empty shop windows became 'filled with artistically arranged pyramids of canned provisions, at prices considerably below those charged twenty-four hours before, and even below those mentioned in the municipal tariff' – a phenomenon which continued to the very end of the siege. But with the advent of the freezing weather and this first hint that the supply of bread might not be infinite and inexhaustible, the threat of famine edged closer.

One crucial mistake in the planning before the siege (which in many ways had been excellent) was to underestimate the numbers of milch-cows required: this led to an early and serious shortfall of milk for babies as well as of every other kind of dairy produce. Obviously fresh fish, beef, lamb, pork and game were soon at a premium – by December they had virtually vanished – but monotony was not a major problem: Vandam noted the sudden passion developed by cooks for what I must be permitted to call culinary literature. As a rule, the French cordon bleu, and even her less accomplished sisters, do not go for their recipes to cookery books; theirs is knowledge gained from actual experience: but at that period such works as *Le Livre de Cuisine de Mademoiselle Marguerite*, *La Cuisinière Pratique* etc. were to be found on every kitchen table. The cooks had simply taken to them in despair, not believing a single word of their contents, but on the chance of finding a hint that might lend itself to the provisions at their disposal.

Ingenuity and the breaking-down of prejudices were the key qualities. A friend of Vandam's gave him a lavish dinner which included a dish of 'sweet macaroni' with a meat sauce made of field mice – tasting it blind, Vandam thought them to be larks. 'Our vaunted superiority as cooks is so much humbug,' the friend lectured him.

The dish of cod I gave you, and which you liked so much, may be seen on the table of the poorest household in Holland and Flanders at least once, sometimes twice, a week, especially in North-Brabant, where the good Catholics scarcely ever eat anything else on Fridays. The sauce, which they call a mustard-sauce, would naturally be better if made with butter, but you could not taste the difference if the cook takes care to sprinkle a little saffron in her fat or marrow. Saffron is a great thing in cooking, and still our best chefs know little or nothing about it. But for the saffron, you would have detected a slight odour of musk in the entrée you took to be larks. You may almost disguise anything with saffron, except dog's-flesh. Listen to what I tell you, and in a month or so, perhaps before, you'll admit the truth of my words. The moment horseflesh fails, the Parisians will fall back upon dogs, turning up their noses at cats and rats, though both are a thousand times superior to the latter. In saying this, I am virtually libelling the cat and the rat; for 'the friend of man,' be he cooked in ever so grand a way, is always a detestable dish. His flesh is oily and flabby; stew him, fry him, do what you will, there is always a flavour of castor oil about him. The only way to minimize that flavour, to make him palatable, is to salt, or rather to pepper him; that is, to cut him up in slices, and leave them for a fortnight, bestrewing them very liberally with pepper-corns. Then, before 'accommodating' them finally, put them into boiling water for a while, and throw the water away.

No such compromises are necessary with 'the fauna of the tiles', who, with his larger-sized victim, the rat, has been the most misprized and misjudged of all animals, from the culinary point of view. Stewed puss is by far more delicious than stewed rabbit. The flesh of the former tastes less pungent than that of the latter, and is more tender. As for the prejudice against cat, well, the Germans have the same prejudice against rabbit, and while I was in the Foreign Legion there was a Wurtemberger, a lieutenant, who would not touch bunny, but who would devour grimalkin. Those who have not tasted couscoussou of cat, prepared according to the Arabian recipe – though the Arabs won't touch it – have never tasted anything.

By November, the staple meat had become horse, and something like six hundred of the creatures were slaughtered every day. Paris was not accustomed to the taste – it was by no means commonly eaten in France – and a certain amount of promotional marketing had to be undertaken by the Société Hippophagique, which informed the public, according to Ernest Vizetelly,

> by means of constant paragraphs in the newspapers that 'viande de cheval' was superior to the flesh of the finest bullock; that the soup produced from it was finer, fuller of flavour, and more suitable to delicate stomachs than any other; and that its fat, of an oily nature, was a good substitute for butter, now very difficult to procure. On application being made to the Archbishop of Paris, that prelate readily authorized the faithful to employ horse fat and oil for culinary purposes on fast days – a fact which the promoters of hippophagie took especial care to announce. One of the successes of the hour was ass's flesh – a kind of veal with a poultry flavour, looking peculiarly white and tempting, and sold at the rate of 2s. 5d. a pound.

Another phenomenon new to Paris was 'the *queue*' (a French word incidentally, not an English one: literally, 'tail'). Vizetelly described it as

> One of the most characteristic inner-life features of the siege. They were first formed in the more populous and poorest districts; but, before a couple of days, had spread to the most aristocratic quarters of the capital. Originally, they commenced about five A.M., in front of the iron railings that invariably shut in the Parisian butcher's shop; and as the mornings were then bright and balmy, the inconvenience,

although considerable, was by no means excessive. But when it was found that only half of those who had waited since five o'clock had succeeded in getting served, the queues began to collect much earlier, and the hours of waiting gradually lengthened, until they extended far back into the night. In the populous quarters two o'clock was commonly the hour when the first dozen women would assemble. Some came to the rendezvous provided with chairs or stools and with chauffe-pieds; and at intervals, members of their family would bring them hot bowls of soup or coffee, or they would arrange to relieve each other every hour or so. These proceedings gave rise to endless disputes. Such as found themselves constrained to wait standing, objected to their neighbours sitting. Frozen-footed individuals, unprovided with foot-warmers, grumbled at those who possessed them; women whose husbands were on duty at the ramparts, and had no one to bring them warm and comforting fluids, protested against refreshment being allowed; while the practice of one member of a family relieving another gave rise to constant vituperation, to struggles, clawings, and blows.

The best joke of the siege: two good bourgeois, husband and wife, had a little dog of whom they were very fond. But a day came when there was nothing to eat in the house, and poor Bijou had to be killed and cooked. His master and mistress sat down to dinner with tears in their eyes, and during the meal the latter mechanically placed the tiny rib-bones on the side of her plate. 'Poor Bijou,' she ejaculated with a sigh, '*what a treat he would have had*!'

8 December

The morale of the Garde Nationale continued to be of major concern to Trochu's government. The problem was not just the Red battalions of Belleville, but a more widespread slovenliness – the inevitable result of a fundamental failure of organization and command. Labouchere translates part of an article in the *Revue des Deux Mondes*, detailing the shocking conduct of the patrols at the fortifications.

Some go away on leave, or disappear without leave; they make excursions beyond the ramparts, or shut themselves up in the billiard-room of some café. Many make during the course of the day frequent visits to the innumerable canteens, which succeed each other almost without interruption along the Rue des Ramparts. Here old women have lit a few sticks under a pot, and sell, for a penny the glass, a horrible brew called 'petit noir', composed of sugar, eau de vie, and the grains of coffee, boiled up together. Behind there is a line of cook shops, the proprietors of which announce that they have been commissioned to provide food. These speculators offer for sale greasy soup, slices of horse, and every species of alcoholic drink. Each company has, too, its cantinière, and round her cart there is always a crowd. It seldom happens that more than one-half of the men of the battalion are sober. Fortunately, the cold of the night air sobers them . . . The abuse of strong drink makes shameful ravages in our ranks, and is productive of serious disorder. Few nights pass without false alarms, without shots foolishly fired upon imaginary enemies, and without lamentable accidents. Every night there are disputes, which often degenerate into fights, and then in the morning, when explanations take place, these very explanations are an excuse for recommencing drinking. Rules, indeed, are not wanting to abate all this, but the misfortune is that they are never executed. The indiscipline of the National Guard contrasts strangely with the patriotism of their words.

The cold snap and some heavy snowfall stimulated more active responses to the enforced idleness. The 7th Company of the 19th Battalion boasted more distinguished artists who became bored with snowball fights (according to Gautier) and turned to a more creative pastime.

A frame was assembled from rubble gathered round about, and the artists, gently supervised by Monsieur Chapu, set to work busily applying the lumps of frozen snow handed to them by their comrades.

Monsieur Falguière made a statue of Resistance and Monsieur Moulin a colossal bust of the Republic. Two or more hours proved enough to complete their inspiration, which can rarely have been happier. All the same, it wasn't the first time that a great artist had deigned to sculpt this carrara marble, sent to earth from heaven in the form of glittering powder. Michelangelo – to satisfy a whim of Piero de Medici – modelled a huge statue out of snow (something not often seen in Florence) in the courtyard of his palace . . . earning him the favour of the new Grand Duke. . . . M. Falguière understood that what should be represented was *moral* rather than *physical* resistance, and instead of personifying a sort of formal Hercules ready to fight, has shown someone with the somewhat fragile grace of a contemporary Parisienne. Resistance, seated – or rather leaning against a rock – crosses her arms over her nude torso with an air of indomitable resolution . . . with a proud fling of her head, she has shaken her hair behind her so that the enemy can clearly see her charming face, more terrifying than the face of Medusa. On her lips plays a light smile of heroic disdain, and, in the crease of her eyebrows is concentrated the obstinacy of defence, which never retreats. No, the coarse fists of barbarism have not been joined to those slim and nervous arms . . . this lithe figure will break sooner than bend. Ethereal strength will win over brute strength, and, like Raphael's angel, kick away the beast's monstrous rump.

9 December

Rumours spread that large numbers of Krupps cannon were now in place for a bombardment, awaiting only the arrival of their carriages. In the Prussian arsenal in Versailles, they were lined up, so they said, like bottles in a cellar.

10 December

Goncourt, on a midnight walk back from Passy to Auteuil:

> The road is covered with snow. The sky melts into a damp fog, pierced only by the diffuse clarity of moonlight. Every branch is coated with a mousse of snow which seems to have turned into candy sugar. . . . It was like passing through the shimmery, glassy, electric glow of an aquarium in the midst of vast white madrepores. It makes a melancholy fantasy, and the idea of death, in this landscape of moon and snow, comes almost sweetly upon you. You could fall asleep without regret in such poetic coldness.

The heroic tracker and freeshooter Sergeant Hoff was feared dead. He had not been seen since fighting on 2 December, and it was now reported that he was in fact a Prussian spy. There was a woman in the case, the recipient of a dubious 57,000 francs.

11 December

Wickham Hoffman of the American Legation breakfasts

> with a French general, who commanded one of the outposts. We had beef, eggs, ham, etc., and, from what I heard, I should say that he and his staff breakfasted as well every day. These noonday breakfasts, by the way, ruined the French army. I reached my general's headquarters at half-past eleven. He and one of his staff were

smoking cigars and drinking absinthe. At twelve we breakfasted bountifully, as I have said, and with champagne, and other wines, followed by coffee, brandy, and more cigars. This was an outpost in presence of the enemy. Had he attacked, what would the general and his staff have been worth? They were very far from being intoxicated, but certainly their heads were not clear, or their judgments sound.

12 December

The papers relate, according to Denis Bingham, how

'La mère Crimée', the oldest *cantinière* in the service, and who is decorated with the military medal for service rendered in the campaigns of Africa, Italy, and the Crimea, has just distinguished herself. She went out with a battalion on Wednesday, which came to a halt one hundred yards from the Prussian sentries, and was distributing *petits verres* all round, when one of the enemy peered out of a hole and was about to take a shot at her. 'Wait a bit, Bismarck!' she cried, and snatching a musket from a corporal, fired and brought down her man. '*Bravo la mère!*' shouted the whole company and the old lady was borne off in triumph. And it is with stories like this that Paris consoles itself.

13 December

An exasperated Henry Markheim was surprised by

the facility with which people believe in 'immense stores' of wheat, just as at the beginning of the siege they believed in immense stores of flour: one would have thought that the first belief having proved false would have carried away with it the second. But Paris hopes against hope, like a patient in the last stage of consumption. I know not of any phase of mind that so exactly corresponds to the present fretful, peevish, dejected and yet hopeful state, in which the Parisians have lived for the last few days.

The Academy of Sciences debated the problem of diseased livestock, inedible themselves, as well as being a further drain on food supplies. No good use could be found for them.

At the sixty-acre depot in Bercy it was estimated that the cellars contained 1,600,000 hectolitres of *vin ordinaire* – about a hundred litres for every inhabitant of Paris.

14 December

The report of the previous night's meeting of one of the *clubs rouges* in Belleville. The discussion began with the question of the slaughter of domestic animals, including privately owned horses. After a ferocious attack on the latter – 'the rich can walk like the rest of us!' – a citizen stands up for dogs and cats: 'It is well known that dogs, particularly poodles, are the most intelligent and faithful animals, almost part of the family. Let us wait awhile before we immolate them for the national good!'

The floor decided unanimously for the slaughter of privately owned horses, but accorded a stay of execution to the dogs and cats. They then moved on to foreign affairs, and the attitude of foreign countries to the war. Belgium and France had been supportive, but England (and *The Times* in particular) was proving ignoble. 'England owes us a lot; it is trade with us that allows it to prosper. We could do without England, because France is the richest nation in the world and self-sufficient. But England could not do without France. This is why Lord Granville the Foreign Secretary had forbidden Bismarck to bombard Paris. Pure self-interest, no concern for us.' ('*hear, hear!*')

Another orator thinks that now is no time to be thinking about foreign affairs: who cares whether Lord Granville had forbidden Bismarck to bombard Paris or not? 'Let them bombard! They say that they will set fire to museums and churches – who cares? Let them burn the Louvre and the pictures of Rubens and Michelangelo – what matters is the triumph of the Republic. He will not be giving money towards the rebuilding of Notre-Dame. (*laughter and applause*) The bombs will rid us of the monuments of superstition and medievalism which are of no interest to socialists. (*more applause*)

'But they will not bombard us. They will take us by famine first. I cannot explain Trochu's inability to act: I think that the government really wants to make peace on shameful terms.'

Another speaker reads out a letter written to the radical newspaper *Le Combat* by some freeshooters from Belleville who had had their arms confiscated.

An outrage. They will be arresting them next. They have been slandered by the forces of reaction. At the same time, they are trying to ban all our committees and deliver us to the tyranny of people nominated by Trochu. They want to push us to the edge. They want a revolution in Belleville. And do you know why they want that? So that they can surrender Paris to the Prussians. (*thunderous booing and hissing*) But there will not be a revolution, we will hold back because we know what Trochu's game is – or rather the game of 'THE SECRET GOVERNMENT OF WHICH TROCHU IS JUST THE INSTRUMENT. (*Yes, yes, the Jesuits are at the bottom of it!*) We will not capitulate. We await the Prussians like the Romans awaited the Carthaginians on their curule chairs. We only have to stop members of the government flying off in a balloon and abandoning us: we must keep the sentries on duty. (*laughter and applause*) We will burn Paris if we need to and blaze a trail through to liberty! (Ten o'clock sounded, and the meeting closed with cries of *Vive la République!*)

16 December

According to Nathan Sheppard, 'the Minister for Agriculture says we still have 10,000,000 kilograms of rice, 10,800,000 of split peas and beans, and a large quantity of cheese.

'As other articles disappear, Colman's mustard becomes more and more conspicuous. It is in every grocer's window. It is tantalizing and aggravating to see windows full of these wasteful little jars of mustard . . . There is something absurdly horrible in the suggestion of a surfeit of mustard and a shortage of meat.'

17 December

My love,
It is now three months since I have heard any news of you. Three months is an age. Two days ago carrier pigeons arrived with dispatches for the government and about twelve hundred private letters. Alas! when I heard that news, my heart started beating with hope. I kept going home at all hours of the day to see if anything had arrived. But another disappointment was in store for me. M. Grimbert, who organizes the mail, has left Paris to return to Amiens. *

We live like animals, or, if you prefer it, beasts penned into a vast

---

* Presumably by balloon, though the records of passengers do not list any such name.

field. All we do is to survive. Just that. Food prices are absurd. A cabbage, ten francs; potatoes, thirty francs a bushel – if you can find one. But thanks to the foresight of Lucie [his sister-in-law] we want for nothing, and relatively speaking we are among the fortunate ones. Potatoes, ham, rabbit, chicken – all these are kept in reserve, if the need should arise. Thanks to a friend of Alfred's [his sister-in-law's husband] we often have contraband horse flesh. This is our amusement and even our lack of concern over our position. They are saying here that we have two months of supplies. Two months to wait: Paris will not surrender until the final extremity.

The government has received news from the provinces. Without being good, they are not bad. Our armies are fighting well. At present they are on the defensive . . .

Public health is generally good; however, about two thousand people die every week. Smallpox and typhoid are making constant ravages, particularly among the peasants who have taken refuge in Paris. They are not acclimatized, they are very badly fed and depressed. . . .

My most tender embrace   DESPLATS
I am in a terrible hurry

19 December

Henry Markheim: ' "15,000 Prussians have been taken." The news is not yet officially confirmed, mais ça se dit sur le boulevard ['that's the word on the streets']. This is our usual cordial before going to bed – the sleeping draught which composes us to rest, the cotton with which we stuff our ears against unpleasant noises – the nightcap of our illusions. Good night, Paris, and may the hosts of Sennacherib vanish like a morning dream.'

20 December

Juliette Adam, on receiving a letter:

My daughter is alive! my daughter is in Jersey! my daughter receives my letters! my mother, my father are living with her, looking after her, loving her, embracing her. And are there still today wretched parents who have no news of their children?

The letter which gives me news of my daughter is sent to me by Madame de Pierreclos, at Mâcon. Thank you, my dear friend! This letter went to New York, in a double envelope. Arriving in Paris, it was sent, with my address, to the Post Office in the Avenue

Josephine. Do I owe this to the American Ambassador? If only I knew who to thank . . .

21 December

Reports that copies of *The Times* seeped into Paris via the American Legation's diplomatic bag meant that its 'personal' columns filled up with messages from friends and relatives of the besieged, many of them, like Juliette Adam's daughter, Parisians who had left before the siege.

LAURIE et tous très bien.

E.S.D., Paris, 29 Boulevard des Capucines. Annie with Uncle A. All well. Receive your letters. Think much of you. If any inside Paris should see this kindly communicate to the above address.

LAVERDURE. All quite well. Children growing and improving. Nothing wanted. Comfortably settled. Climate agreeable. Cheque arrived and cashed. M. Eugène received certificate. Old papa as usual. Coupons of November not in the box. Where are they? All inhabitants of *cour* exceedingly well, and have always been safe. Horses safely in Ch. with John and Alphonse.

Will M. CHARLES DELABRE be kind enough to make known to M. Fred Jourdain, 7 rue de Penthièvre, Paris, that the Granville Colony is still going on well? The Denières and M. Collou are at Louviers, Arthur at Rouen, Maurice at St Petersburg. The Mullers are very well. Louis succeeds at college.

The night-time temperature sank to −14°C. Despite the weather, Trochu ordered another attempt at a major sortie – across the flat plains of Le Bourget to the north-east of the city. Bismarck seemed to have had accurate advance intelligence of the plan. He sneeringly compared French strategy to the behaviour of 'a dancing master, who is leading a quadrille, and shouting to his pupils, now Right! now Left!' In fact, Ducrot's idea was to join up with General Faidherbe's army, which had retaken Amiens and was moving south towards Paris. Again, the execution of the operation was botched. One potentially valuable corps stood by all day in Saint-Denis awaiting orders to advance which never arrived. The French charged and fired with the wild whooping abandon for which they were celebrated – the *furia francese* – but the Prussian clockwork timing and persistence proved ultimately more effective. The ground was so hard that tents could not be erected, nor ditches dug: the wounded simply froze to death. The mistakes of the day cost two thousand French lives and screwed the opposition to Trochu to a state of explosive tension.

22 December
Military report:

> Yesterday was only the beginning of a series of operations. It wasn't – it couldn't possibly have been – definitively successful . . . Had it not been for the adverse weather conditions . . . the valiant energies of our troops . . . a hundred Prussian prisoners taken . . . vigorous response . . . enemy losses

The death was announced of a much-loved Parisian figure, Madame Cornette, aged seventy-five, whose stall on the Pont-Neuf had been celebrated since 1831 for its fried potatoes and doughnuts.

The government sent Tours a stark message via balloon: rations will hold out only until 20 January.

23 December

> A curious new industry has sprung up in Paris. Letters supposed to be found in the pockets of dead Germans are in great request. There are letters from mothers, from sisters, and from the Gretchens who are, in the popular mind, supposed to adore warriors. Unless every corpse has half a dozen mothers, and was loved when in the flesh by a dozen sweethearts, many of these letters must be fabricated. They vary in their style very little. The German mothers give little domestic details about the life at home, and express the greatest dread lest their sons shall fall victims to the valour of the Prussians, which is filling the Fatherland with terror and admiration. The Gretchens are all sentimental; they talk of their inner feelings like the heroines of third-rate novels, send the object of their affections cigars and stockings knitted by their own fair hands, and implore him to be faithful, and not forget, in the toils of some French syren, poor Gretchen. But what is more strange is that in the pocket of each corpse a reply is found which he has forgotten to post. In this reply the warrior tells a fearful tale of his own sufferings, and says that victory is impossible, because the National Guards are such an invincible band. (Labouchere)

25 December
Elihu Washburne's Christmas:

The cold was intense, but I managed to get the *petit salon* and the *salle à manger* quite comfortable by the time the guests arrived. Here is the bill of fare for the 98th day of the siege . . .

1. Oyster soup.
2. Sardines, with lemons.
3. Corned beef, with tomatoes and cranberries.
4. Preserved green corn.
5. Roast chicken.
6. Green peas.
7. Salad.
8. Dessert. Pumpkin pie and cheese, macaroon cakes, nougat cherries, strawberries, chocolates, plums, and apricots, café noir.

Edwin Child's Christmas:

Could not prevent my thoughts reverting to those at home upon this day so sacred to all English hearts, especially while walking up and down upon guard and how often I said to myself What a Christmas! as I pictured them all sitting down to a jolly good dinner, while I was without even a piece of steak or a decent soup to eat and feeling the blank my absence would cause, especially under the circumstances they perhaps thinking me dead or nearly starved, were I at all delicate in my appetite the latter would not be far from the truth.

A French Catholic Christmas:

At mass in the evening, after the blessing, as the congregation was ready to depart, the choir's voices rose in supplication, singing a wonderful, terrible, moving and sublime '*Parce Domine*, spare us, o Lord!' – repeating it three times, the invocation of a whole people, asking for God's mercy – he who had not relented in piling upon us the blows of punishment; and this Christmas Day, a day of joy on which we celebrate the birth of his saviour of the world, finished with a prayer wet with tears and interrupted by sobbing! (Eugène Loudon)

The military's Christmas was celebrated by the continued withdrawal of troops from the ice-packed plains of Le Bourget.

26 December

Advertisements appear, according to Goncourt, proclaiming the virtues of arsenic as a dietary supplement.

Elihu Washburne's Boxing Day:

A case of the terrible suffering of a German family living in the Avenue d'Italie was brought to my notice yesterday. They were literally dying of cold and hunger. I immediately sent Antoine with a little wood, wine, coffee, sugar, *confitures*, etc. He found a family of seven persons cooped up in a little attic about ten feet square, in the last stage of misery – no fire and no food. There was a little boy, some seven years old, lying on a pallet of straw, so far gone as to be unable to raise his head or to talk. I sent Antoine again today to the family with a can of Portland sugar-corn and a very small piece of pork (one-half of my own stock) and two herrings (also one-half of my own stock), and also a little money to buy bread. I told Antoine to take the poor little fellow to my own house to be taken care of by the *maître d'hôtel* and his wife, and when he proposed it to him, he didn't want to go, but preferred to stay with his mother.

Minutes of the Meeting of the Club de la Reine Blanche

The proceedings opened with some minor denunciations: of a woman who was feeding bread to her four dogs; an omnibus conductor who had required a member of the Garde Nationale to pay full fare; and General Clément Thomas, who kept sumptuous apartments in the Élysée Palace, played billiards the whole time, and had slandered certain impeccable battalions of the Garde Nationale.

Citizen Joly took the floor. He was no opponent of the government, he said; he didn't think it was entirely composed of traitors – it was just its total incompetence which amazed him. For three months now they'd been going on about General Trochu's plan – and what had happened? Presumably it was lodged with a notary, like a will. (*general hilarity*) Things were getting steadily worse, and rations diminished daily. Where were the armies outside Paris which were supposed to come to Paris' rescue? Where were our military successes? Yesterday we learnt that operations have been suspended because of the ice – as if our forefathers didn't fight through much worse weather in Holland and Sebastopol. Have we really reached the point at which we can't stand a bit of cold, when it's a matter of saving the Fatherland? Well, they are dragging us gently towards capitulation. They want to exhaust us, to bore and demoralize us into submission. General Trochu, that Breton and Catholic, is waiting for a new Joan of Arc. But there are no more Joans of Arc. Is there a Joan of Arc here, for instance? (*silence*)

Well, we must take matters into our own hands and no longer wait upon the government. The only road to salvation is the formation of an assembly of three hundred members – we should not call it 'the Commune' because it's a name which deters the faint-hearted, reminding them of Robespierre and the Terror. This assembly will elect an executive body which, for the same reason, we should not call the Committee of Public Safety. (*feeble applause*)

Citizen Gase declared that he deplored euphemisms and circumlocutions. We must constitute a Commune and call it a Commune. Of course, this government intended to capitulate: it was in their interests, because they would rather negotiate with Prussians than with socialists. For one thing, they know that socialists send traitors to the guillotine. (*Shocked exclamations and tutting greet this statement.*) Or they shoot them, if that's what you prefer. (*sounds of approbation*)

This government in short wants to make a deal with the Prussians and restore the monarchy. Its members served under the Empire and all that interests them is feathering their own nests.

A lively debate ensued. Citizen Joly's view was that, if you want to create a Terror, you don't brag about it in advance; Citizen Gase believed that it was more honest to announce your manifesto and stick by it. At the end of the meeting, there were cries of *Vive la commune!*

27 December

Prussian shells exploded to the east of Paris, between Fort de Rosny and Fort Avron. The long-awaited bombardment by Krupps cannon was imminent.

29 December

The sheer villainy of the Garde Nationale surpasses anything which the imagination of a decent human being could conceive. I was on a train with three of their number. Their drunken gestures almost strapped their neighbours and every phrase was larded with the word *shit*. One of them embodied imbecile drunkenness; another, sly and cocky drunkenness; the third, brute drunkenness. During the journey, cocky drunkenness told brutal drunkenness that the stationmaster had given orders for his arrest when he left the train, on account of the racket he was making. I saw the man pull out a knife, open it and put it back open into his pocket. I got off the train at the first station, not keen to be present at my travelling companions' descent from the carriage. (Goncourt)

Interior of the
ambulance housed in
the Comédie-Française,
drawn by James Tissot.

A view of the American Ambulance, in the Avenue d'Uhrich.

A tribute to the carrier
pigeons of the Siege
of Paris, painted by
the young Puvis
de Chavannes.

Apparently the only
surviving photograph
of the Siege of Paris:
a balloon launched
from the place
Saint-Jacques.

◀ Albert Robida's drawing of a unit of the Garde Nationale under review. Compare Francisque Sarcey's account on pages 173–4.

An obscene caricature of Thiers and Bismarck by 'Faustin'. Thiers, branded with a royalist fleur-de-lys, is shown pleasuring the German Chancellor – a dig at their supposed complicity against Republican France.

Robida's drawing of rural refugees escaping the Prussian advance by entering Paris.

A barricade in the
rue de Castiglione
during the Commune.

◀ Caricature of
a *pétroleuse*.

Robida's drawing
of a shelter for the
massacred in Belleville.

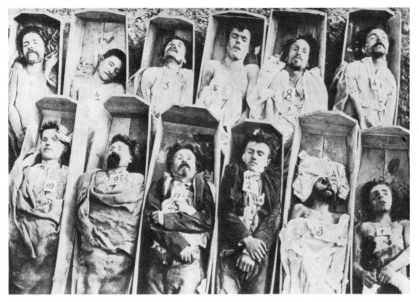

Corpses of anonymous Communards, victims of the Versaillais invasion.

One of several faked propaganda 'photographic' collages of
atrocities perpetrated by the Commune: this one depicts
a fictitious slaughter of Dominican monks on 25 May.

A café sprung up in
the burnt-out ruins
of Paris, June 1871,
by Robida.

◄ The Tuileries Palace
after the fires of
la semaine sanglante.

The Porte Maillot following bombardment.

The new *tendresse*:
Berthe Morisot's
painting 'The Cradle',
exhibited at the first
show of Impressionists
in 1874.

Paris s'amuse:
the Boulevard des
Capucines painted
by the young Monet,
1873–4.

Rimbaud, June 1872,
as Paul Verlaine later
sketched him
from memory.

The cortège of the
Lord Mayor of London
processes towards
the opening of
Garnier's new opera house.

30 December

One of the most infamous events of the siege – the shooting of two popular six-year-old elephants of the Jardin d'Acclimatation, Castor and Pollux, whose corpses had been sold to the 'English butcher' Deboos in the Avenue Friedland. A gunsmith shot Castor with a carbine. He bled profusely, but seemed almost entirely unaffected by the bullet. 'He seemed convinced that wound was due to an accident,' wrote the Comte d'Hérisson, 'and did everything his butchers told him with the greatest docility.' Two conical, steel-tipped *chassepot* bullets were necessary to finish the now screeching creature off. Poor Pollux died likewise. Labouchere found the meat 'tough, coarse, and oily, and I do not recommend English families to eat elephant as long as they can get beef or mutton'. But the blood made good *boudin*.

D'Hérisson printed a table (its provenance unspecified) of other inhabitants of Parisian zoos sold for butchery. Such meat, it should be emphasized, was very expensive and was consumed for its novelty value rather than under pressure of starvation.

Date of Sale	Purchaser	Nature of Animal	Price Francs
Oct. 18, 1870	M. Courtier	1 Dwarf Zebra	350
" 18 "	"	2 Buffaloes	300
" 23 "	M. Lacroix	2 Deer	500
" 23 "	"	12 Carp	150
" 24 "	M. Deboos	2 Yaks	390
" 25 "	M. Groszos	3 Geese	60
" 27 "	M. Lacroix	1 Small Zebra	400
" 28 "	M. Bignon	Lot Fowls, Ducks, &c.	862
" 31 "	M. Deboos	1 Lot of Ducks	115
Nov. 3 "	M. X	11 Rabbits	100
" 17 "	M. Deboos	2 Reindeer	800
" 21 "	"	2 Nilghaus	1,000
" 22 "	M. Lacroix	1 Bengal Stag	300
" 26 "	M. Deboos	2 Wapitis	2,500
Dec. 9 "	"	1 Nilghau	650
" 15 "	"	2 Camels	4,000
" 15 "	"	1 Yak Calf	200
" 20 "	"	2 Camels	5,000
" 29 "	"	2 Elephants	27,000

January, New Year's Day
The Jockey Club celebrated with a dinner of

Potage au Pain
Côte de boeuf rotie
Poule au riz
Epinards au gris
Glace groseille et vanille

The elections which followed included those of Prince de Clermont-Tonnerre; Edward Blount, British Consulate; Baron J. N. de Rothschild; Vicomte d'Haussonville; Richard Wallace; Vice Admiral La Roncière le Noury; Vicomte Edmond de la Panouse. The Jockey Club was one of several such institutions in Paris which managed to maintain a high standard of cuisine and comfort throughout the siege.

New Year's dinner *carte* at Peters, Passage des Princes

Hors d'oeuvre: fresh butter, olives, sardines, saucisson de Lyon et de Boulogne, marinated tuna
Soups: soupe au vin de Bordeaux, Julienne au riz, croûte au pôt.
Entrées: rosbif de mule with puréed potatoes, haunch of goat Sauce Tousenel, filet of elephant Sauce Madère, tenderloin of donkey with turnips, haunch of bear Sauce Bourgeois, Galantine of peacock
Roasts: chickens, ducklings, gigot of lamb
Salade de saison
Vegetables: asparagus à l'huile, petits pois à la crème, artichokes
Sweets: macédoine de fruits, bombe glacée

A story told by the distinguished restaurateur Bignon and related in *Le Gaulois*. A rich and well-dressed gentleman came into the restaurant to order, for 8 p.m. precisely, the following menu for six:

Tapioca consommé
Potage aux herbes
Butter and radishes, sausage, sardines

Rump steak chasseur with soufflé potatoes
Duckling stuffed à la Rouennaise
Salad of celery hearts
Mixed beans
Ceps à la Bordelaise
Apples and assorted fruits
Cheese

It was an extravagant meal, even in pre-siege terms. The man left his card, M. Turpin de Cressé, and went off to the Palais-Royal to buy some flowers.

In the florist's he chose six lavish bouquets and asked the florist to take them to Bignon's and arrange them for his table there. Their cost was 120 francs, but alas! he had only a thousand-franc note in his wallet. So he borrowed ten francs off his coachman and arranged to meet the florist at Bignon's within the hour. Then he disappeared.

But M. Turpin de Cressé never arrived, nor did his guests. Someone suggested that he was a Prussian spy, with intelligence that the city was to be stormed in the morning and determined to celebrate his new masters in style.

Nobody ever saw him again. The florist took back the bouquets and *chez* Bignon they finished the evening with a feast.

2 January

For those without M. Turpin de Cressé's *éclat*, life moved thus. No coal or coke, with firewood very dear and scarce. (Marauding gangs, armed with hatchets and brute force, were pulling up the saplings of the Haussmann era and stripping bare the venerable lime and plane trees of the parks and boulevards.) In winter conditions, no foraged vegetables or fresh foods were available: small children suffered the worst, inflating the week's mortality rate from the five-year mean of 838 to 3,680. Rationing and charity canteens, delivering bread and soup to the most indigent, prevented starvation but could not stem the inexorable spread of cholera, smallpox, and typhoid among the poorest. The Academy of Sciences debated the following: the merits and demerits of green teas; the growth of mushrooms in damp cellars; a thousand and one things to do with a cup of ox blood; the joy of kidney fat; oats. Others proposed candle tallow as a substitute for butter, or suggested that it could be satisfactorily mixed with corn, seasoned with salt and flavoured with onion. A nourishing but disgusting gelatine called *osseine* was devised and celebrated.

Recipes for fluids representing milk abounded. For instance: an ounce of wheat boiled in water with turnips, carrots and sugar, mixed with a small amount of the yellow of an egg; an emulsion made with an egg, sugar and water (but where did you find an egg?); or thirty grams of dried albumen, two grams of soda crystals, sixty grams of olive oil.

Feelings of hunger, the *savants* assured Paris, were no indication of a necessity to eat.

A meeting in the rue d'Arras of delegates from the clubs and other radical combinations and organizations announced that a new committee would be formed, drawn from representatives of all twenty arrondissements, 'with a view to establishing the Paris Commune'. The committee called itself, unimaginatively, 'Delegation of the Twenty Arrondissements of Paris' and it further declared that it would now contemplate 'the measures to be taken in order that it may carry out in a revolutionary way the mission with which it has been entrusted'.

5 January

The bombardment of Paris has begun.

The enemy is not content to shoot on our forts. Now it fires its projectiles on our buildings, it threatens our homes and families.

This violence redoubles the resolution of the city to fight and to conquer.

The defenders of our forts, showered with incessant fire, have lost none of their calm, and know how to inflict terrible reprisals on the assailant.

The population of Paris valiantly accepts this new trial. The enemy believes it can intimidate us, but this will only serve to make its efforts more vigorous. It will show itself worthy of the Army of the Loire, which has repelled the enemy, and the Army of the North, which is marching to our rescue.

Vive la France! Vive la République!

GENERAL TROCHU. . .

6 January

The full impact of Nobel's contemporary development of nitroglycerine into dynamite was mercifully still not fully incorporated into explosives technology, and the shells fired by the Prussian Krupps cannon into Paris were gunpowder-filled, causing more nuisance than slaughter. 'I know nothing of the military impact of a bombardment,' wrote Albert Vandam:

> but have been told that even the greatest strategists only count upon the moral effect it produces upon the besieged inhabitants. I can only say this: if Marshal von Moltke took the 'moral effect' of his projectiles into his calculations to accelerate the surrender of Paris, he might have gone on shelling Paris for a twelvemonth without being one whit nearer his aim; that is, if I am to judge by the scene I witnessed on that January morning . . . At the risk of offending all the sensation-mongers, foreign and native, with pen or with pencil, I can honestly say that a broken-down omnibus and a couple of prostrate horses would have excited as much curiosity as did the sight of the battered tenements at Vaugirard, Montrouge, and Vanves. On the Chaussée du Maine, the roadway had been ploughed up, for a distance of about half a dozen yards, by a shell; in another spot, a shell had gone clean through the roof and killed a woman by the side of her husband; in a third, a shell had carried away part of the wall of a one-storied cottage, and the whole of the opposite wall: in short, there was more than sufficient evidence that life was no longer safe within the fortifications, and yet there was no wailing, no wringing of hands, no heartrending frenzied look of despair, either pent up or endeavouring to find vent in shrieks and yells, nay, not even on the part of the women. There was merely a kind of undemonstrative contempt.

'I would at any time prefer to be for twenty-four hours in the most exposed part of a bombarded town than walk twenty-four times across Oxford Street,' added Labouchere in tones of British sang-froid. The Prussian press and official propagandists had made much of withholding bombardment until the correct 'psychological moment' (the phrase became a great joke and catchphrase of the siege: 'is this the psychological moment for dinner?'; 'is this the psychological moment for the omnibus to arrive?' and so on), but the worse blow to morale was a sudden steep rise in the price of *vin ordinaire*, one of the last unrestrictedly available comestibles. And for the *gamins* and other scavengers, fragments of shell were a useful source of income, gathered for sale as souvenirs. None the less, the bombs served as unmistakable evidence of further deterioration in the military line and fuelled the resentment of the Red left. The hoardings were covered with a poster emanating from the 'Delegation of the Twenty Arrondissements of Paris':

'Has the government charged with national defence fulfilled its mission? No! . . . Through its slowness, its indecision, its inertia, those who govern us have led us to the brink of the abyss. They do not know how to administrate or to fight. We are dying of cold and almost of hunger . . . Futile sorties, murderous and inconclusive battles, repeated failures . . . To perpetuate this regime is tantamount to capitulation . . . The politics, the strategy, the administration of the government of 4 September, heirs to the Empire, are doomed. Yield to the people! Yield to the Commune!'

7 January

The poster of the previous day, printed on red paper, had been displayed principally in the districts of the old suburb of Paris. It incited the people to overturn the government and denounced the governor of Paris as contemplating capitulation. It demanded, moreover, the establishment of the Commune, mass attack, general requisition and free rations – in other words, delivering the mass of the population into the hands of blackguards and promoting the swiftest success to the enemy. The poster was signed by about forty names of the so-called delegates of the capital's twenty arrondissements. Almost everywhere it was torn down or defaced by the people themselves.

General Trochu deemed it proper to reply with the following proclamation: 'At the point when the enemy is redoubling its efforts to intimidate us, the citizens of Paris are being misled by dishonesty and calumny. Our sufferings and sacrifices are being exploited at the cost of our defence. Nothing can force our weapons from our hands. Courage, patience, patriotism! THE GOVERNOR OF PARIS WILL NOT CAPITULATE!'

9 January

The previous night, between 9 p.m. and 5 a.m., nine hundred shells were launched into the city: one projectile fell every two minutes in the area around the Odéon. Casualties were high: twenty-two deaths, thirty-seven serious injuries.

Better by far to be a German prisoner of war, confined in the thick-walled security of La Roquette:

> The Germans had a day-room where they assembled to chat, read, play cards, and amuse themselves as they pleased. They were deprived of nothing but liberty. Their diet was quite as good as that of the majority of the defenders of the city, and they seemed astonished and grateful at the excellent treatment they received. Many of them had imagined they would have been shot when captured. They were mostly very young, and all could read and write . . . A visit was paid to these captives under guidance of one of the chaplains, a venerable white-haired man with benevolence in his mild eyes. He brought a holy zeal to his labour, and as he spoke German, he was peculiarly fitted for his present mission. One very handsome stripling was singing a hymn as the visitors entered, and his comrades joined in with a surprising precision of harmony. At the request of the chaplain, who was a great favourite, they burst into a cheerful sonorous *lied*, a marching chorus. It may be doing them an injustice, but one could not help thinking that the greater part of these martyrs to circumstance were rather better pleased, on the whole, to be under lock and key than to be holding hazardous vigils on a bleak forepost. He who had led the hymn had a flute, and old numbers of the *Gartenlaube* were scattered about the large room, with some copies of the romances of Auerbach and others provided by the broad-minded chaplain. The sole complaint was the impossibility of getting news from home, although the Government had generously allowed them to avail themselves of the balloon-post. (O'Shea)

10 January

As the bombs continued to explode, randomly but incessantly, another poster went up on to the walls of Paris – the work of a lunatic:

THE BOMBARDMENT OF PARIS
Paris must burn, as once did Gomorrah!
God commands it! The flames must devour this den

of debauchery and perdition.
Once we have endured the purification of fire, we
can practise in this impious city the Blessed Requisition.
Signed Abraham DREYFUS

Talk of cannibalism as a means of pepping up the city's diet
was another refuge of the insane. This letter was sent to a
newspaper signed Citizen Gagne, lawyer:

> Paris is today like the raft of the *Medusa* and is about to die stupefied
> with hunger . . . To seize it from the claws of famine and retrieve its
> triumphs, I demand, loudly, the establishment of *philanthropophagy*,
> in other words the fraternal manducation of Man by Man.
>
> I demand that the government issues a decree declaring that all
> men and women over sixty years of age should be sent into retreat
> and delivered up to human butchery! I dare to hope that the
> government will set an example, and whatever its members' ages,
> will sacrifice itself gloriously on the altar of *philanthropophagy*.
> Certainly its members all merit this supreme honour . . .

12 January
A meeting at the Club de la Revendication. Formerly a *café-
concert*, its premises were shabby and pokey. Local women and
children made up much of the attendance, huddling in search of
light and warmth and the comfort of company through the long,
dark evenings.

Yet this was one of the most fervently Red of the clubs, and
the meeting began with an orator declaring that he scorned ham
and sausages and preferred to feed himself on the pure air of
Liberty (a remark which provoked low, pained sighs from the
floor). A Pole, Citizen Strassnowski, tried to defend the
government, only with difficulty making himself heard over the
hissing and catcalls. 'You complain that the government hasn't
sent out more cannon against the Prussians, but where is the
artillery which knows how to fire it?'

'What about us?' someone interjected.

'You? Three months ago you were artisans, factory workers,
shopkeepers. Cannon require trained soldiers. And I think we
must beware of blaming the German people for the war: it is
only their despotic masters we are fighting. I hope one day that

people from all the European nations will hold hands fraternally – from the Pyrenees across the Alps to the Carpathians and Balkans.'

Another citizen begged the floor to excuse Strassnowski's ravings – he was a brave fighting man with six children, but how could he talk such nonsense? Has the government made any serious attempt to provide us with the proper training? What were its real goals? It kept on talking of armies in the provinces coming to our relief – but where were they? We are being lulled to sleep with fairy tales. The government has no moral authority; and this morning by 8 a.m., it was impossible to find any bread in any bakery in the twelfth arrondissement. (Women's voices shout: 'It's true – people have to start queuing at 5 a.m.') The bread we do get tastes like plaster – yet you go into the third arrondissement and it's a different story. That is this government's concept of fairness! How long can this go on? The people should take its own affairs into its own hands! Vive la commune! (cheers all round). Vive la commune!

13 January
Monsieur de Vineuil, by balloon post to his wife:

A bomb falls every minute tonight around Saint-Sulpice, following the shells' preference for areas containing hospitals.

The north wind has brought back coldness that is increasingly insupportable, since the heating here is completely defunct.

A further reduction has been made in the ration of horse meat. . . . And yet there are happy people in this desolate city! I went at the crack of dawn this morning to the Ambulance Chaptal: at the door my path crossed that of Madame —, who was leaving. 'I thought you no longer spent the nights here,' I said to her.

'Normally, I don't,' she said. 'But my 219 is dying. You know how fond of each other we were; he begged me to stay at the end. He suffered little in his final hour, poor boy.'

'Perhaps – but what about you? You'll wear yourself out if the siege doesn't end?'

'Oh don't say that. It's so good to feel useful, to give some consolation. You know,' she added, 'that I have nothing to complain about in my lot upon this earth: and frankly, it is here that I have felt the greatest joy.' . . .

Other women among your friends have also said to me: 'With all its sorrows, this has still been a blessed winter for us. The sufferings are terrible to witness, and it seems that some of the sights will remain unforgettable, but at least one is fighting against pain and evil, and one feels them to some degree lessened by one's efforts. And then we are living for the first time as God wished us to live, there is no tug between the world and our work – everything is devoted to the latter. How many people we love now we might never have known! We could never have believed there was such a wealth of goodness in our people. We have learnt a lot.'

14 January

Edmond de Goncourt shot a blackbird for his supper:

I remember the bird's arrival, every evening at twilight, and the piercing whistle by which he seemed to want to herald himself, and the two or three traversals that he made of the garden, in beautifully swift and smooth flight. I remember the way he would pause for several seconds on a branch – always the same one, a branch on a sycamore near the house . . . Then he would of a sudden vanish into the darkness of the night. It penetrated my consciousness like some superstition that a little of my brother had passed into this winged creature, this bird of grief, and I had a vague terror that I had destroyed with my gunshot something from the world beyond which watched over me and my house. It's stupid, stupid, stupid, it's absurd and crazy, but I was obsessed with the thought all evening . . .

15 January

Firing from the heights of Châtillon, to the south of the city, the Prussians continued to bombard the Left Bank, as well as firing heavily on the forts. The newspapers reported daily laconic catalogues of shell damage to buildings and their inhabitants. A shell fell on the barracks in the rue de Babylonne, on the Sorbonne, in the rue de Rennes, on the Bibliothèque de Sainte-Geneviève. Few casualties, much broken glass. There were horror stories too (a little girl sliced in two on her way home; six women killed in a queue outside a shop; ten children blown to pieces at their boarding school in the rue Oudinot, 'their palpitating flesh pasted against the wall of the dormitory') and tales of miracle escapes (hurrah for the brave *curé* of Saint-Sulpice, who kept his calm when a bomb interrupted mass, begging the faithful to depart quietly and 'walking up and down the aisle like a sea captain pacing his deck in the midst of a tempest').

Between 5 and 17 January, eighty-one Parisians – nearly half of them children – were killed and 207 wounded; in the same period there were over eight hundred deaths from smallpox.

International opinion was outraged by this development in the campaign – only the British failed to make diplomatic protest –but the Prussians were unmoved by appeals to their humanity and clemency. When Trochu formally complained, via parley, of the attacks on hospitals, churches, schools, prisons and convents, von Moltke's chilling reply came to the effect that fog and distance prevented the gunners from taking precise aim, but that as they moved closer to the city it would doubtless be possible to point the cannon more discriminately.

16 January

It was officially announced that all the city's coal supplies were exhausted. Various experiments were made in an effort to develop communication with the outside world, but courier dogs, hollow zinc balls floated down the Seine, and primitive unmanned submarines all failed to function. The harsh weather meant that the pigeon dispatches were becoming rarer and fewer balloons were launched.

17 January

There was talk of imminent capitulation, despite Trochu's unambiguously defiant line of 7 January, and talk of revictualling the city. In response, food prices dropped and shop windows mysteriously filled up with preserved meats, 'even of live fowls and game', according to Tommy Bowles. When restrictions were removed on the sale and distribution of potatoes, they too became more plentiful. 'I am convinced that if they were to shake off all their artificial trammels of requisitions and rations, and were to leave things to take their own course, and provisions to reach their natural prices, we should have no more trouble in this respect,' Bowles added.

But the bread has become 'a very strange and dirty-looking

compound, made of a mixture of wheat, oats, barley and rice'. Some people rather liked its rough, strong consistency; more refined tastes found it inedible and regarded its appearance as the herald of famine.

18 January

A third attempt was made to break out, this time to the west of Paris. A hundred thousand men, half of them Garde Nationale, were marshalled for this last-ditch (some would say suicidal) operation: even to the most patriotic Parisian, they looked sadly bedraggled and unprepared opponents for the world's most efficient professional army. Red battalions of the Garde Nationale had long campaigned to be given a chance to fight on the front line, to run at the Prussians whooping their war cries as part of a torrential *sortie en masse*: but was this another exercise designed to fail – to shut those noisy sections of the Garde Nationale up, if not to dispose of them by means of a smart push into the front line? Or to 'accustom Paris to the idea of capitulation', as Sarcey put it?

A crushing insult to France. In the enemy headquarters at Versailles, during an elaborate and pompous ceremony in the Hall of Mirrors attended by hordes of German nobility, King William I of Prussia was crowned Emperor, Deutscher Kaiser, as prelude to the establishment of a new constitution which created a Second Reich of Germany, dominated by Prussia and the 'Imperial Chancellor' Bismarck.

19 January

Bread was rationed for the first time – a daily 300 grams for adults, 150 for children, at ten and five centimes respectively. This despite previous assurances from the government that the stock of flour was almost unlimited – and indeed there were pavilions of Les Halles visibly stacked with barrels and sacks of it.

At Buzenval, between the forts of Mont-Valérien and Montretout, a sudden thaw, turning frozen earth into glutinous mud below a pall of fog, hampered the French army as much as the usual scandalously incompetent organization and command.

Any early advantages won by the gung-ho courage of the zouaves and the efficacy of the *mitrailleuse* were soon lost and the day ended in chaos, with dreadful casualties. Fifteen hundred of them were members of the Garde Nationale – ill-trained, under-equipped and overparted. Had they suffered simply so that the government could appease public opinion and continue to give an impression of holding to some sort of strategy?

The wounded were ferried back into the city throughout the afternoon and the night. Geneviève Breton prayed in the pages of her diary for her fiancé the painter Henri Regnault. 'My God, my God, protect my sweet, fragile happiness, save my beloved, save him, o just God, and all my life will be nothing but a prayer of thanksgiving and love and I will bless you for what you have done for me,' she raved. In vain: the twenty-seven-year-old white hope of French art was killed by 'a stray bullet' at Buzenval – in other words, by the friendly fire which Trochu himself confessed had probably hit as many as five hundred.

Another golden young man who fell that day was Seveste, the *jeune premier* of the Comédie-Française, widely considered the most promising actor of his generation. The company's director, Edouard Thierry, recalled how he was brought back to be nursed in the ambulance set up inside the theatre that was his home. A charity matinée recitation of Molière's *Le médecin malgré lui* was in progress when the wagon bearing his stretcher drew up. Thierry rushed out of the auditorium when he heard that his young star had arrived. 'The poor boy was screaming horribly. He told me that his leg had been shattered into four pieces and every grating movement of the fragments caused him dreadful pain. Never mind: he was in his theatre, surrounded by his own. He thought that he was saved.' He told Thierry that they must amputate his leg if necessary – 'after all,' he joked, 'you can always make me a director'. They did cut it off, but Seveste died a few days later, still tended by his beloved *comédiens*.

20 January

An armistice, to allow the battlefields to be cleared. Paris held its breath as the siege fell grimly into its final chapter.

21 January

As a consequence of the débâcle at Buzenval, Trochu lost whatever shreds of authority and credibility he had previously clung to. He had governed Paris decently, without cruelty or terror, but he made an uninspiring leader who secretly lacked the necessary blazing belief in the city's ultimate victory. On the field, he was inflexible, unable to adapt his tactics to changing circumstances, be they a matter of the weather or a wall of cannon. In the previous few weeks this stolidly conventional and unimaginative man had succumbed to the primitive super-stitious piety of his Breton Catholic background, declaring that his faith now lay in the intercession of the city's patron saint, Geneviève, who had appeared to him in a vision. This was not enough for the rest of his cabinet, who persuaded him that he must resign. Or rather, to save face, he was nominally to keep the military command, General Vinoy was to become President of the Third Republic, and the governorship of Paris was to be suppressed (thus circumventing the officially proclaimed in-sistence two weeks earlier that 'The Governor of Paris will not capitulate': now there was no Governor of Paris).

Trochu bowed to the inevitable with reluctance. 'I am the Jesus Christ of the situation,' he said bitterly. Paris did not mourn him; he simply faded away.

The *coup de grâce* on what Felix Whitehurst described as 'the worst day of the hundred and twenty-five which Paris has been besieged' was news that the Army of the Loire had been effectively wiped out at a battle near Le Mans. The hope of an outside rescuer was now not even a fantasy.

22 January

Heavy bombardment continued through the fog. A ban on the serving of bread in restaurants was instituted. During the night, about three hundred members of red brigades of the Garde Nationale – goaded by the slaughter at Buzenval and by the government's confession of weakness in disposing of Trochu – marched on the Mazas prison, demanding the release of the flamboyant Gustave Flourens and other jailed instigators of the 'revolutionette' of 31 October. The governor of the prison, either intimidated or sympathetic, soon succumbed and handed over the prisoners, asking only for a receipt of delivery. The liberated and the liberators then marched noisily through the streets to the nearest *mairie* and broke in. Having helped themselves to some bottles of wine and distributed two thousand bread rations from the cellar, they dropped off to sleep.

The following afternoon, however, a posse from this expedition marched to the Hôtel de Ville, banging and shouting abuse at the government. Armed with muskets and led by the notorious Sapia, the lunatic old bore Jules Allix and the fearsome Louise Michel in male uniform, their collective bark was probably worse than their intended bite. Some five thousand onlookers and catcallers had also foregathered. But the government was on a short fuse and disinclined to play a conciliatory game. When a single shot was fired – it is not clear whether it emanated from the Reds or from the Gardes Mobiles defending the Hôtel de Ville – there was immediate panic on both sides and half an hour of furious retaliation and shooting to kill. As further loyalist troops were hastily marched in, the rebels dispersed in all directions, pulling over omnibuses and street furniture behind their lines of retreat. At the end of it all, five corpses and eighteen wounded lay in the square outside the Hôtel de Ville, and for the first time in the siege, ominously, Parisians had fired on Parisians.

23 January

'On the 9th of December 1870, I sent a letter by "mounted balloon" to London. It arrived on the 13th of December, on which day a telegraphic answer was sent, and which I received by pigeon post from Tours on the 23rd of January 1871. Before the Prussian era, I used to send at 7.40 a.m., Monday a letter to the *Daily Telegraph* and buy the paper containing it on the boulevards at 7 p.m. on Tuesday!' (Whitehurst)

In his account of the government of the siege, Vice President Jules Favre would later write of this juncture that 'civil war was a few yards away, famine a few hours'. Of the two, civil war was the more frighteningly imminent. The first result of the previous day's rioting was a decree suppressing two inflammatory red newspapers, *Le Reveil* and *Le Combat*, and closing the *clubs rouges*, prime fomenters of the trouble. The measure had little effect, since the clubs merely convened publicly on the streets, attracting more attention than they would have done indoors.

'We have to break through,' they shouted. 'We have to make a breach.'

'But do we have armies in the provinces or not?'

'If we do, then let's get out there, even if it means the deaths of a hundred thousand men. Let's join up with them and defeat the Prussians together.'

'But we haven't got anything to eat. They're saying that we've got enough bread for a week if we're lucky.'

'Rubbish – there's enough for six months, if they'd only enforce some requisitions on the rich.'

'Then why didn't you vote for the Commune – the Commune would have ordered requisitions . . .'

'Your bloody Commune. The Communards are in league with the Prussians: they were firing on Frenchmen and women yesterday while the Prussians were bombarding us. They are traitors!'

'So what do you want – the Empire back again?'

'It's not a matter of that. It's a matter of whether there are any armies in the provinces and whether we've got any food left. If there's nobody out there waiting to help us, if we haven't got anything to eat, what do you suggest we do?'

Up and down the boulevards, in side streets and passages, through all weathers, day and night, such shouting matches echoed uselessly. Paris was finished, and to seal its fate Favre secretly summoned as envoy the Comte d'Hérisson, empowering him to seek a parley with Bismarck and request an armistice before they were forced into unconditional surrender. This was a decision of the Parisian cabinet alone, necessarily made without consulting Gambetta or the government in Tours, and Favre knew that it was not something the city wanted. 'God only knows,' he said 'what the Parisian populace will do to us when we are compelled to tell them the truth.'

Through the rituals at the House of the Flag of Truce, d'Hérisson explained the situation to the Prussian outpost and arranged for a brief cease-fire. He returned to Paris to collect Favre and together they crossed the Seine in a leaking little boat, whose holes they stopped up with torn handkerchiefs and strips of paper; a tin saucepan served to bale out the water. The night was moonless, illuminated only by a fire at the palace of Saint-Cloud which threw a blood-coloured gleam on to the water. 'It was biblical, magnificent, what you please,' wrote d'Hérisson, 'but it was horrible.'

> With his high hat and badly-made legal black frock-coat, his countenance indented like a crescent of the waning moon, and his ministerial paper-case, Jules Favre was too modern to pose as Dante; while I, with my tunic, scarlet striped trousers, and kepi, could not have given a very accurate idea of Virgil. But if the appearance of the actors left something to be desired, the scene of Hell surrounded them, complete, sombre, mournful, and drawn by reality in proportions certainly more enormous than those of the visions of the immortal Italian poet.

Favre (a histrionic character, whose sincerity d'Hérisson doubted, comparing him to the man in the farce who was always clutching his head and moaning, 'Oh, how I suffer! Oh how it hurts!') was then conducted to the modest house in Versailles occupied by Bismarck. Favre beat his breast, but the Imperial Chancellor was unimpressed, announcing as a bluff that he was currently negotiating with an envoy of Louis Napoleon:

> He explained that nothing would be easier than for him to bring back the dethroned sovereign and impose him on France; that Napoleon III would easily find among the French prisoners detained in Germany a hundred thousand absolutely devoted men, who would be ample to support him when the Germans retired; and that, at the worst, there was still the resource of convoking a certain portion of the old Corps Législatif and treating with it.
> He became more animated as he went on speaking, and he continued almost in these words,
> 'As a matter of fact, why should I treat with you? Why should I give your Republic a semblance of legality by signing a convention with its representative? As a matter of fact you are merely a band of

insurgents! Your Emperor, should he return, has a perfect right to have you all shot as traitors and rebels.'

'But if he returns,' exclaimed Jules Favre, in dismay, 'we shall have a civil war and anarchy.'

'Are you quite sure of that? And besides, in what way can a civil war injure us Germans?'

'Then you are not afraid of reducing us to despair? You are not afraid of driving our resistance to desperation?'

'Ah! you talk of your resistance,' said the Chancellor, interrupting him quickly. 'Ah! you are proud of your resistance? Well, sir, let me tell you that if M. Trochu were a German General I would have him shot tonight. Nobody has a right, do you understand, nobody has any right, in the face of humanity, in the face of God, and for sheer military vain glory, to expose, as he is doing now, a town of more than two million souls to the horrors of famine. The lines of iron are cut everywhere. If we do not succeed in re-establishing them in two days, and that is by no means certain, a hundred thousand of you will die in Paris every day. Do not talk to me of your resistance. It is criminal!'

Jules Favre, thoroughly out of countenance, begged and implored that France, after all her disasters, should not be made to suffer the shame of having to put up with a Bonaparte. He then began to cry up the advantages of the Republic, an impersonal regime which alone could endure the hard and offensive conditions of the conqueror without absolute ruin, which alone was capable of giving adequate assurance to Germany that any treaty should be faithfully observed.

To make a long story short, before they separated, M. de Bismarck had promised Jules Favre to put in writing the conditions which seemed desirable to him and had been discussed by them. On the following morning, after having seen the Emperor and M. de Moltke, the Chancellor delivered to the Minister the plan of a Convention.

Armistice of twenty-one days – The army to be disarmed and to remain prisoners of war in Paris – The old battalions of the Garde Nationale, sixty in number, to remain armed for the preservation of order; the remainder, with all free corps to be disbanded. The army to surrender arms *and colours*: the officers to retain their swords – The armistice to extend to the whole of France, and the respective positions of the armies to be marked out – Paris to pay a war indemnity and to surrender the forts to the Germans – The latter not to enter the *enceinte* during the Armistice – The guns mounted on the ramparts to be thrown into the ditches – Parliamentary elections to be held for the return of an assembly charged with pronouncing on a definite treaty of peace.

Thus did Favre relate the first round of the proceedings to d'Hérisson as he returned to Paris to report to the cabinet.

24 January
At a dinner at Chez Brébant, Edmond de Goncourt and other intellectuals discussed the position. What was criminal about both Trochu and Favre, someone said, was that privately both men had despaired but that publicly they had given the masses to believe in the certitude of deliverance. And would Paris now tolerate a capitulation – not just the revolutionary minority, but the averagely patriotic bourgeois who had made his contribution to the war effort and who now stood to have his arms confiscated?

The scientist Berthelot's view was that the French defeat had nothing to do with the superiority of Prussian artillery. It was simply that the Prussian command studied maps, made precise calculations and considered alternatives, whereas the French command went out in the evenings to enjoy itself, and turned up on the battlefield next morning asking where the troops were and where the attack was coming from.

Finally, the diners wondered how the Prussians would treat the conquered Parisians. Some believed that they would expropriate the contents of the museums, others that they would be more interested in industrial raw materials. Somehow this led to a discussion of dyes, before the conversation reverted to its starting-point. 'Nefftzer, contrary to everyone else, maintains that the Prussians will want to astonish us all by their generosity and magnanimity. Amen! Leaving Brébant's, walking along the boulevard, the word "capitulation" which a few days ago it would have been dangerous so much as to pronounce, is on everyone's lips.'

25 January
Food prices continued to tumble and all manner of provisions were suddenly offered for sale. 'At 11 a.m. when the negotiations between Bismarck and M. Jules Favre could have been but in the preliminary stage,' wrote Albert Vandam, 'I received a note, brought

by hand, from a grocer in the Faubourg Montmartre, asking me to call personally, as he had something to communicate which might be to the advantage of my protégés. An hour later, I was at his establishment, and he offered to sell me five hundred tins of various provisions and two hundred and fifty boxes of sardines at two francs each. It was something like double the ordinary price.

Three weeks earlier the same grocer had claimed to be empty-shelved. The Stock Exchange – which had persistently remained calm throughout the siege and taken a long-term view of the strength of the French economy – rose forty-five centimes on the wing of the rumours of peace.

26 January

Favre continued to negotiate with Bismarck. The sticking-point was the Garde Nationale. Favre knew that to require its Red divisions to surrender their arms would be tantamount to an invitation to revolution – a prospect that had Bismarck snorting contemptuously. Eventually it was agreed that the Garde Nationale would remain armed; that the regular army (except for one division) would surrender all its arms (except officers' swords); that an indemnity of 200 million francs should be paid; that the forts surrounding Paris should be surrendered, but that no Prussians would enter within the walls of the city for the three-week duration of the armistice. Meanwhile a freely elected Assembly at Bordeaux would debate a formal peace, or a resumption of war. Paris would be opened and revictualled.

At 11.45 p.m. Favre took his fifteen-year-old daughter out on to the balcony of his office on the Quai d'Orsay, overlooking the Seine. In silence they listened to the final thunderous dialogue between the French and Prussian artillery. Midnight chimed and the clamour stopped. After a brief pause, the French fired one last shell into the night – a small concession that Bismarck, with uncharacteristic concern for French honour, had granted a city he had besieged for a hundred and thirty-one days, bombarded for twenty-four.

27 January

The news was broken to the people of Paris thus:

So long as the government could count on an army of relief, it was its duty to neglect nothing which could prolong the defence of Paris. Now, though our armies are still on foot, the fortunes of war have driven them back – one under the walls of Lille, the second beyond Laval, while the third is operating on the eastern frontier.*

We have thus lost all hope of their being able to approach us, and the state of our stores will not permit us to wait longer.

In these circumstances negotiation was the absolute duty of the government. These negotiations are now proceeding. Everyone will understand that there is serious difficulty in publishing the details of them. We hope to be able to publish them tomorrow. We can, however, state today that the principle of national sovereignty will be protected by the immediate calling of an Assembly. That the end of the armistice is the convocation of that Assembly; that during the armistice the German army will occupy the forts, but will not enter Paris; that we preserve our Garde Nationale untouched and one division of the army, while no soldier will be sent out of the country.

The announcement caused every conceivable emotion. Felix Whitehurst was plain baffled.

The truth is, the notice is not satisfactory. It speaks of 'the armistice'. Men ask, 'what armistice?' Then there is no word of revictualling, neither is there any allusion to those 'inches of our territory' [about which back in September Favre had declared himself intractable]. Again, do 'soldiers' include Mobiles and National Guards? . . . Things may be better than we expect; but when one remembers the boastful speeches of Trochu, the impossible diplomacy of Favre. . . ; when one recalls the ruinous and unnecessary expense of turning an open into a fortified city; the money expended on the fortifications never manned, and weapons never wielded, and above all the awful sacrifice of life . . . one cannot be astonished if thousands of young National Guards should say 'Our country, our families, our trades are ruined for years. We have given up anything and everything to fight Prussia, and after our Elected Imbecility have kept us in suspense for four months, they have put us by in a corner like an old muzzle-loading musket.'

Juliette Adam was simply devastated: 'I would like to die,' she

* The latter was the army under General Bourbaki, which, owing to an astonishing oversight, was never informed of the armistice. To the Prussian advantage, it continued to fight and was eventually forced back into Switzerland, where it entirely disintegrated.

wrote. The Left furiously contested the government's assertion that famine was imminent; the Right saw only the enemy within, the spectre of Red Revolution, as fearsome a prospect as Prussian occupation. The press fulminated (*Le Rappel*: 'it is not an armistice, it is a capitulation'), wagged its finger (*Le Temps*: 'it is time to put an end to the rhetorical charlatanism, which is one of our worst diseases'), and beat its breast (*Le Siècle*: the Prussians have brought the French race face to face with its decadence; they are the 'fatal gangrene of our virility'). But perhaps Labouchere best summed up the majority's short-term response to the news that they would now be able to eat their old food, without the sound of bombs as sauce to their meals. 'Most of us here,' he commented, 'are much like heirs at a rich man's funeral. We have long faces, we sigh and we groan, but we are not quite so unhappy as we look.'

9 : *A Passage to Civil War*

The government's statement issued on January 29 and detailing further the terms of the armistice, included that 'Paris had suffered much, but the Republic will profit from such long suffering, so nobly sustained. We quit the struggle that has concluded charged for "the struggle to come".' Such rhetoric, designed to placate the bellicose faction, was deplored by, among many, Tommy Bowles, who wrote: 'The idea of presenting the Republic as a consolation for the sufferings and the fall of Paris is one which would just now be extravagant in the wildest burlesque, but it is surpassed in folly by the second phrase I have cited, which seems to have been purposely designed in order at once to irritate the Prussians at the moment when they have their foot on the neck of the country itself in an attitude of resistance, which is now no longer possible.'

Others threw up their hands at a different angle. Flaubert, arch-conservative, refused henceforth to wear his ribbon of the Légion d'honneur, 'because the words "French" and "honour" have become incompatible'; while from England, Matthew Arnold reflected in a sententious letter to his mother that France's position was

mainly due to that want of a serious conception of righteousness and the need of it . . . the fall of Greece, the fall of Rome, the fall of the brilliant Italy of the fifteenth century, and now the fall of France, are all examples . . . the qualities of the French genius, their lucidity, directness of intellect, and social charm, must always make themselves felt, as the far higher qualities of the Greeks did and do. But it is a question whether the practical military and political career of France may not now be ending, not again to revive, as that of Greece did after the Macedonian Conquest.

From within, the architect and historian Viollet-le-Duc was inclined to praise the capital's population, 'decried throughout the world as futile, trivial, dedicated to its own well-being and pleasures, selfish and shiftless', for giving the world an example, 'perhaps unique in history, of constancy, firmness, abnegation and sensitive charity': the problem had been that of a demoralized military leadership, whose attitudes had infected the troops. Labouchere, on the other hand, was not convinced by pious phrases:

> The talk of the people now is, that they mean to become serious . . . If they carry out these intentions, I am afraid that, however their morals may be improved, their material interests will suffer. Gambling tables may not be an advantage to Europe, but without them Homburg and Baden would go to the wall. Paris is a city of pleasure – a cosmopolitan city; it has made its profit out of the follies and the vices of the world. Its prices are too high, its houses are too large, its promenades and its public places have cost too much for it to be able to pay its way as the sober, decent capital of a moderate-sized country, where there are few great fortunes. If the Parisians decide to become poor and respectable, they are to be congratulated upon the resolve, but the present notion seems to be that they are to become rich and respectable – a thing more difficult. Paris – the Paris of the Empire and of Haussmann – is a house of cards. Its prosperity was a forced and artificial one. The war and the siege have knocked down the cards, and it is doubtful whether they will ever serve to build a new house.

But behind the initial flurries of secret relief, the angry debates and hectic influx of news from the outside world, there was no mistaking the city's profound depression – Whitehurst called it 'a complete and idiotic apathy'. In such a political limbo, there was nothing to be done except wait, and 'Paris s'ennnuie' ran the headline in *Le Gaulois*, 'Paris is bored, Paris is bored with itself.' Perhaps the most lowering aspect of these dismal days was the spectacle of soldiers drifting back from the front – the dirty, tattered and drunken remnants of a disarmed and defeated army, lurching through the streets cynically abusing their erstwhile officers and a lost cause. To the first journalists who entered the city, Paris seemed 'eerily stricken, the air haunted by the peculiar, half-sweetish, half-foetid odour which horse flesh gives out in cooking. . . . It permeated the deserted British Embassy, where, asserting my privileges as a Briton, I stabled my horse; it lingered in the corridors of the Grand Hotel, and fought with the taint from wounds in evil case. The Grand Hotel was one huge hospital. Half Paris seemed converted into hospitals . . .'

Thus the *Daily News* correspondent Archibald Forbes. 'Very touching was the ignorance everywhere as to the outside world. "I have seen three English papers since September," said Dr Gordon, our Medical Commissioner. "Is Ireland quiet? Is Mr Gladstone still Prime Minister? Is the Princess Louise married?" '

What excitement there was concentrated on food, and the question of revictualling. It is not at all clear how close Paris was to famine, despite Jules Favre's assertion that it was only days away. There had certainly been widespread hoarding and profiteering, and the moment the armistice was declared Les Halles and the other markets bustled into action, offering a variety of produce which twenty-four hours previously had been considered inconceivable and unobtainable. Down plummeted the prices too: chickens, now twenty-five francs, had been sixty-five; rabbits, now twenty, had been fifty; carrots, potatoes, turnips, even eggs likewise. This caused understandable resentment and a certain amount of rioting and expropriation (its perpetrators declaring that 'they were tired of seeing food kept from them by the cupidity of (not the rich but) their fellow-working people,' wrote Nathan Sheppard. 'The poor have no crueller enemy than the poor').

The foreign press was full of descriptions of starving children and the pressing need for immediate relief supplies, but some post-armistice visitors, including a correspondent of *The Times*, were comfortingly surprised. On 2 February the latter dined at Peters on 'Crécy soup, Seine smelts, excellent roast beef, salad, asparagus, preserved peaches and a bottle and a half of wine, and coffee, for 13 francs each', reporting 'that the people did not look as if they had in any way suffered privation'; five days later he could still talk of 'streets full of provisions of every description at reasonable prices'. All rationing and price control had already been lifted. Despite this impression, the yearning for long-absent oral pleasures remained intense – one man in Les Halles dived into a vat of butter, then ran off covered head to foot in glorious golden grease – and their gradual return to the daily diet brought tremulous happiness to thousands: 'while out in the morning found some eggs at 4*d*. each,' wrote an ecstatic Edwin Child in his diary for 7 February. 'The temptation was too strong bought ½ doz. the first for upwards of 3 months didn't me and Albert enjoy them.' The truly desperate and the more enterprising made their way out to Neuilly, to the west of the city. Here a bridge which led over to the village of Courbevoie provided the one open channel between Paris and the outside world – everywhere else had been bombed or blockaded. On the avenue of approach sat a constant traffic jam of arrivals and departures, the roadside lined with peasants and farmers selling their produce to all comers. 'Nothing is more telling,' wrote Edmond de Goncourt on 7 February 'than the happiness, almost an affectionate tenderness with which people hold in their arms their sticks of bread, of fine white bread, which Paris has so long been denied.'

Gradually the lines of communication eased (although the Prussians maintained a policing cordon) and more systematic supplies managed to reach the city. Conditions improved steadily: by mid February most of the main rail lines were operational and by the end of the month, the gas supply was restored and the mortality rate had dropped appreciably. A journalist called Edward Dicey, writing in the *Fortnightly Review* in London, visited the city at this stage in its reviving fortunes and objectively concluded that there had been 'a great deal of exaggeration about the actual horrors of the siege'. In the centre of the city, the effects of the bombardment appeared negligible (even in the fifth arrondissement, 'where the shells fell thickest . . . as far as I could see, there has not been a single street or public building in this quarter which has been materially damaged by the Prussian cannon'); and the extent of the deprivation was limited, Dicey believed, to one social class:

> The great mass of the working class were by no means badly off. The men had for the most part their thirty sous a day as National Guards; the women and children had their rations; and though there was much sickness, distress, and suffering amongst the operatives, it was scarcely, if at all, greater than in any ordinary hard winter when work is slack. The well-to-do classes, who had money at their disposal, had laid up large stores before the investment began; and though they also were exposed to great discomfort through the curtailment of their accustomed luxuries, they were as a body never brought face to face with actual want. The real pinch and stress fell almost exclusively on the class of small employees, clerks, shopmen, skilled artizans . . . they had no wages or earnings to receive, they had no savings to invest in food; they were too independent to beg for alms, too feeble to hustle and struggle for rations with the crowd. It was amongst this class, which starved and pined away, died and made no sign, that the mortality was the heaviest.

(Dicey goes on to suggest that the reason for the relative restraint of the population through the siege was 'that the governing class and the working class alike never had their resolution tested by the dire extremity of hunger; and that the class which really bore the burden of the siege is the class which never makes barricades or coups-d'état, but, under every administration, obeys the powers that be.')

Getting the food to those who needed it was not an easy job – it never is. Britain and the USA had been notably generous in providing relief (a fund administered by the Lord Mayor of London alone raised the gigantic sum of £100,000 within a month) and mind-boggling train loads of victuals poured in. According to the *Illustrated London News*, the total received between 3 and 7 February alone was as follows:

> 1057 bullocks, 3093 sheep, 14 cows, 31 pigs, 856 tons of cereals, 8050 tons of flour, 500 tons of biscuits, 285 tons of preserved beef; 162 tons of preserved mutton, 8 tons of salt, 80 tons of hams, 1435 tons of salt pork, 26 tons of fresh fish, 210 tons of codfish, 140 tons of butter, nearly 1000 tons of cheese, 74 tons of oil, 1270 tons of vegetables, 10 tons of fruit, 27 tons of forage, 70 tons of cakes, 144 tons of various provisions, 1740 tons of coal, and 94 tons of oats.

The British contribution was stored in two warehouses, one of them at the department store Au Bon Marché: here seven hundred packaged rations were doled out every hour to a line which sometimes contained as many as five thousand applicants. The correspondent for *Blackwood's Magazine* found the scene depressing for several reasons: the appalling destitution of a few; the furiously resentful, grabbing greed of the many; and the presence of 'physiognomies so appallingly depraved, so befouled with degradations and defilements, so denaturalised by hideous appetites, that gorillas would have seemed angels of purity beside them'. But attempts to organize distribution through the *mairies* of each arrondissement proved worse then ineffective: large quantities of foodstuffs vanished and some areas ran dry while others held gluts which turned uselessly sour and rotten on them. One insoluble problem was the *pauvres honteux*, the embarrassed poor, 'many of whom are persons in the upper classes of society' who 'cannot be expected to come and make *queue* for hours in the streets'. Too proud to receive charity, they died shivering and emaciated in the freezing, threadbare gentility of their salons, untraced and unseen, the Prussians' final victims.

Those who weren't hungry may well have found themselves homeless, as the extent of the devastation wrought by five months of modern warfare became stunningly clear. The dull, flat towns around Paris, innocent isolated farmhouses and pleasant suburban villages had been left in silent ruin. The middle classes lost their weekend villas, tens of thousands of refugees lost everything: the land had been cursed in a way that besieged and bombarded Paris had been spared. Most shocking of all was perhaps the fate of Saint-Cloud, 'whose situation' mourned the *Illustrated London News*, 'may be compared to that of Richmond, with respect to London, being the half-rural abode of ancient sovereigns, whose patronage had made it a fashionable residence in former ages, and a prosperous, though quiet, community, including many opulent families'. Destroyed by the Prussians after the sortie of 19 January, it was now nothing but 'a hideous spectacle of blackened and broken walls, through which the German soldiers lounge with cool indifference, while the poor people gather the unconsumed fragments of woodwork from the floors and doorways, to carry away for fuel'. It was still winter, and dreadfully cold.

Yet somehow Paris had to pick itself up from its humiliating collapse, dust off the ashes and begin to walk again – every step overlooked by an icily triumphant enemy whose guns remained at the ready. Nothing was more fundamental to this painful recuperation than the establishment of a government which could credibly negotiate and ratify a treaty of peace with the Prussians. The present regime did not qualify: it had never been properly elected and was theoretically no more or less legal than the Second Empire it had usurped only five months previously. It had also lost the war. Bismarck enjoyed rubbing this salt into the wound when he discussed terms with Favre and other members of the Government of National Defence. Why should he not be talking to Louis Napoleon or the Empress (who had indeed submitted him proposals)? Where was the real control over the population of Paris – with the Garde Nationale? The mob? Nevertheless he knew that a civil war could not be in Prussia's interests and therefore accepted Favre's view that requiring the Garde Nationale to lay down its arms and disband would have provoked mayhem. Making this concession also allowed him to remain intransigent on a number of other fronts.

Another problematic element was the behaviour of Gambetta, who headed the Provisional Government now based in Bordeaux. Infuriated by the armistice, over which he had not been consulted, he spoke out against it, openly advising the troops to steel themselves for further combat – a stance which brought him a sharp telegram from Bismarck, advising him to toe the line. Elections were clearly an urgent priority.* They were held on 8 February and produced a reactionary result: out of 768 seats, over 400 went to those favouring a restoration of the monarchy. Only forty-three seats were allotted to Paris: those elected as its deputies may have been a left-wing republican

---

* They provided incidentally a splendid premise for leaving Paris, something which was only possible with a *laissez-passer* authorized by the police. Over 23,000 of the 100,000 applicants claimed to be standing as candidates in obscure villages where they needed to electioneer.

bunch – Louis Blanc, Victor Hugo, Garibaldi, Gambetta and Rochefort among them – as was the case in most of the large cities, but they were not enough to alter significantly the basically conservative colour of the newly constituted assembly. Chief Executive was the weasel-faced little septuagenarian Adolphe Thiers, who had first been Prime Minister thirty-five years previously under the Orléanist king Louis-Philippe. ('Il n'y a que vous, cher Monsieur Thiers' the duc de Broglie had ambivalently remarked on his election, 'there is no one but you', possibly implying that he wished that there was an alternative.) A celebrated historian of the 1789 Revolution and the Napoleonic era, pragmatic in his politics, but a friend to the business class, to the godly, sober and righteous, he was known for his hard line on urban disruption and his lack of senti- mentality. In private he could be a great charmer, but he was nobody's fool. No idealist, he recognized that, one way or another, France would have to pay a heavy price for its failure. As Emile Zola put it, 'Thiers was for the facts, the Left for principles.'

Like the majority of the new deputies, Thiers was determined to take no nonsense or histrionics from Paris. Paris, for its part, expected its sufferings during the siege to be sympathetically acknowledged. It had always required respect, if not obeisance, from the rest of France; now, in its dark hour, more than ever. Fatally, Thiers did not begin to understand this. Prejudiced and myopic, he had spent the siege in the relative comfort of Tours and lacked the imagination to appreciate what effect those months of privation and anxiety in the capital might have induced.

Thiers was not a man to make subtle observations or fine distinctions, and for him, Red working-class Paris was simply a mob and a menace. He was wrong: it was much more self- controlled than that, and two of its groupings were of lasting importance. One was known as the Corderie, after a building which housed a triumvirate of linked leftist organizations: the Internationale, which contained disciples of both the com- munism of Karl Marx and the anarchism of Mikhail Bakunin (or either of them); the Delegation of Twenty Arrondissements, a 'revolutionary socialist' party which had been plastering the walls of Paris since the beginning of the siege; and the Trade Union Federation. These three drew up a list of shared principles and formed local vigilance committees: they agreed 'to seek to obtain by all possible means the suppression of the privileges of the bourgeoisie, its overthrow as a controlling class and the political accession of the workers. In a word, social equality. No more employers, no more proletarians, no more classes.' Its active membership was probably quite small and largely intellectual – Corderie candidates polled a total of barely 50,000 votes in the election – but it was highly articulate and broadly influential. The other was more numerous and looser. This was the league for the defence of the Garde Nationale, known by various names, but for simplicity's sake here referred to as the Committee of the Garde Nationale. It was controlled by a central body consisting of 'two who kept wine-shops, a house painter, a cook, a door-porter, a lodging house servant, a restaurateur, an acrobat and sword-swallower, an ex-advocate, an ex-zouave, a bookbinder, a concert manager, two inevitable journalists, a wardrobe dealer of the Temple market, a government and a bank clerk (who had been convicted of theft), a former seminarist, a man who had worked in a wash-house, another who had kept some public baths, and a couple of sculptors' assistants.' 'The others,' added Ernest Vizetelly, 'were mostly nondescripts, who had resorted to divers odd ways of making a living.'

Vizetelly's list may not be entirely accurate, but it suggests the flavour: the absence of any industrial workers is particularly notable. It represented what remained of the Garde Nationale after the more bourgeois battalions had disbanded (many of their members had left Paris after the siege was lifted) and it stood firmly opposed to any sell-out to the Prussians. Together the Corderie and the Committee of the Garde Nationale fomented an atmosphere of anger, fear and suspicion, further dividing Paris from the rest of Thiers' smug, craven France. The capital was about to be betrayed, they thought – handed over to the Prussians for some ritual humiliation which might win a softer set of terms for peace. By the end of February the spread of this virus of paranoia – and like all paranoias, it was not altogether unjustified – had left some areas of Paris virtually ungovernable. On one side of the city, shops were reopening, gaslight was shining and water running; on the other, the police were helpless before the barricades, pillaging and lawlessness. On 24 February a red flag flew from the column in the centre of an occupied Place de la Bastille and on 26 February a huge and unruly crowd filled the Champs Élysées, shouting support for the principles of the Committee of the Garde Nationale. One persistent rumour was that Thiers was on the brink of conceding that the Prussians could occupy Paris until peace was settled and that they would be empowered to confiscate any heavy armaments remaining within the city.

What the Garde Nationale felt most possessive about were the cannon which had been bought by public subscription for the defence of Paris. These were currently held in various ineffect- ually protected sites, and the Reds had little trouble in requisitioning them, wheeling the gun carriages through the streets to 'safe' parks in Montmartre and Belleville. The parade caused high excitement, but of an innocent sort compared to the fury which swept through the Place de la Bastille that same day. Here a police spy named Vincensini was spotted taking notes on the demonstrators. Having been lynched, he was strangled and drowned in the Seine, the scapegoat of a crowd of about five hundred, half of them boys. It was an ominous instance of what Dr Lucien Nass gravely described in his interesting book on the social pathology of the era as 'sadism, the faithful companion of revolutionary mobs . . . it is not anger which pushes a crowd to such excess, but the lowest animal instincts'. The beast, it seemed, was out.

The new government monitored the situation from Bordeaux and Versailles. There was not much else that could be done at this stage: Thiers was not one to play softly, softly, but he could scarcely afford to jeopardize the concluding stages of the peace negotiations with the threat of civil war or even the embarrass- ment of a rush of public sound and fury. And the fact was that Red Paris's nightmare was about to be realized. The proposed peace treaty involved the surrender to Germany of most of

Alsace-Lorraine, along France's fertile and prosperous eastern frontier, and the payment of an indemnity of 5,000 million gold francs* towards the cost of the war: until this was paid off – and that might take years – Prussian troops would remain stationed in northern France. Most directly relevant to Paris was a clause which allowed the limited entry of Prussian troops into a part of Paris until the Assembly ratified the initial terms of the treaty. By agreeing to this, Thiers managed to save the besieged town of Belfort from falling into German hands. It was a hard bargain.

Few people had much patience with Paris at this point – 'I am fully convinced,' wrote a fed-up Labouchere, 'that this vain, silly population would rather that King William should double the indemnity which he demands from France than march with his troops down the rue de Rivoli' – but everyone held their breath in anticipation of an explosive reaction. In the event it proved surprisingly muted. The Corderie had persuaded the Committee of the Garde Nationale to take the line (advertised on posters throughout the city) that 'calm' was required and that 'agitation' would be 'counter-revolutionary'.

'With the near-advent of the much-dreaded event,' reported *The Times*, 'Parisian indignation appeared to subside in an extraordinary manner.' Only 30,000 troops would take part, and they were to be confined to a small central area bordered by the Seine, the rue du Faubourg Saint-Honoré and the rue de Rivoli. More barricades were thrown up to prevent any off-bounds incursions and in the Place de la Concorde some unknown genius had hung black veils over the faces of the allegorical statues representing the great French cities, 'that the Barbarians should not triumph in their very faces'. Elsewhere there were no such magnificent gestures. Whether awe-struck, contemptuous or plain terrified, the city fell silent and closed its doors and shutters.

At 8.30 on the morning of 1 March, a first Prussian hussar, name of Lieutenant von Bernhardi, rode through the Porte Maillot and up to the Arc de Triomphe – testing the water, as it

---

* In an attempt to convey the vastness of this sum, *The Times* calculated that in five-franc pieces, this would weigh 25 million kilogrammes, fill 5,000 train wagons, or form a single end-to-end column 1,500 miles high.

were. He was a mere slip of a boy: 'by Jove, if that fellow's mother could see him she'd have something to be proud of for the rest of her time,' gasped an Englishman observing the scene. At ever briefer intervals, larger and larger contingents followed on, but, as *The Times* reported, there was 'scarcely anybody to look at them, except a few scattered groups of spectators among the lower classes, who showed no spirit of ill-will'. Nothing else greeted them. The archway of the Arc de Triomphe had been blocked up. No newspapers were published, no omnibuses ran. The fountains were stilled. No café or shop would have dared to open for business.

Later that morning, the Kaiser, flanked by a full royal, military and political establishment, took the review of the bulk of the troops at the racecourse of Longchamps in the Bois de Boulogne. They then moved down the Champs Elysées 'in a solemn silence, preceded only by drums and fifes'. The crowd was now thicker, although still composed of 'the lower classes' alone. The *gamins* hissed and catcalled, but 'I could feel as I stood among the people,' continued the *Illustrated London News* report, 'that they were becoming more and more impressed in the degree in which they felt they were being completely ignored.' The Kaiser had returned immediately to Versailles, Bismarck came only as far as the Arc de Triomphe: 'smoking a cigar, [he] gazed at the scene for a few moments, and turned round and rode slowly away, without going beyond the crest of the hill'. But thirty thousand of their fellow Prussians and Bavarians were now in possession of the heart of Paris – albeit without access to the standard run of Parisian boulevard pleasures. For all Europe it was a heart-stopping moment.

After they had billeted in the Palais de l'Industrie and the Cirque Impériale, the troops were at leisure and in the mood for sightseeing. Maxime Vuillaume remembered seeing a group of fresh-faced young Prussian soldiers-turned-tourists, leaning in awe over the quai of the Seine and gazing at Notre-Dame, the Sainte-Chapelle, the Palais de Justice and the rest of the legendary panorama. 'Ah, Parisse, Parisse' they sighed in their heavy German accents, 'holding out their arms towards the horizon, as if they wanted to seize hold of and carry away the marvels in front of them.' The Invalides, resting-place of the first Napoleon and a shrine to those fallen in war for France, had tactfully been closed, but it was agreed that officers could visit the Louvre. The museum's treasures were still boxed up in Brittany and the deserted halls of that most charmless of state buildings were hardly anything to write home about. Feeling bored and cheated, some young blades flung open one of the grand windows and gazed indolently out on the Place below. A crowd gathered and after a certain amount of pointing, pouting and jeering, a slanging-match developed: some of the more fool-hardy French began throwing coins up at the invaders, shouting sarcastically that they were a contribution towards the repara-tions. But there was no further significant unpleasantness and all other incidents were isolated ones: a prostitute publicly stripped and taunted for soliciting a Prussian; a lunatic who wove his way round the cavalry in the rue de Rivoli offering cigars and shouting 'Vive la Prusse!'; a drunk who lashed out and had some enemy bayonets pointed menacingly at him in retaliation. Otherwise everyone behaved with amazing restraint: the only souvenirs which the enemy expropriated were laurel leaves plucked from bushes in the gardens of the Tuileries to make triumphal wreaths.

By the following morning a certain normality seems to have re-established itself. Shops began to reopen, people went about their business. In the occupied area, soldiers wandered about, peered through windows and sat on park benches. Parisians trailed them, stared at them, and ganged up to start timid, curious conversations. 'The presence of the enemy was humiliating beyond doubt, but it offered a new sight to look at,' commented *Blackwood's Magazine*, 'and at all times the people of Paris like a sight, whatever be its nature.' However, 'No person of the upper classes was to be seen,' emphasized the *Illustrated London News*: this was only an affair of the streets. It was soon over. The new Assembly in Bordeaux had ratified the initial treaty by 546 votes to 107, Thiers having made it clear that he would resign if it did not go through. There were, naturally enough, many passionate speeches against the terms, some of them direly prophetic of the further wars which the territorial losses would spawn. Gambetta, Rochefort, Victor Hugo and the great majority of the Parisian deputies resigned, as did the betrayed representatives of Alsace-Lorraine. The yeas simply wanted an end and knew how little power they had to determine it.

With provisional acceptance of the peace terms now agreed by the Assembly, the Prussians were obliged to withdraw from the capital. Early on the foggy morning of 3 March, they made a splendid retreat up the Champs Elysées – witnessed, it was reported, by even fewer than had seen the entry. Some of the troops still wore Tuileries laurel wreaths round their helmets, and there was cheering as they passed through the Arc de Triomphe (all obstructions having been firmly removed during the night) and the sun suddenly blazed out in spring glory through the dissolving mist. Before midday, every last man of them was marching outside the city's ring of fortification, and Paris could heave a massive sigh of anticlimax, if not relief. More fervent patriots set about scrubbing floors and pavements trodden by enemy feet with Condy's Disinfecting Fluid, but initially it must have seemed to Thiers that his risky bargain with Bismarck had paid off: Paris had borne its punishment with barely a whimper.

What followed was a fortnight of brisk rehabilitation. No sympathy was shown for the victim: having been flung in rags to the ground, the city was now kicked to its feet and told to brace up. A hard-line conservative, General d'Aurelle de Paladines, was appointed head of the Garde Nationale. Versailles, just vacated by the German High Command, was named as the seat of the new Assembly – a move rudely implying the government's wish to keep the capital at arm's length. The most vicious blows, however, came in the shape of a series of Draconian economic measures. After a period when tens of thousands had lost their livelihoods and before any level of ordinary commercial activity had been given the chance to pick up, the government announced that landlords were entitled to demand full, immediate back-payment on all rents suspended during the siege. Further such legislation on overdue credit, promissory notes and pawnshops, as well as the withdrawal of the Garde

Nationale's universal daily payment of *trente sous* (in effect a dole for those with no other means), made it clear that this was a government prepared to be flint-hearted. The Rothschilds have paid off their creditors, a Minister infamously pointed out to the Assembly, why shouldn't everyone else?

Some grotesque political miscalculation was behind this. Thiers needed to raise money from the banks to pay the first instalments of the indemnity, and the banks required proof that the new government was strong-minded, stable and financially stringent before it would oblige. But at whose expense? It was one thing to clamp down the Reds and leave the poor to charity; it was quite another to antagonize the decent, law-abiding, *patrie*-loving petit bourgeois and small businessman. On 9 March, the Revd William Gibson, a kindly Methodist clergyman on a mission in Paris, recorded in his journal a visit from a mason:

> an honest, respectable Frenchman, who has a real *home* in Paris, with twelve children about him, and his opinion was that the misfortunes to France were to be traced to these four causes:
> 1. Want of religious faith
> 2. Want of respect for authority
> 3. Want of a spirit to *work*
> 4. Want of modesty, shown in a spirit of boastfulness and vainglory.

Here was a man who was a potential supporter of Thiers' line; but the next day, 10 March, he may well have been one of the estimated 150,000 flung into bankruptcy when the new credit laws were enforced. Add these to the city's mass of unemployed – including many migrant workers left jobless by the end of the building boom of the Haussmann era – and you have a bitter black stew of revolutionary emotion: disgruntled working men with time on their hands, nothing to lose and no reason to stay loyal to a government which had scorned them. Their hostility may have been only passive, but it created an invisible barrier – a wall of festering gas – around Paris every bit as dangerous as the more overt demonstrations by the Garde Nationale, busy asserting itself throughout the first weeks of March and now possessed of huge stores of ordnance.

Thiers could only continue to turn the screw tighter. All superfluous troops were evacuated from Paris and the Garde Mobile reservists sent home. Six radical newspapers were summarily banned and two radical heroes, Auguste Blanqui and Gustave Flourens, were condemned to death *in absentia* by a court martial for their role in the Hôtel de Ville uprising of 31 October. The Assembly would move from Bordeaux to Versailles on 20 March, and Thiers was determined to inaugurate its new session with an announcement to the effect that Paris was subjugated or at least in hand. He therefore instructed General Vinoy, Commander-in-Chief of the army in Paris, to make a forceful effort to recover the cannon 'lost' over the past weeks and thereby in effect disarm the Garde Nationale. How fair a picture the government had of the mood of the capital – how far it knew what risks it was taking, how infiltrated the Red sections of the city were with police spies and informers – is not easy to determine. But Picard, the Minister of the Interior, did not seem particularly worried. 'It's nothing, one gets used to all that,' he told General d'Aurelle de Paladines, anxiously facing up to the baying of the Garde Nationale. 'You know what the population of Paris is like.' Sadly he didn't.

Previous attempts to negotiate the surrender of the expropriated cannon had come to nothing, but the situation was far from hopeless. Intelligence reports suggested that if Thiers had been so inclined, a few grunts of tactful compromise, a little back-slapping *bonhomie* and some fulsome compliments might have done the trick – in the absence of the appropriate munitions, much of the artillery was useless and it was only casually guarded. Yet he remained implacable. Despite his later admission that he had realized all along that the 20,000 ragged and weary troops to hand might not be sufficient to secure his goals, he planned a large-scale, city-wide military operation for the early hours of 18 March. Strategic areas – the Place de la Bastille, the railway stations, the bridges – would be occupied and a subsidiary police operation would lead to the arrest of key figures of the Garde Nationale and Red Belleville. Of over four hundred cannon held on seventeen different sites, 171 were in Montmartre: these latter would be the focus of a major attack from the north, under General Lecomte. Success depended on the assumption that there would be little serious opposition. Paris would awake to find itself morally and politically cleansed, its walls plastered with posters explaining what had happened and exhorting *les bons citoyens* to separate themselves from *les mauvais*.

At 3 a.m. on the morning of 18 March, the troops were woken in their barracks and hastily marshalled into shambolic, straggling platoons. It was an icy night of wind and rain. Nobody had thought of providing them with so much as a cup of coffee, let alone a fuelling breakfast: the commanders had been instructed to strike as fast as possible, under cover of darkness, and at first the rush seemed to pay off. In Montmartre, Lecomte found the gun park scarcely guarded and took it at the cost of only one sleepy Garde Nationale sentinel. Successful seizures were similarly made at other sites. Then what? Through some incredible – though far from unprecedented – bungle, the strategists had failed to arrange for an adequate number of harnessed horses to be available to trail the cannon back to lock and key.* So at 8 a.m., some three hours after occupying the Montmartre park, Lecomte's troops were still waiting for the necessary transport, stamping their feet in the cold dawn, slinking off to buy a bit of sustenance, and in some cases not coming back.

Of course by this time, everyone in the area knew what was happening and the alarm had been raised. One of the most fanatical adherents to the Red cause, the schoolteacher Louise Michel, had run down the hill screaming treason. Elsewhere drums were beating, windows opening and Belleville battalions of the Garde Nationale rousing themselves to the defence. Soon a huge and terrifying crowd was gathering round the gun park, jostling the tired and nervous soldiers. 'Where are you taking the cannon? Berlin?' the women asked sarcastically. The Mayor of Montmartre, the bold tiro Georges Clemenceau, strode forward to berate Lecomte for the peremptory invasion and the tempera-

---

* Later, the excuse was that since the siege, during which so many had been eaten, horses were hard to come by. Even if this was the case – which it wasn't – it should have been recognized and allowed for at an early stage in planning.

ture rose explosively. Eventually (according to some sources) Lecomte gave a panicky order to load and fix bayonets. There was no response. Three times he repeated the order: still no response. His soldiers were dropping their arms, tearing off their uniforms and fraternizing with the crowd. As the situation degenerated into chaos, Lecomte and other officers were grabbed by a rabble of Garde Nationale and pushed into the improvised prison of a dancehall while it was decided what to do with them. General Vinoy rushed up, surveyed the scene, and rushed away again, evacuating what remained of the military and leaving his kepi (so it was said) lying on the cobbles of the Place Pigalle.

Things were turning much nastier than either side had anticipated. In the afternoon Lecomte and his officers were flung out of the dancehall. The intention was to transfer them to the relative safety of the Garde Nationale headquarters in the rue des Rosiers on the other side of Montmartre. One of the officers remembered the journey as 'like a march to Calvary': as representatives of a defeated power, they suffered kicking, pelting abuse. The Garde Nationale's headquarters was only a converted family house in a nondescript residential area and there was no chance of defending or securing it from the mayhem which Lecomte had brought in his wake. Attempts to lock up the prisoners and wait for someone 'in charge' to arrive and take control proved futile. Windows were smashed, women screeched for revenge like harpies: as was the case with the lynching of the wretched police spy Vincensini a few weeks previously, only the orgasm of bloody murder would calm the beast.

Meanwhile some eagle eye had spotted the recently retired General Thomas – a distinctively tall and distinguished figure, as well as a former Commander-in-Chief of the Garde Nationale – who had foolishly walked up to Pigalle in mufti to watch what was happening. He was 'invited to join' his *confrère* General Lecomte in the rue des Rosiers. There he was summarily shot in the back garden – a pretty, suburban affair, with trellises and climbers – by what appears to have been anyone who had a weapon to hand. The post-mortem detected forty bullets in his body, as many of them fired from *chassepots* owned by deserters from the regular army as from the rifles of the Garde Nationale. Lecomte was the next to be sent into the garden of execution. He behaved with consummate military dignity. The first of the nine bullets to pepper him was fired by one of his own soldiers, who shot him in the back. When Clemenceau, the mayor of Montmartre, finally fought his way through to the scene, he burst into tears: the bodies had been dumped in the streets and women were pissing over them as the screeching and whistling rose like a hateful threnody.

All over the north and east of Paris that day something of the same pattern asserted itself, with the army's initial success failing as troops deserted and order disintegrated. On the Place de la Bastille, the Red flag which had fallen at 9 a.m. was flying again by noon: only the solemn passage of the funeral procession of Victor Hugo's son, suddenly dead of apoplexy, briefly stilled the hysterical excitement. ('Comme ce peuple m'aime!' sighed Hugo in his diary that evening, 'How these people love me!') The drums of the Garde Nationale rolled relentlessly, barricades rose inexorably, the third, fifth, ninth, twelfth, thirteenth, fourteenth, fifteenth and seventeenth arrondissements were all dominated by revolution. What is equally remarkable is the relative indifference of the more bourgeois west of the city. Attempts to rally loyal battalions of the Garde Nationale failed dismally – it was Saturday, everyone was shopping and *en famille* – and even among the staunchly conservative it was difficult to find a substantial body of citizens willing to exert itself in the defence of the government which had made its loathing of Paris so chillingly obvious.

In the afternoon, an emergency cabinet session was held in the Ministry of Foreign Affairs. Some fractious battalions of Garde Nationale stomped menacingly past the window, and Thiers decided that the moment had come to withdraw the national government and what remained of the troops to Versailles, in effect abandoning Paris entirely until more convincing forces could be marshalled. *Reculer pour mieux sauter*: this was a strategy which had worked for Windischgrätz in Vienna in 1848 (as well as one which Thiers had vainly urged Louis-Philippe to adopt in the same year during Paris's previous bout of revolution), but it proved a dreadfully mistaken one.

By evening, Paris was left for the taking. The *arrondissement* mayors had been perfunctorily briefed to take charge, but they were almost impotent, and posses of Reds, Garde Nationale and disaffected troops were free to occupy the city's major state institutions.* In the Ministry of Justice, they found only a steward locking away the silver plate; at the Prefecture of Police, a caretaker opened the door and invited the insurgents 'to make themselves at home'. The Panthéon, temporarily a huge munitions store, was surrounded with similar ease. Even at the crucial and heavily fortified Hôtel de Ville, the five hundred troops which patrolled it night and day had slipped off via an underground passage. The only body which exerted any sort of co-ordinating control over this pell-mell anarchy was the Committee of the Garde Nationale (whose officers had been re-elected three days previously by 215 out of 245 battalions: it thus held as strong a mandate as anything or anybody else). But it did so reluctantly, *faute de mieux*. Totally unprepared for a task such as governing Paris, its sole advantage was a certain sober seriousness at a moment when everyone else was either running scared or punch-drunk. The Committee of the Garde Nationale took up the reins without having the least idea how to drive the carriage or where to take it.

The violence, the unexpectedness, the sheer suddenness of the day's events cannot be overemphasized. Looking back, from the privileged perspective of posterity, they may look inevitable, but most Parisians were floored. For example: the American Ambassador, Elihu Washburne, had left Paris at noon to spend the day at the weekend retreat of his fashionable compatriots Lillie and Charles Moulton. 'Just as we were starting,' Washburne recorded, 'Mr Moulton said there were rumours flying that there had been a collision between the regular troops and the insurrectionary forces at the Buttes Montmartre, and that two generals had been killed etc., etc. As the city was always full of rumours, frequently of the most absurd and ridiculous

* Although one should remember that this was a Saturday: few offices would have been manned even in the ordinary course of events.

character, which almost invariably turned out to be false, I paid no particular attention to these.' Returning to the city that evening, Lillie Moulton wrote in a letter:

> Mr Washburne thought it more prudent to close the carriage, cautioning the coachman to drive slower. We were stopped at every moment by soldiers and barricades; then Mr Washburne would show his card and his *laissez passer*, after which we were allowed to pass on, until we came to more soldiers and more barricades. Omnibuses turned over, paving-stones piled up, barrels, ladders, ropes stretched across the streets, anything to stop the circulation. Poor Mr Washburne was tired out popping his head first out of one window then out of the other, with his card in his hand.
>
> The men who accosted us were not discourteous, but spoke quite decidedly, as if they did not expect to be contradicted. We did not care to contradict them, either.
>
> 'We know you, Monsieur, by reputation, and we know that you are well disposed towards France. How do you feel towards *la Commune*?'
>
> Mr Washburne hesitating a moment, the man added, cynically, 'Perhaps you would like to add a stone to our barricades.' He made as if he would open the door of the carriage; but Mr Washburne answered, holding back the door, 'I take it for granted, Monsieur, that I have your permission to drive on, as I have something very important to attend to at my Legation,' and gave the man a defiant look, which rather frightened him, and we drove through the crowd. All along the rue de Rivoli we saw the soldiers massing together in groups, a miserable-looking set of men, talking very loud and flourishing their guns as if they were walking-sticks.
>
> This was a sight to behold!

Others were even less impressed: Goncourt went into the centre of the city that afternoon and 'saw nothing except a singular indifference towards everything that was going on in the other districts. The Parisian population has seen so much in the last six months that nothing can move its emotions any longer.'

The next morning brought a sunny and hopeful spring Sunday, and, noted the Revd William Gibson, 'all had a complete holiday air'. 'Anarchie tranquille et complète,' wrote Taine to his wife. On the boulevards and in the cafés the feeling was that Paris had won – that it would now receive its dues from the

Assembly, that Thiers' presumption had been checked, that a restoration of the monarchy was highly unlikely, and that the worst of the bloodshed must be over. The night had been quiet in the Red districts and there was a sense not so much of alarm as of surprise.

For the Committee of the Garde Nationale, however, the brief was awkward. In difficult circumstances, it comported itself with considerable dignity – making clear that it was only a holding body, with a mandate from the sovereign 'people' which had played no part in (and would *ergo* take no responsibility for) Saturday's terrible events in Montmartre. Elections for an autonomous municipal council, a *commune*, would be called as soon as possible: meanwhile, appeals were made for sanity, calm and the maintenance of ordinary daily business. 'I tried to get this people that I love to carry out their great peaceful revolution with the majesty appropriate to a lion waking after twenty years of sleep,' claimed Edouard Moreau, a member of the Committee, grandiloquently. At the door, the hotter Reds barracked for further consolidating action: Louise Michel proposed to assassinate Thiers personally; others pressed for a coup against the Versailles government. But the Committee would only exhort other French cities to imitate Paris's example and establish their own communes: behind this was the dream of a society beyond republicanism, in which small, self-governing units would coexist in a harmonious federation. 'Decentralization', a term that sounds as if it should have originated in the late twentieth century, is in fact one that was commonly used in polemics of the period.*

Sunday in Versailles was less pleasant than it was in Paris. The town's population had swelled dramatically with the arrival of the Assembly and the decamping of the government. Deputies and civil servants were paying ten francs a night to sleep on straw in cellars and corridors. The palace itself, gossiped an article in *Le Rappel*, was full of dormitories for dignitaries, with rows of beds in the Hall of Mirrors and ministers curled up snoring in Louis XIV chairs covered with filched curtains and drapes. Food

---

* For example, in Goncourt's *Journal* for 28 March: 'The newspapers see in what is happening only a question of decentralization . . .'

was at a premium, and shopkeepers could charge what they liked for bread and milk. Tempers were short, and so was time. In emergency sessions of the Assembly (hastily converted from the palace's theatre), Thiers also had to resist precipitate calls to unwise action. Behind him, Bismarck suggested darkly that delay might not be in anyone's best interests. He liked to see France weak and did not mind it enfeebled by squabbling, but he wanted payment of the indemnity that Thiers' regime had negotiated, and a civil war had made a mess of such things. So Favre wrote a mollifying letter to the German High Command in Rouen, apologizing for any interruption in communication with Paris and assuring him that order would promptly be re-established. Thiers, however, simultaneously asked for a little time; he knew Parisian revolutionaries of old; and he had to be sure that when he re-entered the capital he would have enough loyal troops to crush the insurgents by sheer force of numbers if nothing else. For the time being, he cut the capital's links with the outside world, blocking mail deliveries as well as policing roads and searching trains. He also ordered the reoccupation of the fort of Mont-Valérien, an important strategic site overlooking the city.

Paris's Sunday morning cheerfulness was soon unsettled by such measures, and rumours went round to the effect that the Prussians were on their way back. A telegram sent by German High Command to the Committee of the Garde Nationale seemed to clarify the situation: '. . . German troops have received the order to maintain a pacific and passive attitude, so long as events do not involve hostility towards the German army'. This was much advertised: the translator's crafty doctoring of the German word for 'pacific' into the French for 'friendly' made it sound even more reassuring than it was intended to be.

But the Committee of the Garde Nationale's most pressing problem was neither the Germans nor the far left (the Corderie had formally endorsed its temporary mandate); neither Thiers nor Louise Michel. It was cash. Without a *sou* to its name, the Committee was obliged to administrate a city of over one and a half million people. The keys to the municipal coffers in the

Ministry of Finance had been taken to Versailles. Rather than force the locks, a decision was made to approach the banks. Out of naked self-interest, they proved very co-operative. Baron de Rothschild agreed to open them a credit account, and two members of the Committee, Eudes and Billioray, went off to try their luck further at the Banque de France.

They knocked at the door, according to the Comte d'Hérisson's informant. After three taps, it was tentatively opened by a voice asking them who they were and what they wanted.

'We are sent by the Central Committee and we wish to speak to the Director.'

'Are you alone?'

'Yes.'

'Come in then.'

They were led through the banking hall into the office of the Marquis de Ploeuc, a little old man with a disconcerting resemblance to Thiers, but a manner of the utmost urbanity and good humour.

'You have come from the Committee? You need money. Well, I'm not surprised. I've been waiting for you for a long time.'

'You have been waiting for us, Monsieur?'

'Certainly. One cannot govern without money. I know that better than anyone, seeing as I have been paying the Garde Nationale since 4 September. I have read some of your decrees. They are not bad at all. Moreover, I like young people. And in any case, your government can't be worse than the one it replaces. Do you need a lot of money?'

'Yes, monsieur. You see, we don't want to . . .'

'Oh, I understand. I know what you need. You need, say 600,000 francs to tide you over the first few days.'

'Yes please, for the first few days.'

'If that isn't enough, we can take it up to a million. With a million, you can start to sort yourselves out. Come on then, we must get it for you at once. I will ring and have someone bring it up.'

A flabbergasted Eudes stuttered that he was only empowered

to ask for the money, not to take it away. To make sure that everything was regular, he would have to fetch the Committee's treasurer.

'What a good idea,' replied the Marquis. 'You go and get him, and we'll have the money counted by the time you come back.'

Eudes and Billioray politely asked if there was anything the Committee could do for the Bank in return – the services of a protective battalion of Garde Nationale, perhaps?

'No, thank you kindly,' smiled the Marquis. 'That would be useless. We aren't too badly organized here, you know. We have our little way of doing things, and it seems to work rather nicely. We're big fellows, we can look after ourselves. Why bother to complicate what I hope will be very cordial relations between us?'

Eudes and Billioray bowed, took their leave and returned to the Ministry of Finance, overcome with hysterical laughter. Not surprisingly, the Treasurer agreed to the deal – the first priority was paying the Garde Nationale its dole money – and at 6 p.m. Eudes and Billioray were handed 800,000 francs in notes and 200,000 in coin. Contrary to the bank's normal practice, no charge was made for the money bags.

The Marquis de Ploeuc (surely the one true hero of the hour) continued to co-operate with the new government through all the ensuing events, thus keeping his institution free from interference, let alone requisition. What the Marquis understood, as d'Hérisson points out, was 'the attitude to be taken towards children who *asked*, when they could have *taken*'.

The entire episode was typical of the sort of unreality, the state of manic depression, which gripped Paris over the ensuing week. The world's press and the mass of international opinion may have taken a straightforwardly hostile view (*The Times* thundered at 'men given up to mere lawlessness and tigerish ferocity, without any admixture of strength and determination. The insurgents at Montmartre avow no political object; their aims are negative, they desire to do nothing but oppose the executive and retain in their own hands the means of destruction'), but those involved did not know quite what to think or what to expect. The barometer was violently changeable. On 21

March Washburne took 'a long drive through the most important quarters of Paris, and through many important business streets. The stores were all open, the omnibuses were all running, the streets were full of people, and no one would have imagined, from what was seen on all sides, that we were in a city of two millions of people practically without any government whatsoever.'

The next day, *The Times* reported exactly the opposite: 'the Grand Café, at the corner of the Boulevard des Capucines, which, with its many spacious rooms filled with lamps, usually throws a flood of light far into the streets around, was tonight a huge black patch on the scene, silent and grim as a prison wall. The streets were nearly deserted and quite silent, except when now and then the word of command or the tramp of marching men announced the approach of a patrol. Business is said to be duller now than it was during the siege.'

But Martial Senisse's diary simultaneously records that 'the chestnut trees in the squares are budding. How pleasant it is. And the city seems content.'

The direction of the political pendulum was wayward too. The Committee of the Garde Nationale had taken one important initiative, postponing the detested decrees on the repayments on debt and rent. It could do little else, although there was plenty of gossip about its activities: Goncourt was told that 'having destroyed all police records, the priority of these Messieurs has been the elimination of the register of prostitutes. Their mistresses, their wives and sisters were all on it'. In Versailles, before the Assembly, Thiers took a strong but not aggressive line. 'France does not intend to declare war on Paris,' he said 'nor do we intend to march on Paris.' He also said: 'if order is seriously disturbed, count upon our devotion to restore it with the utmost energy; we do not parley with sedition; that has never been my habit in life.'

When a body of the arrondissement mayors went to Versailles to address the Assembly and suggest what today we call 'a peace package', it was shouted down by the Right.

The Assembly may not have been disposed to be conciliatory, but it had to be careful. The army's loyalty under pressure was a doubtful quantity. News came in daily of the declaration of communes in cities all over France: Marseilles, Toulouse, Lyons, Saint-Etienne, Le Creusot, Narbonne. None of them was to last much more than a week, some were a matter of little more than Red flag-waving from the balcony of the town hall, and most of them just dwindled away, but they fuelled the scaremongering of the Right and the hopes of the Left. Paris could not be given preferential treatment, but the Assembly nevertheless debated a nationwide reform of local government, and Thiers replaced General d'Aurelle de Paladines as Commander-in-Chief of the Garde Nationale with Admiral Saisset, a popular figure who had led the manning of the capital's forts during the siege. It was a case of every government's nightmare dilemma – react hard to a situation, and risk overreacting; ignore it, and risk underreacting.

What Thiers could not accurately assess was the degree of grass-roots support he held in Paris. Pockets of loyalist Gardes Nationales in the first and second arrondissements had no strategic significance. Hundreds of thousands of bourgeois had left Paris after the siege and many small businessmen had been antagonized by his 'pay-up or be damned' attitude to their debts. There was a body of conservative opinion which followed the line of the professor of medicine Frédéric Desplats ('at least when we were besieged we knew who the enemy was . . . this is ignoble, and a thousand times worse than a Prussian occupation,' he wrote to his wife) but was it sufficiently militant or numerous to form a real power base or rallying point? On 21 March, a movement called 'The Friends of Order' invited 'good citizens . . . who want order, tranquillity and respect for the law' to gather and march unarmed through the centre of Paris to the Stock Exchange. It was a brave, if not foolhardy, call: in London, Karl Marx noted witheringly that it seemed to assume 'that the mere exhibition of their "respectability" would have the same effect upon the revolution of Paris as Joshua's trumpets upon the wall of Jericho'.

The small success (or not outright disaster) of the march led its organizers to call a more ambitious event for the next day, this time to march to the Hôtel de Ville, again unarmed.

About midday, a couple of thousand men assembled on the Place de l'Opéra. They were led by Admiral Saisset, 'attended by a young man who carried a large tricolour flag,' wrote an eyewitness, Ernest Vizetelly. 'The Admiral intended to harangue the National Guards massed on the Place Vendôme, and to entreat them, in the country's interests, to abandon their revolutionary proceedings and return to discipline and duty. Looking back, I feel that there was not the slightest prospect of the Admiral's eloquence prevailing, and I think, therefore, that the attempt was ill-advised.'

They marched down the rue de la Paix towards the Place Vendôme, sporting blue ribbons on their lapels and shouting 'Vive l'ordre! Vive l'Assemblée Nationale!' Although some of them may have been privately armed, Vizetelly's view was that 'the intention of the demonstrators was undoubtedly pacific. . . . There could be no idea on their part of forcibly seizing the Place Vendôme. Only madmen could have dreamt of any such scheme, and these folk were led by an old officer of great experience, who would have scouted such a project.' As they approached the Place, the two forces confronted each other. The battalions of the Garde Nationale on picketing duty were not inclined to let the Friends of Order pass; the Friends of Order's slogans became more abusive, their *tricolores* more agitated. Then shots rang out – who fired first, on what specific provocation, was never established. There were more volleys, shouting, a stampede, chaos. After five minutes of this, ten demonstrators and two members of the Garde Nationale lay dead, many more wounded. Some smart names were shockingly among the casualties: a director of the Banque de France, an idealistic young American, the Vicomte de Mollinet, the editor of *Paris Journal*. Rumour had it that Louis Napoleon's spies were behind the incident, and that the former Emperor was bent on destabilizing the situation to prepare for his return.

The débâcle of the march of the Friends of Order, and the spectre of a war within Paris between Parisians, made it all the more imperative to establish the city with a credibly legitimate government. After much tedious toing and froing between the mayors, the Committee of the Garde Nationale and the

Versailles Assembly, elections were called for 26 March. There was little time for electioneering, but the manifestos of the various left-wing factions, united to make up what became known as 'the Commune' and endorsed by the Committee of the Garde Nationale, were soon plastered on every available wall in the city. Trumpeting a rhetoric which kept its force for over a century, they set out a new political agenda and a vision of a radically new way of restructuring civil society. 'The whole system of work should be reorganized. Since the aim of life is the limitless development of our physical, intellectual and moral capacities, property is and must only be the right of each one of us to share (to the extent of his individual contribution) in the collective fruit of labour which is the basis of social wealth. The Nation must provide for those unable to work.' Further left, the Internationale lent its support, but pushed the economic creeds of Marx and Proudhon and 'the organization of credit, of exchange, and of production co-operatives in order to guarantee the worker the full value of his labour'. For the Right, such talk was the triumph of barbarism: Goncourt, with a panic typical of the middle-class intellectual, saw only 'the conquest of France by the worker and the enslavement, under his despotism, of noble, bourgeois and peasant. Government passes from the hands of those who have to those who have not, from those who have a material interest in the preservation of society to those who are completely uninterested in order, stability or preservation . . .' Taine compared his feelings about the situation to those of someone who discovers that his parents are 'grotesque, hateful, despicable, absolutely incorrigible and destined for jail or a lunatic asylum'.

The elections of 26 March, it must be said, were not representative of Paris – from an electoral register of 485,000 only 227,000 votes were cast by a new system of proportional representation which favoured the working-class areas, and as many as half a million middle-class Parisian citizens were still absent, taking the air after the siege. But there was no disputing the result – a massive rejection of Thiers, with several arrondissements turning eighty per cent Communard. The government which installed itself in a ceremony outside the Hôtel de Ville on 28 March was the one which the present population of Paris wanted.

10 : *The Commune*

Always anxious to legitimize itself, always a little
bewildered as to its own powers, the Commune was
prone to reassuring rituals of self-consecration and
validation, and the ceremony in which the new government
installed itself was a noble and memorable one. The religious
solemnity of the occasion was emphasized in the left-wing press:
no longer the modern Babylon, Paris had become Jerusalem the
Golden. *Le Cri du Peuple*, a newspaper edited by the
Communard Jules Vallès, called it 'the festive wedding day of
the Idea and the Revolution'. 'Soldier-citizens,' he added, 'the
Commune we have acclaimed and married today must
tomorrow bear fruit; we must take our place once more, still
proud and now free, in the workshop and at the counter. After
the poetry of triumph, the prose of work.'

What exactly was it, this Commune? The dust of confusion is
still not settled, even after so many of the issues it raised are dead
ones. Was this socialism's first run? Or a revival of the municipal
government proclaimed in 1792 by Robespierre, Danton *et al.*
which asserted emergency powers to save *la patrie en danger*? Was
it a freak or a portent? A Good Thing or a Bad Thing? A mistake,
an inevitability, or an instance of what the American philosopher Henry Adams memorably conceived as history's tendency
to develop along the lines of least resistance? If Thiers had not
withdrawn on 18 March, would the tale be substantially
different? Or was the Commune something long burgeoning
which needed only time to flower?

No simple satisfactory answers can be supplied. It sprang

from various historical causes – various exasperations and visions and energies – only to converge immediately into various ideological directions: its unity of identity and purpose was never strong. Its rhetoric and its intentions may seem to be anti-capitalist and pro-labour, setting the political terms for a hundred years or more, but it never had the chance to prove the fine words in reality: from its birth, the enemy was banging noisily on the gates and it could hardly hear itself speak.

But there is one overwhelming emotional truth behind the Commune – a truth which goes beyond questions of socialist faction, of prospect and retrospect, of who was resentful of what. The working class of Paris wanted its city back: wanted to return home with a passion which could not be mollified or modified. Through the Second Empire, Haussmann had done his damnedest to expropriate it: he had bullied and roared, trampled over custom and community, drawn straight lines in black ink and got the traffic moving. But he had seen the city only as a series of equations requiring rational solutions, and had pushed the centralizing logic too hard – Paris refused to become his profit-generating engine, a *machine à vivre*. The siege government had brought another sort of tyranny. Parisians felt the situation thus: Trochu was not a native Parisian, but a Breton; he did not understand the city's honour. Having bungled the chance of victory, he and his cronies were prepared to buy a rotten peace off the Prussians, and had now handed over to their puppets at Versailles.

The Commune was more a furious instinctive response to this trail of humiliation than it was a calculated or conspiratorial political strategy. In this respect, it is futile to look too deep for the 'causes' of the Commune – it simply had to happen, like so much in history, for reasons beyond reason.

Sixty-four men stood red-sashed on the dais in front of the Hôtel de Ville that day, 28 March 1871. To have reached the planned complement, there should have been a further twenty-six, but the immediate resignation of twenty-one right wingers and moderates who felt unable to collaborate (plus two absentees, as well as several candidates elected in more than one arrondissement) meant that a round of by-elections immediately became necessary. The initial sixty-four were, however, fairly representative of the Commune's constitution, and their social origins and orientations have been endlessly examined by historians. Nineteen of them had been members of the Committee of the Garde Nationale; twenty-five were Jacobins, a left-wing republican position, romantic and high-minded, associated with the 1848 revolution and its survivors; nine younger men were Blanquistes, following the more violent, atheistic and conspiratorial line of the veteran Auguste Blanqui, whom the Versaillais had recently captured and imprisoned; twenty espoused the gentle co-operative socialism of Proudhon, which came under the wing of the Internationale; only two had any knowledge of Karl Marx. Thirty-three of them were under the age of thirty-three, but the average age was thirty-eight. Less than a quarter were native Parisians. Eighteen came from middle-class backgrounds; thirty-three of them were artisans – carpenters, decorators, masons. Three were doctors, three lawyers, two soldiers. Antoine Arnaud was well known for his interest in table-rapping and magnetism; Jules Allix was a devotee of female equality and a mystical eccentric who wrote a book called *La Vie Humaine correspond à la vie des astres*, 'Human Life corresponds to life among the Stars'; Jules Babick was another mystic, a founder member of the sect of Fusionism; Alfred Billioray had mixed colours and cleaned brushes for the fashionable painter Rosa Bonheur; Frédéric Cournet had been a *maître de casino*; Jules Johannard was an ace billiards player; Alphonse Lonclas was rumoured to have run a brothel; Dominique Régère was both a vet and a wine merchant; three members were surnamed Clément – Jean-Baptiste was a songwriter whose big hit hymned praise to the nippy waitresses of the Bouillons Duval; Léopold, a concierge; Victor, a dyer.

They were, in other words, a pretty mixed bunch, and the only generalization which can usefully be drawn from the statistics is that none of them had any significant connection with the heavy mechanized industries which had been burgeoning in the suburbs of Paris throughout the Second Empire (and which would eventually become the focal point of Marxist Communism). A few of them had minor police records, a few were crackpot obsessives, but they were not on the whole the parade of roughs and villains which the right-wing press reported on the world over. The majority were respectable, earnest, public-spirited citizens, who worked for their bread and lived by traditional bourgeois values – the sort of men common in any municipal government, open to corruption but not necessarily corrupt. Arthur Arnould is surely right to emphasize in his 1878 history of the Commune that, whatever excesses were committed in its name, this was a government also possessed of a remarkable probity: 'during its short reign, not a man, child or old person was hungry, cold or homeless, even though no government can have been more scrupulous on matters of money, even though it never touched any of Paris's countless riches, belonging to the city's most implacable enemies. Never was more done with less.'

What they crucially lacked was a leader, natural or otherwise. They had an elected president in a seventy-five-year-old engineer of moderate and dignified demeanour, Charles Beslay, but his executive authority was minimal, and the Commune hoped to rule Paris by a system of democratic committees rather than dominating personalities. How things might have turned out if a Robespierre or a Lenin had emerged is an interesting speculation; but the Commune is one of the rare revolutionary episodes not primarily remembered for the heroic or charismatic individuals it threw up. If its great stroke of bad judgement was the decision to leave the Banque de France untouched, its great stroke of bad luck may well have been the absence from Paris of Auguste Blanqui – he had been locked up by the Versaillais in Toulon, far out of harm's way, only days before the declaration of the Commune. He alone would have possessed the hardened revolutionary professionalism required to push out the well-intentioned and concentrate the effective, as well as the amoral courage to be dictatorial. Without him, the Commune began to disintegrate before it had even coalesced.

None of this was evident on that golden afternoon of 28 March. To see beyond one's prejudices at such a point was impossible, and those who were not plain hostile had to admit to bafflement at the appearance of a form of government which made no sense in a world of nations and empires. Rather than the shape of things to come, the Commune seemed primitive, a throwback. 'He would be very clever who should succeed in arranging under one form of doctrine the varied and often contradictory ideas with which the adepts of this great sect are inspired. Most of them only understand one thing: they wish to possess and enjoy,' pronounced *The Times* sarcastically. 'What a curious idea to wish to throw us back four or five centuries, to wish to imitate the small Italian republics or the Flemish communes, at the moment when other nations are grouping together and condensing in order to club their forces and their interests! Is not this a sign of decomposition and decline? Is this what the Communalists call "Progress"?'

Those of the city's middle and upper class who had not already decamped in anticipation of trouble surveyed the scene uneasily. One small consolation was recorded in the diary of the Revd William Gibson of the Methodist Mission. 'I have never seen the streets of Paris so well swept since the siege as they were this morning. The heaps of rubbish had been cleared away, the centre of the road as well as the causeways well swept, and the men were busy watering the roads.' Cleanliness, it seems, would have to make up for Godlessness.

29 March

The council of the Commune met for the first time and decided for reasons of security to hold its plenary council sessions in secret. This measure interrupted important links of democratic communication with the clubs, the Garde Nationale, and the arrondissements, as well as the press and the city at large. Ministries were established under 'Delegates' of the Commune and control of all public services and facilities assumed. Abolition of the death penalty and military conscription were debated.

30 March

Measures vital to ensuring the support of the poorest and most volatile sections of Paris were taken. Decrees placarded throughout Paris announced that no rent was payable on any property since the beginning of the siege, and that rebates must be given on any monies already paid for that period. The sale of goods pawned to the Mont-de-Piété shops was also suspended. Flaubert snorted in a letter to George Sand: 'now government meddles in Natural Law and interferes in contracts between individuals. The Commune asserts that we don't owe what we do owe, and that one service is not to be paid for by another. It's monstrous ineptitude and injustice. . . . It seems to me that we have never sunk lower.'

The British Ambassador Lord Lyons wrote to his Foreign Secretary, Lord Granville: 'The great hope appears to be that the members of the Commune will quarrel among themselves.' As Lyons anticipated, the cracks were already deepening. A faction of moderates led by Antoine Tirard of the largely middle-class second arrondissement quit the Commune's Council; and the Committee of the Garde Nationale, although no longer officially empowered, took the initiative over the reorganization of its legions. Gustave Cluseret, a veteran of the American Civil War, was put in charge.

The youngest and perhaps most unpleasant member of the Council of the Commune was twenty-four-year-old Raoul Rigault, who served notoriously as Prefect of Police. A brilliant student from a prosperous background, he had run the gamut of *la vie de Bohème* in the Quartier Latin and come out a savage political journalist, unhealthily obsessed with the ubiquity of imperial spies. In his self-appointed uniform – scarlet- and gold-fringed, with yellow gloves – he shamelessly used his power to pull women. But alongside his *Sadique* tendency to self-indulgence was an insistence on the moral purity of a revolution (imbibed from Marat and other such). 'Revolutionary laws are never strong enough,' he wrote, proposing a new system of justice in which 'sons would judge fathers . . . convicts the judges' – a chilling foretaste of the horrors of Maoism. His atheism was violent to the point of silliness. In conversation he eliminated all references to religion: the Boulevard Saint-Michel became the Boulevard Michel, the Cross the Guillotine. In his prefectorial role he boasted that he would issue a warrant for God's arrest, condemn him to death for contempt of court, then execute his effigy. To one of the many priests he arrested and interrogated he is said to have quipped: 'Whom do you serve?' 'God,' replied the accused. 'Where does he live?' 'He lives everywhere,' persisted the priest. Rigault turned to his scribe and said: 'Write down: serves God, a vagrant.'

The brazen American socialite Lillie Moulton applied to him for a passport to leave Paris.

Peering across the table to see whether my eyes were brown or black, or my hair black or brown, he never lost an opportunity to make a fawning remark before writing it down. He described my *teint* as *pâle*. I felt pale, and think I must have looked very pale, for he said: 'Vous etes bien pâle, Madame. Voudriez-vous quelque chose à boire?' ['You are pale, Madame, would you like something to drink?'] Possibly he may have meant to be kind; but I saw BORGIA written all over him. I refused his offer with effusion.

When he asked me my age, he said, *insinuatingly*, 'Vous êtes bien jeune, Madame, pour circuler seule ainsi dans Paris.' ['You are very young, Madame, to run around Paris thus.']

I answered, 'Je ne suis pas seule, Monsieur. Mon mari (I thought it best to tell this lie) m'attend dans la voiture de Monsieur Washburne et il doit être bien étonné de ma longue absence.' ['I am not alone, Monsieur. My husband is waiting for me in Mr Washburne's carriage and he must be extremely concerned at the length of my absence.']

I considered this extremely diplomatic.

Turning to the man at the mantelpiece, he said, 'Grousset, do you think we ought to allow the *citoyenne* to leave Paris?'

Grousset (the man addressed)★ stepped forward and looked at Mr Washburne's card, saying something in an undertone to Rigault, which caused him instantly to change his manner toward me (I don't know which was worse, his overbearing or his fawning manner).

'You must forgive me,' he said, 'if I linger over your visit here. We don't often have such luck, do we, Grousset?'

I thought I should faint!

Probably the man Grousset noticed my emotion, for he came to my rescue and said, politely, 'Madame Moulton, j'ai eu l'honneur de vous voir à un bal à l'Hôtel de Ville l'année dernière.' ['I have the honour of having seen you at a ball at the Hôtel de Ville last year.']

I looked up with surprise. He was a very handsome fellow, and I remembered quite well having seen him somewhere; but did not

★ Pascal Grousset, twenty-six, another prominent Communard and later Delegate for External Affairs. A journalist involved in the affair of Victor Noir (see pp. 129–30), he was frequently complimented on his genteel manners.

remember where. I was happy indeed to find any one who knew me and could vouch for me, and told him so. He smiled. 'I venture to present myself to you, Madame. I am Pascal Grousset. Can I be of any service to you?'

'Indeed you can,' I answered eagerly. 'Please tell Monsieur Rigault to give me my passport; it seems to have been a colossal undertaking to get it.' I preferred the *Pascal* G. to the *Rascal* R.

Grousset and Rigault had a little conversation together, and presto! my longed-for passport lay before me to sign. No Elsa ever welcomed her Lohengrin coming out of the clouds as I did my Lohengrin coming from the mantelpiece.

1 April

Skirmishes with Versaillais troops around Courbevoie and the strategically important bridge across the Seine at Neuilly broke out: but Thiers held back. He had played a large part in the construction of Paris's fortifications in the 1840s, and he knew the problems of attempting to storm them (the cynics, indeed, claimed that vanity caused him to exaggerate their impregnability).

The Commune agreed that the highest annual salary for any of its functionaries should not exceed 6,000 francs – what a master carpenter or mason might expect to earn.

A new newspaper, *La Sociale*, called for the abolition of inheritance under a headline 'The Liquidation of Property'; *Le Cri du Peuple*, the popular radical organ edited by the Communard Jules Vallès, applauded the idea.

In England – as the public's attention was diverted by the glamorous wedding of the pretty Princess Louise to the handsome Marquis of Lorne – Louis Napoleon, released from Prussian captivity on 19 March, had joined Eugénie and the Prince Impérial at Camden Place in Chislehurst. They were living off the £50,000 proceeds of the sale of some of Eugénie's diamonds, smuggled from a bank vault out of Paris. The Emperor's reception at Dover and in London had been wildly enthusiastic, and he was inundated with letters of sympathy and surrounded by loyal exiles of his court: once mistrusted, he was now cast as a victim, if not a martyr. How seriously he plotted his return to France and the throne is uncertain, as everything about him invariably was. Queen Victoria received him at Windsor Castle and found him 'much depressed' with 'tears in his eyes', as he spoke of 'the dreadful and disgraceful state of France, and how all that had passed during the last few months had greatly lowered the French character, the officers breaking their parole included. There seemed to be "point d'énergie" [no energy].'

2 April

The previous day's skirmishes suddenly intensified: the Versaillais took possession of Courbevoie. At 3 p.m. the news reached Paris and the Garde Nationale rallied hysterically in Montmartre and Belleville. Nine months previously the war cry had been 'A Berlin!'; now it was 'A Versailles!' The hoardings were covered with the announcement that 'the royalist conspirators have ATTACKED. Despite the moderation of our attitude, they have ATTACKED. Elected by the population of Paris, our duty is to defend our great city against the guilty aggressors. With your help, WE SHALL DEFEND IT.'

In the Commune's Council it was confidently anticipated that the discipline of the Versailles troops would not hold, that in the event of a face-to-face encounter, the 'fraternization' of Montmartre on 18 March would recur, and that already the cannon of the Versailles-occupied fort on Mont-Valérien had refused to fire on the Fédérés, as the Commune's troops were known. On this dangerous assumption, an ambitious plan for a three-pronged offensive was adopted.

A decree had separated Church and State, adding that freedom of conscience was 'the first of liberties'. But this unexceptionable statement held contradictory implications. A deep-seated, often paranoid distrust of the Catholic clergy took possession of various sections of Paris during the Commune and efforts to stamp out its influence – actual or imagined – were often irrationally hostile and occasionally downright violent. The Catholic Church was regarded not only as the Establishment, unrestrained in its amassing of wealth and privileges, but as an instrument of repression and superstition operating behind closed doors. It became identified as the enemy within and many churches were attacked accordingly. More militant battalions of the Garde Nationale, abetted by some rowdier elements of the populace, harassed and pillaged; there were several more organized attempts to expropriate church property (feebly justified by reference to the French laws of mortmain). Versaillais apologists and propagandists made hay with the idea of a systematic campaign of persecution, but the reality of the violence was random and sporadic – and all the more terrorizing for that.

3 April

The sortie which began at midnight was, in the words of the historian Robert Tombs, 'the highpoint of the Fédérés' military strength, both in numbers and enthusiasm'. But the day went badly against them, as one wing was decimated by fire from the 'traitors' in Mont-Valérien and two prominent leaders, Flourens and Duval, were killed. (Flourens died spectacularly, much to the gratification of his enemies. Wandering aimlessly into an *auberge* after the battle was over, his presence was betrayed. The officer arresting him, infuriated at his impudence, simply cleft his head in two with one cut of his sabre.) 'Fraternization', the Commune's secret weapon, conspicuously failed to work. Hundreds of prisoners were herded off to the dreadful prison camp of Satory, near Versailles.

Another rousing poster appeared on the walls of Paris, amid rumours of victory. Issued by the Committee of the Garde Nationale, its tone was more fiercely socialist than the Council of the Commune would have dared to be:

> Workers, do not be deceived. This is the great struggle. It is parasitism and labour, exploitation and production that are at stake. If you are tired of vegetating in ignorance and coughing in misery, if you want your sons to be men and not types of animals reared for the factory and the battlefield, if you no longer want your daughters – whom you cannot raise and protect as you would like – to be the instruments of pleasure in the hands of the aristocracy of wealth, if you would like to see the reign of Justice – workers, arise!

Meanwhile, Paris's contact with the outside world was once again curtailed. To the north, through territory still occupied by

Germans officially disinterested in the city's internal affairs, communications were better, though unreliable. With the right *laissez-passer* and documents, it was still relatively easy to leave the Gare du Nord for Brussels or Boulogne, the Gare Saint-Lazare for Rouen. Tens of thousands did so, many of them creeping off to dodge the draft into the Garde Nationale which now officially applied to all able-bodied males (one such being the future composer of *Carmen*, Georges Bizet, who sat out most of the crisis in a hotel in Compiègne).

The surburban town of Saint-Denis, a mile or so outside the city walls, was the first stop beyond the frontier of the Commune. If you reached here, you were doing well (Edwin Child queued five hours for his *laissez-passer*). From the south, Thiers had done all he could to stop mail services into Paris: inward-bound letters were stored in the Galerie des Batailles in the palace of Versailles and all stores of postage stamps had been removed from the capital when the government decamped on 18 March. But in Saint-Denis you could post out, hire couriers, buy Versaillais newspapers, talk to German soldiers and pick up one of the horde of prostitutes drawn there since the outbreak of war. At no point in the Commune's brief existence was Paris as completely invested as it had been during the siege: but psychologically the breaches increased the sense of insecurity as much as they opened a safety-valve.

4 April

The sortie of 2 April was clearly a failure, with many casualties and prisoners taken. Fighting dragged on around the south-western forts of Issy and Vanves. Cluseret announced a fundamental reorganization of the Garde Nationale and mobilized all single men between the ages of seventeen and thirty-one. Amid news of the maltreatment and even summary execution of captured Communards, women rallied from all quarters of Paris: dressed in black, adorned only with red rosettes in their caps, they planned a peace march on Versailles. The Garde Nationale forbade it to proceed.

5 April

The rumours of reprisals taken by the Versaillais stung the Commune to extreme retaliation. 'Any person suspected of complicity with the government of Versailles will be immediately charged and incarcerated.' In other words: we can arrest anybody, for anything. A jury would bring a verdict within forty-eight hours and the guilty would remain – in a fatal, chilling phrase – 'hostages of the people of Paris'. Then came a terrible threat: 'any execution of a prisoner of war or a partisan of the legal government of the Commune of Paris will immediately be followed by the execution of a triple number of hostages.'

Over three hundred would be held under the first decree, about two-thirds of them priests and a quarter gendarmes. Most prominent among them was the liberal, pacific Archbishop of Paris, Mgr Darboy, arrested the previous day on Rigault's express instructions and held in solitary confinement in the Mazas prison.

No measure of the Commune provoked more antagonism: in public relations terms, it was a catastrophe, provoking even a radical republican like Victor Hugo to write a poem ('Pas de représailles' 'No reprisals') in protest. To those of a moderate or right-wing persuasion, the point was blackly proved: the men of the Commune were beasts let out of a cage or brigands who should be locked up in one, blackmailers whose only motives were personal gain, envy and revenge. There could be no discussion of the matter, let alone negotiation of terms: this was a conflict of Law against Crime. Such was the line persistently taken, from a distance, by France's intellectual establishment – Taine, Flaubert, du Camp, Gautier, Goncourt, Renan, George Sand – one followed throughout the civilized world, from bourgeois breakfast tables to senates and parliaments. The Commune was left with few friends, none of them influential.

6 April

In the 1960s, left-wing historians with an agenda high on matters of personal liberation and ecstasy, wrote of the Commune as an early exercise in spontaneous street politics. It was a *fête*, a carnival, full of joy and hope and free love. By the 1990s, the vision has darkened, and the celebrations of the Commune seem more like rituals of exorcism than feasts of fun.*

This was the day, for example, when a bonfire was solemnly made of the guillotine. The 137th Battalion of the Garde Nationale wheeled it from its depot in the rue Folie-Méricourt to the foot of a statue of Voltaire, where it was broken up and immolated to cries of 'Vive la Commune!' In the name of 'the purification of the arrondissement and the consecration of the new liberty'. At the famous church of the Panthéon, the cross was removed from the pediment by the 59th Battalion and replaced, after a speech, by a huge red flag. Later twelve battalions lined up to fire salvos as the flag was blessed. In the name of the Commune and the future.

Most dramatic of all, those who had fallen in the great sortie of the previous week were commemorated in a grand processional. Three catafalques, each bearing twelve coffins draped in red and black, paraded through Paris to the cemetery of Père Lachaise, escorted by a guard of honour carrying their arms reversed. Muffled drums and muted trumpets accompanied them, witnessed by hundreds of thousands of Parisians lining the streets with their heads bowed. At the cemetery, one of the grand old men of the Commune, Charles Delescluze, a veteran of 1848 imprisoned under the Second Empire, gave a solemn peroration. 'Let us not weep for our brothers who have fallen heroically, but let us vow to continue their work!'

The Army of Versailles was being reorganized under General MacMahon, one of the non-heroes of the Franco-Prussian War. The lull in the military offensive was due to Thiers' wisely cautious insistence on building up loyalty, expertise and morale of forces battered by nine months of failure. Punishments were strictly enforced; twice-daily drill was ordered. Shortages of everything from boots to bugles were remedied. A new railway station was built at Versailles to improve supply and communication links. Rations were increased and pay bonuses doled out, along with free copies of right-wing newspapers such as *Le Soir*.

* Although it seems that the traditional gingerbread fair ran through the Commune in the Place de la Bastille, donating half its proceeds to the war-wounded.

Although the Commune's socialism was scarcely to his political taste, Bismarck cleverly maintained his sniffy attitude to the Versailles regime, and Thiers had to beg for the repatriation of badly needed officers from the German prisoner-of-war camps. Until Germany signed a final peace treaty with France, Bismarck did not want to see the French army cockily rearmed and flexing its muscles, albeit against a domestic enemy. It was therefore in his interest to keep diplomatic channels with the Commune open, unsettling Versailles' status as the legitimate government and making it work all the harder at the negotiating table. Thiers could not count him an ally until he had confirmed that Germany would get what it wanted out of France.

Thiers was keenly aware of the threat of 'fraternization' in the event of open face-to-face confrontation with the Commune and trained up the more conservative and malleable recruits from rural areas over the more fractious and suggestible townees. In Paris, the word 'peasant' was uttered with as much contempt as the word 'priest'.

Monitoring the situation from London, Karl Marx was exasperated. He wrote to his disciple Wilhelm Liebknecht that he believed 'the Parisians are succumbing. It is their own fault . . . due to their too great decency.' Marx's view was that the Commune should have taken more immediate and aggressive advantage of their victory on 18 March instead of wasting time scrupulously establishing their legality with elections, 'giving that mischievous abortion Thiers time to concentrate hostile forces'. What Marx wanted was 'the dictatorship of the proletariat'.

7 April, Good Friday

Paris was slackly policed, not least because of the defection of many gendarmes and *sergents de ville* to Versailles. There were fears of a crime wave. A letter in *The Times* reported an *affiche* 'telling us to beware of our pockets, for 4,000 London thieves have appeared in Paris.' There were many tales of depravity – 'performances of the wildest cancan,' continued *The Times*, 'were never more numerous nor more run after than at the present moment' – most of them nonsense. Any atrocity could be believed of these men in this city. Easter irritated the anti-clerical factions. Notre-Dame was invaded and closed. Many other churches were allowed to continue to hold services only on condition that they made their premises available to the *clubs rouges* for evening meetings of their infamous talking-shops. This led to some strange incidents and juxtapositions: at Saint-Sulpice, a timetabling clash meant that the *Salve Regina* was counterpointed by the *Marseillaise*, both choirs attempting to drown out the other. At Saint-Germain-l'Auxerrois someone anticipated dada by fifty years when he stuck a pipe into the mouth of a statue of the Virgin Mary, while at Saint-Jacques de Haut-Pas a Garde Nationale washed his dog in the font. One bright idea at Saint-Nicolas des Champs was to bag the corpses of the city's 60,000 priests and use them to build barricades; at Saint-Eloi a woman less creatively proposed throwing all nuns into the Seine. Talk, talk, talk: the Commune talked pie-in-the-sky, fantasies of Utopia and bloody revenge, the oldest levellers' dream of 'seven halfpenny loaves for a penny' and the common-wealth.

8 April

Versaillais troops invested Neuilly and seized the bridge over the Seine. *The Times*'s correspondent archly attempted to translate the military situation into terms that a Londoner might appreciate:

> The Reds are at the Mansion House; their army is in ruined forts about Clapham; the other army is about Sydenham and Wimbledon; the other government is at Richmond; and the invaders are at Highgate and Harrow and all over the north. Spectators are at the waterworks at Campden Hill, looking south. A cloud of white smoke rises about Clapham, another smaller cloud appears about the Crystal Palace, and a spectator remarks 'That is a bomb which explodes on the plateau of Clamart.' A white puff rises among some trees on a rise to the right towards Wimbledon; a cloud appears above the fort at Clapham, and two reports follow as fast as sound can travel after light. 'Behold the chateau of Meudon which has cast an *obus* into Issy' '*Ah ça*! That is sad.' Crrrrrrash. '*Ah! la mitrailleuse*!' Pop, pop, pop. The small arms, the skirmishers. 'Oh that ought not

to be.' 'To nourish soldiers to come and fire upon Paris! That is too bad!' Oh! another bang. 'That is too strong, for example.' 'There is Issy which gives. There is Vanves. There is Montrouge. Ah! It is terrible' . . . And so the curious cluster at the Trocadéro and converse and watch the battle which has been going on ever since Sunday. There is no danger whatever for them.

Ironically, the brunt of the bombardment fell on the middle-class western areas of the city, where most of Versailles' supporters were concentrated. (The north and east remained Prussian zones, and the south was strategically irrelevant.) With the help of an entrepreneur employing a thousand men over ten days, a huge battery was assembled at Montretout. It was from here that the puffs and pops mostly emanated – Paris's merest background muttering. Some clever person dug up a speech made in 1848 by Thiers on behalf of Palermo, then being bombarded by its own government 'because that unfortunate town demanded its rights'. The irony needed no pointing.

Women

The French Revolution of 1789–94 had brought women to the streets in protest at the price of bread and thrown up some remarkable campaigning heroines, Théroigne de Méricourt and Olympe de Gouges (who challenged Robespierre to swim against her across the Seine) among them. The female sex played little part, however, in the events of 1848 – the Club des Vésuviennes, an association of Amazonian virgins of the Republic, was just a newspaper joke – and the 'advanced' socialist-romantic thinkers of the era, such as Proudhon, Comte and Saint-Simon, tended to enshrine women in a silent temple of wifedom and motherhood.

Throughout the Second Empire there persisted various fringe publications and organizations (such as the Société de la Revendication du Droit des Femmes, the Society for the Vindication of the Rights of Women) earnestly dedicated to improving women's social and political status, in terms not much different from those proposed in England seven years earlier by Mary Wollstonecraft. The influence of this movement was minuscule, confined to the politically sensitive wing of the intelligentsia –

the same people who lapped up the novels of George Sand and their defence of a woman's sexual emotions.

The Siege of Paris quickened the pace. The memory of Joan of Arc's militant patriotism was a vivid inspiration (not only to those with lunatic delusions★) and there were jobs to be done. Many of them were traditionally feminine: tending the wounded, queuing for bread and shouting against the cold. But there was also a new dimension. Women began to barge into the debates of the *clubs rouges* and to identify their own positions with the socialist politics of the exploited worker against the capitalist profiteer. Come the Commune, their presence had become more insistent, their voices more strident. Men were shocked at being contradicted, let alone shouted down. Hyenas, viragos, and whores, they called them (Maxime du Camp characterized the participants as 'vacationing residents of Saint-Lazare' – a reference to the prostitutes' prison hospital implying venereal infection). This impression was confirmed by the statistical fact that the revolutionary cause was not an occupation for pale, intense young maidens: the women in the clubs were a largely unrefined and uneducated lot, coarse-tongued and toothless. The majority were over thirty-five and worked not just for their living but their survival: washerwomen, street-vendors, seamstresses and the other slaves of the sweatshops of the garment trades.† They smoked cigarettes, coughed, drank *absinthe* and cohabited. Fearless from having nothing to lose, they vented their most passionate anger on butchers and bakers, whom they suspected (often rightly) of profiteering and corruption. Nuns were another target of their venom. Many of the women of the clubs must have been victims of their finger-wagging piety and Draconian discipline in schools, orphanages and hospitals; more pressingly, there was running resentment at the way convent ateliers undercut ordinary commercial prices in various women's industries (artificial flower-making, button-

★ See pp. 199–200.
† A baffling oddity pointed out by Richard Cobb in his excellent essay 'The Women of the Commune' (in *A Second Identity*, London, 1969) is the absence of domestic servants from their ranks. The fact that so many middle-class families had decamped from Paris during these months can only partially explain this mystery.

stitching and so on). Such scenes were not rare. Profaning religion in general gave much satisfaction. In the church of Saint-Pierre du Montmartre, according to Paul Fontoulieu, 'the nave was transformed into a workshop for the manufacture of military uniforms in which fifty women of all ages toiled, singing non-stop the most obscene songs. They had lunch in the church, and the altar was turned into a buffet table, piled with glasses, plates and bottles'.

During the Commune, several exclusively female clubs were established. None of them was particularly important or successful, although one must bear in mind that our records of their proceedings come via sceptical male journalists who colour their reports with the varnish of cheaply condescending satire. Yet occasionally the fanatic earnestness of these unattractive women comes through authentically. Here, for instance, is the speech of a murderous little old lady who attended the meetings in the church of the Trinité:

> If tomorrow we executed a hundred of those who are refusing to fight – which is not a lot – and exhibited their bodies on the boulevards with notices showing the crimes they committed, you can be sure that the day after tomorrow crowds of people would come forward to serve the Commune. What the Hell! The ends justify the means. But our leaders want to make omelettes without breaking any eggs and that cannot be done; on the contrary, you need to break lots of eggs. What are the lives of a few unworthy citizens when our future liberty is at stake? That's my opinion. We must frighten the reactionaries and the Versaillais by showing them that we are capable of punishing the guilty ones.

More conventional feminist themes also emerged, argued to the extreme. Male government, male religion, male institutions, male society, male sexuality were all hauled into the pillory. 'Men are like monarchs, softened by their too constant power,' one woman cried. 'It is time that women replace them in the direction of public affairs. Make way for women, for their talents, their courage, their patriotism.'

Some of the rant was as radical as anything heard a hundred years later. 'Marriage, *citoyennes*, is the greatest error of ancient humanity,' claimed a member of the Club of Saint-Eustache, according to John Leighton.

> To be married is to be a slave . . . Marriage, therefore, cannot be tolerated any longer in a free city. It ought to be considered a crime, and suppressed by the most severe measures. Nobody has the right to sell his liberty, and thereby to set a bad example to his fellow citizens. The matrimonial state is a perpetual crime against morality. Don't tell me that marriage may be tolerated, if you institute divorce. Divorce is only an expedient, and, if I may be allowed to use the word, an Orleanist expedient!' (*Thunders of applause*). 'Therefore, I propose to this assembly, that it should get the Paris Commune to modify a decree which assures pensions to the legitimate or illegitimate companions of the National Guards, killed in the defence of our municipal rights. No half measures. We, the illegitimate companions, will no longer suffer the legitimate wives to usurp rights they no longer possess, and which they ought never to have had at all. Let the decree be modified. All for the free women, none for the slaves!'

The decree on pensions to which she refers – a measure by which widows who were not officially married to casualties of the conflict received the same state pension as those who were – was one of several which suggest the seriousness with which the Commune took the question of women: another was the admission, for the first time in history, of the principle of equal pay for equal work, when female teachers' salaries were levelled with those of male.

A poster proclaimed 'A Call to the Women Citizens of Paris'. It required them to assemble to form committees in each arrondissement 'aimed at organizing a women's movement for the defence of Paris,' in the event that Reaction and its gendarmes should attempt to capture it'. In response there developed the Union des Femmes, the statutes of which announced that it would 'give assistance in the work of the government's commissions and serve at ambulance stations, at canteens and at the barricades'. Its personnel was not genteel or bourgeois (during the siege, a Union des Femmes would have been a meekly respectable matter of bandages and poetry readings). Out of its 128 core members, the professions of sixty are recorded: 'fifteen seamstresses, nine waistcoat-makers, six sewing-machine operators, five dressmakers, five linen drapers, three makers of men's clothing, two bootstitchers, two hat-makers, two laundresses, two cardboard-makers, one embroiderer of military decorations, one braid-maker, one schoolteacher, one perfume-maker, one jeweller, one gold-polisher, one book-stitcher and one bookbinder,' according to the historian Edith Thomas.

Of necessity at such a time, much of the work of the Union des Femmes would have been routine errands of welfare, but nevertheless its perspectives were broader and its sights higher than the kitchen stove and the hospital bed. At the end of April it sent the Commune's Commission of Labour and Exchange a proposal for a system whereby 'free producer associations' would share out 'profits from various industries'. Points of reform were set out thus:

(a) Variety of work in each trade – a continually repeated manual movement damages both mind and body.
(b) A reduction in working hours – physical exhaustion inevitably destroys man's spiritual qualities.
(c) An end to all competition between male and female workers – their interests are identical and their solidarity is essential to the success of the final world-wide strike of labour against capital.

The Association therefore wants:
(1) Equal pay for equal hours of work
(2) A local and international federation of the various trade sections in order to ease the movement and exchange of goods by centralizing the international interests of the producers.

The general development of these producer associations requires:
(1) Informing and organizing the working masses . . . The consequence of this will be that every association member will be expected to belong to the International Working Men's Association.
(2) State assistance in advancing the necessary credit for setting up these associations: loans repayable in yearly instalments at a rate of 5 per cent.

The reorganization of female labour is an extremely urgent matter, when one considers that in the society of the past it was the most exploited form of all.

Behind this Utopian-socialist programme – none of which was ever realized – was the quixotic figure of Elizabeth Dmitrieff, one of several adventurous and interesting women to make their mark on the Commune. Born in Pskov in 1851, she was the illegitimate daughter of a hussar and a nurse. Highly educated in her adolescence, she left Russia for Switzerland in the hope of entering a university (still impossible in Russia, as indeed it was in France). Marriage to a wealthy and elderly turbercular colonel gave her a status and independence of which she took full advantage. Through her contacts with *émigré* revolutionaries in Geneva, she joined the Internationale and went to London, where she became friendly with Marx and his daughters. It seems that she arrived in Paris, some weeks before the declaration of the Commune, with an unknown mission from Marx. Events overtook her and she found a more public destiny at the centre of the Union des Femmes. Superbly dressed in a black velvet riding habit with a red silk scarf wrapped boldly round her breast, her mysterious alien beauty was long remembered by the Communards – a striking contrast no doubt to the grim, lumbering giant figure of the 'Red Virgin' schoolteacher Louise Michel (a Joan of Arc II if ever there was one), stomping up and down the Commune's front line, a tunnel-vision revolutionary with no life beyond the cause.

12 April

As Versaillais bombs pummelled the Champs Élysées from the fort of Mont-Valérien and battle raged at Asnières, Thiers rejected out of hand the Commune's proposal for an exchange of the Archbishop of Paris for Auguste Blanqui. Blanqui, Thiers claimed, was a criminal, the Archbishop an innocent hostage. There could be no deals or compromises. But he was embarrassed by a letter from the Archbishop sternly asking for fair treatment of prisoners of war.

The Commune declared a moratorium on prosecutions for non-payment of bills. On the Boulevard de la Madeleine, the Revd William Gibson was amazed by

what I never expected to see in the centre of the metropolis of France

– a man in the middle of the broad asphalted pavement, with a crowd around him, performing feats with heavy weights, lifting them and throwing them over his head; a sight such as you might see on the green of a provincial village on a *fête* day. Paris, the gay, the fashionable, is reduced to this. The empty state of the city – *i.e.*, as far as carriages are concerned, has, however, some advantages. One can cross the Boulevard reading a newspaper all the time without any fear of being run down. Fancy this in the Strand or Cheapside.

13 April

Four hundred artists packed the lecture hall of the School of Medicine at the Sorbonne to hear the manifesto of the Federation of Artists of Paris read out. It proposed that Art should be run by Artists, free of commercial considerations, and promised unexceptionably to preserve the treasures of the past, to illuminate the work of the present and to educate for the future. Plans for a programme of exhibitions and a journal were established and teaching reforms instituted.

For all this encouragement, the Commune stimulated no art of note and signally failed to inspire the great painters and sculptors of the day to anything more than the odd sketch. Corot, Manet and Degas had decamped from Paris; Millet, Renoir and Daumier kept their heads down and did not get involved. The one enthusiast was Gustave Courbet, the fifty-two-year-old pioneer of the new Realism, celebrated for his paintings of peasants, workers and the hard life of the rural poor. A fervent Republican, he had turned down Louis Napoleon's offer of the Légion d'honneur, and was now a leading light of the new Federation, an artist turned committee-man. 'I get up, I eat breakfast, I sit down and preside twelve hours a day,' he wrote. 'My head begins to feel like a baked apple. But despite all this unaccustomed turmoil of the head and brain, I'm in a state of enchantment. Paris is a real paradise.' *Paris est un vrai paradis.*

For heaven's sake, Courbet, get back to painting, grumbled Catulle Mendès in his journal. It's spring and you should be in the woods, sketching the rustling young leaves, not debating and federating in the Hôtel de Ville. How will any of this make anyone a better artist? What can matter to an artist except his solitary conscience and imagination? 'Help us, if you like, but

without obligation, without partisanship or regulation . . .
Leave us in peace, Monsieur de la Fédération!'

15 April
The first coins of the Commune were struck – 400,000 five-franc
pieces, never widely circulated. The design was simple, and by
some oversight, *Dieu protège la France*, God protects France, was
engraved on their rims.

The Banque de France continued to pay a clever game, doling
money out regularly with some generosity and thereby allowing
the Commune no excuse to assume direct control. Thiers knew
about this, and nodded assent to the tactic. Karl Marx's view was
that this situation constituted the Commune's most feeble
naïvete, arguing that had the bank's assets (over 1,000 million
francs of shares and securities and 500 million of cash) been held
hostage, Versailles' attitude would have been far more conciliatory. Francis Jourde, a former bank clerk, was the Commune's
Delegate for Finances. He behaved with impeccable book-
keeper's integrity and not a *sou* of the finances went un-
accounted. Apart from bank loans (finally totalling over twenty
million francs), money was also raised from the normal tax on
goods entering the gates of the city and a backdated levy on the
profits made by the railway companies.

By-elections for the seats on the Commune left vacant by the
immediate resignations of 28 March made the Reds restless. Not
enough was being done, the pace was too slow and the attitude
too moderate. The chairman of the Club that met in the church
of Saint-Séverin wrote to Raoul Rigault with some advice on
how to hot things up:

> It [the Commune] is certainly in need of some fresh, virile blood, for
> it is barely moving. If I were a member, I would do everything
> possible to eliminate a good two-thirds of the members and I would
> want to crush the bourgeoisie once and for all. I see only one way of
> achieving this: take over the Bank of France, imitate that timberman,
> Abraham Lincoln, grant a five-thousand-franc bonus to each
> volunteer, take care of the families of the dead and wounded, shoot
> any deserter, send two hundred million francs to serve as treasury for
> the International, return immediately all objects in the National
> Pawnshops . . .

16 April

The results of the by-elections suggested a disgruntled electorate. Turnout was low – in some arrondissements, where the middle-class exodus had been highest, it fell by as much as half of what it had been on 28 March – and some winning candidates did not attract even the required minimum votes from one-eighth of the electoral roll. Nine seats remained uncontested. One of those newly elected in the sixth arrondissement was Gustave Courbet. Why the loss of faith?

A decree encouraged workers' co-operatives to take over abandoned factories and workshops. This had been a popular idea in France for twenty years or more, and Paris boasted over fifty co-operative enterprises before the Commune began. But the decree had little impact: there were only ten instances of anyone taking advantage of it. Paris's mind was elsewhere.

In Hyde Park in London, republicans and sympathizers organized a demonstration of support for the Commune. *The Times* pronounced it 'a signal failure in every respect'.

17 April

Complaints about the supply of food centred on hoarding and profiteering rather than shortages. The Revd William Gibson, however, noted that 'the price of provisions is rising rapidly'. His explanation for this was a sound one: 'country people don't care to bring their provisions into a city bristling with cannon and abounding in barricades. Naturally prudent, they prefer to sell their provisions to the Prussians, who surround the city on the north and east, and to the French who surround it on the south and west, to running the risk of penetrating into the city at the risk of losing their lives by shells and bullets.' Ironically, this meant that the rewards for those who were prepared to run the risk increased: 'veal, which sold at 1 franc, 40 c, now sells at 2 fr the pound; leg of mutton, which a week ago was selling at 1 fr. 30c, is now 2 fr. 90c'.

The clubs grumbled for more requisitions from the well-stocked larders of the rich and complained that whereas the muncipal butchers closed for two hours a day, 'the aristocratic butchers' remained open. Why could the employees of the former not take staggered lunch breaks?

18 April
The Versaillais took the station at Asnières and many prisoners. William Gibson's view was that the two leaders in the field – the naturalized American Cluseret and the *émigré* Pole Dombrowski – were both handicapped by not being fully-fledged Frenchmen. (This notion, that 'foreigners' were 'behind' the Commune, was widespread, and the Internationale was a convenient focus for such a suspicion. 'They have recruited the tramps and brigands from all over Europe,' wrote Paul de Saint-Victor. 'Polish forgers, Garibaldian adventurers, Slavic pimps, Prussian agents, Yankee filibusters all frolic at the head of its battalions. Paris has become the main sewer for the scum and dregs of two continents.') 'The more I get to know about this insurrectionary movement the more I am convinced that it is a great effort of the Red Republican party in Europe to gain their ends,' Gibson continued.

[They have] been on the look-out for years for a field of operations; they could not find it in England or Germany, but in Paris, at this particular juncture, they have found exactly what they have long wanted. And to make their cause more popular they have turned the legitimate desire on the part of the Parisians, to have the municipal management of Paris in their own hands, to suit their own nefarious purposes. Two entirely distinct things have been blended together. Hence Paris gets blame which she does not deserve. The Assembly is angry at Paris. The anger and complaint should be directed against that which Paris happens to contain at the present moment. The 'word of order' to these people in Paris is said to come from the International Society in London!

Paranoia about the Internationale such as this was fed by a book by one Oscar Testut, who painted it luridly as a sort of Red incarnation of the Freemasons, with an undercover network stretching all over Europe and fomenting strikes, crimes and plots in various sinister collaborations. There was a grain of truth in this, but only a grain. The Internationale was in fact a very loose and diverse organization, not unduly secretive about its operations. According to Eugene Schulkind:

> membership could be based on anything from payment of dues to merely voting for affiliation of one's club or union, and necessitated no explicit commitments to specific points of the Internationale programme. Since members held a wide range of socialist beliefs, it is not surprising that although one-third of the members elected to the Commune were also members of the Internationale, they were as divided politically as were the other members of the Commune.

19 April

The Commune published its only attempt at a manifesto. *The Times* called it 'a confused medley of contradictory and ill-conceived ideas, of absurdities, of arrogant pretensions, and of lies . . . "You are free" the Commune says to France, "but on condition that I am at liberty to do everything, and that you do as I do".'

Drawn up in a hurry by the Proudhonian journalist Pierre Denis and waved through various committees without much debate, it is not a very gripping or stirring document. Perhaps the most interesting aspect is its vision of a France split up into a collection of autonomous Communes. Political unity, it states, is not a matter of empire, monarchy or parliamentarianism but 'the voluntary association of local initiatives, the spontaneous and free concourse of all individual energies with respect to a shared goal, that of the well-being, the liberty and security of all'. The Revolution of the Commune, begun by the people's initiative of 18 March, inaugurates a new era of 'experimental, positivist and scientific politics'.

20 April

An intelligent middle-class lady, Madame Talbot of the rue Godot-le-Mauroy, near the Madeleine, to her sister in Bordeaux:

> The cannon didn't stop yesterday or last night – nor did the shooting – and the noise continues this morning. The general view is that the Fédéré Garde Nationale are absolutely beaten, but because it boldly

fights on and the troops of Versailles advance slowly, we haven't made much progress in the last week.

What makes us think that the struggle on the ramparts is moving in favour of Versailles is the construction of huge barricades at the gate to the Place de l'Etoile, at the Place de la Concorde, at the Marine Ministry in the rue Royale, and at the start of the rue de Rivoli, near the rue Saint-Florentin. They continue to fortify the Place Vendôme . . . Many people wonder why M. Thiers has allowed the time for these formidable defences to be built in the streets. He has a plan, they say; but people are sceptical of plans nowadays and put little faith in them. We wonder what might be 'the two great infallible measures' which he says must be used if he is not victorious in the present campaign. Famine and bombardment are a terrible prospect; I don't believe an alliance with the Prussians is possible.

It is astonishing how accustomed one becomes to the noise of cannon. For two or three days now, even though it seems to be drawing closer, everyone has been pursuing their ordinary routines; we come and go, and if Paris is sad and deserted, that is because half the population has left the city and commerce has ceased. The situation becomes graver day by day, it is true; they have just suppressed five newspapers. Soon there will only be those put out by the Commune. I think only *Le Temps*, *Le Siècle*, *L'Avenir National* are now appearing, and yesterday and this morning they protested vigorously against the arrests made by the Commune, regarding it almost as a disgrace to have been spared closure.

Everyone says: 'This cannot go on much longer'; but people have been saying that for the last nine months of tragedy – and still the weeks, the months pile up and God alone knows when an end will come.

21 April

One major new appointment in the reorganization of the Commune's administration was that of Edouard Vaillant, a Blanquiste delegated to the Commission for Education. The French state provided for only secondary and higher education; Vaillant pushed to extend this, following a report made by a committee of male and female teachers, into compulsory free schooling of both sexes up to the age of twelve. Special emphasis would also be put on the provision of professional training opportunities for women and on nursery facilities. The first obstacle was the stranglehold exerted on schools by nuns and priests. The Commune wanted to secularize education and rear its young on 'experimental, positivist and scientific' principles, but the church would not let go without fighting back and there were some violent incidents in the ensuing sporadic attempts at a purge. Like so many of the Commune's measures of social reform, this educational policy had no time to establish itself, let alone develop. But how good were the intentions behind it!

22 April

George Sand to Alexandre Dumas: 'The Commune is the result of an excess of material civilization throwing its scum to the surface on a day when nobody was watching the boiler.'

Moderate bodies continued to plead with Thiers to negotiate. He remained intransigent: asked why he bombed the capital, and what would be the end of it, he replied: 'A few buildings will be damaged, a few people killed, but the law will prevail.'

The Funny Side

Jokes were at a premium during the Commune, a much more earnest episode than the siege had been. Gruesome political caricatures, of varying degrees of obscenity and wit, lined the booksellers' windows, providing a grim knowing chuckle; that dumpy pocket dictator Thiers with his wispy pate and owl-eyed spectacles was an easy target: General Boum, Four-eyed Tamburlaine, Little Caesar, they called him, General Tom Thumb, The Nation's Undertaker. The odd theatre played on – there was a satirical revue called *J'ai mon plan!* (in reference to Trochu) at the Folies-Athènes, and according to Catulle Mendès, performances of the boulevard farce *The Duck with Three Beaks* were packed with audiences guffawing at the idiocy and treating themselves to *violette praliné* chocolates.

But there wasn't much else on offer, and *Le Petit Journal pour rire*, the city's most popular magazine of escapist humour, announced on 21 April that it was closing down for the duration, considering its flippant tone inappropriate to the situation. Most of the remaining laughs came from a pocket-size daily news-sheet, price one *sou*, with a circulation of some 70,000. It was called *Le Père Duchêne*, after a comparable publication of the first Revolution, and it was largely written by a brilliant twenty-six-year-old poet, journalist and Bohemian, Eugene Vermersch. *Le Père Duchêne* provided a daily blast of blatant populism, delivered as if from the bar-room by a foul-mouthed but plain-speaking son of Belleville. 'Père Duchêne' was a friend to the Commune, but not afraid to be critical of it. As he knocked back his booze (*boit sa chopine*), he divided the world into the decent buggers (*les bons bougres*) and the bastards (*les jean-foutres*). He could be violent (*en grande colère*) in his review of the day's events and policies, advocating that *tous ces bougres-là* be shot forthwith but he could also be bloody pleased (*bougrement content*) when the Commune acted for the best. Behind this rather tiresome persona was a keen political intelligence, sensitively attuned to the feelings and thoughts of the working-class people who had voted the Commune in and were prepared to fight for its survival. The quips and jibes of Père Duchêne became the Commune's streetwise talk, a hundred times more effective and influential than the stiff rhetoric of official posters and publications.

The foreign correspondents scrabbled around desperately for items of light relief. One wonders who cooked up the story that café waiters, those staunch members of the working class, were banding together to complain about tipping malpractice. John Leighton sank to reporting that in a Belgian newspaper's view 'the world of fashion' had deserted Paris in its time of trouble and that 'London henceforth dictates to all the modistes of the universe'. English leather, mushroom-shaped bonnets, the colour of magenta – all apparently vulgar or *passé* – would come to invade the streets of the French capital as the final humiliation of its fallen pride.

24 April
Elizabeth Dmitrieff, of the Union des Femmes, to a fellow member of the Internationale in London, in a letter sent by courier:

> It is impossible to write by the post – communications are interrupted and everything falls into the hands of the Versaillais. . . .
> How can you stay there doing nothing, when Paris is perishing

because of such inaction? The provinces must be agitated, at all costs, to come to our aid. The population of Paris fights bravely on the whole, but we never thought we would be abandoned as we are. However, up to now, we have managed to hold all our strategic positions. Dombrowski fights well and Paris is truly revolutionary. There is no shortage of food. As you know, I am a pessimist and never look on the bright side, so I expect to die one of these days on the barricades. We await a general attack . . .

I am very ill. I have bronchitis and a fever. I work hard, we are looking after all the women of Paris. . . . I think we are doing everything we can. I cannot say too much, for fear that the fine eyes of M. Thiers might be inspecting these lines – there is some question whether the bearer of these lines, a Swiss publisher from Basle who brought me news of the Internationale in London, will arrive safe and sound in London . . .

One may assume that this is a fair example of the 'conspiracy' of the Internationale's 'secret network' – hardly very sinister.

25 April
An eight-hour truce was called at Neuilly to permit evacuation of civilians from the theatre of the single hardest-fought engagement of the war against Paris. Ambulances rushed to this formerly elegant and bustling suburb – closely followed by posses of gawping spectators and journalists – to help with the casualties of a battle that had scarcely relented for three weeks. They discovered shocking scenes of starvation and desolation – two women, for example, were hauled out of a cellar where they had been huddling for eighteen days beside the dead body of a friend. Thiers uses the truce to install three hundred new pieces of heavy artillery which began to fire the second the truce was over, most of them aimed at the southern forts of Issy and Vanves. For the Commune, Dombrowski fought on.

27 April

Could hear a continuous cannonade, but suppose as usual that it is simply gaspillage of munitions. Wish the whole affair was finished one way or other, it is becoming absolutely sickening, during the siege at least people knew why they were suffering and for what end, but now it would be difficult to say which is the most preferable the Commune or the Government, both give such proofs of their incapacity. It's a great pity that the whole affair cannot end like the battle between the two Kilkenny cats, then I think everybody would be satisfied & some means might be found of forming a new government in accordance with the desires of the country. [From the diary of Edwin Child]

The Commune prohibited night work in bakeries. This proved a highly controversial measure, bitterly opposed by the bakery owners and enforced with great difficulty. Some historians, however, have deemed it the Commune's one lasting achievement in the field of social legislation. Other reforms included the requisition of vacant lodging; the abolition of workplace fines (one factory exacted three francs for being caught smoking on the job, and twenty-five centimes for combing your hair); and liberalizing changes to the regulations governing the *livret de travail*, a much-disliked workers' identity card, instituted during the Second Empire and stamped with the holder's employment record. But again, these were only shakily enacted.

28 April

Despite the reorganization of 21 April, the Commune was becoming increasingly enfeebled by fractious internal divisions. Louis Rossel, the Commune's twenty-seven-year-old Chief of Military Staff, a veteran of the siege of Metz who had defected from a brilliant career in the French army in disgust at its surrender to the Prussians, began to plot a military dictatorship with members of the Committee of the Garde Nationale – anything, he said, to stop the waste of energy in a futile war of words. In the Assembly of the Commune, the establishment of a Committee of Public Safety was proposed, modelled on the notorious cabal which took the reins of the revolution in 1793, suspended the liberties of democracy and ruled by Terror instead. But something drastic had to be done: the 8th Battalion of the Garde Nationale had just mutinied and military discipline was slipping.

A letter received by Jules Audoyaud of the Committee of the

Garde Nationale embodied the frustration felt by the mass of the Commune's working-class supporters – the level of public opinion that *Le Père Duchêne* so unerringly reflected:

> Things are not working out right, citizen; the Commune is not rising to the occasion and something should be done about this as soon as possible. All we see are the same old monarchist and parliamentary procedures. Nothing but that. Concern for old economic, philosophic and social prejudices. But no revolutionary measures such as the people have in mind.
>
> The moratorium on payment of rents? Instead of a determined policy of housing the people in the homes of the rich and the bourgeoisie, there is only the humiliating postponement of three of the quarterly rent payments which the landlord vultures will easily recoup in the future. The people are left in the slums. . . .
>
> What has been done about food? Municipal canteens have been set up where they dish out awful grub, while, next door, luxury restaurants are still in evidence, where the rich and the bourgeoisie have their feasts. And all this, when it is a simple matter to confiscate the storehouses and provisions of the merchants who supply them.
>
> Yet what can be heard at the town hall? Worn-out, high-sounding words about respect, justice, integrity, decency and – damn it – even refinement. This is all nothing but twaddle to cover up and excuse the oppression of the proletariat by the rich and the bourgeoisie. And, believe me, citizen, they also talk about capital and interest.
>
> I ask you and your colleagues, citizen, if this isn't weakness, surrender and treason?
>
> The air of gilded drawing-rooms has already corrupted you! I tell you that if you don't expropriate things through sweeping, regularly enacted legislation, then we will have to take everything when and how we decide. But we will take it. And your posters, 'Death for looting', 'Death for stealing', won't make a difference, for we will be the stronger. . . . Instead of enacting a general law restituting all that is due to us, you talk and act like people who have not the least idea of what the proletariat demands . . .

Thousands of such letters were sent to all the institutions of this participatory democracy, concerning every imaginable subject and offering a wide range of counsel and injunction. One old fellow wrote to propose a loosening of the Commune's straightlacedness and a little free love:

There is no such thing as public decency, shame, vice or prostitution. Nature is not concerned with such stupidities. She has her needs, her demands, and she must be satisfied as is thought best, in her way, when and where one wishes, taking any opportunity, as one pleases, completely by chance, after waiting a long time or at the first meeting, with whoever one wants to, as we do, we other proletarians, among ourselves. Only today what we need are your girls, O idle rich, your women. What is needed is that they return for the benefit of the proletarians, and of everyone in the great communal family. Enforce this measure at once, prudish Commune, or else we will see to it ourselves, and gleefully so, I assure you. Sadly I do not speak for myself, for I am too old to do anything but simply watch the show of this great and magnificent priapic festival that will be the inauguration of the true community.

29 April

Over the previous week or so the Freemasons had taken a lead in making overtures of conciliation and peace between the Commune and Versailles – it was they who had negotiated the truce at Neuilly on 25 April.

Encouraged by the granting of that small concession, the Freemasons of Paris had called a meeting at the Théâtre du Châtelet on 26 April. They voted to march to the front line, where they would plant their banners on the ramparts and wait for the shooting to stop. A delegation went on to the Hôtel de Ville to inform them of this initiative.

Whose side were they on? There was some confusion over this question. Conspiracy theorists believed that the Internationale was behind Freemasonry or that Freemasonry was behind the Internationale, and it was certainly true that at least fifteen Masons sat on the Commune. But there were probably twice as many involved in the government of Versailles, and one can only assume that their agenda was sincerely pacific and disinterested.

The important Grand Orient lodge disassociated itself from a parade which would violate the Masonic code of secrecy and there was some argy-bargy about the ethics of Masonry being seen to take such an active and partisan political stand. Nevertheless, in golden sunshine, a magnificent procession assembled on the morning of 29 April. Led by a white banner inscribed in red

'Love One Another', fifteen thousand Masons from sixty-five male lodges and one women's lodge paraded from the Place de la Bastille down the rue de Rivoli up the Champs Élysées to the Porte Maillot, chanting their ritual hymns and sporting their ritual robes and insignia, never before seen in public. A small balloon emblazoned with the Masonic triangle was launched and it was rumoured that irresistible magical powers passed down from the biblical King Solomon would be released into the ether.

Arriving at the ramparts as the Versaillais guns continued to fire, the Masons planted their glittering scarlet, gold and purple banners, interspersed with white flags. After more hymns and emanations, the shooting quietened (but not before bullets had pierced a banner and killed two Masons). A deputation went on to Courbevoie, where Thiers received the mellifluous injunctions with an indifference bordering on irritation. There could be no negotiation with the Commune. Criminals must be punished: Paris must surrender or face the consequences.

30 April
Amid heated debate as to the merits of establishing a Committee of Public Safety, Rossel was made the Commune's Delegate for War and took immediate action to intensify the building of barricades. His predecessor, Cluseret, had just reoccupied the fort of Issy, abandoned by its governor the day before. Inside, Cluseret found only a weeping sixteen-year-old clutching a powder-keg with which he planned to explode the fort when the Versaillais entered. Cluseret burst into tears too and embraced the youthful patriot of the Commune. On his return to Paris, Cluseret was arrested on totally unfounded suspicion of disloyalty.

Colonel Mayer, administrator of the Garde Nationale, assessed the military strength of the Commune at 6,507 officers and 162,651 troops. These figures were made up of the twenty legions of the 'regular' Garde Nationale, divided into battalions of vastly varying efficacy: some of those drawn from middle-class areas scarcely functioned except on paper, while others from working-class areas were little better than bands of drunken pilferers. Although theoretically most able-bodied men under the age of fifty were obliged to serve, nothing seems to have been easier than excusing yourself by simply failing to turn up at the appointed place or time. Much more useful were the ten thousand-odd men who belonged to thirty-four 'irregular' brigades,* some of them (like the Vengeurs de Flourens) crack urban guerrillas.

From Rouen, Flaubert let rip to George Sand. He was sick of the whole business, sick of the modern world and its cant:

> We will become a big, dreary, industrial country – a kind of Belgium. The disappearance of Paris (as the seat of government) will make France dull and stagnant. She will have no heart, no centre – and, I think, no mind?
>
> As for the Commune, which is in its death throes, it's the latest manifestation of the Middle Ages. Will it be the last? Let's hope so!
>
> I hate democracy (at least as it is understood in France), because it is based on 'the morality of the Gospels', which is immorality itself, whatever anyone may say: that is, the exaltation of Mercy at the expense of Justice, the negation of Right – the opposite of social order.
>
> The Commune is rehabilitating assassins, just as Jesus forgave thieves; and they are looting the houses of the rich because they have learned to curse Lazarus – who was not a *bad* rich man, but simply a rich man. The slogan 'The republic is above all argument' is on a par with the dogma that 'The Pope is infallible.' Always slogans! Always gods!
>
> The God-before-last – universal suffrage – has just played a terrible joke on his faithful by electing 'the assassins of Versailles'. What are we to believe in, then? Nothing. That is the beginning of

---

* Called: Carabiniers Volontaires; Cavaliers Bergeret; Foot Chasseurs; Polish Chasseurs; Contre-Chouans; Defenders of the Republic; Eclaireurs Bergeret; Eclaireurs of the National Guard; Eclaireurs of Neuilly; Eclaireurs of the Hôtel-de-Ville; Enfants Perdus of Paris; Enfants de Paris; Enfants of the Père Duchêne; Squadron of the Eclaireurs of the Marseillaise; Federals of the 1st arrondissement; Francs-tireurs of Paris; Francs-tireurs of the 12th arrondissement; Francs-tireurs of the Republic; Francs-tireurs of the Commune; Lascars of the Commandants Janssoulé; Mounted National Guard; Italian Legion; Alsacian Legion; Belgian Legion; Marines of the National Guard; Marines-Sauveurs; Mobilisés of Seine-et-Oise; Tirailleurs of the Marseillaise; Tirailleurs of the Commune; Tirailleurs Eclaireurs; Vengeurs of Flourens; Vengeurs of Paris; Volunteers of the Column of July; and Volunteers of Colonel Lenfant.

Wisdom. It is time to rid ourselves of 'Principles' and to espouse Science, objective inquiry. The only rational thing (I keep coming back to it) is a government of Mandarins, provided the Mandarins know something – in fact, a great many things. The *people* never come of age, and they will always be the bottom rung of the social scale because they represent number, mass, the limitless. It is of little importance that many peasants should be able to read and no longer listen to their priests; but it is infinitely important that many men like Renan or Littré be able to live *and be listened to*. Our only salvation now lies in a *legitimate aristocracy*, by which I mean a majority composed of something more than mere numbers. . . .

For the moment, Paris is completely epileptic. It's the result of congestion of the brain caused by the siege. Besides, during the past few years France was living in an abnormal mental state. The success of the *Lanterne*, and Troppmann, were very clear symptoms.

This madness springs from excessive stupidity; and the stupidity from a superfluity of nonsense. Our lying had turned us into idiots. We had lost all notion of good and evil, of the beautiful and the ugly. Remember what criticism has been like these last few years. Could it tell the difference between the Sublime and the Ridiculous? What lack of respect! What ignorance! What a muddle! 'Boiled or roast, it's all the same!' And, at the same time, such servility toward the 'opinion of the day' – *le plat à la mode*.

Everything was fakery: fake realism, fake army, fake credit, and even fake whores. . . .

Foreign opinion

Flaubert's brilliant outburst, flinging himself crazily against the ropes on the right of the political boxing ring, can be countered by Frederic Harrison's temperate defence of the Commune, published in the issue of the *Fortnightly Review* current in London:

There is a point, and we have reached it, at which national greatness and glory pass into national tyranny and pride. The idea of imperial grandeur is a simple evil – reactionary, oppressive, and demoralising. This pride in vast State aggregates which do not correspond with true political and social units, made up of dissimilar parts bound together by force or craft, is not a good thing, but an evil. The grand State systems having done their part in Europe, like the Roman Empire, like it are growing oppressive. These empires, cemented by 'blood and iron', have no true vitality. They gratify the ambition or the vanity of the professional classes, but the people throughout Europe abhor them, and they are doomed. The imperial spirit is the Nemesis of patriotism. Look at the history of the late war, and of its authors on both sides, and judge how profoundly hostile to civilisation this pride of imperial greatness has become. Events have given this sentiment a momentary strength, but the people do not share it in France, in Germany, or in England. It is the honour of the Paris workmen that they definitely repudiate this coarse ambition. They look forward in the future to a nation greater than any – the people of the West of Europe. They repudiated the league of the bourgeoisie against the Germans. A Prussian★ sits on the Commune. Their dream of a universal Republic means no absurd extension of national territory. It means the union of men in their true political aggregates, bound together as a nation in a federal bond, forming for many purposes but one people, without the barriers of jealous nationality or the oppression of centralised states. . . .

The idea of the Commune, the idea of the gradual dissolution of nations into more similar aggregates and truer political unity is the idea of the future. It lives deep in the instincts of every people of Europe, and now that 200,000 workmen in Paris have taken up arms to conquer it its ultimate triumph is assured.

Another prominent English intellectual, Matthew Arnold, did not share Harrison's confidence, but was forced to acknowledge that the Commune was more than just a criminal *coup* or an historical aberration: 'Paris does not make me so angry as it does many people,' he wrote, 'because I do not think well enough of Thiers and the French upper class generally to think it very important that they should win. What is certain is that all the seriousness, clear-mindedness and settled purpose is hitherto on the side of the Reds.' Later he would add that 'the Paris convulsion is an explosion of that fixed resolve of the working class to count for something and *live*, which is destined to make itself so much felt in the coming time, and to disturb so much which dreamed it would last for ever'.

But the world at large could see no further than the end of its nose. The press was ignorant of the facts and immovably

★ Presumably a reference to Léo Frankel, in fact the son of a Hungarian doctor, but a member of the Internationale in Germany.

prejudiced towards one party or the other. In England, the *Daily Telegraph* unsurprisingly talked of the Communards as 'assassins and convicts' and the *Daily News* averred that 'the most humane among us would not be too scrupulous about the repressive measures which might be necessary'; for the left, the Chartist *Reynolds News* equally unsurprisingly talked of 'clever-headed, noble-hearted men . . . awarding themselves the very modest sum of twelve pounds a month for their services'. In the USA, the *New York Times* worried that its own workers might be infected with the Parisian disease: 'let some such opportunity occur as was presented in Paris . . . let this mighty throng hear that there was a chance to grasp the luxuries of wealth, or to divide the property of the rich, or to escape labour and suffering for a time, and live on the superfluities of others, and we should see a sudden storm of communistic revolution even in New York such as would astonish all who do not know these classes.'

2 May

The *Journal Officiel* announced that:

1. A Committee of Public Safety will be immediately organized.
2. It will be composed of five members, nominated by the Commune from open ballot.
3. The most extensive powers over all the delegations and commissions will be given to the Committee, which will answer only to the Commune.

In the Assembly of the Commune forty-six voted for this drastic measure, twenty-three against (Courbet among them: 'I wish that words and terms belonging to the Revolution of 1789 or 1793 would be applied only to that epoch . . . we are behaving like plagiarists and re-establishing to our detriment a Terror that is out of keeping with our time.' This tendency was also indicated by the committee's decision to adopt the Revolutionary calendar, making today not 2 May but 13 Floréal). Those elected were Antoine Arnaud, Leo Méillet, Gabriel Ranvier, Félix Pyat and Charles Gérardin – a tough line-up. The dominating figure was Pyat, who also edited the influential newspaper *Le Vengeur*. Bottomlessly ambitious, scheming and slippery, he had Marat's gift for inflammatory speechifying and would sink to any excess to make an effect – 'he needs muzzling to stop him turning our revolution into a melodrama,' one Communard colleague aptly remarked. Aged sixty, he combined a steel will with a fund of revolutionary experience. It was not easy to gainsay him; it was impossible to outwit him. Rossel was his mortal enemy – a straightforward military man who could not tolerate Pyat's blood-and-thunder posturing and had once dared openly to laugh at him. Pyat was determined to see his downfall.

The seventeenth and eighteenth arrondissements were bombed for the first time. After much debate, it was decided that the majority of goods deposited at the state pawnshops, the Monts-de-Piété, could be freely reclaimed.

3 May

The case of the church of Saint-Laurent, on the Boulevard Magenta. It had been closed on Good Friday by the Garde Nationale, which took only the petty cash and some postage stamps, then for some reason insisted on providing the priest with a receipt for same. A week later some more adventurous Gardes Nationales were exploring the crypt, where they found some human remains ('what else did they expect to find?' Paul Fontoulieu asked drily). Someone who had worked on repairs in the church ten years previously came forward to claim that he had heard strange underground moans and groans while he was there. Two magistrates and a chemist were brought in to examine the bones and fourteen skeletons, some of them female, were reconstructed. Everyone enjoyed believing that there must be a secret attached to all this and a lurid little brochure entitled *Les Cadavres de Saint Laurent* was published complete with illustrations and tales of the iniquities of the Catholic Church.

Starved for entertainment, the Parisians flocked to the crypt (entry, fifty centimes) and drew their own conclusions, based on the more paranoid fantasies of the anticlericals. The bones later proved to be at least a hundred and fifty years old.

Another popular brochure was *Le Pilori des mouchards*, published by the left-wing rag *Paris-Libre*, which for days had been featuring lists of paid informers, or *mouchards*, and their addresses, culled from the files of the Second Empire's secret police. The newspaper assembled these in book form, including many cringing letters of application for the honour of becoming a grass, as well as several applicants' verses of loyalty and admiration humbly addressed to the imperial family.

5 May
In the provinces, the results of municipal elections signalled a reaction against Thiers' hard-line attitude to the Commune and a move in national opinion towards some sort of conciliated settlement with Paris.

'The cowardice, the indifference of this population, living in the midst of this horror, under the sway of this gloating scum, infuriates me,' complained Goncourt.

> I can't watch it continuing calmly to live its ordinary life without flying into a rage. You would suppose that out of this vile parade of men and women, some anger or indignation would spring – some indication of our underlying natural moral sense. But Paris quite simply behaves as though it was experiencing nothing but a hot flat summer season. Today's Parisians, I tell you, would stand back while their wives were raped – worse, they would let you steal their wallets from their pockets, just so long as they could remain what they are: the most abominable moral cowards I have ever known.

In Tours, Hippolyte Taine heard a rumour from someone who had slipped out of the capital that there was a suicide squad of 25,000 Gardes Nationales prepared to brave all for the Commune.

6 May
The palace of the Tuileries was opened to the public, with admission charges donated to the wounded, widows and orphans. For sums ranging from five francs to fifty centimes, the publicity announced, you could visit 'the tyrant' Louis Napoleon's family apartments and attend a concert 'whereby these rooms might at last be rendered useful to the people'. *The Times*'s correspondent took his ticket 'and joined myself to a

thick stream of people who belonged to every nationality and rank of life':

> Every class of Parisian society was represented in the throng that swayed and hustled through the rooms, but the saddest sight of all was a knot or two of decrepit veterans from the Invalides who leant against the balustrade of the grand staircase, and gazed with pinched-up lips and dry eyes at the National Guards on duty, lounging and carousing down below. The stairs were littered with bedding and cooking utensils, shirts and stockings hanging to dry over the gilt railings, while in the square at the stairs' foot were ranged benches and boards on trestles, and there the soldiers of the Guard sat in picturesque groups enough, contrasting in the careless-ness and dirt of their general appearance with the lavish ornaments of marble and gilt work which served as a background to their figures. Marching orders, more or less thumbed and torn, hung in fragments from the panelled walls; names in pencil and names in ink, and names scrawled with a finger-nail, defaced the doors and staircase wall. A sentry stood at every door to see that the citizens behaved themselves – a precaution by no means unnecessary, the outward aspect of certain members of the crowd being taken into consideration. In the Salle de la Paix a number of women were busy uncovering a number of chairs for the promised concert, and in the Salle des Maréchaux beyond, where the concert was to be given, velvet benches were already occupied by old ladies in white caps with baskets in their hands, who presented a stern aspect of endurance, as though they were determined to sit there through the preparations as well as the promised entertainment, and still to continue sitting until turned out by sword and bayonet.

Posters screamed that 'the gold that drapes these walls is your sweat and toil' and great efforts had been made to obliterate anything reminiscent of the imperial past – busts of generals lining the corridors, for example, were covered with white sheets. (*The Times*'s correspondent considered this 'a rather foolish proceeding, considering that the bee-spangled imperial curtains still hang over the doors'). The palace was otherwise strangely denuded:

> Not a chair or a window blind, or even a door-plate or handle, is to be seen in any of the rooms, except in those used for the concerts, and the question arose, naturally enough, 'Where is it all gone to?' The same demand was made so often of an elderly bourgeois on duty at the end of the Salle de Diane that he was fairly bewildered, and

looked round for Help, and hailing the gold stripes on my cap as a haven of relief, he forthwith seized upon me as a superior officer, and insisted on an explanation. 'You know there were quantities of cases carried off during the time before Sedan,' he said, 'but, with all their cunning, they can't have dismantled a whole palace of this size, can they?' . . . The looking-glasses which spring from the walls called down ejaculations of delight from a party of dressmakers, who carefully took notes of the mechanism, 'in order to imitate it, my dear, when Paris becomes itself again.' There was a large placard upon the wall of a kind of library, inviting the attention of the public to the secret arrangements in a recess whereby the Empress obtained her dresses and linen from some manufactory of garments above, and an old lady, after having carefully examined the elaborate details, turned away with a sigh and a shake of the head. 'How foolish of them, after all, not to have done a little for us in order that they might have continued to abide in this paradise!'

The concert itself was a variety show, staffed by Gardes Nationales in their Sunday-best white gloves and slicked-down hair. Alongside the turns by amateur violinists and minor celebrities of the boulevard theatres, two great stars gave their services. One was La Bordas, a popular *chanteuse* of the *café-concerts*. She wore a scarlet gown, her hair loose, her *décolletage* and arms bare – a suburban goddess of Liberty, as Louis Barron put it. What would this boldly vulgar and voluptuous creature sing in such circumstances? Thrillingly, she dared her worst, shaking her fist at the class enemy with a defiant rendition of the revolutionaries' favourite – a song of Brechtian ironic defiance called 'La Canaille'. 'So you think they're muck?' went its refrain: 'well, let me tell you – I'm muck too'! The audience joined in enthusiastically.* Next came the magnificent trage-

---

* 'La Canaille' was one of the two most popular songs of the Commune. The other was a sentimental ballad, 'Le Temps des cerises' (Cherry-blossom time) which wistfully captured the seasonal hopes and dreams of the period of the Commune:

> J'aimerai toujours le temps des cerises
> Et le souvenir que je garde en cœur

(I will always love cherry-blossom time, and the memory of it that I keep in my heart). The scenario concerns a boy who falls in love with a beautiful girl who sells him some of the fruit in question. But he can never find her again, and she becomes just a 'souvenir'. The song's lyrics were written by a member of the Council of the Commune, Jean-Baptiste Clément, in 1867, and 'rededicated' in April 1871 to an ambulance nurse. The author would like to thank Patrick O'Connor for singing 'Le Temps des cerises' to him.

dienne of the Comédie-Française, Mademoiselle Agar, a brave woman who was no special friend to the Commune (her house sheltered several fugitive priests) but who would never refuse to help the victims of war. She declined to deliver the *Marseillaise*, on the grounds that 'I sang it several months ago, when the Germans were at our gates. I now see only Frenchmen': instead she recited poems by Victor Hugo.

From the city walls and beyond, the audience could hear the competing artilleries continuing their low thump and flash and boom – like a culminating fireworks display, remarked Catulle Mendès grimly.

7 May

Rossel and Dombrowski combined to plan a counter-offensive to save the beleaguered fort of Issy. Nobody listened, even though it was a key to the city's weak western defences. A meeting of the Council of the Commune was cancelled when the appointed hour found the hall three-quarters empty. All effective central power seemed to have passed to the Committee of Public Safety.

Paris continued to consume vast amounts of alcohol. The Commission for War received reports of an absinthe-soaked Colonel of the Garde Nationale and there were persistent rumours that the defence of Issy and Neuilly had been badly handicapped by the incapacity of drunken troops. Versaillais propaganda made much of all this, portraying Paris as one reeling, vomiting mass of intoxicated vagabonds, criminals and lunatics. Several futile attempts were made by arrondissements of the Commune to legislate against the indisputable problem of public alcoholism, including the institution of fines against anyone serving liquor to those already drunk. Doctors claimed that alcoholism lowered resistance to infection and that it was killing off soldiers with only minor wounds.

8 May

Rossel and Dombrowski's plan was abandoned, as the generals could not muster the necessary twelve thousand troops, and the fort of Issy was finally evacuated and abandoned. Thiers' spies offered Dombrowski 500,000 gold francs and a safe conduct to his native Poland in return for information on the guarding of city gates. Dombrowski secretly suggested to the Committee of Public Safety that this could be turned into a way of trapping the Versaillais, but this was a possibility not taken seriously.

Another ecclesiastical scandal: the case of the convent at Picpus, in the Faubourg Saint-Antoine, far more sinister than that of Saint-Laurent. In cells measuring seven by six feet at the back of its garden were discovered three incarcerated old women, clearly lunatic, who had been kept there for nine years in conditions of hopeless squalor. 'They were idiots when they arrived,' claimed a tight-lipped Mother Superior when questioned, the daughters of 'good families' who had been 'put away'.

The conductor of the inquiry replied that, if such were the case, it was illegal to have admitted them to the Convent at all [reported *The Times*] and that even supposing them to have been admitted, the place where they were found was not a fit dwelling-place for a dog. A key was discovered, . . . labelled 'key of the great vault'; but where this great vault may be has not yet been found out. The Superior and her nuns keep a uniform and persistent silence upon the point; excavations have been made at different points in the garden, and under the high altar of the chapel, but hitherto without effect. At one end of the nuns' garden stands an isolated building, in which were found mattresses furnished with straps and buckles, also two iron corsets, an iron skull-cap, and a species of rack turned by a cog-wheel, evidently intended for bending back the body with force. The Superior explained that these were orthopaedic instruments – a superficial falsehood. The mattresses and straps struck me as being easily accounted for; for I have seen such things used in French midwifery, and in cases of violent delirium; but the rack and its adjuncts are justly objects of grave suspicion, for they imply a use of brutal force which no disease at present known would justify. On our way back through the gardens our guide made a *détour* in order to show us a great subterranean warehouse, where an enormous quantity of potatoes was stored, as well as barrels full of salt pork, while in a yard hard by lay grunting a fat pig. 'Look at this!' cried our National Guard indignantly. 'Look at these stores, which might have helped to feed the starving poor of the arrondissement during our six months' siege, and think that these people were begging from door to door the whole time for money to buy broken victuals for their pensioners!' Arrived at the entrance gate our guide nudged me, telling me in whispers to look at the old woman who was wandering about, followed by a younger one, stooping from time to time to pick up a leaf or rub her hands with sand and gravel. 'That is Soeur Bernadine,' he said, 'one of the three prisoners of the wooden cages. She is the most sane in mind of the three, and we keep her here under the care of one of our wives to cheer her up. She is only 50, though she looks past 70. The other two have been removed, as they were rendered violent by the crowd and change of scene.' I passed close to her and she looked up – a soft, pale face, with sunken eyes shaded by the frills of a great cap. She looked at me dazedly, without taking any notice, and stooping again, filled her hands with refuse coffee grounds, which she put into her mouth until prevented by her companion.

A treatise on abortion and two female skulls were also discovered. The nuns of Picpus were imprisoned in Saint-Lazare, alongside the whores.

9 May

An exasperated Rossel refused to co-operate in the cover-up over the shambolic evacuation of the fort at Issy. He distributed ten thousand posters announcing the unpleasant truth that 'the flag of the tricolore flies over the Fort of Issy, abandoned by its garrison'. The Commune issued a rebuttal: 'It is not true that the flag of the tricolore flies over the Fort of Issy. The Versaillais do not occupy it and will not occupy it.'

Sick of the lies, the back-room tussles and factions, the hopeless lack of discipline and crumbling organization, as well as the chronic shortage of able fighting troops, Rossel resigned. 'Citizen Members of the Commune,' he wrote in a letter he also copied to all the major newspapers.

You entrusted me provisionally with the post of War Delegate. I no longer feel able to accept this position of authority when the men under me do nothing but hold discussions and refuse to obey orders. . . . I do not want to initiate tough measures and find myself alone in bearing the opprobrium of the executions that are necessary to turn this chaos into organization, obedience and victory. If I were at least protected by the people knowing about my efforts and my impotence, I would feel able to retain my mandate. But the Commune has not had the courage to make the situation known to the public. Twice already I have made the situation clear to you, but twice you have insisted on the matter being debated in a secret committee.

My predecessor [the unjustly disgraced Cluseret] made the mistake of trying to struggle with this absurd situation.

His example is a lesson to me. Since I am convinced that the strength of a revolutionary rests entirely on his refusal to compromise, I have the choice between two courses of action: to overcome the obstacle impeding my actions or to withdraw.

The obstacle cannot be overcome, for it is you and your weakness; I do not wish to offend against popular sovereignty.

I am therefore resigning and request a cell in the Mazas.

Rossel.

This letter provoked further slinging of insults and accusations of treachery. The Committee of Public Safety was re-elected without Pyat: 'you are the evil genius of the Commune,' the Internationalist Bénoît Malon shouted at him. 'It is time your influence was abolished.' Having been replaced by the veteran Charles Delescluze, Rossel managed to slip away and hide out in a hotel on the Boulevard Saint-Germain under an assumed name.

10 May

Arrest of more Communards accused of treason.

The treaty of Frankfurt was signed, finalizing peace between France and Germany. Bismarck now became very friendly towards Versailles and offered a degree of help in the campaign against the Commune. Thiers reluctantly decided that any active interference from the Germans in this delicate matter would be politically unacceptable; he was pleased, however, that Bismarck agreed to allow more troops to repatriate from the prisoner-of-war camps and that Versaillais forces would be allowed free passage through the German troops still in occupation north of Paris.

11 May

Ten more newspapers suppressed. The Committee of Public Safety decided that in reprisal for the continued bombardment of Paris and the murder of innocent women and children, Thiers' property in Paris would be requisitioned by the Commune, and his house, standing empty on the Place Georges, destroyed.

12 May

'Up at 8. At the shop nearly all day, reading & writing. Tea at my room in eve, aftn. stroll on Chps Elysees. Fine day.' (Edwin Child's diary)

13 May

In one of the club meetings, *Citoyenne* Thyou was passing by the Place de la Bourse when she stopped a citizen to ask for some information. He replied that there were no 'citizens' in that neighbourhood, only ladies and gentlemen. The *Citoyenne* asks that cannon be set up on the Place de la Bourse to 'silence all these reactionaries'. She was not altogether joking.

After a tip-off unintentionally provided by a disgruntled seamstress complaining to the Hôtel de Ville that she had not received her wages, twenty thousand *tricolore* armbands were seized from an atelier run by a certain Madame Legros. These seemed to be intended for distribution to pro-Versaillais elements of the Garde Nationale in the event of an invasion of Paris, and they suggested the existence of a network of spies and agents within the city, fed by Versaillais funds. A few names circulated: one Colonel Corbin, one La Mère de Beaufond, one Georges Veysset (who seems to have approached Dombrowski with Thiers' bribe) and various figures associated with the ill-fated Friends of Order movement which had crumbled in the Place Vendôme on 23 March. But although everything and anything could be blamed on their machinations, there was virtually no solid evidence of their conspiracy.

14 May

Félix Pyat's rag *Le Vengeur* announced that 45,000 troops were amassed in the Bois de Boulogne, waiting for an opening to attack. The road from Versailles was said to be blocked with the traffic of artillery and siege-breaking equipment. But the Commune could not altogether believe that Versailles would dare a full invasion of Paris and remained ill-prepared for such a contingency. The dismantling of Thiers' house began. It was an impressive but severe mansion in which he had lived for over half a century, throughout his career as politician and historian.

In theory all its chattels were to be expropriated for the common good – the linen passing to hospitals, the works of art and books to public collections, the furniture sold to raise money for orphans of the war; and the house razed to the ground so that the site could be turned into a public garden. But what occurred was inevitably reported as a free-for-all pillage. Thiers himself was deeply shaken by news of the vandalism, exaggerated as it may have been (Courbet later claimed that he had personally intervened to safeguard the works of art). The Assembly voted him full compensation, at a final cost to the nation of over a million francs.

15 May

As the Commune's military position became more precarious – the Versaillais had just taken the fort at Vanves – the squabbling and name-calling intensified disastrously. The Council of the Commune was pitted against the Committee of Public Safety, which was pitted against the Committee of the Garde Nationale, which was pitted against its own troops. Internationalists would not co-operate with Blanquistes, and Jacobins would not talk to either party. 'Who was the great conspirator against Paris?' asked the left-wing journalist Prosper Lissagaray. 'The extreme left.' Rises in the price of food and shortages of basic products tested the people's patience further, and in an effort to maintain public security and order, the introduction of compulsory identity cards was announced. The Commune was collapsing from within.

16 May

The Commune's single most infamous act was the destruction of one of Paris's most prominent monuments, the column in the Place Vendôme. A commemoration of the expansionist campaigns of the first Napoleon, its bronze reliefs depicted scenes of French military triumph, forged in recast gun metal captured from the enemy. To veteran soldiers, it was a sacred war memorial, a cenotaph. Ever since the declaration of the republic, there had been pressure to remove what Félix Pyat interpreted as 'a symbol of brute force and false glory, an affirmation of militarism, a negation of international law, a permanent insult to the conquered by their conquerors, a perpetual insult to one of the three great principles of the French Republic, Fraternity'. The bee buzzed particularly loud in the bonnet of Gustave Courbet, who talked obsessively about the need to be rid of the column, even if he played no part in the official decisions surrounding its fate.

After being voted through the Assembly, the deed was postponed several times, partly for engineering reasons (nobody was quite sure whether the column was hollow or not) and perhaps because of a certain pussyfooting around the issue – to all opponents of the Commune it raised fundamental matters of French nationhood, as well as the honour of the war dead, and the Commune may have felt reluctant to inflame such volatile emotions. However, the date was finally set for 16 May and great excitement generated. In anticipation of the debris, windows were pasted over with strips of paper and crowds jammed the surrounding streets sardine-solid (admittance to the Place itself was by invitation only; security was intense). Bands of the Garde Nationale played rousing tunes and dignitaries of the Commune stood on draped balconies.

It was all a splendid anticlimax, costing a total of 15,000 francs. A pulley snapped and a rumour circulated among the restive onlookers to the effect that the engineers were still arguing as to what they were up against. Finally, at 5.35 p.m., the bands struck up the inevitable *Marseillaise*. Then came a momentous silence. The column had been partially sawn through at the base and would be toppled by a series of ropes turned in on capstans: after a whistle they creaked into action and after a tense half-hour the column fell with a pathetic flop, raising a huge cloud of dust, on to a bed of sand and brushwood. There was no crash, only a clatter. 'Like a piece of theatrical decor,' is how Louis Barron described it. 'How fragile it was, how empty and sad. It seemed to have been eaten out from the middle by a horde of rats.' The red flag was planted on the column's empty pedestal and the dust settled. From a window in the Place came the unexpected sound of the anthem 'Hail Columbia!', 'played violently on a piano', according to

Vizetelly, 'by some Yankee girl belonging to a party of Americans in the Hotel Mirabeau' (not, presumably, the anti-Communard Lillie Moulton). All evening, the enterprising foraged among the fragments, and little souvenir pieces of the Vendôme Column were soon on sale alongside the glass paperweights filled with black bread* of the siege.

If the world was appalled, Paris was faintly disappointed.

Another comparable project was the proposal for the demolition of the chapel built in 'expiation' of the first revolution's execution of Louis XVI. Then someone called Libmann, claiming to be a rich American, offered to buy it for 50,000 francs and transport it across the Atlantic brick by brick. The trick worked: Libmann was in fact an ardent Catholic royalist and his phoney scheme persuaded the Commune to sell the chapel instead of sacrificing it to Liberty.

Rather more significant was the invasion of the Grand Hôtel du Louvre in the early hours of the morning. Three hundred armed 'irregulars' of the Commune had stormed in at 1 a.m., claiming that fugitives were being sheltered and that the basement concealed a secret passage to Versailles (this latter notion providing a good excuse to raid the wine cellars). By 6 a.m. they had stripped the entire vast establishment of food, cigars, alcohol, clocks, cutlery, crockery, linen and the pettier contents of the staff's quarters. Such empty intimidation and vandalism was becoming increasingly frequent and vicious.

Le Figaro urged Thiers on: 'Never has such an opportunity presented itself for curing Paris of the moral gangrene that has been consuming it for the past twenty years.'

17 May

Following yesterday's comedy in the Place Vendôme, a tragic surprise. About 6 p.m., a vast and unprecedented explosion stunned the centre of Paris. 'A pyramid of flame, of molten lead, human remains, burning timber and bullets showered down,' reported Lissagaray: Smoke 'exactly in the shape of a mighty balloon', accompanied by a noise like 'the roaring of an express

---

* An example of which can still be seen in the Musée Carnavalet.

train through a station, but more lasting,' thought *Blackwood's Magazine*.

It transpired that the arms depot on the Avenue Rapp near the Champ de Mars had blown up, causing horrifying carnage and damage, as well as destroying literally millions of cartridges. Five arrondissements were now under bombardment – eight thousand shells were today fired on the Porte Maillot – but nothing in the last eight months had had such a terrible impact. Entire roads were ripped up by the blast; buildings collapsed continually; glass and rubble were spattered with blood; fires raged wild; those not outwardly injured stood literally frozen with shock. Above the city that evening the mushroom cloud loured over Paris, darkening the sky like a pall of death. Agents of Versailles were blamed – the infamous Corbin was thought to be in possession of nitroglycerine – and there were calls for the retaliatory execution of hostages, but the true cause of the disaster was never established.

The Commune continued in its attempts at moral reform. Today, the discrimination between legitimate and illegitimate children was abolished and the formalities governing marriage liberalized. The second arrondissement declared the closure of all the *maisons de tolérance*. Officers caught dining in the Café Américain with high-class tarts were sent off to dig trenches, while the girls filled sandbags at Saint-Lazare. Increasingly heavy policing of public prostitution in general – the eleventh arrondissement, embracing Belleville and the Place de la Bastille, enacted something like a purge of the streets – sent posses of fed-up *filles* down to the Hôtel de Ville offering their services as nurses on the ramparts.

But it made little difference. As a friend of Catulle Mendès put it:

After Paris has been entirely destroyed, when its houses, palaces and monuments have been overturned and crumbled, littering the cursed ground beneath them and leaving no more than a vast ruin – then, from this shapeless heap, we will see, rising as if from an immense tomb the phantom woman, a skeleton dazzlingly dressed in a low-cut gown with a skull covered by a fur hat. And this phantom, gliding through the debris and occasionally turning its head to see if some libertine, resuscitated as she has been, is following her through the lonely landscape – this phantom will be the dreadful soul of Paris!

18 May
Suppression of ten further newspapers and journals, with an overall ban on the appearance of anonymous or unsigned articles. Abolition of all titles, privileges, liveries, armorial bearings and honorific distinctions.

19 May
The Council of the Commune was reduced to debating the condition of the Theatre in Paris. It was not, admittedly, healthy. More establishments had closed. Actors and musicians either served in their own independent (and signally inactive) battalion of the Garde Nationale or slipped away. The Comédie-Française had officially decamped to London, where it was enjoying enormous success. Audiences wanted only frothy comedy, if that.

To stop the rot, the Commune decided that all theatres should pass into the hands of the Commission of Education. All subsidies and monopolies were to be withdrawn and all companies and troupes should henceforth be run as self-managing co-operatives.

20 May
'All teachers of both sexes are invited to the meeting which will take place next Sunday, 21 May 1871, at precisely 11 a.m., in the École Turgot, rue Turbigo 69, first floor. Order of the day: detailed explication of the universal language invented by François Sudre; and, if there is time, a decision on its introduction into public education.' (*Journal Officiel*)

In the club held in Saint-Ambroise, *Citoyenne* Valentin 'urged that clothing in convents and monasteries be distributed to dress the poor and that the flowers on the altars in the chapels and around the madonnas be given to schoolchildren as prizes.'

The Commune had run out of good ideas.

21 May

Edwin Child's Sunday: 'Up at 8. Church at 11. At 1 o'clock met Madame Clerc (rendezvous) at the Madeleine, breakfasted au Cafe du Helder . . . afterwards strolled to Ch. Elysees. There rested best part of afternoon. About 5 p.m. saw her home (Avenue Friedland), walked to my room, had tea, and then took bus to Johnson's, where I passed the evening. Lovely day.'

Edmond de Goncourt walked into the Place de la Concorde, where a noisy crowd was surrounding a carriage. A woman told him that it contained a gentleman whom the Garde Nationale had just arrested for shouting that the Versaillais had entered the city. For Goncourt, this was good news – but was it true?

> I walk for a long time in search of information or clarification . . .
> Nothing, nothing, nothing. The people who are still in the streets
> look very much as they did yesterday: just as sanguine, just as
> dismayed. Nobody seems to know anything about the shout on the
> Place de la Concorde. So it was a false report.
>
> Finally, I reached home. I went to bed in despair and could not
> sleep. Through the tightly shut curtains, I thought I heard a distant
> rumbling. I got up and opened the window. It was just the regular
> sound, on far-away streets, of companies marching to relieve each
> other, as happens every night. Nothing, in other words, but my
> imagination. I go back to bed . . . but now I can clearly hear drums
> and bugles! I jump up again and go over to the window. They are
> beating a recall throughout Paris; and soon the drums and bugles, the
> cries and shouts mount in waves: *Aux armes*! . . . a sinister noise
> which fills me with joy and sounds for Paris the death-knell of an
> odious tyranny.

22 May

The Versaillais troops had finally breached the walls of Paris, after someone's tip-off that the gate at the Point du Jour, to the south-west of the city, just north of the Seine, was unguarded. The previous evening they had marched, with little resistance, through unbarricaded Passy and the Trocadéro up as far as the Arc de Triomphe. Those troops that Goncourt had heard in Auteuil soon melted away and were let off lightly: some of them immediately donned *tricolore* armbands and turned to fight their former comrades in the Garde Nationale. An even dirtier activity was the writing of unsigned denunciations: needless to say, the army received thousands of them. All through the night and today, the invaders poured effortlessly through – 130,000 of them within twenty-four hours.

But they were initially hesitant. Unsure as to what they would confront, fearful of traps and rumours of secret chemical weapons, the Versaillais now made their way gingerly through side-streets and round the northern fortifications (despite a clause in the armistice which forbade them to do so: the occupying Prussians happily turned a blind eye to the infringement), edging towards the centres of the revolutionary working class, Montmartre and Belleville, to the east of the city.

They had one enormous advantage, of which they were not yet aware. The Commune had no real strategy and poor internal defences. Had the Committee of Public Safety listened to Rossel, a coherent structure of barricades would have been built: as it was, they were thrown up in pell-mell and panicky fashion, often to the detriment of their own lines of communication, patched out of the urban detritus of upturned vehicles and old furniture as well as paving-stones. Nor had anyone seriously thought of tactics appropriate to fighting on Haussmann's wide boulevards. Worse, the Garde Nationale and the irregular forces of the Commune never acted in concert. Largely because of the absence of firm leadership, they seemed to lose interest in Paris and retreated instead to their own arrondissements, clinging to familiar small patches with animal defensiveness. Thus the Commune literally disintegrated.

From the Delegate of War, Charles Delescluze, the seventy-one-year-old veteran of 1848, came a proclamation which called hysterically not for Total War so much as anarchy: 'Enough of militarism, no more officers bespangled and gilded along every seam! Make way for the people, for fighters, for bare arms! The hour for revolutionary warfare has struck. The people know nothing of intricate manoeuvres; but when they have a gun in hand, paving-stones underneath them, they have no fear of all the strategists of the monarchical school. To arms, citizens, to arms!'

Another of the day's posters pointed to the strength of the

Commune's delusion that the enemy was a basically friendly force which could never fire face to face on fellow Frenchmen:

> *The People of Paris to the Soldiers of Versailles!*
> Brothers!
> Do as your brothers did on 18 March! Unite with the People of whom you are part! Leave the aristocrats, the privileged, the executioners of humanity to defend themselves and the rule of Justice will easily be established.
> Desert!
> Come into our homes. Come to our families. You will be welcomed fraternally . . . The people of Paris can never believe that you would be able to point your arms against theirs when you come into close contact; your hands would recoil from an act of such fratricide.
> Like us, you are proletarian; like us, you have no interest in allowing the conspiracy of monarchists the right to drink your blood as it drinks the sweat of our brows.
> What you did on 18 March, you will do again . . . Come to us, brothers, come to us, our arms are open! . . .

In vain: these were not the rain-soaked and hungry recruits who had dropped their arms on 18 March in a state of exhausted bewilderment, but drilled and energetic professional soldiers, as well fed with propaganda as with red meat. They were not so easily fazed.

In the Assembly at Versailles, Thiers claimed that the army represented the triumph of 'the cause of justice, of order, of humanity, and of civilization'; it would behave 'in the name of the law and by the law'. But everyone knew what he meant.

Madame Talbot wrote breathlessly to her sister at 5.30 that day, as the fighting edged towards her house near the Madeleine. She was awaiting 'deliverance' from the Commune:

> They have dug up all the cobbles on our street and requisitioned all empty barrels – one of ours among others – to make a barricade in the rue Neuve-des-Mathurins, thus lengthening the street.
> The whistling bullets hamper them considerably. They fill the barrels with cobbles. I think they are making another barricade in the rue de Sèze. The battalion [of the Garde Nationale] is in our street, men rest on the ground while others work.
> There is also a barricade in the rue Caumartin, near Jacob's

grocery. You can have no idea what our street looks like: men working on their knees or flat on their stomachs to get the barrels and cobbles into place; the whistling bullets and explosions are terrifying.

An old woman has been brought to our house. She isn't wounded, but she has been taken ill. But I can see a poor wounded man being taken into the house opposite. He looks terrible! One of the men wounded this morning is dead; I fear the same for this one – and how many more when the barricade is taken!

The owner of the house opposite, who for a long time has refused to open his door and has expressed rather too much verbal hostility, has had the fine idea of receiving the wounded and turning his unpopular house into an ambulance. I have just sent him over a trestle-bed, a mattress and some linen.

What will we see before the day is out? Before the night is out? . . .

23 May

Resistance to the Versaillais continued to be sporadic. Most of Batignolles and Montmartre fell to the *tricolore*, but the Left Bank, the Hôtel de Ville and the east of the city were still Red. With the Communard retreat from the centre, a series of massive fires began to rage. Who started them was contended: the Commune claimed that the cannon of Versailles were largely responsible, but it was also clear that the Commune was operating a 'scorched earth' policy as it evacuated, slowing the Versaillais advance. Over the next three days, for no good military reason, many of central Paris's monuments and governmental buildings were in some degree gutted by fire, turning the city into an apocalyptic inferno: the Conseil d'État, the Tuileries, the Palais Royal, the Ministry of Justice, the Ministry of Finance (the national accounts had fortunately been 'multiplied microscopically', copied by photograph, and safely deposited in other locations), the Prefecture of Police, the Belle Jardinière department store, most of the rue de Rivoli and the Boulevard de Sébastopol were all in flames, as well as docks, warehouses, factories and an estimated thousand private houses: contrary to reports that hit the world's newspapers, Notre-Dame and the Louvre were largely spared. The former lost only its chairs to the flames, the latter a small part of its roof.

Another persistent rumour was that women were behind the conflagration. The image of the *pétroleuses*, female incendiaries, has proved one of the most powerful and persistent in the story of the Commune,* and it remains difficult to establish its veracity. Women were certainly prominent on the barricades – they held the rue Racine and the Place Blanche, and an English medical student, working in an ambulance at the Château d'Eau, records the existence of an entire female battalion, 'armed with Snider carbines . . . they fought like devils'. After their defeat, one bold creature was taken away and 'undressed' by four soldiers. When interrogated 'she began to laugh ironically and replied roughly: "May God punish me for not having killed more. I had two sons at Issy; they were both killed. And two at Neuilly. My husband died at this barricade – and now do what you want with me".' The medical student crawled away, 'but not soon enough to avoid hearing the command "Fire" which told me that everything was over'. Twenty-five women were reported shot for pouring boiling water over the heads of passing Versaillais.

There were many such incidents, some of them doubtless true. But what are we to make of the idea, springing from nowhere but suddenly everywhere, that Paris was full of women carrying 'small tickets, of the size of postage stamps', marked with the letters 'B. P. B.' – *bon pour brûler*, good for burning? 'Some of the tickets were square, others oval, with a bacchante's head in the centre' and they were found pasted upon walls of houses in different parts of Paris. In their wake would follow women (according to Catulle Mendès) who walked rapidly, 'along the shadow of a wall. They are poorly dressed, generally between forty and fifty, their brows bound with red-checkered handkerchiefs from which hang hanks of uncombed hair. Her complexion is ruddy, her gaze shifty.' John Leighton continues:

> Her right hand is in her pocket, or in the bosom of her half-buttoned dress; in the other hand she holds one of the high, narrow tin cans in

* A celebrated fictional *pétroleuse* is the heroine of Karen Blixen's tale 'Babette's

which milk is carried in Paris, but which now, in the hands of this woman, contains the dreadful liquid. As she passes a post of regulars, she smiles and nods; when they speak to her she answers, 'My good Monsieur!' If the street is deserted, she stops, consults a bit of dirty paper that she holds in her hand, pauses a moment before the grated opening to a cellar, then continues her way, steadily, without haste. An hour afterwards, a house is on fire in the street she has passed. Who is this woman? Paris calls her a *Pétroleuse*.

For each house she was paid ten francs by the commander of her squadron: altogether there were eight thousand such agents, some of them small orphan girls. Not content with kerosene, they had brought nitroglycerine and vitriol into their armoury. Sometimes they dropped their fire-bombs down chimneys, sometimes through letter-boxes. A woman *en grande toilette* seen escorted in chains down the Champs Élysées was assumed to be a *directrice* of the operation. The fantasies multiplied, divided and intersected. Although it is not inconceivable that there were women doing such things, it is highly unlikely that there was an organized conspiracy on the scale imagined. The fact that no woman was ever convicted of incendiarism by a court of law is not conclusive: anybody armed was shot on sight, not charged and handcuffed.

For Madame Talbot, it was all over at 5 p.m.:

It is finished. We are delivered, but at what a price. How can I describe our joy, our cries, our terror, our anguish, our horror?

We heard the shout of 'every man for himself' and we saw the Gardes Nationales rushing down the boulevard, screaming 'They're here, run for your life.' We heard gunfire in our street as we closed the windows. Then, a few minutes later, I carefully reopened one and saw, on the left in the rue Neuve-des-Mathurins, a regular army officer followed by his soldiers. What joy, what delirium! There were tears and cheers and we assured them that we were no traitors.

Such great joy was checked by the gunfire at the end of the street, near the boulevard; how to paint our despair and horror when we saw regular soldiers take away an officer of the battalion of the Garde Nationale which for the last two days had been so close to us – and shoot him!

Feast'. Incidentally, her career as a great chef is historically implausible: at its highest levels, the profession was entirely staffed by men.

The noble Polish-born general of the Commune's forces, Jaroslav Dombrowski, was killed on the barricade of the rue Myrrha. First his men laid him out on Madame Haussmann's blue satin bed in the Hôtel de Ville. Then on the way to burial, according to Lissagaray, the funeral cortège stopped in the Place de la Bastille to lay the corpse at the foot of the column commemorating the events of 14 July 1789. One by one, by the light of flaming torches and to the sound of rolling drums, Dombrowski's soldiers processed past and gently kissed his brow: the Commune's last, saddest ceremonial.

24 May

Against an early summer sky, azure blue, windy but cloudless, Paris continued to burn. Human chains passing fire buckets proved quite ineffectual. Sheets of flame and billows of smoke obscured the brilliant sunshine; musketry and *mitrailleuse*, cannon and shell rattled and roared. 'We could not but recall some passages in the 18th chapter of the Book of Revelation,' wrote the Revd William Gibson. ' "Alas, alas, that great city that was clothed in fine linen and purple and scarlet and decked with gold, and precious stones, and pearls" . . . "and they cried when they saw of her burning, saying, What city is like unto this great city!" ' From London, Captain Shaw, the ace fire-fighter later immortalized in Gilbert and Sullivan's *Iolanthe*, offered his services. An estimated £20m (say, £300m or $500m today) of damage was caused. Raoul Rigault, Prefect of Police, was killed as the Commune lost control of the Left Bank. The Versaillais officer who shot him pointed the pistol at his temple and ordered him to shout 'Vive l'armée de Versailles!' but Rigault's last words were 'Vive la Commune!' His body was left lying in the gutter, his wallet, watch, even his shoes and socks, stolen, his pockets turned out.

From the Committee of Public Safety's new headquarters in Belleville, orders were signed, according to the measures of 5 April, for the execution of six of the hostages, following reports of Versailles' wanton massacre of prisoners. At 7 p.m., the Archbishop of Paris and five other clerics were shot by a squad of eager volunteers. Their courage and dignified deaths instantly brought them the status of martyrs and increased public sympathy for the Versaillais worldwide. Thiers may well have calculated on this.

25 May

Delescluze climbed boldly to his death, standing on top of the barricade at the Château d'Eau.

The poet Paul Verlaine, who worked in the Commune's press bureau, sat in his apartment only a stone's throw – a bullet's trajectory – away and ate a hearty dinner with two blackened refugees from the fighting. He was preoccupied with the seduction of his wife's maid. At 4 a.m. he was awoken by his terrified mother, who had walked from Batignolles and witnessed a horrible massacre in the street. In the rue du Temple, Edwin Child played cards all night with his friends the Johnsons. All Paris was now 'liberated', except for Belleville and the surrounding heights of Buttes Chaumont and Père Lachaise. According to *Le Petit Moniteur Universel*, a London travel agent was already booking excursions to the ruins of Paris.

The full horror of the reprisals was only now beginning to emerge. The Versailles army, nominally under General MacMahon, inglorious commander of the Franco-Prussian campaign, was allowed, if not encouraged, to shoot to kill without restraint. It took full advantage of this: Frenchmen were slaughtering Frenchmen and Frenchwomen in a spirit of blind vengeance which witnesses could scarcely credit. The next few days constitute one of the most terrible episodes in nineteenth-century history. How, one futilely asks, did such a black murderous hatred come to master men reared in an apparently civilized, Christian country? What was it that they were trying to kill?

26 May

Not that the Communards were innocent. As the advent of heavy rain began to quench the strings of fire, the last vestiges of the Committee of Public Safety's authority perished and alongside those fighting desperately behind the last hopeless barricades ran a crazy mob with nothing to lose except its individual lives. The governor of the prison of La Roquette confronted it when he was forced to surrender another fifty of the Commune's hostages – eleven priests, thirty-five gendarmes and four imperial informers – entrusted to his safe-keeping.

They were dragged through the streets to the rue Haxo, behind the cemetery of Père Lachaise, and pushed into a high-walled garden. A few members of the Commune made efforts to intervene, but they only increased the hysteria. The hostages were then shot in screaming chaos, 'like rabbits', as one witness put it, running in all directions. At the final count there were fifty-one corpses; one body had been peppered with sixty-nine bullets.

Back at La Roquette, a warder released the remaining hostages. They, however, decided they would be safer remaining where they were and proceeded to barricade themselves in with their mattresses and bedsteads. A squad of Garde Nationale tried to smoke them out and a few who ran off in panic were instantly mowed down. When the Versaillais arrived, they turned the prison into a pitch for their own slaughtering, colder in spirit than the Garde Nationale's. 'At first about 120 were shot right off,' wrote the anonymous correspondent of the *Illustrated London News*.

> Then the officers began to get tired of it, and took to inspecting the prisoners. He had only allowed those to be punished who had blue marks on their shoulders of the recoil of the gun or had black hands from powder or smelt of powder: of course the marks of a *forçat* or returned convict were also looked for. At first the firing was done at too great a distance and often death did not result. They were sailors who had this duty to perform, and the officer ordered them to stand nearer, when they came so close that the muzzle of the gun almost touched the victim. To make sure of the 120 first shot, they went up to each again, and fired a revolver into his ear. Strange to say, there was one man only slightly wounded, but who managed so well to mimic the appearance of death that the sailors said 'He has no need of an extra touch' and passed him over. As the others were shot, they were piled over him, and in this dreadful position he lay seven hours. He at last got up and approaching the sentinels he said. '*Dieu m'a sauvé! Sauvez-moi!* ['God has saved me! Save me!'] This only resulted in the use of the revolver which he had escaped at first. All the insurgents are reported to have died what is vulgarly called 'game'.

One gave 20 francs to the man who was about to shoot him, saying 'I shall not want this in the next world'. A woman who was said to have killed about twenty of the Versaillais said she had killed enough and '*il faut faire vôtre devoir*' ['you must do your duty'] as she bared her breast to be shot . . . Seven railway-vans took them away.

Perhaps the most depraved of all was General de Galliffet, previously celebrated for his womanizing and dandified ways. 'Madame, j'ai frequenté tous les théâtres de Paris, ce n'est pas la peine de jouer la comédie', he told one suppliant, tear-stained woman: 'Madame, I have been in regular attendance at all the theatres in Paris. It's not worth trying to play-act with me.' Others were picked out to face the firing-squads on the grounds of their height, hair colour, ugliness, age, youth or no pretext at all. 'I am known to be cruel,' he told them. 'But I am even crueller than you can imagine.' At which Louise Michel is said to have begun whistling a cheeky children's song about a braggart 'C'est moi qui suis Lindor'. The other prisoners could not help laughing; Galliffet ordered his soldiers to shoot into the crowd and restore order. But they would not shoot.

MacMahon later told an investigative tribunal that his soldiers had been given clear instructions on the treatment of all those apprehended: 'When men surrender their arms they must not be shot: that was agreed. Unhappily, in certain cases, the instructions I had given were forgotten.' This is a lie. Commanders were clearly as reprehensible as their troops, and the mass killing was not hysterical or accidental, although its savagery was often oriental.

An estimated five thousand children took part in the fighting for the Commune (there were 651 arrests of boys under sixteen, forty of them under thirteen). A battalion a hundred strong, so it is said, fought at Château d'Eau, barracked there and paid ten *sous* a day: many of them must have died. Victor Hugo wrote a moving tribute to one young hero of the hour:

> *Sur une barricade . . .*
> Sur une barricade, au milieu des pavés
> Souillés d'un sang coupable et d'un sang pur lavés.
> Un enfant de douze ans est pris avec des hommes,
> —Es-tu de ceux-là, toi? – L'enfant dit:
> > [Nous en sommes.

—C'est bon, dit l'officier, on va te fusiller.
Attends ton tour. – L'enfant voit des éclairs
                        [briller,
Et tous ses compagnons tomber sous la muraille.
Il dit à l'officier: Permettez-vous que j'aille
Rapporter cette montre à ma mère chez nous?
—Tu veux t'enfuir? – Je vais revenir.
                        [—Ces voyous
Ont peur! Où loges-tu? – Là, près de la fontaine.
Et je vais revenir, monsieur le Capitaine.
—Va-t'en, drôle! – L'enfant s'en va.
                        [—Piège grossier!
Et les soldats riaient avec leur officier.
Et les mourants mêlaient à ce rire leur râle;
Mais le rire cessa, car soudain l'enfant pâle,
Brusquement reparu, fier comme Viala,
Vint s'adosser au mur et leur dit: Me voilà.
La mort stupide eut honte, et l'officier fit grâce. . . .

(On a barricade, among cobbles stained with guilty blood and washed with innocent blood, a child of twelve is taken with some men. 'Are you one of them?' The child said: 'We are together.' 'Good,' said the officer. 'We're going to shoot you. Wait your turn.' The child sees lightning flashes and all his companions fall beneath the wall. He says to the officer: 'Will you allow me to go home and give this watch back to my mother?' 'Are you trying to escape?' 'I will come back.' 'These little rascals are scared! Where do you live?' 'Over there, near the fountain. And I will be back, Monsieur le Capitaine.' 'Go on, joker!' The child goes. 'That's a dumb trick!' And the soldiers laugh with their officer. And the groans of the dying blend with the laughter. But the laughter stops – because suddenly the pale child has reappeared, as proud as Viala [a boy hero of the first French Revolution], leans his back against the wall and says to them: 'Here I am.' The fool death was ashamed and the officer had mercy.)

The pro-Versailles press remained adamant. In *Le Soir* a leader sternly admonished liberal opinion that 'Paris has morally ceased to be the capital of France. When a city can contain so much crime and folly, it is condemned to degenerate and if it at present escapes the Biblical fire from heaven, it cannot escape the pity and contempt of men.'

27 May

The members of the Commune were now on the run. Some, like Félix Pyat, escaped, having assured his comrades with tears in his eyes that he did not know what 'more glorious end' he could hope for than death on the barricades. Some, like Courbet, were falsely believed dead (in his case, of self-administered poison, 'in great agony', it was reported). Others were humiliatingly captured: Pascal Grousset was dragged on to the street wearing one of his mistresses' black skirts and a chignon. Many died vile deaths: Eugène Varlin, who had tried to prevent the massacre of the hostages in the rue Haxo, was arrested while slumped asleep on a bench. He then endured an hour's march to the Versaillais death centre in the rue des Rosiers (where the Generals had been shot on 18 March) which left him with an eye dangling from its socket and his head beaten to a pulp; half-dead, he had to be tied to a chair before they could shoot him. Many behaved with unbroken pride: Francis Jourde, the Commune's impeccable Financial Commissioner, insisted almost absurdly when arrested that he should officially hand over the 9,770 francs in the coffers, subtracting only his personal salary of 120 francs.

As the west of Paris fell silent and some even began to think about tomorrow, the killing in the east continued, hour after hour, with numb relentlessness. Escape routes to the north were blocked by the Prussians, who had moved 10,000 troops up to the city walls as a way of supporting the cause of Versailles and who turned back a march of 3,000 refugees, led by a delegation of Freemasons. The cleansing of the working-class areas that Haussmann had tried to effect through social engineering was now achieved by massacre.

There was nowhere to go now, nowhere left sacred. If the Commune had been blasphemous, the troops of Versailles proved no great respecters of religion either. Three hundred Fédérés were hauled out of sanctuary in the Madeleine to be shot; and some of the fiercest fighting of the last hours of the Commune took place in the cemetery of Père Lachaise, in the heart of Belleville. Two batteries of guns and two hundred Gardes Nationales defended it. The Versaillais had little trouble blasting through the gate, but there followed a bizarre battle, skirmishing between the stone sentry boxes, vaults and gravestones which make up its forest of the dead: the last shots were fired where the memorials to four important French authors (Balzac, Nerval, Nodier and Delavigne) impressively face each other. Any Communards who survived until surrender were lined up against a wall at an empty eastern corner of the cemetery and shot. The site was much favoured by the Versaillais over the next week and the *mitrailleuse* was used three or four times daily for mass execution of 'suspects'. The bodies fell straight into a ditch – hundreds of bodies. All over Paris such slaughter continued mechanically: behind the walls of La Roquette, of the Ecole Militaire, the Lycée Bonaparte, the Gare du Nord, the Jardin des Plantes, and in the open too – on the Place du Châtelet, for instance, Catulle Mendès witnessed the process: 'They take the Fédérés, by twenties; they condemn them; they are led into the square, their hands tied behind their backs, and they tell them to turn around. A hundred paces away is a *mitrailleuse*; they fall by twenties. In a courtyard in the rue Saint-Denis there is a stable filled with their corpses. Even those in hospital were not safe: the Versaillais gunned their way through the ambulance at Saint-Sulpice. A thousand bodies were piled up in the Trocadéro; in the courtyard of the Ecole Polytechnique they were laid out three deep in a gruesome ring a hundred yards in circumference.

Those who were not thus eliminated were rounded up and marched through the city to vast concentration camps set up around Versailles. There are several accounts of these horrific convoys, which contained as many as two hundred men, women and children, treated with the utmost brutality. Following body searches, many of the women were left bare-chested and the men were instructed to wear their coats and jackets inside out. 'It was the astonishing effect of that livery of shame, worn by such a mass of men at once that rendered the scene so matchlessly abject,' wrote the correspondent of *Blackwood's Magazine*. The most detailed and first-hand of these accounts is contained in an article written by the anonymous 'Victim of Paris and Versailles', published in *Macmillan's Magazine* later that year. The author is a young Englishman involuntarily swept into the maelstrom when he was press-ganged into the Garde Nationale. Having been captured, he was marshalled with other prisoners and waits to hear his fate:

We stood there bare-headed in the sun for some time, until our attention was called to the sound of shooting, and then a whisper went round, '*On va nous fusiller tous.*' ['They will shoot us all.'] Oh, the agonized look on the faces of some I can never forget! It was a complete index of what was passing in their minds. To die thus, and leave wife, children, parents, brothers, or sisters, without one word of farewell, to be thus suddenly cut off, is fearful. I could see this on some countenances near me as plainly as if it had been written on them. But these were men of the better sort, and but few in number; the greater part looked sullen and stolid, shrugged their shoulders and said, "*C'est bientôt fini! Un coup de fusil et voilà tout.*' ['It will soon be over. One shot, and that'll be that.']

One boy about four files behind me was a pitiable object; he had a document which was enveloped in a piece of newspaper in his hand, and this he presented to every soldier or officer near him, screaming out amidst floods of tears, '*Oh, je suis innocent! Oh, mon capitaine, ne me fusillez pas!*' ['I'm innocent, oh, my captain, don't shoot me!'] till at last an officer gave him such a blow with his cane that, though he cried louder than ever, he was forced to desist from his entreaties for mercy. Those around him kept exclaiming, '*Tais-toi, crapaud,*' ['Shut up, toad.'] but the '*crapaud*' only turned to them, and with fresh bursts of tears produced his document, and explained the nature of it to his companions in misfortune.

Great was the contrast between this boy, who must have been at least fifteen years of age, and a poor child of nine who stood next to me; he never cried nor uttered a word of complaint, but stood quietly by my side for some time, looking up furtively in my face. At last he ventured to slip his little hand within mine, and from that time till the close of that terrible day we marched hand in hand, he never relaxing his grasp except when absolutely necessary. Meanwhile the executions went on; I counted up to twenty, and after that I believe some six or seven more took place. They were nearly all officers of the National Guard who were thus put to death. One who was standing near me, an *officier payeur*, had his little bag containing the pay of his men, which he had received the day before, but had been unable to distribute among them. He now gave it away to those standing about him (I among the number getting a few francs), saying as he did so, '*Je serai fusillé moi-même, et cet argent peut vous servir, mes enfants, dans votre triste captivité.*' ['I will be shot and this money may be of use to you, children, in your sad captivity.'] He was led out and shot a few minutes afterwards. They all, without exception, met their fate bravely and like men; there was no shrinking from death, or entreaties to be spared, among those that I saw killed. Had they exhibited as much bravery while actually fighting for their cause, as they did when it became necessary to pay the penalty of death for their share in the insurrection, I doubt not that the reign of the Commune would have been of longer duration, and might have even succeeded in its design of government.

After remaining for more than an hour at the Buttes Chaumont, we were marched to a large open space at La Villette, passing on our way through some of the batteries used by the Government troops against Paris. Here we again halted, and orders were given that all rugs, *bidons, gamelles* [cans, mess tins] and knives must be delivered up to the non-commissioned officers of our escort; that all those wearing uniform coats of whatsoever description should turn them inside out, and wear them in that fashion; and that we were to form ourselves by fives. All these orders having been carried out, though some time was expended therein, a staff of officers rode down our ranks and inspected us, after which we again set forth, escorted this time by regiments of cavalry.

From La Villette we proceeded down the Rue Lafayette as far as the Nouvel Opéra, being greeted as we went with the choicest selection of curses and epithets that I ever heard: '*Ah, les salots! les voyaux! les assassins! les incendiaires! les voleurs! les crapauds! Fusillez nous tout ça! A Cayenne la Commune et ses soldats!*' ['Murderers! Thieves! Shoot them all! Send the Commune and its soldiers to a convict island!'] were the mildest expressions used, but there were many others which it would be impossible for me to write down.

From the Nouvel Opéra to the Madeleine, down the Rue Royale (a strange scene of ruin, where the bystanders called on us to look at the ruin we had caused), into the Place de la Concorde, up the Champs Elysées to the Arc de Triomphe, on we marched bare-headed under a burning sun, exposed to the taunts and insults of the passers-by, running every minute in obedience to the cry of '*Serrez vos rangs,*' ['Keep in line'] and then relapsing into a walk for a few seconds: we were glad indeed when in the Avenue de l'Impératrice the order to halt was given. There, weary and footsore, many dropped down on the ground, and rested themselves as best they could, waiting for death, which we were now convinced was near at hand for all of us. For myself, I felt utterly numbed and quite content to die, as I would at that time have received with equal indifference the news of my release. I remember thinking and plotting in my mind how I could possibly get the intelligence conveyed to my parents in England. Could I ask one of the soldiers to convey a message for me should I have any opportunity of so doing? and, if so, would he understand what to do? With such thoughts, and mechanically repeating the Lord's Prayer to myself at intervals, I whiled away more than an hour, until *'Levez-vous tous'* ['Get up everybody!'] broke the thread of my meditations.

Up we started, and placed ourselves in our ranks.

Presently General the Marquis de Galliffet passed slowly down the line, attended by several officers. He stopped here and there, selecting several of our number, chiefly the old and the wounded, and ordered them to step out from the ranks.

'*Sors des rangs toi, vieux coquin! Et toi par ici, et toi tu es blessé! Eh bien, nous te soignerons,*' ['Leave the ranks, you old fool. And you, and the wounded one. Come on, we'll look after you.'] said he sharply and decisively, now to one, now to another. A young man about five men from me called out to him, waving a paper as he spoke, '*Eh, mon général, je suis Americain moi; voilà mon passeport, je suis innocent.*' ['General, I'm an American, here is my passport, I'm innocent.']

'*Tais-toi, nous avons bien assez d'étrangers et de canaille ici, il faut nous en débarrasser,*' ['Shut up, we have enough foreigners and scum here, we have to get rid of them.'] was the reply, as the General proceeded on his way. All chance was over now, we thought, and we should be shot in a few minutes; for our idea was, that those who had been placed aside were to be spared from the general massacre, perhaps released, the wounded sent to the hospitals to be cured, and old men, after a short confinement, given permission to return to their homes: '*C'est juste, on ne peut pas fusiller les vieillards et les blessés.*' ['It's true, you can't shoot the old and the wounded.'] Alas! we were soon to be undeceived.

As for me, while the General went by, I took a good look at him. I remember remarking his uniform particularly, comparing it in my mind with that of a general in our own service, and wondering whether it was as expensive as the scarlet coat of dear old England, which at that time I never thought to see again.

We soon started off, and proceeded in the same order, except that we were obliged to march arm-in-arm to the Bois de Boulogne, where we again halted.

There we soon had our minds set at rest as to the ultimate destination of those who had been picked out at our last halt. They were all shot, old men and wounded together (over eighty in number, I believe), before our eyes. We, however, were struggling for water, of which there was a scant supply, whence obtained I know not, for I was not fortunate enough to get any.

The execution being over, we again set forth, with the knowledge that Versailles was now our destination, though what our fate would be when we were once there, none of us could conceive.

Oh, the misery and wretchedness of that weary march! The sun poured fiercely down upon our uncovered heads, our throats were parched and dry with thirst, and our blistered feet and tired legs could scarce support our exhausted and aching bodies.

The first division consisted almost entirely of soldiers of the line, and their condition must have been even more pitiable than our own. The road was strewn with knapsacks which the poor wretches had thrown down, and the men composing our escort made us pick up any object which they thought could be of use to them, and hand it over for inspection. Now and again, a man, utterly worn out both in mind and body, would drop down exhausted by the wayside; one of our guards would then dismount and try, by dint of kicks and blows with the butt-end of his rifle, to induce him to resume his place. In all cases these measures proved unavailing, and a shot in our rear told us that one more of our number had ceased to exist; the executioner would then fall into his place again, laughing and chatting gaily with his comrades as if nothing had happened.

We passed over the Seine and by the ruins of the Palace of St Cloud, then through the park, where the cool shade of the trees brought unspeakable relief. Oh! how I longed for a draught of water, – for my tongue was so glued to the roof of my mouth that I could not utter a word, – but though some managed to obtain a little, I was not among that number.

Towards eight o'clock in the evening, we at last marched into Versailles; and if the execrations that we had endured in Paris had been numerous and varied they were here multiplied tenfold. '*Ah! il y a des bombes-à-pétrole que vous connaissez pour vous là-haut! Il y a des mitrailleuses, sacrés coquins,*' ['There are some of your petrol bombs up there! There are some *mitrailleuses*, you bloody fools.'] and so on in the same strain.

We toiled up the hill leading to Satory, and when we reached the summit struggled on as well as we were able through mud more than ankle-deep.

'*Voilà les mitrailleuses pour nous,*' said one of my companions, pointing to what, in the distance, seemed like a small park of artillery; '*c'est vraiment fini cette fois-ci.*' ['Here are our *mitrailleuses*; the game is really up now.'] Then for the first time I did feel afraid, I thought of the horrors of being mutilated by shot and shell, and wished that I had been among those who had been executed in the day-time, knowing that death by the rifle was quick and sure; whereas here, to be horribly wounded and linger on in misery, ah! I could not think of it.

The order came to halt, and I waited and waited to hear the whirring sound of the *mitrailleuses*; but thank God, I waited in vain. We set ourselves in motion once more, and were turned into an immense yard surrounded by walls, and having on one side three large sheds, in which we were destined to pass the night. With what eagerness did we throw ourselves on our faces in the mud, and lap up the filthy water in the pools.

After further misadventures, the Englishman was eventually released and returned to England to tell his tale. His summary of the moral merit of the Commune is as succinctly fair as anyone's:

The greater part of those who served the Commune (for all, with but few exceptions, did serve) were 'pressed men', like myself; but those who had wives or children to support, and were without work – nay, without means of obtaining even a crust of bread (for the first siege had exhausted all their little savings) – were forced by necessity to enrol themselves in the National Guard for the sake of their daily pay.

In the regular army of the Commune, if I may so style the National Guard, there were but few volunteers, and those were in general orderly and respectable men; but the irregular regiments, such as the Enfants Perdus, Chasseurs Fédérés, Défenseurs de la Colonne de Juillet, were nothing but troops of blackguards and ruffians, who made their uniform an excuse for pillaging and robbing all they could lay their hands on. Such men deserved the vengeance which overtook the majority of them.

All I can say in conclusion is, that the crimes and excesses laid to the charge of the Commune seem to me to have been greatly exaggerated: that they were greatly to blame is indisputable, but the old proverb is a true one, – 'The Devil is never so black as he is painted,' and it certainly holds good in this case.

28 May

'The last barricade of the days of May was in the rue Ramponeau [in Belleville]. For a quarter of an hour a single Federal defended it. Thrice he broke the staff of the Versailles flag hoisted on the barricade of the rue de Paris. As a reward for his courage this last soldier of the Commune succeeded in escaping.' (Lissagaray).

At midday the following proclamation reached the hoardings:

Republic of France!
Inhabitants of Paris, the Army of France has come to save you. Paris is delivered. Within the last four hours our soldiers have taken the last positions held by the insurgents.

Today, the struggle is terminated. . . .
*The Marshal of France, MacMahon, Duke of Magenta,
Commander-in-Chief*

Some figures: 877 Versaillais soldiers had been killed since the beginning of the fighting in April; something in the region of 3,500 Communards had fallen in the defence of Paris up to 21 May. Since then, in the ensuing slaughter – which continued into early June: what was baptized *la semaine sanglante*, 'the blood- soaked week', should more accurately be called *les quinze jours sanglants*, 'the blood-soaked fortnight' – Versailles admitted to causing 17,000 fatalities: the real total must have been considerably more. There were 34,522 official male arrests,* 1,058 female.

But facts and numbers meant little to Paris. There were those who lived in the middle-class west of the city and had witnessed little or none of the carnage which had decimated the working-class east. Spared the horror, they did not conceal a certain smug sense of good riddance to bad rubbish: 'It was well done,' wrote Goncourt in his diary on 31 May. 'There was no conciliation or negotiation. The solution was brutal. Pure force.' Such

---

* Classified by occupation, they break down thus:

Agricultural   398   1.1%
Woodworkers   2,791   8%
Textiles   1,348   3.9%
Cobbling   1,496   4.3%
Leather   381   1.1%
Crafts   2,413   6.9%
Books etc.   925   2.7%
Metalwork   4,135   11.9%
Construction   5,458   15.7%
Day labourers   5,198   14.9%
Retail, catering and office workers   2,790   8%
Servants   1,699   4.9%
Small businessmen   1,516   4.3%
Professionals   1,169   3.3%

Many analyses have been made of these statistics, many conclusions drawn. One of them emphasizes that construction workers and day labourers – mostly young, single, country-born men who had come to Paris during the Haussmann building boom and who had suffered from the slump since the Baron's dismissal eighteen months previously – accounted for nearly a third of the total.

bourgeois would have brushed aside the fact that the Commune had in any case been on the verge of internal collapse on 21 May and hardly needed the Versaillais to destroy its political existence, let alone 17,000 of its citizens. All that mattered was that the Commune was gone, whatever the price.

But for anyone a degree closer to the reality of the war, the experience was shattering, whatever their views. Thus Catulle Mendès:

> We are without anger or pity; we are broken, resigned, haggard; we see the convoys of prisoners being led to Versailles without looking at them . . . Even the soldiers are silent. As conquerors, they are mournful; no carousing, no singing. Paris is like a city seized by mutes; nobody loses their temper, nobody weeps. The *tricolore* flags, hung from every window, amazed us: why hang flags from windows? It isn't that – particularly in the most recent period – the triumph of Versailles wasn't ardently desired by the majority of the population; but we are so exhausted that we haven't time to be pleased.
>
> Think about it! The siege, famine, boredom, absent parents, poverty, and then the Montmartre insurrection, the shock, the hesitations, cannon firing all day and night, the unremitting fusillade in the distance, mothers in tears, sons hunted down – every calamity has fallen on this unfortunate city. It is like Rome under Tiberius, Rome after the barbarians. . . . Corpses in the streets, corpses in doorways, corpses everywhere! Yes indeed, they were guilty, the men who were captured and killed; they were criminal, these women who poured eau-de-vie into their glasses and petrol into houses! But in that first flush of zeal, is one never mistaken? Were they guilty, all those who were killed? Moreover, the sight of these tortures, deserved or not, is always appalling. Innocents are saddened while justice is done. Oh yes, Paris is quiet now, as quiet as a battlefield the day after a victory, as quiet as the dead of night or a tomb. A horrible lassitude oppresses us. Will we ever emerge from under this shadow and this apathy? A weary and overwhelmed Paris turns sadly from the past and doesn't yet dare lift its eyes towards the future.

Epilogue

In November 1989 – towards the end of another tumultuous year of hopeful revolutions aimed at turning full circle on the ideologies and rhetoric that the Commune had brought to parturition – I visited the cemetery of Père Lachaise. It is a strange oasis to the south of Belleville, itself a flavourless, ugly suburb, seemingly unaware of its terrible past as it endures the ordinary problems of Western urban life in these last bleak years before the second millennium.

The cemetery is now most famous as the resting-place of the mystical American rock star Jim Morrison, as well as of the great descendant of Theresa, Edith Piaf, and that tragic champion of the Commune, Oscar Wilde. The Mur des Fédérés, the wall against which perhaps fifteen hundred Communards fell to the *mitrailleuses* fired by their compatriots in the last days of *la semaine sanglante*, is not much of a pilgrimage any longer. Its bricks are not all the original ones and the neat municipal flower-beds in front of it hardly pay a dramatic tribute to the carnage that lies beneath. A large horse chestnut tree spreads a sleepy benevolence over the place. In the distance, a landscape of tower blocks and bungled town planning stretches emptily.

Behind stand more impressive monuments both to all shades of Red politics – heroes of the Resistance like Colonel Fabien, those who served in the International Brigade against Franco, Communist notables such as Paul Eluard and Maurice Thorez – and their unspeakable mirror-image – stark memorials to the French victims of Buchenwald, Dachau, Belsen, Mauthausen, Ravensbrück, Auschwitz, and other charnel-houses of Bismarck's nationalism run rotten. The ghosts of the Dreyfus case, Action Française and the Vichy regime must haunt the ground too. An old woman in a blue coat puts down a bag of shopping and sits on a bench to stare, motionless in her secret mourning even as the rain begins to patter through the last autumn leaves.

The Mur des Fédérés is still a moving sight. Facing it are the graves of several of those who survived May 1871: among them Jean-Baptiste Clément, composer of 'Le Temps des cerises', Charles Longuet, who married Marx's daughter Jenny, and

Valery Wroblewski, another Polish romantic who had bravely held out on the Butte-aux-Cailles. On the wall itself is a simple plaque which reads only 'AUX MORTS DE LA COMMUNE' – 'To the dead of the Commune'. Around it are nailed several rusty iron prongs, used for a century or more to hang commemorative wreaths from. Today they are hung no more. Communistic socialism is dead and discredited, and the Commune has passed safely into history, its lineage extinct.

Yet a sense of lost honour lingers on. A plastic red carnation lies on the ridge of the plaque and the graffiti *Vive la Commune!* looks freshly scrawled. The Commune had its days of hope and good intentions. Its politics were blunderingly innocent, its enemies third-rate. 'They were madmen,' said the painter Auguste Renoir of the Communards, 'but they had in them the little flame that never dies.' Does this much-quoted judgement strike an unwarrantedly sentimental note? I don't believe so. How can one not be deeply moved by the Commune's helplessness, the sheer abandoned pathos of its last stand – endured, as Edwin Child put it, 'with a courage, or despair, worthy of a better cause'? The Commune may not have deserved a future, but at the very least it did not deserve its fate.

Part III

11 : *Repentance and Revenge*

'Fifty or sixty thousand Communards remain scattered round the suburbs, all ready to massacre and pillage!' wrote the trembling old Comtesse de Ségur, a popular fairy-tale author, from her château in Normandy on 5 June. Outside Paris provincials still locked their doors against bogeyman rumours, but within its battered, concussed walls, people averted their eyes and went about their business – this was not Berlin in May 1945, even though *la semaine sanglante* had involved thousands more deaths than that invasion would. Whole swathes of the western sides of the city bore no physical scars of the Commune and were therefore able to give a fair impression of normal smiling hustle and bustle. On 3 June Ludovic Halévy noted that 'at 9.30 p.m., along the boulevards all the shops were open, the cafés lit up and bursting with customers: a huge crowd was gay, noisy and animated; on every face was an expression of something like astonishment at the speed and the ease of the revival'. By 12 June Edwin Child was reflecting that come 'another six months & we shall wonder where all the fires took place'. To the east of the city the atmosphere was icier, of course: Belleville and Montmartre and Ménilmontant mourned in cowed, surly silence. '*Solitudinem faciunt, pacem appellant,*' wrote the Roman historian Tacitus, 'they make a wilderness and call it peace' – words which meant something in the Paris of 1871.

Meanwhile, tourists flocked to the eerie beauty of the burnt-out ruins, as though Paris were the modern Pompeii. A guidebook, *A travers les ruines*, was rushed out to enlighten visitors in search of picturesque desolation. Even the natives were impressed: Goncourt marvelled at the remains of the Hôtel de Ville, 'all pink and green, and gleaming agate where the stonework had been burnt by petrol . . . like the ruin of an Italian Renaissance *palazzo*, tinted by centuries of sunshine'. The statue of the Venus de Milo, lifted from its protective wooden coffin in the basement of the Prefecture of Police, was solemnly restored to its plinth in the Louvre. How long before the old chimes of 'Paris s'amuse, Paris s'amuse' rang out again?

First, some reconstruction was required. (Reorientation too: for some reason none of the city's public clocks seemed to agree as to the correct time, as if the horror of it all had swayed and stopped their hands.) Hampered only by the shortage of manual labourers – so many were dead or now awaiting trial – the rebuilding proceeded 'with extraordinary rapidity', as Edwin Child noted on 12 June, barely three weeks after the fires had started. The state subsidized work on private as well as public property and extra funds were raised through an issue of Premium Bonds (the principal repayable in seventy-five annual instalments!) which yielded £20 million over five years; the versions of the Palais Royal, Palais de Justice, Cour des Comptes, Légion d'honneur and Hôtel de Ville which we see today are the result.

Only the palace of the Tuileries was left to lie. For many years its husk rotted away in Ozymandias-like warning to all would-be despots and majesties – 'there is not one little blackened stone which is not to me a chapter in the bible of democracy,' pronounced Oscar Wilde in 1883 as he contemplated the site – and not until 1889 was it finally cleared to make way for a public park. Some of the debris was sold off: the couturier Worth, with fond memories of Tuileries splendours which he had himself dressed and styled, created a garden folly from his pickings.

There were more urgent scores to be settled. On 29 June 100,000 troops of the French army paraded at Longchamps. The occasion was solemn and funereal rather than triumphant, as befitted a ceremony marking both a crushing defeat at the hands of a foreign invader and a blood-soaked victory in civil war. The spectators doffed their hats in silence when the soldiers presented arms and even those hardened leaders Thiers and MacMahon were seen to weep as they embraced. In Paris, a strict political censorship was enforced over the Internationale and all its friends; the government also 'encouraged' an anti-Communard trade union, the Ouvriers Compagnons, pledged to patriotism and a no-strike policy.

The 35,000 prisoners taken during the *semaine sanglante* were at the same time being distributed to prisons all over northern France. Many of them were dumped in hulks moored off the Britanny coast, where conditions were said to be unspeakably dreadful (although *The Times*'s eyewitness correspondent thought them acceptable enough).* Justice was long in coming, and dubious when it arrived. On 7 August the trial of the fifteen captured members of the Council of the Commune began in Versailles, which remained the seat of government. They were variously charged with complicity in the murders of the Generals on 18 March, the riot which broke up the Friends of Order rally on 23 March, the explosion in the Avenue Rapp, the execution of the hostages, as well as arson, theft and other footling infringements. The prosecutions were altogether un-satisfactory, but it was politically necessary to establish guilt and bring decisive convictions. There were plenty of stool-pigeon witnesses (the authorities had received a reputed 400,000 neighbourly denunciations from citizens anxious to drop the hot potato of blame for the Commune at everybody else's feet) and the press obligingly painted the defendants in the familiar lurid terms: beasts, brigands, scum.

In court there were some craven attempts to save face and apologize, alongside the heroic but suicidal defences of such as Théophile Ferré, Rigault's four foot six deputy, who earned one of the two death sentences. 'A member of the Commune,' he declared, 'I am in the hands of its victors. They want my head; they may take it. I will never save my life by cowardice. Free I have lived, so I will die. I add but one word. Fortune is capricious; I confide to the future the care of my memory and my revenge.' Two of his comrades were given hard labour for life, seven were condemned to transportation, one was given three

* See also the painter Alexandre Pouthier's account, reported by Goncourt on 12 January 1872.

months' jail and the rest were acquitted. Except, that is, for Gustave Courbet, who was given six months' jail and then, having served his term, required to pay 500,000 francs towards the rebuilding of the Vendôme Column – a preposterous fine which he evaded only by fleeing to Switzerland. Those released had no present hope for making a life for themselves in France; many made their way to London, where they joined three thousand other fugitives from the war against the Commune, falling in with Soho Internationalist circles and eking livings from teaching and radical journalism. Gladstone refused requests to extradite those who had not been tried.

Twenty-six courts martial sat in the coming months. Their proceedings were widely considered farcical, if not tragic. 'Some of the Judge Advocates really seem to have no legal conscience,' complained *The Times*, 'but go upon the principle – not uncommon perhaps in private life, but strangely out of place in a court of justice – that if you only throw enough mud some of it will stick.' The accused were dealt with at breakneck speed – one court handed out six hundred sentences within two months – and most of them were simply pushed through perfunctory legal procedure without any real regard to the possibility of establishing the truth behind the charges. Those actually responsible for the assassinations of the generals and the executions of the hostages were never discovered, although several were punished for their peripheral roles in the affairs. Similarly, many of the women were ludicrously charged with indulging in 'obscene bacchanals in the midst of burning houses' and condemned as *pétroleuses* on evidence which normally would have collapsed under proper cross-examination. Louise Michel behaved with magnificent contempt for those who faced her in the dock. Bluntly imperious in black, she threw back her veil and challenged them to do their worst. 'If you are not cowards, kill me. If you let me live, I shall never cease to cry for vengeance.' They were cowards, in the event, and ordered only transportation: Louise Michel lived on, intense and unrelenting to the point of sheer battiness, until 1905.

Most of the trials were over within a year and public opinion's appetite for vengeance on the beasts, brigands and scum was gorged. There was a total of twenty-five executions (including, most controversially, that of the Commune's honourable head of armed forces, Louis Rossel. He was shot alongside Ferré, who brushed aside the white blindfold and puffed nonchalantly on a last cigar as Rossel, a pious Protestant, was refused a last request to command the fire) and 20,000 acquittals.

The remainder were either imprisoned or – in 4,500 cases – transported, the majority to the islands of New Caledonia, a French colony about 700 miles east of Queensland. The first ship left in May 1872, the journey took up to five months, and those who weathered its privations found little comfort on arrival. Propaganda had presented the islands as pleasant, pastoral places in which those convicts not specifically sentenced to confinement within a fortress and a regime of hard labour might cheerfully cultivate smallholdings, with the state providing basic amenities, tools and accommodation. But the reality of New Caledonia was no such thing: barren, fearsomely hot, rotten with plague and pests, it could scarcely have been worse, had it not been for the camaraderie which grew up among its wretched inhabitants. Only a few escaped – most sensationally, Jourde, Rochefort and Grousset, whose successful break-out via an Australian merchant vessel was painted by Manet (Grousset made his way back to London and later became the first French translator of Stevenson's *Treasure Island*). The others waited and endured or died. In 1880, following years of lobbying led by Gambetta and Victor Hugo, an amnesty was granted. The Communards returned to take their place as citizens of the Third Republic of France.

This constitution, born spontaneously on 4 September 1870, had had some trouble legitimizing itself. The elections ensuing in February had returned to the Assembly a majority of representatives favouring restoration of a monarchy. Most of them were wealthy conservative landowners of established families whose immediate priority was the swift negotiation of a decent peace with Germany, and they gave Thiers the necessary parliamentary support for his hard-line campaign against the

Commune in Paris and similar agitations elsewhere in France. With the end of the crisis of civil war, longer-term questions as to the fundamental nature of the regime governing France could be raised and the monarchists began to flex their muscles against the puny and exhausted republic. There were two serious claimants to the throne – the Legitimist comte de Chambord, son of Charles X, King of France from 1824 to 1830 and great-nephew to Louis XVI and XVIII; and the Orléanist comte de Paris, a descendant of Louis XIII and grandson of Louis-Philippe, King of the French from 1830 to 1848. Their respective factions were scarcely amicable, let alone united, but there was hope of a viable compromise between them – the comte de Chambord was childless and might be persuaded to pass the succession to the offspring of the comte de Paris, under a monarchical constitution that he had approved.

But the comte de Chambord was a strange and isolated romantic, who lived in Austria lost in clouds of mysticism and medievalism. In July 1871 he made a mysterious visit to Paris for the first time in many years and spent the morning praying in Notre-Dame, the Sainte-Chapelle and Saint-Roch. This excited the right-wing Catholics led by the journalist Louis Veuillot and fascinated everyone else – what was the political agenda here? – but it turned out that the blessed comte would only deign to accept the throne of France if the *tricolore* was replaced by the white flag and fleur-de-lis of the *ancien régime*. As a symbolic repudiation of the greater part of French history since 1789, this was a political impossibility and it proved a fatal, albeit faintly ridiculous, sticking-point for the cause of monarchist restoration.

The slippery Thiers continued to hold the balance of power and stave off the prospect of a further descent into constitutional anarchy. Only a few looked to the socialist republic espoused by Gambetta and Victor Hugo; only a few contemplated the return of the Bonapartes – in Chislehurst Louis Napoleon's health was poor and his son, the Prince Impérial, was still a slip of a teenager. The majority supported the principle of either a monarchy or a conservative republic, and Thiers miraculously maintained a foot in both camps, the inhabitants of each believing that secretly the weight of his sympathies lay with them. In fact, his primary consideration was the consolidation of his own power and position. In June 1871 he had supervised a highly successful issue of government bonds at five per cent, raised to pay off the war indemnity. Then, following elections which substantially increased the number of republicans in the Assembly, he was voted in as President of the French Republic – itself still a 'provisional' institution – for a term of three years, sponsoring autocratic and protectionist policies considerably less liberal than those of Louis Napoleon.

In 1872 a second 'patriotic' bond issue was fourteen times oversubscribed and the entire indemnity was paid off nine months ahead of the schedule set out by the Treaty of Frankfurt – an amazing achievement which was a tribute both to the underlying strength of the busily industrializing French economy and to the assurance of stability which Thiers unattractively represented. Yet ironically, with the last occupying Prussian off French soil and the Communards packed off to New Caledonia, Thiers' prestige began to fade. He had done his job, and done it ruthlessly, but he was in his mid-seventies, he was cantankerous and intransigent, and he had been there long enough. In an attempt to re-establish his power base there, he began making visits to Paris, holding a series of political soirées (at which gooseberry juice and exiguously buttered sandwiches were the meagre refreshments) as if to test a numbed patient for signs of a return of normal responses. He seems to have misread the evidence, however, because Charles de Rémusat, the candidate he supported as deputy for Paris in the 1873 election, was crucially defeated by an anticlerical, Red-tinged Freemason from Lyons called Désiré Barodet. This was deeply embarrassing to Thiers, who could no longer claim to stand as a bulwark against the Left, and it broke his coalition. It was a bad year for old men. Louis Napoleon died; Marshal Bazaine was sentenced to death (although he was never executed) for his treason in surrendering Metz to the Prussians; and Thiers was finally toppled.

The Assembly was now dominated by Gambetta, whose

republicanism had become more centrist since the siege and who was untainted by any liaison with the Commune, but Thiers' successors were right-wing. Marshal MacMahon, a patriot before he was a politician, was appointed as a figurehead President with limited powers, and the post of Chief Executive went to the Orléanist duc de Broglie, who led what he called 'a government of moral order' which lasted until May 1874. During this period, restoration of the monarchy again seemed a possibility and the Prince Impérial, now eighteen and personable, stirred the hopes of the Bonapartists. Finding some more broadly satisfactory and permanent arrangement became imperative, if France were not to become again vulnerable to extremism: so, early in 1875, by 353 votes to 352, an amendment was passed whereby the President would be elected for seven years by a majority vote of the Senate and the Chamber of Deputies (the latter itself elected by universal suffrage). This seemed to hold, and the Third Republic was *de facto* established. Although there were several more turns of the screw in store for this regime – and although it never quite shook off its grumpily indecisive and mediocre character – it lasted through the First World War and France's recovery of Alsace-Lorraine until the Nazi invasion of 1940.

On French souls and minds the Commune had an intense short-term effect. In the longer term it came to be regarded as a crucial station in the eschatology of communistic socialism and its martyrs were enshrined in the glow of myth. Marx had been sceptical of the Commune fulfilling the 'scientific' requirements of a successful Red revolution – the wrong people, he believed, had been using the wrong tactics in the wrong circumstances – but his disciples Lenin, Trotsky and Mao all made the events of 1871 their profound and seminal study. Relics and images of the era remained potent for a century to come: one old Communard, Adrien Lejeune, continued to trot round making guest appearances at rallies and conventions in the Soviet Union until his death in Siberia in 1942; even more recently, the student insurrection of May 1968 raised old spectres and brought the barricades of a springtime civil war back to Paris. As History, it is all scarcely dry on the page.

Yet in the middle term, it meant oddly little, as though the episode had been only a hideous aberration, a blip on a steady flow-chart. By the mid 1870s, the Commune had come to seem like the end of a cycle – one which had begun with Louis Napoleon's *coup d'état* of 2 December 1851 – not the beginning. Having restored some sort of order and administered some sort of justice, France had to expiate deeper levels of guilt and point longer fingers of blame upon itself: the angles of national self-analysis opened by the Franco-Prussian War and the Siege of Paris had to expand, as it were, over a perspective of 360 degrees. Official committees investigated, reported and recommended a familiar clutch of reforming measures (more education, better public housing, stricter policing) which were never whole-heartedly enacted. More rigorous was the overhaul of France's military system, a process involving wider conscription, generous investment in new weapons and forts (particularly along the border with the annexed Alsace-Lorraine), and the introduction of the study of war into the *lycée* curriculum. Bismarck looked on beady-eyed, in expectation that France would not let its honour lie lost for long.

The debate on the catastrophe of 1870–1 offered no easy or hopeful answers. The doctrines of moral and social progress, proclaimed earlier in the century by thinkers such as Saint-Simon, Fourier and Comte, collapsed and dissolved; darker ideas about racial degeneracy prevailed instead.

The Comte de Gobineau's baneful view, originally published in 1855, that the 'purity' of black, white and yellow bloods had been fatally mixed by intermarriage and the movements of trade and colonization, suddenly assumed great resonance. France, it was thought, had lost the war and massacred itself because of some ingrained racial weakness and a failure to maintain the hierarchy and discipline that the Prussians lived by. Look back at the Roman Empire and the pattern was already evident: the fierce, hard energy of Nordic Aryan tribes invading the softer, more reflective and sedentary Gallo-Roman civilization. The materialism of the Second Empire had literally poisoned France: the fall in the birth rate, the recourse to prostitution and the spread of venereal disease, the consumption of *absinthe*, the overindulgence in illicit sexual activities leading to impotence and mania, the comforts and pleasures of modern Parisian life – all these had enfeebled French blood and muscle, poisoning the race with the vices of envy and greed and sloth. Many pamphlets, essays and books circled round these notions; one of the most striking was *La Dégénérescence Physique de la Nation Française*, written by a German, Dr Karl Starck, and published in 1871.

How to stiffen the national sinews? The attempt to invigorate all aspects of French culture, to the exclusion of foreign influence, was one course. Everyone, in whatever sphere they toiled, could play a part: the chemist Louis Pasteur set to work to improve the quality and hygiene of native beer, so as to circumvent the necessity of importing German lagers; the composer Camille Saint-Saëns established the Société Nationale de la Musique, solely dedicated to the performance of new French works. Paris, they all thought, could no longer be the tolerant and cosmopolitan capital of high consumption and low morals: its sins had to be expiated in sobriety. For a while, the effects were palpable. 'The streets are kept in better order and are more thoroughly cleaned than ever before,' wrote *The Times*'s correspondent in October 1872; three months later he remarked that 'never was there such an outcry against luxury, never were so many attempts made to inculcate in ladies' minds the propriety of simple dressing, as since the period of the Commune.' The police doubled the annual number of arrests for prostitution between 1870 (7,841) and 1875 (15,415). The blurring of the natures and responsibilities of the sexes had to be clarified. Reiterating arguments posed in Jules Michelet's tract *La Femme* in 1860, Alexandre Dumas' *L'Homme-femme* (1872) lambasted *les féministes* as he called them (after the term *féminisme*, coined by Fourier in 1837 to suggest the philosophy which exalted the noble destiny of women in the world): women who emasculated men by competing with them and invading their domains, as well as neglecting their domestic roles as wife and mother. The effeminacy of men who were less than men – quite apart from the unmentionable class of *femmes-hommes* who dressed as women and indulged in Greek vice – was another evil to be eradicated.

The newly christened disease of alcoholism or dipsomania (previously people had simply fallen drunk *ad hoc*) was considered a primary evil. Reports in the medical press analysed the prevalence of alcoholism among Communards and confirmed the convenient idea that the entire insurrection had been the doing of the deranged and intoxicated. A new Société Française de tempérance was established in 1871 by a Dr Barth, whose house had been burned down during *la semaine sanglante*: it campaigned for the moderate and 'hygienic' use of wine, beer, tea and coffee and deplored *absinthe*, eau-de-vie and the other distilled spirits. A tough and unpopular law against public drunkenness was passed in 1873: Zola, shortly to write *L'Assommoir*, his masterly study of the laundress Gervaise who 'inherits' her alcoholism through her 'degenerate' Macquart ancestry, thought the measure hypocritical – why was alcohol not taxed more heavily, why was it the wretched, impoverished victims of a highly profitable industry who took all the blame?

Against all the nineteenth-century drift towards atheism, science, positivism, materialism and a humanized, historically plausible Christianity, the Catholic Church now saw an opportunity for a reactionary whiplash. In Paris, the proposal to build an ecumenical Temple to Jesus Christ on the Trocadéro as 'an expression of belief in God' and 'national regeneration' was deemed too expensive, but in 1873 public credit was voted by the National Assembly to a scheme to build a basilica on the highest ground in the city, on land in Montmartre previously squatted by boozy cabarets, shacks and slums – the dead heart of the Commune. The site had originally been consecrated during the siege by a Jesuit priest praying for divine protection from Protestant attack; the Romano-Byzantine monstrosity subsequently to rise as the Sacré-Coeur was thus a thanksgiving as well as a symbolic assertion of the city's return to its spiritual duties. Elsewhere penitential and pietistic cults, such as the Bleeding Heart of Jesus, flourished; all over France ancient ritual observances – the stations of the cross, the months of Mary – brought people to their knees. In the countryside, so many prodigies, miracles, visitations and visions were reported that the Bishop of Orléans felt obliged to issue a circular discouraging the faithful from believing them. Ultramontane Catholicism, fervently supporting the Pope's absolute political independence and infallibility, gained the ascendant over reforming Gallican Catholicism. Joan of Arc, saviour of her nation in time of war, was commemorated in a five-act drama, several biographies and two new statues in Paris alone. There was a positively medieval vogue for pilgrimages: Lourdes became for the first time a popular destination, the town being newly linked to the railway system.*

The state looked on approvingly. Legislation increased by three and a half million francs the annual state subsidy of the Church – the *budget des cultes* which the Commune had abolished – and enforced strict moral and religious teaching in schools, as well as encouraging the setting-up of exclusively Catholic universities. Factories and ateliers instituted prayer-circles, attendance at which was compulsory for apprentices: 'Espérance de la France, ouvriers – soyez Chrétiens!' ('Workers, France's hope, be ye Christians!') There was to be no more mealy-mouthing. Paris was the Sodom that God had destroyed for its wickedness. Basic values had to be reclaimed, and everyone in France would live by them.

But the intellectuals weren't satisfied. Flaubert, Renan, Taine, Goncourt, Michelet, Gautier, Zola, George Sand and their *confrères* could not swallow the panacea of unreconstructed Catholicism. In their diagnosis, the virus went deeper – perhaps to the unacknowledged level of guilt at their own inactivity and cowardice. Yet what was there in good conscience to defend? Théophile Gautier, no cynic by nature, returned to Paris from Versailles in June 1871 and wrote to Maxime du Camp in despair: 'I am saturated with horror. I want only one thing: to

---

* Bernadette had claimed to have had visions of the Virgin Mary between 1858 and 1862. In 1860, the baby Prince Impérial had fallen ill with sunstroke while the imperial family were holidaying in Biarritz. Much to the excitement of Eugénie, the 'cure' proved to be a phial of holy water from the grotto at Lourdes – a 'miracle' which greatly contributed to the myth of the place. Bernadette retired to a convent in 1866; a basilica was constructed 1868–76; and the first national pilgrimage, organized by the mystical Assumptionist sect, took place in 1873, with nine bishops leading a flock of 20,000. The following year was the first in which parties of the chronically ill and disabled were brought to the waters. See Patrick Marnham, *Lourdes* (London, 1980).

sleep . . . If I knew some kindly Turk who liked French poetry, I should go and settle with him in Constantinople, and I should exchange a few sonnets to the glory of the prophet for a plate of *pilaf* to eat, a *chibouk* to smoke and a carpet to lie on – and I would try to forget that I belonged to western civilization. I don't want to die . . . I want to be dead.' Within months, he was – 'poisoned by the filth of modern life', in Flaubert's view.

Gautier had never been politically committed; George Sand, on the other hand, had been an earnest and idealistic Republican. Her disappointment was all the more tragically intense: 'I imagined that all the world could become enlightened . . . could correct or restrain itself; that the years I had passed with my fellows could not be lost to reason and experience; and now I wake from a dream to find a generation divided between idiocy and delirium tremens,' she wept in a letter to Flaubert, who himself gave way to total and uninhibited disgust. During the trial of the Communards he wrote to George Sand that 'they should have sent all the Commune to the galleys and forced the blood-stained fools to clean up the ruins of Paris. But that would have upset humanity. People feel sorry for mad dogs, not for those that bite. . . . Hate: that is what you lack. Despite your great sphinx-like eyes, you have seen the world through a golden haze.' A year later, in November 1872, he wrote to another friend of sweet temperament, the Russian novelist Ivan Turgenev, who had asked him why he let 'the rabble' bother him so much, that 'the state of society' was still 'crushing' him: 'Seeing my country die has made me realize that I loved it . . . I have always tried to live in an ivory tower, but a sea of shit is beating up against its walls, it's enough to bring it down.'

As to the causes of the mess, two social developments of the Second Empire were widely blamed. One was universal suffrage ('Society is dying of universal suffrage,' wrote Goncourt on 11 July 1871); the other was a misguided attitude to education. Taine's view, in a letter of November 1871, was that 'the essential thing is that the enlightened and wealthy classes lead the ignorant and those who live only for the day'. Flaubert, rather more cogently, agreed (in a letter to George Sand of 7 October 1871) that 'the most urgent thing is to educate the rich, since they know nothing, absolutely nothing', but then wondered whether 'the entire dream of democracy' was not 'to raise the proletariat to the level of bourgeois stupidity':

> The three levels of education have shown within the past year what they can accomplish: (1) higher education caused Prussia to win; (2) secondary education, bourgeois, produced the men of the fourth of September; (3) primary education gave us the Commune. Its Minister of Public Education was the great Vallès, who boasted that he despised Homer.
> Suppose that three years from now *all* Frenchmen know how to read. Do you think we'll be the better for it?

These are all personal reactions, privately communicated. But there was also a flood of published literature on the subject – the catalogue of the Bibliothèque Nationale is said to contain 216 novels, tracts and pamphlets related to the Commune, issued in 1871 alone. The overwhelming majority of them were attacks (the more balanced defences, for example Jules Vallès' autobiographical novel *L'Insurgé* and Zola's clear-eyed *La Débâcle*, came later, 1886 and 1892 respectively) which made the absolute assumption that the Commune had been a Bad Thing. A few were more supple than that. One of these, *La Reforme intellectuelle et morale de la France* (1871) by the liberal theologian Ernest Renan, provoked controversy by suggesting that France should learn from Prussia and reshape society on the latter's authoritarian and hierarchical model. France had been corrupted by philosophies of revolutionary egalitarianism for a century and now risked becoming 'a second-rate America' (*sic*); as a result the French had fallen prey to 'presumption, puerile vanity, indiscipline, a want of seriousness, application and honesty, weakheadedness, inability to keep command of several ideas simultaneously, absence of scientific spirit, naïve and vulgar ignorance'. Now they must bow their heads and look to the future. *Laboremus*, let us set to work, is Renan's last word.

Elme Caro's *Jours d'épreuve*, 'Days of Hardship' (1872) located the problem more specifically. In his view, Bohemianism was to blame for the Commune. The vogue for romanticizing Latin Quarter students, artists, poets and philosophers had all begun charmingly enough, made fashionable in the 1850s by Henri Murger's short stories (on which Puccini's *La Bohème* was later based). In themselves these characters had been innocent of politics, but they had been disrespectful of bourgeois values and standards, making the margins of society glamorous to the impressionable young. When this clashed with the Second Empire's get-rich-quick outlook, a spirit of emulation and dissatisfaction was stimulated. From there it was only a short step down to the political cynicism of Rochefort's *La Lanterne* and Eugene Vermersch's *Le Père Duchêne*; and from there to assassination, nihilism, anarchy. 'The modern novel must therefore take some responsibility – serious responsibility – for recent events,' Caro claimed. 'One of the most essential conditions for this regeneration of France to which everyone aspires – a condition even more essential than the shape of the institutions which must govern us – is that literature and the press must reconstitute themselves on the principles of serious thought, labour, dignified living and the respect of writers for each other and for ideas.'

12 : *This Wild Parade*

In such a stifling cultural climate, the story of Arthur Rimbaud and his coming to Paris is all the more remarkable. This brilliant boy – more astonishingly precocious in his way than Mozart – had been born in the north-eastern industrial town of Charleville in 1854. Locked up with his fanatic mother, he had endured an oppressive and isolated hothouse childhood of a type conducive to literary precocity. He read Rochefort's *La Lanterne*, sneered at Louis Napoleon and the bourgeois banalities of his surroundings, and wrote his first rapturous and intense poems, a couple of which were published in avant-garde quarterlies. A sympathetic schoolmaster, Georges Izambard, introduced him to the work of Baudelaire and Hugo. He may also have seduced the boy; he certainly tried to stabilize him. In the summer of 1870, while Izambard was on holiday, Rimbaud ran away to Paris to seek his literary fortune. This first assault on the capital was a miserable failure: because of railway detours necessary to avoid the war zone, he found himself thirteen francs short of the full fare and was arrested and imprisoned in the Mazas as a vagabond.

Izambard secured his release and return to Charleville, where he rejoiced in the collapse of the Second Empire, was turned down for national service on the grounds of his youth, and drew up his own plans for a communistic state. As soon as the Siege of Paris was over and rail links reopened, Rimbaud sold his watch and made his way back to the capital. The second trip was scarcely more successful than the first – for two weeks he wandered around, staring into bookshop windows, sleeping on coal barges and picking food out of the garbage. Then he walked back to Charleville. What happened in the ensuing months is uncertain. It seems possible that he spent a couple of weeks in Paris during the Commune, where – if thus we are to interpret his poems 'Coeur volé', 'Stolen Heart', and 'L'Orgie Parisienne' – he was buggered by some soldiers in a barracks. It is equally possible that he mooched around Charleville smoking, drinking and writing some of the great poems of French literature. In either case, the two significant documents of this period of Rimbaud's life are a pair of letters, dated 13 and 15 May, in which he sets forth his anarchic literary credo. 'The poet makes himself a seer through a long, immense and systematic derangement of all his senses,' he wrote. The poet is a magician, in other words, exploring forbidden or unknown imaginative terrain, and seeking out the extremes of experience that life in Charleville eliminated or ignored: Rimbaud had leapfrogged the bombast of Victor Hugo and his imitators, as well as the precious salon lyricism of the fashionable 'Parnassian' poets like Gautier. Baudelaire, whom he much admired and learnt from, had written of sensuality in terms of cool classical lucidity; Rimbaud's originality was to ignore the formal conventions of metre, grammar and logical association, chasing instead only the promptings of a mind intoxicated by an unedited tumble of words, impressions and images. To make sense was to be very dull indeed: but that did not mean he was joking. Deeply fascinated by the occult and Cabbalistic, he thought of poetry in terms of spells, incantations and mysteries, which he alone could unlock. 'J'ai seul la clef de cette parade sauvage,' he wrote as a sort of epigraph to his collection of poems known as *Les Illuminations*: 'I alone have the key to this wild parade.' Nothing illustrates all this better than his magnificent outpouring, written in that bitter and gloomy summer of 1871, 'Le Bateau Ivre', 'The Drunken Boat'. The sixteen-year-old Rimbaud had never so much as seen the sea, but here he takes an inner journey through the most exotic rivers and furthest oceans, where the night is green and the sun is bitter:

> Je sais les cieux crevant en éclairs, et les trombes
> Et les ressacs et les courants; je sais le soir,

L'Aube exaltée ainsi qu'un peuple de colombes,
Et j'ai vu quelquefois ce que l'homme a cru voir!

(I have knowledge of skies bursting with lightning, and torrents/and
surf and currents; I have knowledge of the evening/ and of Dawn as
exalted as a mass of doves/ and sometimes I have seen what man
thought he saw!)

Still ablaze with literary ambitions, Rimbaud sent a clutch of
his work off to one of the few living poets for whom he admitted
an ounce of admiration – the twenty-seven-year-old Bohemian
Paul Verlaine, who had escaped the nemesis of the Commune
and was now living with Monsieur and Madame Mauté, the
genteel parents of his seventeen-year-old wife Mathilde
(Verlaine's piano-teacher mother-in-law numbered the young
Claude Debussy among her pupils). The letter told a sob story,
but Verlaine spotted genius. He invited Rimbaud to Paris with a
flourish ('venez, chère, grande âme, on vous appelle, on vous
attend', 'come, dear great soul, you are called, you are awaited')
– he, Verlaine, would look after him, introduce him here and
there, talk poetry with him. He would also pay his train fare.
And so, one afternoon in September 1871 into the Mauté
drawing-room, peremptory and unannounced, came a beautiful
dirty boy with long blond hair, his wrists and ankles protruding
awkwardly out of an ill-fitting jacket and trousers. He had no
luggage, his socks were an alarming electric blue and he
comported himself like a monosyllabic lout; in his pocket was
the manuscript of 'Le Bateau Ivre'. Verlaine had gone to meet
him at the Gare de l'Est, but had missed the arrival of his train;
nor had he forewarned the Mautés. What ensued could have
been farcical had its consequences not been so dreadful.

On his return, Verlaine explained that his young friend
needed somewhere to stay. The Mautés stupidly showed him to
a spare room in their apartment and immediately regretted it.
The *farouche* Rimbaud thieved and sulked and showed no
politesse, let alone gratitude. He smoked a pipe, stank of alcohol
and sweat and crawled with lice: after a fortnight he had to leave.
By this time the highly susceptible Verlaine was infatuated with
the boy – to the bafflement of his naïve and pregnant wife, who

was quite at a loss to understand what was happening. Rimbaud moved on from garret to garret, behaving atrociously wherever he went. One friend of Verlaine's who kindly took him in was appalled to discover that he wiped his arse on pages torn out of the expensive journal *L'Artiste*; at a dinner party, he lost his temper and attacked his host with a carving knife. He was drunk, he smoked hashish, he was foul-mouthed, and although rumours of his genius spread round what remained of Paris's Bohemian quarters, it was hard to see him as anything other than a nightmare adolescent with a chip on his shoulder. At the Café de Cluny, where the poets met to read, he would lie across the seats, feigning sleep or snorting when the verse being declaimed met his disapproval. When Verlaine took him to the Louvre, his only comment on the paintings was 'Let's get out of here: what a pity the Commune didn't burn all this stuff.' Eventually, Verlaine drummed up some cash to rent his beloved 'Rimbe' an attic of his own. The boy was thrilled: so thrilled, perhaps by the room's bareness, that he christened his tenancy by ripping all his clothes off and flinging them out of the window. Even in the decadent atmosphere of 1869 such conduct would have been considered objectionable: in straitlaced 1872 it was positively outrageous.

Sophisticated literati gossiped knowingly about Verlaine's relationship with 'Mademoiselle Rimbaud', but Verlaine's wife and family remained astonishingly innocent of its nature: they seemed to have assumed that the dreadful youth was just a difficult poetic type. This should not surprise us: homosexuality was unarticulated in the bourgeois consciousness, except in the vaguest terms. Among the medical and intellectual communities, the generally accepted idea was that certain males felt a compulsion to cross-dress and take a 'passive', 'female' sexual role and that certain men found this prospect exciting and piquant: the word 'homosexual' did not exist – instead they talked about 'weak' men, effeminates or hermaphrodites chemically lacking in full-blooded male brawn. (The Goncourts' journal for 22 February 1863 mentions one such transvestite called André who made big money cruising the *bals publics* and who was livid when a cat ate one of his false breasts, made of boiled sheep's innards.)* The Bureau des Moeurs, the city's police department which enforced matters of public decency, had been beset with hushed-up corruption scandals throughout the Second Empire and its records are unreliable, but we do know that over three thousand charges for 'pederasty' were brought between 1860 and 1870. There were regular raids on bushy areas of the Parc de la Muette and the Bois de Vincennes and several public baths and lavatories, notably those newly constructed below Baltard's Les Halles, where the walls between the closets were notoriously riddled with holes. Otherwise we know virtually nothing about this aspect of Parisian life during these years.

Nor can we be certain what went on sexually between Verlaine and Rimbaud, except that it seems to have been torridly passionate, horribly violent and drunkenly insane: nothing camp or effeminate about it at all. Verlaine continued to reside nominally at the Mautés' apartment, but he came and went at all hours, explosions of temper alternating with episodes of mawkish tenderness and moroseness. At his worst, he started beating up his poor little wife, setting fire to her hair and throwing their month-old baby against the wall. Presumably he was tortured with a mixture of guilt and frustration, but Mathilde not surprisingly left him.

There followed months of toing and froing. Rimbaud returned to Charleville and wrote some more poetry – the excitements of Paris seem to have suffocated his muse; Mathilde returned to Verlaine, who promised to behave; then Rimbaud returned to Paris and the affair resumed with all its old knife-edge intensity: fighting with knives, indeed, seems to have been a compulsive part of their sexual agenda. 'I am of Scandinavian descent!' Rimbaud once screamed at Verlaine. 'My ancestors

---

* One Dr Cox-Algit, investigating the phenomenon of male prostitution in a bizarre pamphlet entitled *Anthropophilie* (Nantes, 1881) noted how many of them referred to each other by women's names, generally of a theatrical flavour: Cora Pearl, Salome, Adrienne Lecouvreur – interesting evidence of the early existence of a camp argot.

used to pierce their flanks and drink their own blood. I shall slash my body, I shall tattoo myself all over, because I want to become as terrifying as a Mongol!' In July 1872, following one particularly bad patch, Verlaine prostrated himself before Mathilde yet again and made further protestations of self-reform. One morning, she announced that she was feeling ill and asked her husband to buy her a remedy. Verlaine went out, met Rimbaud in the street and never went back home. The two poets fled together to Brussels, where, in July 1873, after an interim trip to London, the suicidal Verlaine shot Rimbaud in the arm. Rimbaud turned him over to the Belgian police and he was given a two-year prison sentence, which he served in Mons. There he was belatedly seized with the spirit of revivalist Catholicism sweeping post-Commune France, and his poetry would henceforth bow in that direction; Rimbaud meanwhile wrote the unique cycle of prose poems, *Une Saison en Enfer*, 'A Season in Hell', encoded autobiography of the most potently magical and impenetrable kind. In 1874, still only nineteen, he was back in Paris, hawking bootlaces and keyrings on the boulevards. He and Verlaine met, briefly and disastrously, for the last time in 1875. (Rimbaud then left France and gave up literature, dying of cancer in 1891; Verlaine survived until 1896, writing exquisite poetry of divine grace and repentance and living off drink and charity.) In the context of a France huffily enjoining its citizens to regenerate their morals, it makes an ironically salutary tale.

In 1873, the clouds over French morale began to lift. That June, *The Times* noted the return of 'gaiety' to the capital, and there were good reasons for it – the rapidity with which the indemnity to the Germans had been paid off and the consequent withdrawal of occupying troops from the north-east, the fall of Thiers and the spectacular reconstruction of Paris among them. Nowhere was the brighter mood more evident than in the little exhibition held in the studio of the photographer Nadar in April 1874 by a co-operative of young painters calling themselves the Société Anonyme des Artistes. Rejected by the official salon which was favouring canvases of post-war sackcloth and ashes, earnest scenes of country life, symbolic or historical patriotism and pomposity, the Société Anonyme turned its attention to the everyday sights of urban and suburban life – inspired to some degree by the Flemish genre painters of the seventeenth century. There was no rhetoric of hectoring triumphalism in the spirits of Claude Monet, Alfred Sisley, Auguste Renoir, Camille Pissarro, Paul Cézanne, Edgar Degas; their palettes were pastel, their outlines blurred, their focus small-scale and almost haphazard: in a sense, snapshots. In these familiar landscapes and domestic scenes, the sun shone on life, but otherwise there was no real message communicated. Some of the critics lambasted the style uncomprehendingly – a child of three could do it; what did it *mean*? – others nervously accepted that it might be the way forward. A reviewer in the weekly journal *Charivari* came up with the label 'Impressionist'; and the label stuck.

The most telling expression of this recovery of 'gaiety' came, however, with the opening of Charles Garnier's new opera house. Conceived in 1861 as one of the crowning glories of Haussmannization, the Opéra had been left unfinished at the fall of the Second Empire and was used as a munitions store during the siege. Everything about its architecture spoke of the regime of Louis Napoleon and its values. 'What style is that?' Eugénie had asked irritably when Garnier had originally presented his plans. 'That's no style – not Greek, not Louis XVI, not even Louis XV.' Garnier bridled: 'Madame, those styles were for those times. This is the style for the time of Napoleon III and you're complaining!'

After the fall of the Commune there had been a certain amount of discussion about the building's future, with republican opinion inclining to the view that the project should be abandoned on grounds that it represented a politics and an extravagance that were now scorned. But such a monster could scarcely be left to moulder in its nine-tenths state, nor could it easily be transformed into something of a more acceptable ideological character; and when the old opera house in the rue Le Pelletier fortuitously burnt down in 1873, the Assembly voted the budget necessary for completion. On 30 December 1874,

Garnier solemnly handed the 1,942 keys unlocking the mysteries of his creation over to the newly appointed management.

The preceding autumn had been a quiet and contented one in Paris. A young American correspondent, Henry James Jr., had reported in his column for the *New York Tribune* that:

> the numerous Americans who have been spending the summer in Europe congregate doubly during September and October upon the classic region, about a square mile in extent, which is bounded on the south by the Rue de Rivoli and on the north by the Rue Scribe, and of which the most sacred spot is the corner of the Boulevard des Capucines, which basks in the smile of the Grand Hotel. The ladies, week after week, are treading the devious ways of the great shops – the Bon Marché, the Louvre, the Compagnie Lyonnaise; the gentlemen are treading other ways, sometimes also, doubtless, a trifle devious. Paris seems more than ever, superficially, a vast fancy bazaar, a huge city of shop fronts.

The new Opéra looked like the most brazen shop front of them all, ostentatious beyond all canons of vulgarity and good or bad taste. Paris was thrilled. 'Be proud of being French as you look at our Opéra!' boomed *Le Sifflet*. 'Foreigners who come to visit this marvel will see that, despite our misfortunes, Paris is and will ever be without rival.' The statistics confirmed this view. At a total cost of over 36 million francs, the new Opéra was a triumph of art and engineering. Almost literally built on water – eight steam-pumps had been used round the clock for seven months to drain the foundations* – it incorporated green granite from Sweden, yellow marble from Italy, red porphyry from Finland and *brocatello* from Spain; the grand foyer staircase was 32 feet wide, with steps of white marble, balustrades of *rosso antico* and handrails of Algerian onyx; the stage was 196 feet high, 178 feet wide and 74 feet deep; the chandelier in the auditorium held 340 burners. Ceilings were decorated with murals of mythological scenes and walls were studded with

---

* Damp has remained a chronic problem of the building and now threatens the building's future, so great is the estimated cost of eliminating it.

niches and medallions of musical worthies. The *ensemble* embodied precisely the gilt and stucco heaviness and pretentiousness which the exhibition in Nadar's studio had ignored. Yet Paris fell in love with Garnier's Opéra, its passion tinged with nostalgia for the glamour of the dead regime it represented.

On 5 January 1875 a gala evening of operatic and balletic extracts christened this wonder of the world. There was great excitement when the prima donna Christine Nilsson cancelled her appearance at the last moment – not that this abated the fever for tickets (a Peruvian was said to have paid an astonishing £700 on the black market for a box). In the audience was the King of Hanover, King Alfonso XII of Spain, the Prince and Princess of Hohenlohe, the Ali Pasha, the Orléanist pretender to the throne the Comte de Paris, the Duc de Nemours of the blood royal of France, and, most sensationally of all, the Lord Mayor of London in his state robes and gilded carriage (the French press went mad for 'Sir Stone', as they called the Rt. Hon. Sir David Stone, and he caused a further furore the following evening when he turned up at a boulevard theatre to see the long-running hit *Around the World in 80 Days*).

'Everyone who had succeeded in getting inside the edifice was certainly a power in the land,' gasped *The Times*. The *Illustrated London News* added that 'the honours of the evening were for Madame Krauss and Mdlle Sangalli, the first in the part of Rachel in Halévy's *La Juive*, the second in the role of Naila in [Delibes'] ballet of *La Source*. Only while these ladies were performing was any particular interest taken in what was passing on the stage. Marshal de MacMahon who looked very gloomy, spent the evening conversing with the Duc de Broglie.' The newspapers could not stop crowing. 'France can be proud of the spectacle that it gave Europe on Tuesday night,' proclaimed *Le Monde Illustré*, 'a spectacle which is also a triumph for our beloved city of Paris. Such a celebration among a people who were dying of hunger four years ago is more than a sop to pride; it is the beginning of a renaissance.'

One could be forgiven for thinking that nothing in Paris had changed since 1869; for thinking that Paris had not learnt from its humiliation and was prepared to resume its old sins and pleasures; for thinking that it takes more than a war, a siege and a revolution to change a city and its people.

Conclusion

In 1869, a hack journalist called Tony Moilin, who would play a small role in the Commune, wrote a Utopian fantasy called *Paris en l'an 2000*. As the city approaches that millennium, it is amusing to consider how near and far of the mark Moilin's predictions were. The city, he thought, would be ruled from a huge single Palais International covering all of the Îles de la Cité and Saint Louis, the headquarters of 'the Social Republic'. A central bank would control all money, wages and commerce; there would be full employment, total equality and a comprehensive national insurance scheme. The fertility rate would have dropped and crime be virtually eliminated. The streets would be multi-layered and railways would run through them; the day's events would be communicated not through newspapers but *théâtres-journaux*, in which they would be accurately represented.

Moilin, in sum, envisages the triumph of a benevolent regime which exerts complete control over all aspects of society, a Brave New World of human beings dovetailing with technology to become a model of efficiency. It was a dream which in some degree Louis Napoleon and Baron Haussmann shared with the men of the Commune – a sharing which in our concluding century became the terrible confluence of Fascism and Communism. From this dream turned nightmare the world has now awoken, and we have lost faith in the idea that society responds rationally to enlightened reform, according to the laws of cause and effect.

Perhaps this is one moral of the story. The idea which we

casually use in daily speech that 'Paris' has one entity with one will – that a city has an identity of its own which to some extent will be shared by all its inhabitants – is a very doubtful one (even though I admit it is one used journalistically in this book as much as anywhere else). If anything, Paris in the years 1869 to 1875 illustrates precisely the opposite: a noisy multifariousness and confusion, and a hostile resilience to all attempts to placate or silence them. Like every city, it argued with itself, constantly pulling in a thousand different directions, growing like a virus, in an unreasonable organic fashion. The reality of Paris is its people's voices and stories, motivated by the pressure of immediate daily experience and the ceaseless flow of mis-information we call 'news'; it cannot be reduced to a thesis, an image or a generalization. Given the modern intellectual's natural tendency to unify and simplify, we must remember that.

Yet even as I have been writing this book, rejoicing in the variety and unpredictability it embodies – the sheer *panic* of a city – I have sensed a thudding counterpoint to the events it describes. If it takes more than a war, a siege and a revolution to change a society, it also seems to take more than a hundred and twenty-five years (and perhaps history is less a progress down a road or up a hill, from darkness to light or vice versa, and more a camera issuing versions of the same image through different exposures and tints). Tyrannies which liberalize themselves too late and crumble into nothing; rampant economies which bring no true prosperity; governments with entirely misconceived views of the potency of other great powers; the long slow fuse of revolution, so shocking when it explodes, so inevitable in retrospect; the apocalyptic gloom of the intelligentsia, seized with the idea that the end of civilization is nigh; the more widespread malaise which overpowers societies which have become too materially comfortable; the tension between the government of a capital city and the nation to which it belongs; the boredom, the excitement, the spending, the headlines, the homeless, the hype, the serial killers, the sex, the traffic, the weather – all these belong there as much as here, in ghostly immanence.

Acknowledgements

I am enormously grateful to the staff of the library of the University of Sussex, which houses Professor Eugene Schulkind's unique Commune collection – a treasure trove to which I was cordially allowed free access. In London, my thanks also to the staff of the London Library, the British Library, the Victoria and Albert Museum and the library of King's College, London (which holds the delightful Edwin Child collection); in Paris, the Bibliothèque Nationale, the Louvre, the Musée Carnavalet, the Musée de la Commune and the Bibliothèque Historique de la Ville de Paris; in Compiègne, the Musée du Second Empire; in New York, the New York Public Library.

I have been very fortunate in my editors and their efficiency, encouragement and acumen: Penny Hoare, Amanda Vaill and Dawn Drzal are all happily of the old school of publisher which puts the good of a book before the immediate claims of the corporate profit margin (I hope this doesn't get them into trouble). My mother, sister and many friends have helped me in various ways through the book's long gestation – not least by refraining from asking too insistently when it might be completed: I must mention in particular Hero Granger-Taylor; Meredith Etherington-Smith; Marion and Robert Turnbull; Rose Garnett, David Farr, and the cast of *Les Grandes Horizontales* (for last-minute inspiration); and Ian Macready (who advised on the furniture). John Hay did useful, boring work on the bibliography, for which he was shamefully remunerated; Roger Cazalet and Richard Dawes did a splendid job of copy-editing, Victoria Hutchinson battled valiantly with the picture research and Douglas Matthews has provided what I believe to be a meticulous index.

Two debts are unrepayable. I finished this book in a wing of the house of my friends Bill and Virginia Nicholson. Their hospitality over eighteen months has been unfailing, and I am inclined to rank them among history's most noble literary patrons (I don't know, for instance, how they have put up with the daily tap-tap-tap of my archaic manual typewriter, now alas replaced with a soulless electronic thing). Finally, my agent

Acknowledgements

Caroline Dawnay at A. D. Peters Fraser and Dunlop. Caroline is a good deed in a naughty world: patient yet persistent, entirely reliable, miraculously good-humoured and sympathetic as well as a tiny bit strict, she is more than I deserve. This book is dedicated to you, my dear Caroline, with love, wonder and gratitude.

A Note on Sources

This book is primarily a narrative which makes no claim to analytical profundity or originality, although it does use many unfamiliar sources. I only want to add, I hope not defensively, that there are peculiar difficulties in writing about the Second Empire and the Commune (less so the Siege of Paris): both rank among those eras which have suffered intensely from the posthumous partisanship of historians, novelists and memorialists. For instance, take the best-known of them, Emile Zola, whose Rougon-Macquart cycle gives a subtly misleading account of the last years of the Second Empire – even the department store in *Au Bonheur des Dames* operates commercially in terms of 1883, the year of the book's composition, rather than 1863.

This tendency affects all shades of the political spectrum: stories about the courtesans and the court of the Tuileries are as blatantly fabricated and elaborated as those of the excesses of the Communards. There is of course no way that one can strip away all falsehood, leaving only pure, unvarnished truth, and like everyone else I have been obliged to act on my own instincts and sensibility in assessing the reliability of witnesses and interpreters. But I came to the subject as I leave it, with no conscious ideological commitment to any of the parties involved. Pluralism is an overused term, too often an excuse and an evasion, but I hope that in this book every side of the question is allowed its voice.

Translations, unless otherwise attributed, are my own and free in spirit.

Bibliography

I owe large general debts to the following works of modern scholarship in English, all of them available through any substantial public library. On the broad context of French culture and society, Theodore Zeldin's magnificent two-volume *France 1848–1945* (Oxford, 1973 and 1977), and on the Second Empire in particular, Alain Plessis, *The Rise and Fall of the Second Empire*, translated by Jonathan Mandelbaum (Cambridge, 1985), as well as Joanna Richardson's lavishly illustrated *La Vie Parisienne 1852–70* (London, 1971). Alastair Horne's *The Fall of Paris* (London, 1965; new edition, 1989) is a deservedly popular straightforward account of the Siege and the Commune, wisely and wittily narrated; Michael Howard's *The Franco-Prussian War* (London, 1961) is a classic text of military history; Theo Aronson's *The Fall of the Third Napoleon* (London, 1970) is irresistibly gossipy and entertaining. Stewart Edwards's *The Paris Commune, 1871* (London, 1971) may be wayward in detail, but is still a rich chronicle and interpretation of the episode; Robert Tombs's *The War Against Paris* (Cambridge, 1981) is a fascinating study of the campaign mounted by the Versaillais. Roger L. Williams's *The French Revolution 1870–1* (London, 1969) is thoughtful and provocative; for those who read French, I would also recommend William Serman's balanced and reasonable *La Commune* (Paris, 1986) and long browsing in Pierre Larousse's *Grand Dictionnaire Universel* (Paris, 1866), 17 vols. First and last, two excellent reference books: *Historical Dictionary of the French Second Empire*, edited by William Echard (Westport, Conn., 1985) and *Historical Dictionary of the Third French Republic 1870–1940*, edited by Patrick H. Hutton (Westport, Conn., 1986).

Paris Partout! A Guide

This introductory chapter is drawn entirely from contemporary guide-books and pamphlets, most of them to be found in the Bibliothèque Historique de la Ville de Paris. *Almanach de l'étranger à Paris* (Paris, 1867); *American Travellers' Guide to Paris* (Paris, 1869); Baedeker, Karl, *Paris*

(Koblenz, 1865) and *Paris and its Environs* (Leipzig, 1874); *Chambers' Handy Guide to Paris* (London, 1867); Delvau, Alfred, *Les Plaisirs de Paris: Guide pratique et illustré* (Paris, 1867): *Eight Days in Paris, or Paris in the Hand* (Paris, 1866); Fosca, F., *Histoire des Cafés de Paris* (Paris, 1934); Gaze, Henry, *Paris: How to See it for Five Guineas* (London, 1864); *Gowland's Guide to Paris: How to Go and What to See When You Get There* (London, 1867); Jerrold, William Blanchard, *Paris for the English* (London, 1867); Joanne, Adolphe, *Nouveau Guide de l'étranger dans Paris* (Paris, 1866); *Kirkland's Guide to Paris* (London, 1867); Murray, John, *Handbook for Travellers in France* (London, 1867); *Paris Nouveau* (Paris, 1861); *Paris Partout: Guide général* (Paris, 1868); Renaudin, Edmond, *Paris-Exposition* (Paris, 1867); *What's What in Paris* (London, n.d.).

PART I

1: *Autumn Pastoral*

Many of the memoirs of the Second Empire are hopelessly coloured by hindsight, and beset by either blind animosity towards Louis Napoleon or hopeless nostalgia for the glamour of his court. Among modern biographies of the Emperor and Empress, J. M. Thompson's *Louis Napoleon and the Second Empire* (Oxford, 1954), T. A. B. Corley's *Democratic Despot* (London, 1961) and Jasper Ridley's sympathetic *Napoleon and Eugénie* (London, 1969) are outstanding; Roger L. Williams's *Gaslight and Shadow: The World of Napoleon III* (New York, 1957) and *The Mortal Napoleon III* (Princeton, NJ, 1971) are both more speculative than solidly informative. On Compiègne, the best publication is undoubtedly J. M. Moulin's *Le Château de Compiègne* (Paris, 1987): on Worth, Diana de Marly's *Worth: Father of Haute Couture* (London, 1980). Other works consulted include: Bac, Ferdinand, *Intimités du Second Empire* (Paris, 1931), 3 vols.; Baroche, Celeste, *Second Empire: Notes et souvenirs* (Paris, 1921); Bicknell, Anna, *Life in the Tuileries under the Second Empire* (New York, 1895); Bouchot, Henri, *Les Elégances du Second Empire* (Paris, 1896): Camp, Maxime du, *Souvenirs d'un demi-siècle* (Paris, 1949), 2 vols., hostile but intelligent; Feuillet, Mme Octave, *Quelques années de ma vie* (Paris, 1894); Filon, Augustin, *Recollections of the Empress Eugénie* (London, 1920); Fleury, Comte Maurice, *Memoirs of the Empress Eugénie* (New York, 1920); Fleury, Comte Maurice and Sonolet, Louis, *La Société du Second Empire 1867–70* (Paris, 1911), 2 vols.; Haymann, Emmanuel, *Pauline Metternich* (Paris, 1991); Hegermann-Lindencrone, Lillie de (Lillie Moulton), *In the Courts of Memory* (New York, 1912); Mérimée, Prosper, *Correspondance générale* (Paris, 1961–4), vols. 15–17; Metternich, Pauline, *Souvenirs 1859–71* (Paris, 1922); Vandam, A. D., *Undercurrents of the Second Empire* (London, 1897) and *An Englishman in Paris* (London, 1892), 2 vols.; Vizetelly, E. A. (Le Petit Homme Rouge), *The Court of the Tuileries 1852–*

1870 (London, 1907), perhaps the best work of its eyewitness kind; Whitehurst, Felix, *Court and Social Life in France under Napoleon the Third* (London, 1873), 2 vols.; Zola, Emile, *His Excellence Eugene Rougon*, translated by E. A. Vizetelly (London, 1897). The Musée du Second Empire at Compiègne gives vivid evidence of the painting and fine arts of the period, as do the new Second Empire rooms in the Louvre.

2. *The First Thunderclap*
The major text on the Troppmann case is Pierre Drachline's *Le Crime de Pantin* (Paris, 1985). See also Bolitho, William, *Murder for Profit* (Garden City, NJ, 1926); Duveau, Georges, *La Vie Ouvrière en France sous le Second Empire* (2nd edition, Paris, 1946); Flaubert, Gustave, *Letters*, edited and translated by Francis Steegmuller (Cambridge, Mass., 1980–2), vol. 2; Lachaud, C. A., *Plaidoyers* (Paris, 1885), 2 vols.; Moreau, Georges, *Souvenirs de la Roquette* (Paris, n.d.); Troppmann, Jean-Baptiste, *Mémoires secrets* (Paris, 1870), a forgery; Turgenev, Ivan, *Literary Reminiscences*, edited and translated by David Magarshack (New York, 1959); Williams, Roger L., *Manners and Murders in the World of Louis Napoleon* (Seattle, 1975), not as good as it may sound; Wolff, Albert, *Mémoires d'un Parisien* (Paris, 1888). Also journals and newspapers, notably *La Gazette des Tribunaux*, *Le Moniteur Officiel*, *La Parodie*, *The Times*. Disappointingly little has been written on the subject of crime and criminality in the period covered by this book; but see Camp, Maxime du, *Paris: ses organes, ses fonctions, sa vie* (Paris, 1869–75), 6 vols.

3: *Monuments of Hypocrisy*
On Carpeaux, see *'La Danse' de Carpeaux*, Dossiers du Musée d'Orsay (Paris, 1989) and Anne Wagner, *Carpeaux* (New Haven, 1986). On cabaret, cancan and operetta, see Appignanesi, Lisa, *The Cabaret* (London, 1975); Condemi, Concetta, *Les Cafés-Concerts* (Paris, 1992); Delvau, Alfred, *Les Cythères Parisiennes* (Paris, 1864); Gasnault, François, *Guingettes et lorettes* (Paris, 1986); Harding, James, *Jacques Offenbach* (London, 1980); Theresa, *Mémoires* (Paris, 1865). On the theatre, Hemmings, F. W. J., *The Theatre Industry in Nineteenth-century France* (Cambridge, 1993). On ballet, Guest, Ivor, *The Ballet of the Second Empire* (London, 1953). On grand opera, Crosten, William L., *French Grand Opera* (New York, 1948); Fulcher, Jane F., *The Nation's Image* (Cambridge, 1987); Walsh, T. J., *Second Empire Opera* (London, 1981).

On intellectual life in Paris, Baldick, Robert, *Dinner at Magny's* (London, 1971), a collection of contemporary table talk; Bellet, R., *Presse et Journalisme sous le Second Empire* (Paris, 1967); Camp, Maxime du, *Souvenirs d'un demi-siècle* (Paris, 1949), 2 vols.; Goncourt, Edmond and Jules de, *Journal*, edited by R. Ricatte (Paris, 1989), vols. 1 and 2; Seigel, Jerrold, *Bohemian Paris* (New York, 1986); and Taine, Hippolyte, *Notes sur*

Paris: Vie et opinions de M. F. T. Graindorge (Paris, 1867). On painting and fine arts, *Les Origines de l'Impressionisme*, Grand Palais (Paris, 1994); *L'Art en France sous le Second Empire*, Grand Palais (Paris, 1979); *William Bouguereau*, Petit Palais (Paris, 1984); Clark, T. J., *The Painting of Modern Life* (London, 1985); Hanson, Anne Coffin, *Manet and the Modern Tradition* (New Haven, 1977); Mainardi, Patricia, *Art and Politics of the Second Empire* (New Haven, 1987); *Manet*, Grand Palais (Paris, 1983); Reff, Theodore, *Manet: Olympia* (London, 1976). On photography, Freund, Gisèle, *La Photographie en France en dix-neuvième siècle* (Paris, 1936); McCauley, Elizabeth, *Industrial Madness* (New Haven, 1994), fascinating on pornography; Rouille, André, *L'Empire de la Photographie* (Paris, 1981); Rouille, André and Marbot, Bernard, *Le Corps et son Image* (Paris, 1986); Scharf, Aaron, *Art and Photography* (London, 1968).

On literature, Auerbach, Erich, *Mimesis*, translated by Willard R. Trask (Princeton, NJ, 1955), ch. 19; Baudelaire, Charles, *Oeuvres complètes*, edited by Claude Pichois (Paris, 1975–6), 2 vols.; Flaubert, Gustave, *Letters*, edited and translated by Francis Steegmuller (Cambridge, Mass., 1980–2), vol. 2; Goncourt, op. cit. and *Germinie Lacerteux*, translated by Leonard Tancock (Harmondsworth, 1984); Hemmings, F. W. J., *Emile Zola* (London, 1966) and *Culture and Society in France 1848–98* (London, 1971); Levin, Harry, *The Gates of Horn* (New York, 1963); Prendergast, C. J., *Paris and the Nineteenth Century* (Oxford, 1992), deconstructionist in tendency; Richardson, Joanna, *Théophile Gautier* (London, 1958); Williams, Roger L. *The Horror of Life* (Chicago, 1980); and Zola, Émile, *Thérèse Raquin*, translated by Andrew Rothwell (Oxford, 1992). Roger L. Williams's *Gaslight and Shadow: The World of Napoleon III* (New York, 1957) contains useful chapters on leading figures in Second Empire culture, including Offenbach and Courbet.

4. The Spermal Economy

The best modern research in this area has been conducted by the admirable French scholar Alain Corbin. His collection of essays *Le Temps, le Désir, L'Horreur* (Paris, 1991) has yet to be translated into English; *Les Filles de Noce* fortunately has – *Women for Hire*, translated by Alan Sheridan (Cambridge, Mass., 1990).

See also Adler, Laure, *Secrets de l'alcove* (Paris, 1983) and *La Vie Quotidienne dans les maisons closes* (Paris, 1990); Armengaud, A., *La Population Française du XIXème siècle* (Paris, 1971); Bergeret, Louis, *Des Fraudes dans l'accomplissement des fonctions génératrices* (Paris, 1868) and *Les Passions* (Paris, 1878); Briais, Bernard, *Grandes Courtisanes du Second Empire* (Paris, 1981); Camp, Maxime du, *Paris: ses organes, ses fonctions et sa vie* (Paris, 1869–75), 6 vols.; Debay, Auguste, *La Vénus Féconde* (Paris 1871) and *Hygiène et Physiologie du mariage* (48th edition, *sic*, Paris, 1868); Delvau, Alfred, *Dictionnaire Érotique Moderne* (Brussels, 1864); Gasnault, François, *Guingettes et lorettes* (Paris, 1986); Harsin, Jill, *Policing Prostitution in 19th-century Paris* (Princeton, NJ, 1985); Jeannel, Julien, *De la Prostitution* (Paris, 1868); John, Nicholas (ed.), *Violetta and her Sisters* (London, 1994), essays around the courtesan heroine of Verdi's *La Traviata*; Lecour, C.-J., *La Prostitution à Paris et à Londres* (2nd edition, Paris, 1872); Mayer, A., *Des Rapports Conjugaux* (6th edition, Paris, 1874); Michelet, Jules, *L'Amour* (Paris, 1858); Perrot, Michelle, *From the Fires of Revolution to the Great War*, A History of Private Life, vol. 4, translated by Arthur Goldhammer (Cambridge, Mass., 1990); Richardson, Joanna, *The Courtesans* (London, 1967), full of fascinating stuff, but perhaps too credulous in the face of sensationalizing evidence; Vintras, Dr, *On the Repressive Measures Adopted in Paris* (London, 1867).

5. Social Engineering

The most important postwar study of Haussmannization is that of David H. Pinkney, *Napoleon III and the Rebuilding of Paris* (Princeton, NJ, 1958), a sterling work perhaps a little tired after thirty-five years of service to historians of the period. See also Allem, M., *La Vie Quotidienne sous le Second Empire* (Paris, 1948); Alphand, Jean, *Les Boulevards de Paris* (Paris, 1867–73), 2 vols.; Benjamin, Walter, *Paris, capitale du XIXème siècle*, translated from German by Jean Lacoste (Paris, 1989), disappointing notes towards an unfinished major study by a fashionable Marxist *savant*; Cabaud, Michel and Eliette, *Paris et les Parisiens* (Paris, 1982), a spectacular picture-book; Camp, Maxime du, *Paris: ses organes, ses fonctions, sa vie* (Paris, 1869–75), 6 vols.; Claudin, Gustave, *Mes Souvenirs* (Paris, 1884); Descars, Jean and Pinon, Pierre, *Paris: Haussmann* (Paris, 1991); Duveau, Georges, *La Vie Ouvrière sous le Second Empire* (2nd edition, Paris, 1946); Ferry, Jules, *Les Comptes Fantastiques d'Haussmann* (Paris, 1868); Fournel, Victor, *Paris nouveau et Paris futur* (Paris, 1865); Gaillard, Jeanne, *Paris 1852–70* (Paris, 1977), serious and somewhat indigestible, but challenging and original; also 'Le Baron Haussmann' in *L'Histoire* (September 1981), xxxvii; Girard, Louis, *La Deuxième République et le Second Empire 1848–1870*, Nouvelle Histoire de Paris (Paris, 1981); Goncourt, Edmond and Jules de, *Journal*, edited by R. Racatte (Paris, 1989), vols. 1 and 2; Haussmann, Baron Georges-Eugène, *Mémoires* (2nd edition, Paris, 1890); Loyer, François, *Paris: 19th-century Architecture and Urbanism*, translatd by Charles Lynn Clark (New York, 1988); Maneglier, Hervé, *Paris Impérial: la vie quotidienne* (Paris, 1991); North Peat, A. B., *Gossip from Paris* (London, 1903); Olsen, Donald J., *The City as a Work of Art* (New Haven, 1986); Oster, Daniel and Goulemot, Jean (eds.), *La Vie Parisienne* (Paris, 1989), an interesting anthology of lesser-known texts, presented in coffee-table format; Plessis, Alain, 'L'Age d'or de la Banque de France' in *L'Histoire* 1 (February 1983); Saalman, Howard, *Haussmann: Paris Transformed* (London, 1971); Sutcliffe, Anthony, *The Autumn of Central Paris: The Defeat of Town Planning 1850–1970* (London, 1970); Véron,

Pierre, *Paris s'amuse* (Paris, 1861); Veuillot, Louis, *Les Odeurs de Paris* (Paris, 1867); Whitehurst, Felix, *Court and Social Life in France under Napoleon the Third* (London, 1873), 2 vols.

On food and restaurants, see the guidebooks cited in Chapter 1 and Aron, Jean-Paul, *Le Mangeur du 19ème siècle* (Paris, 1974); *The Epicure's Yearbook 1868-9* (London, 1868); Langle, H.-M. de, *Le Petit Monde des cafés* (Paris, 1990); Maneglier, op, cit.; Mennell, Stephen, *All Manners of Food* (Oxford, 1985); Shaw, Timothy, *The World of Escoffier* (London, 1994); Whitehurst, op. cit. On shops and shopping, Miller, Michael B., *The Bon Marché: Bourgeois Culture and the Department Store* (London, 1981); Perrot, Michelle, *From the Fires of Revolution to the Great War*, A History of Private Life, vol. 4, translated by Arthur Goldhammer (Cambridge, Mass., 1990); Uzanne, Octave, *Fashion in Paris* (London, 1897); Zola, Émile, *Ladies' Delight* (Au Bonheur des Dames), translated by April Fitzlyon (London, 1960). Contemporary magazines such as *Charivari*, *L'Illustration*, *Le Monde Illustré*, and *Le Petit Journal* pleasantly repay browsing.

6: *Too Much, Too Soon?*
Apart from Alain Plessis' lucid and simple *The Rise and Fall of the Second Empire*, translated by Jonathan Mandelbaum (Cambridge, 1985), there are a few other books which provide a basic understanding of the politics of the period, notably Alice Gérard's *Le Second Empire: Innovation et réaction* (Paris, 1973), J.-P. Miquel's *Le Second Empire* (Paris, 1979) and Adrien Dansette's *Du 2 Décembre au 4 Septembre* (Paris, 1972); also Theodore Zeldin's *The Political System of Napoleon III* (London, 1958) and *Émile Ollivier and the Liberal Empire of Napoleon III* (Oxford, 1963). To supplement Michael Howard's *The Franco-Prussian War* (London, 1961), turn to A. J. P. Taylor's famous study of nineteenth-century diplomacy *The Struggle for Mastery in Europe 1848-1918*, Oxford History of Modern Europe (Oxford, 1954) and Gordon A. Craig's *Germany 1866-1945* (Oxford, 1978). Other more specific studies include Nancy Nichols Barker's revealing portrait of Eugénie's attitude to foreign policy *Distaff Diplomacy* (Austin, Texas, 1968) and Sandra Horvath-Peterson's account of one of the brighter areas of the Second Empire's legislation, *Victor Duruy and French Education* (Baton Rouge, Ind., 1984). Louis Chevallier's *Classes Laborieuses et Classes Dangereuses* (Paris, 1958), Georges Duveau's *La Vie Ouvrière en France sous le Second Empire* (2nd Edition, Paris, 1946) and Alain Faure's 'The Public Meeting Movement in Paris from 1868 to 1870' in *Voices of the People*, edited by A. Rifkin and R. Thomas (London, 1988), deal with the working-class politics of this period. See also Bergeron, L., *L'Industrialisation de la France au XIXème Siècle* (Paris, 1979) Kulstein, David, *Napoleon III and the Working Class* (San José, 1969) and Poulot, D., *Question Sociale: Le Sublime ou le travailleur comme il est en 1870 et ce qu'il peut être* (Paris, 1870), which is every bit as odd as its title suggests.

See also Bicknell, Anna, *Life in the Tuileries under the Second Empire* (New York, 1895); Boilet, G. E., *La Doctrine Sociale de Napoléon III* (Paris, 1969); Camp, Maxime du, *Souvenirs d'un demi-siècle* (Paris, 1949), 2 vols.; Carette, A., *Souvenirs Intimes* (Paris, 1889), 3 vols.; Case, L. M., *French Opinion on War and Diplomacy* (Philadelphia, 1954); Filon, Auguste, *Recollections of the Empress Eugénie* (London, 1920); Flaubert, Gustave, *Letters*, edited and translated by Francis Steegmuller (Cambridge, Mass., 1980–2), 2 vols.; Goncourt, Edmond and Jules, *Journal*, edited by R. Racatte (Paris, 1989), vol. 2; Halévy, Ludovic, *Carnets*, edited by Daniel Halévy (Paris, 1935) 2 vols.; Ollivier, Émile, *L'Empire Libéral* (Paris, 1895–1915), 14 vols.; *Revue d'Histoire Moderne et Contemporaine*, January– March 1974; Taine, Hippolyte, *Notes sur Paris: Vie et opinions de M. F. T. Graindorge* (Paris, 1867); Vatré, Eric, *Rochefort et la comédie politique* (Paris, 1984); Victoria, Queen, *The Letters of Queen Victoria 1862–1885*, edited by G. E. Buckle (London, 1926), vols. 1 and 2; Viel-Castel, Marc, *Mémoires* (Paris, 1883); Vizetelly, E. A., *The Court of the Tuileries* (London, 1907); Wagner, Cosima, *Diaries 1869–1877*, translated by Geoffrey Skelton (London, 1978); Wellesley, Henry, *The Paris Embassy during the Second Empire*, edited by F. A. Wellesley (London, 1928); Willard, Fletcher, *The Mission of Vincent Benedetti to Berlin 1864–70* (The Hague, 1965); Williams, Roger L., *The Mortal Napoleon III* (Princeton, NJ, 1971), dealing particularly with the state of the Emperor's health and its effect on events.

7: *Too Little, Too Late*
In addition to the texts listed for the previous chapter, see also Carson, Gerald, 'The American Dentist and the Empress', *American Heritage* (1980) xxxi, 4 and Evans, T. W. *Memoirs* (London, 1905), 2 vols., for a full account (though not necessarily an infallibly veracious one) of the Empress's escape from France. The terrible events at Hautefaye, men- tioned on p. 148, are detailed in Alain Corbin's *Village of Cannibals* translated by Arthur Goldhammer (London, 1992). Both *The Times* and the *Illustrated London News* had admirable anonymous foreign correspon- dents in Paris at the outbreak of the war. An interesting discussion of the ways in which historians have interpreted the Second Empire is contained in Stuart L. Campbell's *The Second Empire Revisited* (New Brunswick, NJ, 1978).

PART II

8: *The Siege*
The sources for this section are as follows: Adam, Juliette, *Mes Illusions et mes Souffrances* (Paris, 1902); Arnold, Matthew, *Letters 1848–1888*, edited by G. W. E. Russell (London, 1895), vol. 2; Arsac, J., *Mémorial du Siège de Paris* (Paris, 1871); Bingham, Denis, *Recollections of Paris* (London, 1896), 2

vols.; Blount, Sir Edward, *Memoirs*, edited by Stuart J. Reid (London, 1902); Boissonas, Mme B., *Une Famille pendant la guerre* (Paris, 1873); Bowles, Thomas G., *The Defence of Paris* (London, 1871); Breton, Geneviève, *Journal* (Paris, 1985); Cadol, Victor, *Paris pendant le siège* (London, 1871); Cailler, Pierre, and Courthion, Pierre, *Portrait of Manet*, translated by Michael Ross (London, 1960); Carlyle, Thomas, 'The Latter Stage of the French-German War' in *Critical and Miscellaneous Essays* (London, 1872), vol. 7; Caro, Elme, *Les Jours d'épreuve* (Paris, 1872); Chamoissier, Leon, *La Poste à Paris pendant le siège* (Paris, 1919); Chevalet, Émile, *Mon Journal* (Paris, 1871); Claretie, Jules, *Paris assiégé* (Paris, 1871); Cornudet, Michel, *Journal du siège de Paris* (Paris, 1872); *Correspondance Impériale*, Documents Authentiques, Les Papiers Secrets du Second Empire (Paris, 1870–1), 13 vols.; Cresson, Guillaume, *Cent jours du siège* (Paris, 1901); Dabot, Henri, *Griffonages quotidiens* (Paris, 1985); Dalseme, Achille, *Paris pendant le siège* (Paris, 1871) and *Paris sous les obus* (Paris, 1883); Daudet, Alphonse, *Contes du lundi* (Paris, 1873); Desplats, Frédéric, *Lettres d'un homme à la femme qu'il aime*, edited by Pierre Lary (Paris, 1980); Deschaumes, Edmond, *Journal d'un lycéen* (Paris, 1890); Drapeyron-Seligman, Ludovic, *Les Deux Folies de Paris* (Paris, 1872); Dubois, Lucien, *Chapitres nouveaux* (Paris, 1872); Duruy, Anatole, *Souvenirs du siège* (Paris, 1873); Duveau, Georges, *Le Siège de Paris* (Paris, 1939); Eliot, George, *Letters*, edited by Gordon S. Haight (New Haven, 1955), vol. 5.; Evans, Thomas W., *History of the American Ambulance Establishment* (London, 1873); Fisher, John, *Airlift 1870* (London, 1965); Flaubert, Gustave and Sand, Georges, *The Correspondence*, translated by Francis Steegmuller and Barbara Bray (London, 1992); Flourens, Gustave, *Paris livré* (Paris, 1871); François, L., *Les Correspondances par ballon monté* (Paris, 1925); Gautier, Théophile, *Tableaux du siège* (Paris, 1886); Girard, G., *La Jeunesse d'Anatole France* (Paris, 1925); Goncourt, Edmond and Jules de, *Journal*, edited by R. Racatte (Paris, 1989), vol. 2.; Harrison, Frederic, 'Bismarckism' in *Fortnightly Review*, 1 December 1870; Hérisson, Comte Maurice d', *Journal of a Staff Officer* (London, 1885); Heylli, Georges d', *Journal du siège* (Paris, 1871–4), 3 vols.; Hoffman, Wickham, *Camp, Court and Siege* (New York, 1877); Houssaye, Arsène, *Les Confessions* (Paris, 1885–91), 6 vols.; Hugo, Victor, *Carnets Intimes*, edited by Henri Guillemin (Paris, 1953); *Inside Paris during the Siege* by an Oxford Graduate (Henry Markheim) (London, 1871); *Journal du siège*, by 'Raoul B.' (Paris, 1984); Kranzberg, Melvin, *The Siege of Paris* (Ithaca, NY, 1950); Labouchere, Henry, *Diary of the Besieged Resident* (London, 1871); Lecour C.-J., *La Prostitution à Paris et à Londres* (2nd edition Paris, 1872); Loudun, Eugène, *Journal d'un Parisien* (Paris, 1872); Maillard, Firmin, *Les Publications de la rue* (Paris, 1874); Martial, A. P., *Paris pendant le siège* (Paris, 1982); Marx, Karl and Engels, Friedrich, *Collected Works* (London, 1986), vol. 22; McMullen, Roy, *Degas: His Life, Times and Work* (London, 1985); Michel, Louise, *Mémoires* (Paris, 1886); Michell, E. B., *Siege Life in Paris* (London, 1870); Molinari,

Gustave de, *Les Clubs Rouges* (Paris, 1871); Moland, Louis, *Par ballon monté* (Paris, 1872); Morley, John, *The Life of Gladstone* (London, 1903), vol. 2; Nass, Lucien, *Le Siège de Paris: essais de pathologie* (Paris, 1914); O'Shea, John Augustus, *An Iron-bound City* (London, 1886); Quepat, Nérée, *Simple notes* (Paris, 1871); Palat, Barthélemy, *Bibliographie Générale de la Guerre* (Paris, 1896), an astonishing tome; Piedagnel, Alexandre, *Les Ambulances de Paris* (Paris, 1871); Pratt, Michael, 'A Fallen Idol', in *International History Review* (1985), vii.4; Richardson, Joanna, *Paris under Siege* (London, 1982) and *Victor Hugo* (London, 1976); Robida, Albert, *Album du Siège* (Paris, 1971), 2 vols.; Saint-Edmé, Ernest, *La Science pendant le siège* (Paris, 1871); Sarcey, Francisque, *Le Siège de Paris* (Paris, 1871); Schuler, P., *Journal d'un Suisse pendant le siège de Paris* (Bienne, 1871); Segur, N., *Dernières conversations avec Anatole France* (Paris, 1927); Sheppard, Nathan, *Shut up in Paris* (London, 1871); Thierry, Edouard, *La Comédie-Française* (Paris, 1887); Thiers, Adolphe, *Notes et Souvenirs* (Paris, 1903); Thomas, Edith, *The Women Incendiaries*, translated by James and Starr Atkinson (London, 1967); Trailles, Paul and Henri, *Les Femmes de France* (Paris, 1872); Vandam, A. D., *An Englishman in Paris* (London, 1894); Victoria, Queen, *The Letters of Queen Victoria 1862–1885*, edited by G. E. Buckle (London, 1926), vol. 2; Viollet-le-Duc, Eugène, *Mémoires sur la défense* (Paris, 1871); Washburne, E. B., *Recollections of a Minister to France* (New York, 1889); Whitehurst, Felix, *My Private Diary* (London, 1875), Journals and newspapers consulted include *The Athenaeum*, *L'Eclipse*, *Le Figaro*, *Fortnightly Review*, *Le Gaulois*, *Illustrated London News*, *Pall Mall Gazette*, *The Times*. The catalogue of the exhibition, *The Franco–Prussian War and the Commune in Caricature*, Victoria and Albert Museum (London, 1971) is both fascinating and amusing.

9: *A Passage to Civil War*

Detailed accounts of the complicated gestation of the Commune and the background to Thiers' rearguard action are contained in Stewart Edwards's *The Paris Commune, 1871* (London, 1971), Georges Lefebvre's *La Proclamation de la Commune* (Paris, 1965) and Robert Tombs's *The War Against Paris* (Cambridge, 1981).

Other sources include Adolphus, F., *Some Memories of Paris* (Edinburgh, 1895); Arnold, Matthew, *Letters 1848–1888*, edited by G. W. E. Russell (London, 1900); Dansette, Adrien, *Les Origines de la Commune* (Paris, 1944); Desplats, Frédéric, *Lettres d'un homme à la femme qu'il aime*, edited by Pierre Lary (Paris, 1980); Dicey, Edward, 'Paris after the Peace' in *Fortnightly Review*, 1 April 1871; Flaubert, Gustave, *Letters*, edited and translated by Francis Steegmuller (Cambridge, Mass., 1980–2) vol. 2; Gibson, Revd W., *Paris During the Commune* (London, 1872); Goncourt, Edmond and Jules de, *Journal*, edited by R. Racatte (Paris, 1989), vol. 2; Hegermann-Lindencrone, Lillie de (Lillie Moulton), *In the Courts of Memory* (New York, 1912); Hérisson, Comte Maurice d', *Nouveau Journal d'un officier d'ordonnance* (Paris, 1889); Labouchere, Henry, *Diary of the Besieged Resident* (London, 1871); Lissagaray, P.-O., *Histoire de la Commune* (Brussels, 1871); Nass, Lucien, *Le Siège de Paris: essais de pathologie* (Paris, 1914); O'Shea, John Augustus, *An Iron-bound City* (London, 1886); Sarcey, Francisque, *Le Siège de Paris* (Paris, 1871); Senisse, Martial, *Les Carnets d'un fédéré*, edited by J. A. Faucher (Paris, 1965); Sheppard, Nathan, *Shut up in Paris* (London, 1871); Thiers, Auguste, *Notes et Souvenirs* (Paris, 1903); Thomas, Edith, *The Women Incendiaries*, translated by James and Starr Atkinson (London, 1967); Vizetelly, E. A., *My Adventures in the Commune* (London, 1914); Vuillaume, Maxime, *Mes Cahiers Rouges au temps de la Commune* (Paris, 1971); Washburne, E. B., *Recollections of a Minister to France* (New York, 1889); Whitehurst, Felix, *My Private Diary* (London, 1875); Yriarte, Charles, *Les Prussiens à Paris* (Paris, 1871).

Journals consulted include *The Times*, *Illustrated London News*, *Pall Mall Gazette*, *Journal Officiel* and *Le Gaulois*.

10: *The Commune*
The sources for this section are as follows: Adamov, A., *La Commune* (Paris, 1959), the best of several anthologies; Adolphus, F., *Some Memories of Paris* (Edinburgh, 1895); Alméras, Henri d', *La Vie Parisienne pendant le siège et sous la Commune* (Paris, 1925); Amodru, Abbé Laurent, *La Roquette* (Paris, 1887); Andrieu, J., 'The Paris Commune' in *Fortnightly Review*, 1 November 1871; Arnould, Arthur, *Histoire populaire et parlementaire de la Commune* (Brussels, 1878): Arsac, J., *La Guerre Civile et la Commune en Paris en 1871* (Paris, 1871); Barron, Louis, *Sous le drapeau rouge* (Paris, 1889); Barrows, Susanna, 'Alcoholism, Temperance and Literature in the Early Third Republic' in *Consciousness and Class Experience in 19th-Century Europe* edited by J. M. Merriman (New York, 1980); Blanqui, Auguste, *La Patrie en danger* (Paris, 1871); Bruhat, J., Dautry, J. and Tersen, E., *La Commune de Paris* (Paris, 1960), a picture-book; Chevalet, Émile, *Mon Journal pendant le siège et la Commune* (Paris, 1871); Claretie, Jules, *Histoire de la Révolution de 1870–1871* (Paris, 1872); Cobb, Richard, *A Second Identity* (London, 1969), containing a superb essay on the historiography of the Commune; Dabot, Henri, *Griffonages quotidiens* (Paris, 1895); Daudet, Alphonse, *Lettres à un absent* (Paris, 1871); Delaroche-Vernet, André (ed.), *Une Famille pendant la guerre et la Commune* (Paris, 1912); Desplats, Frédéric, *Lettres d'un homme à la femme qu'il aime*, edited by Pierre Lary (Paris, 1980); Dommanget, Maurice, *L'Enseignement, l'enfance et la culture sous la Commune* (Paris, 1964); Edwards, Stewart, *The Communards of Paris, 1871* (London, 1973); Flaubert, Gustave, *Letters*, edited and translated by Francis Steegmuller (Cambridge, Mass., 1980–2), vol. 2; Fontoulieu, Paul, *Les Églises de Paris sous la Commune* (Paris, 1873); Forbes, Archibald, 'What I saw of the Paris Commune' in *The Century*, October

1892; Gaillard, Jeanne, *Communes de Province, Commune de Paris* (Paris, 1971), dealing specifically with the communes established outside Paris; Gibson, Revd W., *Paris during the Commune* (London, 1872); Goncourt, Edmond and Jules de, *Journal*, edited by R. Racatte (Paris, 1989), vol. 2; Greenberg, L. M., *Sisters of Liberty* (Cambridge, Mass., 1971); Halévy, Ludovic, *Notes et souvenirs 1871–1872* (5th edition, Paris, 1935); Harrison, Frederic, 'The Commune' in *Fortnightly Review*, 1 May 1871 and 'The Fall of the Commune', *Fortnightly Review*, 1 August 1871; Hérisson, Comte Maurice d', *Nouveau journal d'un officier d'ordonnance* (Paris, 1889); Lefebvre, Henri, *La Proclamation de la Commune* (Paris, 1965), excellent on the early stages; Leighton, J., *Paris under the Commune* (London, 1871); Labarthe, Georges, *Le Théâtre pendant les jours du siège at de la Commune* (Paris, 1960); Lecour, C.-J. *La Prostitution à Paris et à Londres* (Paris, 1882); Leith, James A., *Images of the Commune* (London, 1978); Lissagaray, P.-O., *Histoire de la Commune* (Brussels, 1871), the most readable and sympathetic of the pro-Communard eyewitness accounts; Maillard, Firmin, *Affiches, professions de foi, documents officiels pendant la Commune* (Paris, 1871); Marx, Karl and Engels, Friedrich, *Collected Works* (London, 1986); vol. 22; Mendès, Catulle, *Les 73 journées de la Commune* (Paris, 1871); Michel, Louise, *Mémoires* (Paris, 1886) and *La Commune* (Paris, 1898); Nadar (Félix Tournachon), *Sous l'incendie* (Paris, 1882); Nass, Lucien, *Le Siège de Paris: essais de pathologie* (Paris, 1914); Noël, Bernard, *Dictionnaire de la Commune* (Paris, 1978), 2 vols., useful and imaginative – compiled entirely from contemporary newspapers; Reclus, Élie, *La Commune au jour le jour* (Paris, 1908); Renoir, Jean, translated by R. and D. Weaver, *Renoir my Father*, (London, 1962): Roberts, J. M., 'The Commune from the Right', *English Historical Review Supplement 6* (London, 1973); Rougerie, Jacques, *Procès des Communards* (Paris, 1964) and *Paris Libre 1871* (Paris, 1971); Schulkind, Eugene, 'The Activity of Popular Organisations during the Paris Commune' in *French Historical Studies* (1960), i.4 and 'Socialist Women in the Paris Commune' in *Past and Present*, February 1985, also *The Paris Commune of 1871: The View from the Left* (London, 1972); Seigel, Jerrold, *Bohemian Paris* (New York, 1986); Senisse, Martial, *Les Carnets d' un Fédéré*, edited by J. A. Faucher (Paris, 1965); Serman, William, *La Commune de Paris* (Paris, 1986); Taine, Hippolyte, *Life and Letters*, translated by R. L. Devonshire and E. Bayly (London 1902–8), 3 vols.; Testut, Oscar, *L'Internationale* (Lyon, 1871); Thiers, Auguste, *Notes et souvenirs* (Paris, 1903); Thomas, Edith, *The Women Incendiaries*, translated by James and Starr Atkinson (London, 1967); Tombs, Robert, 'Harbingers or Entrepreneurs? A worker's co-operative during the Paris Commune', in *The Historical Journal* (1984), xxvii.4 and 'Paris and the Rural Hordes', in *The Historical Journal* (1986), xxix,4, also 'Prudent Rebels' in *French History* (1991), vol. 4; Victoria, Queen, *The Letters of Queen Victoria 1862–1885*, edited by G. E. Buckle (London, 1926), vol. 2; Vizetelly, E. A., *My Adventures in the Commune*

(London, 1914); Vuillaume, Maxime, *Mes Cahiers Rouges au temps de la Commune* (Paris, 1971); Washburne, E. B., *Recollections of a Minister to France* (New York, 1889); Williams, Roger L., *The French Revolution of 1870–1871* (London, 1969); Winock, Michel and Azéma, Jean-Pierre, *Les Communards* (Paris, 1964); Wright, Gordon, 'The Anti-Commune: Paris 1871' in *French Historical Studies* (1977), x.1; Zeldin, Theodore, *France: 1848–1945*, vol. 1, 'Ambition, Love and Politics' (Oxford, 1973). The catalogue of the exhibition, *The Franco–Prussian War and the Commune in Caricature*, Victoria and Albert Museum (London, 1971) repays further investigation.

The account of the march on pp. 361–5 appeared anonymously in *Macmillan's Magazine*, September–October 1871. Other newspapers and journals consulted include *The Times*, *Illustrated London News*, *Pall Mall Gazette*, *Le Combat*, *Le Cri du Peuple*, *Le Drapeau Rouge*, *Le Moniteur de la Garde Nationale*, *Le Moniteur des Citoyennes*, *Le Père Duchêne*, *Le Réveil* and many miscellaneous publications housed in the University of Sussex's Commune collection. The Edwin Child letters are to be found in the archives of King's College, London. In Paris, original documents are held in the Archives Historiques de Guerre, the Musée de la Commune in Saint-Denis and the Bibliothèque Historique de la Ville de Paris.

PART III

12: *Repentance and Revenge*

On the aftermath of the Commune, see Lissagaray P.-O., *Historie de la Commune* (Brussels, 1871); on the deportations, Baronnet, Jean and Chalon, Jean, *Communards en Nouvelle-Calédonie* (Paris, 1987). The first years of the Third Republic and the postwar settlement, Brogan, D. W., *The Development of Modern France* (2nd edition, London, 1967); Halévy, Daniel, *The End of the Notables*, edited and translated by Alain Silvera and June Guichanand (Middleton, Conn., 1974), an elegant essay on a turgid and convoluted political situation; Mayeur, J. M. and Robérioux, Madeleine, *The Third Republic from its Origins to the Great War*, translated by J. R. Foster (Cambridge, 1984), a useful modern textbook; Mitchell, Allan, *The German Influence in France after 1870* (Chapel Hill, NC, 1979); Vizetelly, E. A., *Paris and her People under the Second Republic* (London, 1919); and Williams, Roger L., *The French Revolution of 1870–1871* (London, 1969). See also Cheneviére, J., *La Comtesse de Ségur* (Paris, 1932); Guest, Ivor, *Napoleon III in England* (London, 1952); Thomas, Edith, *The Women Incendiaries*, translated by James and Starr Atkinson (London, 1967). On racism and worries about national moral and physical decline, see Barrows, Susanna, 'Alcoholism, Temperance and Literature in the Early Third Republic' in *Consciousness and Class Experience in 19th-Century Europe*, edited by J. M. Merriman (New York, 1980); Barzun, Jacques,

Race (2nd edition, London, 1965), which gives a reasonable account of
Gobineau; Caro, Elme, 'La Fin de la Bohème' in *Revue des Deux Mondes*,
July 1871; Charton, D. G., *Secular Religions in France 1815–70* (Hull,
1963); Copley, Anthony, *Sexual Moralities in France 1780–1980* (London,
1989); Dansette, Adrien, *A Religious History of Modern France*, translated by
J. Dingle (Edinburgh and London, 1961); Digeon, Claude, *La Crise
Allemande de la pensée française* (Paris, 1959); Dubos, René J., *Louis Pasteur:
Freelance of Science* (Boston, Mass., 1950); Dumas *fils*, Alexandre,
L'Homme-Femme (Paris, 1872); Flaubert, Gustave and Turgenev, Ivan, *A
Friendship in Letters*, edited and translated by B. Beaumont (London,
1985); Goncourt, Edmond and Jules de, *Journal*, edited by R. Racatte
(Paris, 1989) vol. 2; Harding, James, *Saint-Saens and his Circle* (London,
1965); Harsin, Jill, *Policing Prostitution in 19th-century Paris* (Princeton, NJ,
1985); Hayem, A., *Le Mariage* (Paris, 1872); McManners, John, *Church and
State in France 1870–1914* (London, 1972); Mohrt, Michel, *Les Intellectuels
devant la défaite* (Paris, 1942), an obvious parable for the Nazi Occupation;
Renan, Ernest, *La Réforme Intellectuelle et Morale de la France* (new edition,
Paris, 1967); Richardson, Joanna *Théophile Gautier* (London, 1958); Seigel,
Jerrold, *Bohemian Paris* (New York, 1986).

12: *This Wild Parade*

On French poetry in general during this period, see Kenneth Cornell's *The
Symbolist Movement* (New Haven, 1970); on Rimbaud in particular, see
Enid Starkie's unsurpassed *Arthur Rimbaud* (revised edition, London,
1961), as well as Chadwick, C., *Rimbaud* (London, 1979); Hanson,
Elisabeth, *My Poor Arthur* (London, 1959); Hare, Humphrey *Sketch for a
Portrait of Rimbaud* (London, 1937); Reed, Jeremy, *Delirium* (London,
1991); and Ross, Kristin, *Rimbaud: The Emergence of Social Space* (London,
1988), fanciful in thesis. Rimbaud's *Complete Works, Selected Letters*, edited
by Wallace Fowlie (Chicago, 1966) is a useful parallel text; *Arthur Rimbaud:
Portraits, Dessins, Manuscrits*, Dossiers du Musée d'Orsay (Paris, 1991)
catalogues visual representations of the poet. On homosexuality in Paris,
see Carrier F., *Des Deux Prostitutions* (Paris, 1887); Copley, Anthony,
Sexual Moralities in France 1780–1980 (London, 1989); Cox-Algit,
Anthropophilie (Nantes, 1881); Hahn, Pierre, *Nos Ancêtres les pervers* (Paris,
1979), which dredges the exiguous seam of evidence; Tardieu, A., *Étude
Médico-légale sur les attentats aux moeurs* (Paris, 1857).

On the new painting, see Moffat, C. S. (ed.), *The New Painting:
Impressionism 1874–1886* (Oxford, 1986), especially Paul Tucker's essay,
'The First Impressionist Exhibition in Context'; Clark, T. J., *The Painting
of Modern Life* (London, 1985); Hamilton, G. H., *Manet and his Critics*
(New Haven, 1954). On Garnier and the Paris Opéra, Mead, Christopher
J., *Charles Garnier's Paris Opéra* (Cambridge, Mass., 1991) and *L'Ouverture
du Nouvel Opéra*, Dossiers du Musée d'Orsay (Paris, 1986), as well as the

reports in *The Times* and *Illustrated London News* and documents in the Musée de l'Opéra. Henry James's Paris journalism is reprinted in James Henry, *Parisian Sketches*, edited by Leon Edel (London, 1958).

Index

A Selected List of Non-Fiction Titles Available from Mandarin

While every effort is made to keep prices low, it is sometimes necessary to increase prices at short notice. Mandarin Paperbacks reserves the right to show new retail prices on covers which may differ from those previously advertised in the text or elsewhere.

The prices shown below were correct at the time of going to press.

All these books are available at your bookshop or newsagent, or can be ordered direct from the address below. Just tick the titles you want and fill in the form below.

Cash Sales Department, PO Box 5, Rushden, Northants NN10 6YX.
Fax: 01933 414047 : Phone: 01933 414000.

Please send cheque, payable to 'Reed Book Services Ltd.', or postal order for purchase price quoted and allow the following for postage and packing:

£1.00 for the first book, 50p for the second; **FREE POSTAGE AND PACKING FOR THREE BOOKS OR MORE PER ORDER.**

NAME (Block letters) ....

ADDRESS ....

....

☐ I enclose my remittance for ....

☐ I wish to pay by Access/Visa Card Number ☐☐☐☐☐☐☐☐☐☐☐☐☐☐☐☐

Expiry Date ☐☐☐☐

Signature ....

Please quote our reference: MAND